THE NEPALI DIASPORA

Migrants, Ministry and Mission

THE NEPALI DIASPORA

Migrants, Ministry and Mission

Dr Valerie M Inchley OBE
MA, MB ChB, DObstRCOG, Dip HE (Theol)

Val Inchley

EKTA BOOKS
Kathmandu, Nepal

THE NEPALI DIASPORA

Migrants, Ministry and Mission

First Published in 2014 by Ekta Books

Distribution Information
Ekta Books Distributors Pvt. Ltd.
Prashutigriha Marga, Thapathali
GPO Box: 6445, Kathmandu, Nepal.
E-mail: ektabook@mos.com.np
http://www.ektabooks.com

Language
English

Computer Type
VM Inchley

Cover
Kishor Joshi

ISBN 978-9937-1-0331-2

Printed in Nepal at **Monaj Offset Press Pvt. Ltd.**, Kathmandu

"नेपाली र आलु

जहाँ पनि

पाइन्छन् ।"

"Nepalis and potatoes

are found

everywhere."

ACKNOWLEDGEMENTS

I wish to thank Mr RC Timothy of EKTA for challenging me to write this book, and also Dr Cindy Perry for allowing me to use some of her maps and base my updates on her original masterpiece *Nepali Around the World*.

Without the help and support of my colleagues in the International Nepal Fellowship (INF) and Nepali Pravasi Ekata Sanjaal (NeMUN), not to mention all those who responded to my requests for information, it would have been difficult to achieve my aim. My thanks are also due to all those who checked and edited the work in part or whole.

Last, but not least, I thank God who cares for migrants: this book is dedicated to Nepali migrants wherever they are.

The subject, however, is such that the information is sometimes the best possible 'guesstimate'. Much will also soon go out of date. All mistakes are mine. Please inform of any errors so that they may be corrected in any future revisions.

Valerie M Inchley

July 2014

ABBREVIATIONS

AIDS	Acquired Immune Deficiency Syndrome
CSW	Commercial Sex Worker
DoFE	Department of Foreign Employment
EPS	Employment Permit System
FEPB	Foreign Employment Promotion Board
FNWRC	Foreign Nepali Workers Rescue Center
GoN	Government of Nepal
HIV	Human Immunodeficiency Virus
HRW	Human Rights Watch
ICMW	International Convention on Migrant Workers
IDP	Internally Displaced Person
ILO	International Labour Organisation
INF	International Nepal Fellowship
IOM	International Organization for Migration
MoFA	Ministry of Foreign Affairs
MRI	Migrant Rights International
NAFEA	Nepal Assn. of Foreign Employment Agencies
NeMUN	Nepali Pravasi Ekata Sanjaal (Nepalese Migrant Unity Network)
NGO	Non-Government Organisation
NIDS	Nepal Institute for Development Studies
NRN	Non-Resident Nepali
PNCC	Pravasi Nepali Coordination Committee
SAARC	South Asian Association for Regional Cooperation
TIA	Tribhuvan International Airport
WMW	Women Migrant Worker

PREFACE

Dr Cindy Perry's 1997 definitive work on Nepali Christians in the Nepali Diaspora, based on her PhD research up to 1994, was mainly concerned with the dispersion of Nepalis in India (with Sikkim) and Bhutan. This included both Nepali speakers and ethnic Nepalis, whether having Indian citizenship or not. Chapter 14, however, was a meagre 9 pages covering "Nepali Overseas," mostly in Asia. On page 351 she quoted a figure of perhaps 5-6,000 Nepalis in 'Arab' in 1992 and stated that the Nepali pioneers in the Middle East were ex-servicemen "searching further afield for employment opportunities", who were later joined by other labour migrants after these 'Gurkhas' had established a good reputation for Nepali workers. Dr Perry also noted that the Nepalis in Malaysia were also mostly descendants of Gurkha soldiers, who had settled there and gained citizenship after the 2nd World War.

The subsequent 15 plus years have seen vast changes both in Nepal and in the Nepali Diaspora, notably due to the Maoist Peoples' War. The associated socio-economic and political disturbances at home have caused a steady and increasing stream of Nepalis to leave their homeland such that today conservative figures are of more than 700,000 Nepalis in each of 'Arab' and Malaysia, most of whom are labour migrants. And that does not take into account the vast numbers in India or of the increasing numbers of students who find their ways to the 'West'.

Sections 1 and 2 are an outline of the socio-economic factors involved in migration in the Nepali context as well as giving some information about some of the different types of migrants. Section 3 looks in more detail at Diaspora destinations for Nepalis and Section 4 summarises how all this is already changing Nepali ministry and mission, both to, for, and through Nepalis. My conclusion is a challenge as to how we might further respond.

The sources that I have used are mainly personal experiences or contacts, and press cuttings rather than academia. This book is not a scholarly treatise but rather an attempt to fill in the gap of those important years since Nepali migration became a flood. I have recounted the history and geography of Nepali migration, explained the push and pull factors in some detail and outlined the problems that have become associated with this extensive labour migration and remittance economy, but have also illustrated the account with individual anecdotes. Like Dr Perry, I have written from a Christian perspective and have tried to highlight important Christian issues. The final chapters look specifically at the way God is working in the Nepali Diaspora in order to present a challenge concerning ministry among migrants as well as a vision for mission through migrants. I hope therefore that this book will not only be a source of information about the Nepali Diaspora, but that it will also be a stimulus to pray for Nepalis, and their families who are in any way affected by migration.

INDEX

SECTION 1

DIASPORA & MIGRATION

"*...scattered among the nations*" (NIV)
"*...dispersed throughout the world*" (New English Bible)
"*...living abroad*" (Twentieth Century New Testament)
~ James 1:1 ~

Migration is one of the great global realities of our era.

> People are on the move as never before. The [20th century] capacity for long-distance travel has contributed to the vast numbers of immigrants, refugees, displaced persons, and migrant workers… [and they] have had bad effects as well as good… family disruption, the drain of skilled workers from developing nations...[1]

By 2010, there were about 200 million people in the world[i] living outside their countries of origin, either voluntarily or involuntarily.[2] Even in 2003, there were 20 million refugees,

---

[i] This figure is expected to double in the next 10 years, even without counting the descendants of earlier migrants.

30 million 'displaced' persons, and 150 million 'economic' migrants scattered around the globe.[3] These figures are now more than 5 years out of date, and, considering the socio-economic reasons for such people movements, figures for the second decade of the 21st century, are surely even higher.

Looking specifically at figures from Nepal, it is humorously stated that 'a third half of the population is living outside Nepal'. Excluding those in India, the actual figure is now probably nearer 3 rather than 2 million, of whom the majority are labour migrants in various Asian countries, notably Qatar, Emirates, Saudi Arabia, Kuwait and Malaysia.

A third of all Nepalis live outside their country!

"Until the 19th century, there were more Nepalis in Tibet than anywhere else outside Nepal."[4] This was because of the historic trade links between the two countries. This business later decreased, but long-distance trading has continued. For example, the Manang-pa, who traditionally travelled to Bangkok, Singapore and Hong Kong, deal these days "in gold, electronic goods, clothing and, in some cases, drugs, on the world markets."[5]

In the mid-1950s it was estimated that about 200,000 people were absent from Nepal long-term, but by 1981 that figure had doubled.[6] Again, the Himalayan News service reported that the number of overseas migrant workers almost doubled in the 5 years between 2001/2 and 2006/7 from just over 1 *lakh*[ii] to just over 2 *lakh*.[7] Neither source states the specific destinations, but the contexts indicate that the first referred mainly to those going to India; the second counted only legal departures to destinations other than India.

During the following 5 years, migrant figures increased further by a factor of ten! In March 2013, the Department of Foreign Employment (DoFE) calculated that about 2% of the working age population of Nepal was going overseas for employment. This works out at about 3-4 *lakh* every year.[iii]. Of these, around three-quarters are unskilled workers. Monthly departures have varied over the years but the overall trend has been an annual increase, which still shows no sign of abating. In recent years, Malaysia and Qatar have alternately vied for top place in recruitment.

One positive result of this movement of people is that it is changing or adding to what we have traditionally thought of as 'the mission field'. "The beginning of globalization is the end of geography."[8] Many people in the world can no longer be defined by their traditional country boundaries. The implication is that "the phenomenon of diaspora requires a new missiological paradigm to cope with the opportunities and challenges emerging… [and that] Missionaries should flow ever more freely from and to all six continents…"[9]

Diaspora requires a new mission paradigm.

[ii] 100,000.

[iii] The figures the DoFE quoted were that 1.83% of the 15.09 million working age population of Nepal, or 276,787 individuals, had left for destinations overseas in the preceding 9 months.

Chapter 1

DIASPORA DIMENSIONS

"... 'I have spread you [or scattered you] abroad as the four winds of the heavens', declares the LORD."
~ Zechariah 2:6 (ESV) ~

The phenomenon of people of all nations living outside their homelands is what makes for diaspora. Before we consider the Nepali Diaspora in detail, it may be helpful to study this issue in general and historical terms.

WHAT is DIASPORA?

"...The kingdom of God is as if a man should scatter seed on the ground."
~ Mark 4:26 ESV ~

Diaspora is a Greek word (διασπορά) which literally means 'scattering' or 'dispersion'. Nowadays it is used to refer to the movement, migration, or scattering of any people away from their ancestral homeland. In Ancient Greece it originally referred to empire-building colonists, but it is best known as the term applied to the Jewish people exiled to Babylonia in 587 BC and later forced to flee from Jerusalem in AD 70. In this form it appears in the Septuagint (Greek)

Bible and it continued to be used, almost exclusively, in this specific way for many centuries. Only at the end of the 19th century does the word start to appear in English usage. By the middle of the 20th century, however, it was in much more common usage in English and referred to the growing numbers of permanent expatriates from various different countries. Our 21st century now knows only a borderless world, with 3% of the world population (i.e. more than 200 million people) living outside the borders of their own original homelands – in Diaspora. "People are on the move – from everywhere – to everywhere," but the exciting and challenging fact is that God Himself is also on the move.[iv]

People are on the move.

Interestingly, according to the *Oxford English Dictionary Online*, the first known recorded usage of the word *diaspora* in the English language in 1876 spoke of the "extensive *diaspora* work of evangelizing among the National Protestant Churches on the continent." Then, for over a century, God's role in diaspora seems to have been largely overlooked by most theologians and missionaries. However, Samuel Escobar has reminded us that "The *migration model* has... functioned through the centuries. Migrants from poor countries who move in search of economic survival carry the Christian message and missionary initiative with them..."[10]

Since the 1990s, other Missiologists have again taken up this idea and begun to search for new ways to address the new opportunities and challenges of Diaspora populations.

[iv] This was the main theme of Lausanne III, Cape Town, 2010

Protestant Evangelicals, through the various Lausanne Conferences since 1974, and also the Roman Catholic Church in the USA recognised this in their official document *One Family Under God*, Sept 1995, revised 1998. This dealt comprehensively with the matters of migration and mission.[11] Slowly the worldwide church is coming to realise that "migration is not just one of the dominant features of our globe; it is one of the most significant opportunities for mission today."[12]

Migration is one of the most significant opportunities for mission today.

What has been happening in the Nepali Diaspora is a powerful illustration of this as significant numbers of Hindu Nepalis have gone to work overseas, often in Muslim nations, and returned home as Christians.

The Chinese and the Indian Diasporas are well known, but it is the Filipino Diaspora that is especially important for us to note in the Christian context. About 11% (or between 6.8 to 11 million) of the total population of the Philippines are living in Diaspora. Each year more than 1 million Filipinos go overseas to work. "A majority of them are women applying as domestic helpers and personal service workers."[13] A large number of these migrants see themselves as missionaries, and the churches in the Philippines see diaspora as one avenue for mission in creative access countries. This vision has been well-documented in *Scattered – The Filipino Global Presence* by Pantoja et al, 2004. Some would suggest that it was God himself working behind the Filipino government's diaspora policy which has enabled many Filipino Christians to become Christ's witnesses to so many remote corners of the earth.[14] Luis Pantoja Jr. says that Filipinos "need to be awakened to and challenged with the religio-missiological implications of their scattering..."[15] The fact is that many have already woken up to it and left an example to be followed by others like the Nepalis. The Filipino global presence and their Christian witness "caught the attention of missiologists" as they saw many Filipinos accepting Christ while working overseas, local indigenous churches being established, not only in countries with religious freedom, but also in some restricted access nations, and Filipino pastors starting to go overseas as 'tentmakers'.[16] What has particularly caught my attention is that Filipinos helped Nepali migrants in Qatar to establish a Nepali fellowship. (see p.232ff)

GOD is on the MOVE

"...Be strong and courageous.
Do not be frightened, and do not be dismayed,
for the LORD your God is with you wherever you go."
~ Joshua 1:9 ESV ~

The over-arching theme of the landmark Christian conference, Lausanne III, in Cape Town, 2010 – arguably the largest single diverse, yet united, Christian congress ever – was 'GOD IS ON THE MOVE', meaning that as people move back and forth across the globe, so too God is moving in them and with them and on behalf of them. Several of the sessions

> ***God is on the move.***

centred around Diaspora issues i.e. People on the Move. A souvenir booklet produced by the Lausanne Diasporas Leadership Team was entitled *Scattered to Gather – Embracing the Global Trend of Diaspora.* As these leaders prepared for the conference, they considered the redistribution of people that has come about through Diasporas and saw that "a new strategy [was] necessary to effectively reach the millions of migrants wherever they are." (p.9) They called this 'Diaspora Missiology' and defined it as "a missiological framework for understanding and participating in God's redemptive mission among people living outside their place of origin." (p.10)

DIASPORA & the BIBLE

"Now those who were scattered went about preaching the word."
~ Acts 8:4 ESV ~

The Bible is full of stories of migrants, though the words used are generally 'foreigner', 'stranger', 'sojourner', 'alien', or 'exile'. Since God expelled Adam and Eve from the Garden of Eden (Gen. 3:24), and later commanded the sons of Noah to spread out through the earth (Gen. 9:1; 10:5), mankind has been migrating to and fro across the world. Abraham was called to leave his home city of Ur and travel to the 'Promised Land'. In the time of Joseph, all the family of Jacob (Israel) migrated south to Egypt where they remained for 430 years until, under the leadership of Moses and then Joshua, they were able to return to their homeland. The Babylonian Captivity (or Exile) – which lasted 70 years – was the next major migration of the Jewish people, although in the periods of the Judges and Kings there were individual migrants. Well known examples are Naomi and Ruth as well as the little girl who served Naaman's wife. (2 Kings 5) Jesus himself, was taken as a small child to Egypt, to escape the wrath of King Herod (Matt. 2:13-15). In New Testament times, we see Aquila and Priscilla moving between Rome, Corinth and Ephesus for political and Gospel reasons. Paul and the other Apostles were moved out by God in order to spread the Gospel (Matt. 28:18-20). The final major dispersion of the Jews occurred after the rout of Jerusalem by the Romans in AD 70, and it was only after the Second World War that Jews were once again allowed to return to their homeland as a people.

The Jewish Christian Diaspora was related to Christian missions in Bible times. In James 1:1 and 1 Pet. 1:1 the noun, 'scattered' / diaspora is used and in Acts 8:1, 8:4 and 11:19 the verb, 'to scatter'. "The persecution of Acts 8:1 and the subsequent missions' efforts in Acts 8:4 resulted in the formation of 'the church throughout Judea, Galilee and Samaria [i.e. in Israel]'" and then in Acts 11:19-20 "those who were scattered by the persecution related to Stephen's martyrdom went to the northern portions of Phoenecia [sic], Cyprus, and Antioch [i.e. Gentile territories]". Diaspora, along with suffering and persecution, is one of God's chosen tools for the spread of missions.[17]

Christianity is a migratory religion.

Jehu Hanciles has said something very similar: "Christianity is a migratory religion, and migration movements have been a functional element in its expansion."[18] Roger Greenway goes even further, saying that, "… the migratory phenomenon of diaspora… is a divine provision of making those who traditionally had been unreachable and resistant to become reachable by and receptive to the gospel."[19] They all agree that God deliberately chooses to use diaspora as one of his mission methods.

There are many Bible verses which address the issues of migration and diaspora, but three are of especial importance for us today, especially in relation to the extent of labour migration among Nepalis:

The first declares for us how God himself sees migrant people. Psalm 146:9 (NIV) says, ***"The LORD watches over the alien…"*** Because God loves migrants and cares for them, this is a solid foundation for our Christian involvement in migrant ministry. It is not a command but an example for us to follow. If we do not heed this challenge, then we are missing something that is obviously close to God's own heart. The very fact that so many Nepalis are meeting God while working overseas is surely evidence of his love and concern for them. It is far from unusual to hear the testimony of returnees, 'I went to Malaysia, Arab... to make money. I did not find fortune there but I did find a Saviour.' I heard a heart-warming testimony of a young man I met in Malaysia:

The LORD cares for migrants.

He had come from a Christian background but had backslid. Nevertheless he was working conscientiously and had become the foreman of a group of others. One day he was approached by an older man in his unit, who requested an hour off. When he enquired the reason, the man said, "I want to spend time reading my Bible and praying before I die." His strange request was granted and shortly afterwards the young supervisor also went off duty for a short break. On his return, he found the older man had collapsed and his dying words were, "Please come back to the Lord." The young man did.

The second verse speaks to the people in those nations who host migrant communities. ***"When an alien lives with you in your land, do not ill-treat him... Love him as yourself, for you were aliens in Egypt."*** (Leviticus 19:33-34 NIV).

Even secular bodies recognise the value of trying to achieve mutual benefit for both migrants and their hosts, "improving dialogue and the management of labour migration so as to benefit both sending and receiving countries and better protect the rights and equal treatment of migrant workers."[20] However, it is insufficient to simply not treat foreigners or migrants badly. As Christians, we are commanded to treat them as God would and, insofar as it is possible under the laws of the land, to treat them the same as native citizens. Many specific suggestions concerning fair recruitment, effective services for migrant workers, skills training and ensuring safe migration, especially for women, have been made over the years but sadly, most have not yet trickled down to benefit Nepali migrants. This is an issue for host country churches, for it seems that those who are really maturing in their Christian lives are more likely to exhibit greater concern for the living conditions of migrants.[21]

Do not ill-treat a migrant... love him as yourself.

Many migrants leave their own countries because of intolerable situations back home. Sadly, in the new countries to which they go, they are often treated equally badly – if not worse. At best they are regarded as 'second-class citizens' even if they are given formal citizenship. At worst they may be ill-treated and abused psychologically, physically and even sexually. Migrants are often "victims of exclusion by the host society," being segregated and forced to live in migrant ghettos or discriminated against in various social situations.[22] Even 'enlightened' western countries all too often cite rules, regulations, and quotas as excuses for not providing migrants with their due human rights.

I met a Nepali who had been living and working in the UK for several years but recently been deported. He may, of course, have omitted some embarrassing details when talking to me, but his story does not speak well for the authorities in Britain. He told me that a friend who had 'overstayed his welcome' in the UK had been arrested. This man then went to visit his friend in order to help. When the authorities discovered that his own visa had expired – despite the fact that he had a legal case pending over this situation – he himself was immediately arrested and detained. Two weeks later he was duly sent back to Nepal. In the meantime he had not been allowed to return to his home – even with an escort – to collect his belongings.

In the Middle East and even Malaysia, many migrants are treated far worse than this by their employers, but not all Malaysians behave in this way. Like the Israelites, who were reminded of their own earlier migrant status in Egypt, most non-Malay (i.e. ethnic Chinese or Indian) Malaysians are themselves migrants, albeit several generations back. Although they are themselves, to some extent, second class citizens in their own country, many Christians have developed a real concern for the huge numbers of new (labour) migrants in their midst. Churches all over Malaysia are involved in migrant ministries, offering various kinds of practical and spiritual help.

The third verse is addressed to the migrants themselves. ***"… seek the peace and prosperity of the city to which I have carried you in exile. Pray to the Lord for it, because if it prospers, you too will prosper."*** (Jeremiah 29:7 NIV). Migrants are to behave well and show concern for the place of their adoption, whether it is temporary or permanent. If they are Christians, they are also to pray for the people of their host country. There are migrants who flout the laws of the country in which they work. There are migrants who commit crimes.

Pray for the land you go to.

In Malaysia, in 2011, my Nepali friends received an urgent phone call from one of their group, who, the night before had gone to help a friend, returning to Nepal, take his luggage to the airport. Because the Nepal Airlines flight leaves very early in the morning, they spent most of the night camped out in the departure lounge. Then this man left his friend at the airport, and travelled into the centre of Kuala Lumpur to catch a bus back to the south. It was still very early in the morning when few people were around. Suddenly, he was set upon by a group of 10 youths – migrants from a different national group. He was stabbed but happily only sustained minor wounds.

This is not an isolated incident. The year before, I heard of two Nepalis stabbed to death while walking home from work late at night. In some countries, despite enjoying all the benefits of their adopted country, some migrants have turned against it and its people. Some have committed horrendous atrocities, though Nepali migrants have never, to my knowledge, been involved in anything as radical as suicide bombing. The most common crime among (Nepali) migrants in Malaysia and the Middle East seems to be illegality. Some know this is wrong and hope to hide their illegal status. Probably many are unaware of the consequence of running away from their contracted place of employment. Even Christians have become illegal, often through little fault of their own. In contrast, the many Christian groups try to help fellow migrants with their problems. In this, where they can, they work together with local Christian believers.

In this Biblical context, we are reminded of the challenge of massive migrant populations as identified by Samuel Escobar, a Peruvian Missiologist:

> First is *the challenge to Christian compassion and sensitivity*... The second challenge is *the need for the churches to take a prophetic stance in the face of society's unjust treatment of immigrants*... The third challenge is the fact that *migration is an avenue for the evangelistic dimension of mission*... (his original emphasis).[23]

I will return to this important issue in Section 4.

Chapter 2

MIGRATION MATTERS

"The LORD had said to Abram, 'Leave your country, your people and your father's household and go to the land I will show you.'"
~ Genesis 12:1 ~

The title of this chapter has been deliberately chosen for its ambiguity of meaning. It is about the matters or issues of migration. It also emphasises that migration, as a phenomenon, is important, that is, it matters; and not only to those who participate in it personally.

WHAT IS MIGRATION

"By faith he went to live in the land of promise, as in a foreign land, living in tents with Isaac and Jacob, heirs with him of the same promise."
~ Hebrews 11:8-9 ESV ~

At its simplest, migration is the movement of peoples. However, many scholars have attempted to define or categorise migration in greater detail than this.

Hornby and Jones speak of mobility as the over-arching term, and circulation, which seems to imply returning as well as outgoings. Migration, they defined as a much narrower term, describing a usually permanent change of residence from one administrative area to another.[24] This is helpful as it is clear that most people travelling to and from a country are not migrants in a strict sense. "Tourists, business executives, temporary workers and asylum seekers… are not usually defined as migrants."[25] If permanency is the most significant criteria, it begs the question of how permanent is permanent – or how long does one have to reside overseas, or plan to do so, before being called a migrant? Both these definitions significantly predate the latest massive wave of Nepali migration and it is arguable that they are no longer wholly valid distinctions at least in the Nepali context. One thing is clear and that is that migration leads to further migration as later migrants observe the benefits and follow on.[26] This phenomenon has been demonstrated in the Nepali Diaspora as the early ex-Gurkha migrants to the Middle East became the forerunners of the present-day labour migrants.

Many long-term (or permanent) migrants do not completely break their ties with the homeland but maintain family links across international borders – witness the popularity and growth of associations of non-residents in many nations. Perhaps therefore we should call international migration 'Transnational Migration' or 'Transmigration'? Transmigrants try, as far as possible, to participate socially, economically and politically in both their host country and their homeland. Many continue to send back remittances, make regular visits, and vote (if that is legally possible).

Most migrants maintain family links back home.

They are usually bilingual and often lead dual lives with homes in two countries.[27] Even the Nepali labour migrants in Asia, who may only reside overseas for 2-10 years are vastly changed by their experiences and return home with broadened world views and knowledge.

PUSH & PULL FACTORS

Joseph was 'pushed' out of Canaan by his family: later his family was 'pulled' out by Joseph. (Genesis 37:28; 45:25-28) *The early Christians were 'pushed' out of Jerusalem: Paul was 'pulled' towards Macedonia.* (Acts 4:4-5; 16:9)

Most secular scholars divide the factors that influence migration into two categories: the 'Push' and 'Pull' Factors. Push Factors are usually socio-economic difficulties in the homeland, natural disasters, war, unemployment and poverty. Pull Factors are those real *or imagined* benefits that entice people to another place and include the hope of employment, a good salary, the chance for a better livelihood, educational opportunities and safety. Both have been active in the migration of Nepalis – in the past and still are today.

Scholars usually separate these factors into different categories, but the reality is that there is a very significant overlap and interaction between the demographic, environmental, economic, educational, socio-cultural, religious and political factors. A poor, largely uneducated family, with too many sons and too little land is already at risk. It only needs a crop failure or a threat to their safety, like that which was posed by the Maoists in Nepal, to push them out. Similarly, the lure of a job with anticipated high wages and better conditions for their families along with safety and freedom and, maybe even the chance to find education and general betterment, all combine to lure Nepalis from their homeland. However, the significance of each of the factors has varied over the years. Even before the population explosion, land was becoming scarce for ordinary people, at least partly because of political oppression by the elite rulers. More recently, during the Maoist crisis, economic and political factors have worked together.

Push and pull are themselves not mutually exclusive. They are the two sides of the same coin, which work together like the way Nepalis use a spade with one man digging and the other pulling back. For example, lack of employment opportunities in Nepal is linked with perceived (even if not, in the event, actual) job opportunities elsewhere. Political oppression, religious discrimination and criminal violence push people out, while their desire for personal and family safety, security and freedom pull them out. It is rare for any one factor to work alone, although it may well be the straw that breaks the proverbial camel's back and so triggers the migration which has gradually been becoming inevitable.

Push and Pull factors are like two men digging with one spade.

Another way of describing these factors is to speak about opportunity-seeking migrants – for whom the pull factors are the stronger, and survival-driven migrants – who are literally pushed out of their homeland.[28]

Combining all the lists of possible factors results in about a dozen of each, but I am going to describe only those which have particular relevance in the Nepali context.

PUSH FACTORS

1. Shortage of Land

Loss of land was one of the earliest causes of Nepali migration in the late 18th and early 19th centuries. It was not, however, an absolute shortage, but rather a politically precipitated problem as common usage land was taken from villagers and given as rewards to the political elites.[29]

Nepal's population has been increasing at the rate of at least 2.1% per annum.[30] In actual terms, it has increased from around 8 million, when Nepal first opened up in the 1950s, to around 27 million in the 2011 census. Over the intervening years this has become an ever-increasing problem for the 80% who remained as village farmers. Apart from unjust land laws and gifts (as above) the Nepali cultural tradition of dividing the land between the sons of the family has resulted in halving the land ownership almost every generation. When combined with the lack of industry and inadequate education in the villages, migration became unavoidable.

2. Lack of employment opportunities

Apart from farming and its related occupations, Nepal has never developed any significant alternative employment for its rural population. Before the 1950s, there were no village schools that could have equipped young men for other kinds of work. Nowadays there are plenty of schools but still no alternative work in most of the villages. This is largely because in Nepal employment depends on education and training, gender and 'who you know.'[v 31] Internal migration to the towns has become almost inevitable although village youths with low levels of education cannot compete with their urban counterparts for the few jobs that are available. They are the ones, however, who are eligible for the overseas 'brawn drain'. Gugler suggests that there are only 3 options for 'peasants' like this caught in rural poverty. They can rebel. This was one of the main factors in the recruitment of members for the Maoist insurgency. They can retreat into subsistence farming. This is no longer a viable option in Nepal because of the diminishing land. Or they can migrate to the towns or beyond. This is what has caused the current flood of emigrants.[32]

Entrepreneurism (a specific area of employment opportunity) has been adversely affected by the deteriorating situation in Nepal in recent years, but especially in the towns. Capital funding is not the only prerequisite needed for establishing any kind of business. New enterprises also require a reliable infrastructure – something that is sadly lacking in modern Nepal. With few and badly maintained roads, long hours of load-shedding (i.e. power cuts), shortages of fuel and other essential commodities, as well as frequent politically inspired strikes, even the rich have problems starting up a new business. No new enterprises mean no new jobs for potential employees. However, economic development on its own will not bring migration to an end. Some suggest that it could even increase it depending on the state of market forces.[33]

---

[v] In Nepal, patronage works through the *aaphno manche* system.

3. Armed Force(s)

In Nepal there has, thankfully, been nothing like the inter-tribal wars of Africa that led to huge population movements across that continent. However, the ethnic cleansing of Nepali-speaking Hindus from Bhutan contains an element of cultural conflict. In addition, the **Maoist 'so-called' Peoples' War** was one of the most significant push factors in the decade plus that it lasted.

The Maoist people's war was one of the most significant push factors.

In fact, when armed force – or rather armed forces – are mentioned in connection with Nepal, one immediately thinks of the **Gurkhas,** who have played a very different and unique role in the history of Nepali migration, but originally as a strong pull factor. This has been well documented by Dr Perry. The Gurkha soldiers, the 'lahures' who first went to Lahore for enlistment in Ranjit Singh's army were, in a very real sense, the first Nepali (specialised) labour migrants. During the two world wars, around 45,000 Gurkhas lost their lives. Later, their survivors spearheaded the next significant wave of labour migration as retired Gurkhas started to work in the Gulf countries, Singapore and Brunei. In the beginning, joining the army was essentially a pull factor for it represented almost the only way that young Nepali men could hope to obtain any education and opportunity other than farming their ancestral lands. Enlisting in the British or Indian army is perhaps now both a push factor and a pull factor.

4. Religious Intolerance & Persecution

From the unification of Nepal (in 1768-9) until recently, Nepal was regarded as a Hindu country, although many Buddhists have traditionally, and usually peacefully, coexisted within the state. Until 2006, Nepal was proud to be the only Hindu kingdom in the world. Since then, despite becoming in 2008, what I facetiously call the only Federal Democratic (Communist) Republic in the world, still the majority of the population (approx. 80% in the 2011 census) are practising Hindus. Every so often there are uprisings prompted by those who would like to put the clock back, returning Nepal from its secular status to a Hindu one.

In the century before unification, the three Malla kings of the Kathmandu Valley allowed Roman Catholic Capuchin monks to settle and practise their Christian religion. Thus a small church was established. However, when King Prithvi Narayan Shah overthrew the Mallas, he also threw these fathers and their Christian disciples out of Nepal. This is an isolated example of involuntary migration for the 57 Newari Christian converts who had to leave Nepal at that time. They settled in Bettiah in North India[34] and never returned.

In the subsequent years – under the Shah Kings and then during the 104 years of the Rana Regime – no Christians were allowed to migrate into Nepal, although there were several attempts to do so. Only in the middle of the 20th century were Nepali Christians allowed to return to their homeland. These were the descendants of earlier waves of migration into India; Nepalis who had accepted Christ while in the diaspora. Nevertheless, between 1952 and 1990 there were sporadic instances of Christians being exiled from

Nepal because of their faith. I personally knew Ps. David Mukhiya (of Ramghat Church, Pokhara). He was forced to remain in exile in India when a warrant was put out for his arrest in 1960 and only able to return to Nepal in 1969. Another pastor from a church in Kathmandu was also forced to leave the country or face a long spell of imprisonment. Strictly speaking, these pastors made their own decisions – regarding where they should stay – in fact both are really examples of compulsory migration on religious grounds.

Migrant Nepali Christians were the first missionaries back to their homeland.

In Nepal it has always been difficult to separate religious and political issues. This is still so in modern secular Nepal.

5. Lack of Human Rights & Political Oppression

From one perspective we may even consider HM King Tribhuvan a victim of the oppressive Rana Regime. He was forced to seek temporary asylum in India in 1950 before the change in political situation, and the fall of the Ranas allowed him to return and take over the reins of government in Nepal.

During the Maoist insurgency, which began in the mid-1990s, thousands of Nepalis fled from their homeland. The vast majority opted to take work in India, SE Asia or 'Arab'. These are the modern labour migrants – the flood that constitutes the latter phase of the third wave of Nepali migration. For one young man from Arghakhanchi, in West Nepal, it happened like this:

I had a small shop in the village. Everything was all right. One day, out of the blue, some of the youth were taken by the Maoist army. We suspected that they were killed but later, information was given that they too joined the Maoist army. Our villagers were told that the Maoists were in need of more people in their force. My parents decided to send me away from the village. I was in a dilemma: what to do? I couldn't wait any longer in the village. I just crossed the border and came to Delhi. I was in touch with some of my villagers who had already been working here. I also joined a hotel. Since then I am working here and support my family. I had to sacrifice my study due to the political crisis. What to do when you don't get work in Nepal? Even if you get work, youth like us are not secure. Now, I can visit my parents during the festival time. Earlier it was tough even to visit.[35]

A smaller number sought asylum in a wide variety of countries, either in Asia, or in the west – if they could afford to travel there. I remember acting as interpreter for the British Home Office in the late 1990s. In one day I sat in on two interviews. One was of a former Maoist who claimed his life was in danger if he remained in Nepal. In fact, he admitted that his family hoped he would find educational opportunities in the UK. The other was of a lady who belonged to the Rastriya Prajatantra Party and also said she went in danger of her life while remaining in Nepal. She had arrived via India and other countries and it was not clear why she had ended up in the UK. I doubt if either were successful in their requests, partly because of the way they presented themselves. However, others with more convincing stories were undoubtedly worthy of gaining asylum.

The extent to which the Maoist People's War and the long drawn-out revolution affected out-migration from Nepal is hard to separate from all the related factors. Although strictly speaking these migrants were also not expelled by any armed force, threats and actual violence were undoubtedly trigger factors for thousands of families to decide to send at least one member overseas. The reality of this threat was brought home to my friend in a rather sad way in 2007.

> *A Nepali migrant she met in Malaysia mentioned that a former hospital laboratory colleague of hers, with whom she had worked for 2 years in Nepalgunj, had been kidnapped by the Maoists and apparently 'disappeared'.*[vi]

In a few cases, a more direct involvement from one or other of the antagonists was discernible. I remember meeting two Nepali men in Malaysia:

> *One had been a high school teacher, who with several of his colleagues, had been arrested by the Maoist forces. Some of these colleagues were killed but just as he was expecting the same fate for himself, and for no obvious reason, he was released. Soon after, he decided to flee the country and ended up working in a factory, where he met Christians and accepted Jesus as his Saviour.*
> *The other man, Bhim, had joined the Maoists to take revenge for the killing of his brother and aunt apparently by the Nepal Army. He subsequently took part in many battles in west Nepal, but after Beni, he was captured by the Government forces, accused of multiple murders as a Maoist red army commander and fully expected to 'be disappeared' and die at their hands. In fact, for more than 2 years he was tortured and imprisoned in a dark underground tank. Then, again for some unknown reason, someone arranged a ticket to Malaysia for him. He also started to work in a factory, where he met Christians and himself eventually became a believer in*

[vi] This usually means that they have been killed.

Christ through hearing the good news that Christ can forgive and cleanse even from sins as bad as his.

Now these two 'brothers in Christ' were present together in the same Christian meeting.

During the period of ethnic cleansing in Bhutan in the 1980s, those who were of Nepali origin and mostly of Hindu religion, were forced to leave, regardless of whether or not they held Bhutanese citizenship. Some left before they were pushed out, but most would have chosen to stay in their adopted country. This is an example of **expulsion by coercion**, albeit not carried out physically by armed force.

6. Lack of Security due to Revolution, Violence, Lawlessness & Crime

Revolution spawns violence and crime. This has been the experience in Nepal for many years. Protests originally started peacefully but frequently became increasingly violent and lawless. Students and others clashed with police, threw stones, burnt tyres, called for *bandhs*.[vii] Ordinary people were intimidated and frightened. Taxi drivers lost income. Sick people were unable to reach hospital. Schools and colleges were frequently shut down and students missed classes, sometimes for weeks on end.

In September 2004, there was an unprecedented day of violence, bizarrely triggered by a tragedy in the diaspora. 12 Nepalis had been assassinated in Iraq. Suddenly, within one hour, tyres were burning and blocking every *chowk*[viii] on the

[vii] Closure, strike.
[viii] Road junction, cross-roads.

ring road and every major intersection in Kathmandu city centre. The contents (furniture, computers, records, etc.) of dozens of Manpower Agency offices were trashed, thrown into the roads and set on fire. This uprising was attributed to the distraught relatives of the 12, but in fact that is highly unlikely. Distressed and mourning families are unlikely to organise anything like this. Also, the demonstrations were so highly synchronised, within the space of one hour, that this could not possibly have been a spontaneous reaction from ordinary people. It was rather a violent outburst of anger against the agencies who had sent people to Iraq and against the government who had not tried hard enough to rescue the victims. The organisers had just seized the opportunity.

That very morning, I found myself away from home, on the wrong side of town. Riding my scooter to get home to safety through the flames and ashes, and dodging the stone-throwing angry youths was quite an adrenaline-raising experience. One expatriate family almost immediately left the country – they could not cope with the trauma. On the other hand, the natural fatalism of the Nepali people enabled them to live with this, not that they had much choice! Maybe, until the initial furore died down and in relation to a few countries like Iraq, it did temporarily slow the flood of migrants. However, people continued to look and hope for something better. They were searching for something safer for their families. And so in the long run, the exodus of labour migrants continued unabated.

7. Slavery & Trafficking

The issue of trafficking of Nepali girls has been widely publicised in the Nepali media, partly because it relates to the growing problem of HIV/AIDS[ix]. Many NGOs[x] have thus become involved in the rescue and rehabilitation of these unfortunate sex slaves, although successful extraction of girls from the brothels of India is extremely hard to achieve.

I once heard the story of a pastor's daughter who had, I think, through the agency of some unscrupulous relatives, been trafficked into a brothel in Bombay. Immediately the father heard the true facts, he and his son set off for Bombay, without any real idea of where to start looking, and almost certainly, with no concept of how difficult it would be to make contact, let alone rescue the girl from the clutches of the pimps and madams. They reached Bombay and located the red light area. They prayed as they wandered the streets. Suddenly, they looked up and there was the girl, at one of the windows. Amazing! Even more amazing – they were able to extricate her and take her home to safety.

This is one happy ending in the midst of thousands of unhappy ones. All too many girls ultimately become infected with HIV and are then returned to Nepal to face ostracism, rather than a loving welcome back by their families.

The size of this problem is hard to tell exactly but it is certainly very significant. In 2012, the National Human Rights Commission (NHRC) suggested that 12,000 women and girls were trafficked out the country each year, but this may be an over-estimate as it is based on NGO figures which are sometimes duplicated. On the other hand, official figures of just under 300 are grossly underestimated as most cases never reach the courts.[36] Baruah says something interesting

---

[ix] Human Immunodeficiency Virus / Acquired Immune Deficiency Syndrome.

[x] Non-Government Organisations

but not too surprising: "The ban [restricting women under 30 going for domestic work in the Gulf] has only proved counter-productive as many women are now going through extra-legal routes via India and therefore remain undocumented and even more vulnerable."[37]

8. Natural hazards, Famine & Drought

Although Nepal lies in an **earthquake** zone and is subject to both **floods** and **famine** from time to time, the response to these calamities has usually been one of temporary internal migration until such time as the victims have been able to return to their own land. However, in the wake of some disasters, despite return, survival is no longer feasible in the affected areas. This then leads to longer term solutions, of which overseas migration is now probably the number one choice, at least for the young men.

> ***There is a longstanding tradition of seasonal migration from the NW hill districts of Nepal to India.***

In some districts of western Nepal (e.g. Mugu, Achham, Bajhang, Bajura), which are the least developed in the country, there has long been a **crop deficit**. The hillsides are extremely steep, the land is poor and the crop yield quite insufficient to feed the population. In Bajura, for example, food production is only sufficient for 6 months of the year, but 83% of the people there lack alternative income skills. This is what has led to a tradition, stretching back over several generations, of seasonal migration into NW India by the men from the villages in this area. However, the Maoist insurgency intensified it. About 25% of the population from these hills are seasonal migrants,[38] and the womenfolk they leave behind have to shoulder the burden of caring for the family and doing all the field-work.[39] Until 2001 most Nepali migrants originated from the hills: now more come from the *Terai*.[xi][40] This is serious, as migration from the country's 'breadbasket' has therefore resulted in lowered agricultural productivity there.[41]

9. Poverty

With a per capita GDP of only 1,300 USD, Nepal is one of the poorest countries in the world.[42] Poverty is a ubiquitous problem and related to almost all the other factors – population increase, lack of land, poor education, limited employment opportunities and the Maoist insurgency, to name only the principal ones. Most modern international migration is ultimately economically driven.[43] The poor are always at greater risk. Poverty is not only an important push factor but also the degree of poverty determines the destination of the migration.[44] The poorest Nepali migrants have always gone to India as there are no significant overheads involved in crossing the open land border.

42% are under the poverty line

46% are unemployed

Most modern international migration is economically driven.

[xi] Southern plain of Nepal.

However, the poorest of the poor are tied down by debts being repaid locally through their labour and do not have the resources even to go to India.[45] The real benefit for very poor families is often not the remittances (which may be negligible) but the fact that one member away in India has reduced the burden on the family food stocks.[46]

Those slightly less poor tend to opt for other destinations in Asia. However, after paying outrageous fees to the agents, these migrants invariably begin their new overseas careers with huge outstanding loans. Amnesty International has reported that "migrant workers take loan for up to 35 percent interest rate against 14 percent determined by law."[xii] All spare salary from their first year of work has to go towards the repayment of these strangling debts. If illness or accident occurs during this time, or if the promised job never materialises due to the dishonesty of the agents, they face a critical situation. These returnees have no money, no job, huge interest repayments on their loans and are maybe even too disabled to ever find a suitable job. Research done by Third Alliance in the eastern district of Mahottari revealed two sad facts. Almost half of migrant earnings goes towards paying back loans, and many do not manage to clear these debts despite years of hard labour overseas. The other half of their earnings is spent on

Half of migrant earnings pays back loans: the other half pays for living essentials.

[xii] Several figures quoted in the 2011 AI report are almost certainly over-estimates. However, many migrants definitely do repay their loans at rates far higher than the legal limit – even up to 60%.

essentials like food, clothes, health and education for family members. There is therefore nothing left over or saved to fulfil their dreams of buying a plot of land and building their own family house. This means that the workers are forced to go abroad repeatedly.[47] In contrast, the rich and the educated have been able to travel to the west to take up opportunities for education and professional advancement.

PULL FACTORS

10. Acquisition of Land & Right of Settlement

The original expansion of the borders of Nepal with associated settlement in Gadhwal-Kumaon in the west and Darjeeling in the east may have included an element of land acquisition, but overall this period of Nepali 'colonialism' was more political than related to individual settlers.

The more recent waves of migrants cannot normally hope to acquire land in another nation. The best many of them can expect is slum settlement in the cities of India or temporary contract employment with squalid hostel accommodation in other parts of Asia. This hope of land is therefore no longer a pull factor for most Nepali migrants.

However, the attraction of acquiring a Green Card with its associated right of residence in the USA (or the equivalent in other western countries) is nowadays a significant pull factor, especially for richer and better educated Nepalis.

11. Better Opportunities for Self & Children

There are two ways in which family betterment is perceived.

If the 'rice-winner' (i.e. Nepali bread-winner) of the family works overseas for a period of years, the expectation is that the whole family will benefit from the remittance economy. Earnings, which are positively correlated with education and skills,[48] are to be sent back to Nepal and used, not only for day-to-day expenses but to buy land, build a house and pay for education for their children. This is investment for the future, the way to betterment and an escape from the poverty trap, but as noted in No. 9 above, the reality is often not the same as the vision. Usually, very little goes towards any productive enterprise back in Nepal, and there may be three reasons for this. There is not enough money for projects over and above the more immediate family needs. Nepalis actually see their house and children's education as future investments for themselves. Most returnees do not have the necessary skills to start up new enterprises.

The other possibility is for the whole family to migrate overseas. In India it is possible for them to relocate together. This has the advantage that it keeps the family intact but all too often fails to provide the betterment they are looking for. Many of the families in India discover that they do not easily have access to the same welfare and schooling facilities that their Indian colleagues have. Children living with their parents in Indian slums frequently miss out on schooling. There are plenty of opportunities in India, but most of them go to the richer migrants.

To my knowledge, therefore, the only group of migrants who are significantly motivated by improved welfare and educational facilities are those who manage to travel to the west. In particular, the ex-British Gurkhas, settling in the UK, now receive pensions commensurate with their English counterparts and also all the facilities of the UK welfare state. Two older couples (both in their 70s) said they had come to the UK "because we are ill and the health service is free."[xiii] Some younger Gurkha families have migrated largely to help their children. With attacks on private schools in Nepal and frequent strikes that often close down schools and colleges for long periods, the benefits of the educational system in the west are clear.

In contrast, labour migrants in most other parts of the diaspora often discover the welfare facilities there are worse, rather than better. Many employers do not provide adequate industrial medical insurance, and in the Gulf, Nepali housemaids frequently complain that their employers refuse to let them access hospital services if they fall sick.

A further drawback that affects the family is that most labour migrants in SE Asia and the Middle East are 'geographical bachelors'. Those who are already married, have to leave their families behind: those who are not, tend to delay marriage until they return from overseas. A few get married on a short holiday back home and immediately leave behind their new wives. None of these scenarios strengthens family life; rather the reverse. The Third Alliance report particularly highlighted the difficulties faced by the wives of migrants, saying that they "are exposed to violence, harassment and

Young male migrants – 'geographical bachelors'.

[xiii] Personal communication from Joyce Odell, who says that they are now so lonely and miss their grandchildren, they are planning to return permanently to Nepal.

mental torture, mainly over financial issues. Hemmed in by their desires and traditional values, these women are often vulnerable to various threats."[49] They face other problems too: "around 90% of the husbands of ladies attending the Tansen hospital Ante Natal Clinic are overseas."[50]

12. More Work Opportunities

Of the more than 400,000 Nepalis who enter the job market every year, most of them go overseas: only 30,000 get jobs in the domestic market.[51] For those with only basic levels of education and no skills training and who no longer wish to work in the fields, or who have no fields in which to work, the vision of a factory job in Malaysia or 'Arab' is very attractive. Such jobs are readily available for non-skilled migrants but, all too often, at the end of their contracts they are back 'at square one'. To date, most overseas labour employment has not provided the migrants with any significant new (trade) skills that they can use back home in Nepal. It seems that those who migrate without skills, stay in very low-level jobs, whereas those who have at least some basic skills to start with do sometimes manage to increase these and improve their position overseas. If there were some way to ensure that migration became a source of new skills as well as of income, it could change what is currently an 'act of desperation' into a hope for a better future back in Nepal.[52] As it is, migrants return with a broader world-view but the same limited skills and

Migration is very often an 'act of desperation'.

after only a month or so back home, they are again on their way back to the same or a different location in the diaspora.

13. Higher Salaries

Most labour migrants expect to be paid significantly higher wages than they could ever hope for in Nepal. In this they are often deceived by dishonest agents and employers.

The usual procedure is to issue the migrants with a work contract. Until recently this was printed in English (or Arabic), languages with which most are quite unfamiliar. No one points out to them that the figure of salary quoted is often the maximum possible they can achieve, but only if they work inhuman overtime hours. In reality, much of their 'instant wealth' goes on repayment of loans and other overheads about which they have also never been warned.

The 2011 Amnesty International report claimed that "recruitment agencies have been charging on an average Rs. 100,000 as service fees from the migrant workers… three times more than the average annual income of Nepal in 2010," while the Nepal Government (GoN) limit is 80,000.

As the majority of Nepalis still do not pay income tax, migrating to a tax haven is clearly not a relevant factor – yet! However, some have found their way to the Cayman Islands.

14. Marriage & Other Family Reasons

This factor is only really relevant to migrants in India. Nepali communities living in the *Terai* form marriage alliances with communities just over the border, and Nepali families may join their migrant husband/father in Indian cities. In the same way some Indians have migrated into Nepal, but the numbers are far fewer and many are businessmen, industrialists and professionals as well as semi-skilled and unskilled labourers.[53]

In many of the countries to which labour migrants go, there are restrictions that preclude marriage with locals: if a Nepali wishes to marry a local Muslim, he must convert to Islam. This is usually sufficient deterrent. However, there have certainly been sexual entanglements.

In contrast, those who succeed in obtaining right of residency in the west, often try to bring over their relatives, a privilege sometimes abused by migrants from Asian communities (who bring over large numbers of their extended families or arrange marriages deliberately to bring others over) although I am not aware that Nepalis have been major culprits.

15. Political/Religious Freedom & Security

This factor is the pull for the asylum seekers. It reached its zenith during the Maoist conflict but is less significant now.

For most Nepalis influenced by one or more of these factors, the result is usually overseas migration, but this is not inevitable. Suman, a Christian student, tells his story:

> ***Suman** believed that God had given him the desire to become an engineer and serve Him and His people through this career in the future. However, he comes from a poor family and his parents faced financial problems to help him continue his studies. Instead, they suggested he go overseas to make money. "But my heart was not allowing me to do that. Deep in my heart, there was a voice: 'by any means I have to achieve what the*

Lord has stored for my life'". He prayed and God answered. His parents took a bank loan to invest in his studies, he obtained a 50% scholarship for Kathmandu University and then received further help from FOCUS[xiv]. In the middle of his engineering studies, Suman made a promise to God that when he graduates, he will return to his village and invest his skill to make use of the water resources, especially to produce hydroelectric power.[54]

THE GOD FACTOR

"And I heard the voice of the Lord saying, 'Whom shall I send, and who will go for us?'
Then I said, 'Here am I! Send me.'"
~ Isaiah 6:8 ~

For Christians I suggest that there is a third factor that should be at work in migration. I call it the 'God Factor'. This is perhaps better known as the missionary call, although this term tends to imply a limitation to those who are full-time Christian ministers. However, this God Factor should be active in the lives of all Christians, wherever they live and work and regardless of whether they have a secular or Bible College training. In diaspora terms, the God Factor should become the over-ruling reason why Christians venture overseas, regardless of any other push and pull factors that may also be working in their lives. This is because they need to know that working overseas is God's purpose for them, and this applies equally to those who have professional training and to those who go as unskilled labourers.

[xiv] FOCUS is a Christian organisation that provides scholarships for Christian students studying for secular professions.

Up until now, a significant number of Nepali Christians have gone overseas for exactly the same reasons as their non-Christian friends – without necessarily taking into consideration whether this is God's plan for their lives. One reason is that they have the same financial needs as others. Another possible reason is that until recently, in the Nepali church, only full-time ministry was regarded as 'the Lord's work'. This erroneous belief is now slowly changing and a new generation of Nepali Christians is beginning to understand, not only that the Lord has a plan for everyone's life, but that for some this is actually secular employment. The exciting thing is that such workers can be witnesses for God in a place where no pastor is welcome. Few pastors can hope to secure a full-time church role in fellowships in the Asian Diaspora, although India is a notable exception, and a few are also able to do this in Malaysia. However, some dedicated pastors have taken up the challenge to be 'tent-makers': working in factories by day and pastoring in their spare time. More such lay leaders and part-time pastors are needed to respond to this challenge.

'Tentmaking' is <u>the</u> opportunity in the Diaspora.

Right from the earliest days of Christianity this God Factor has been the main motivating force in the outward spread of the Gospel across the world. The Apostles, including Paul, responded to the challenge of the Great Commission and moved out from Jerusalem, throughout Israel and into the Gentile world, both to the east and the west. Within four centuries, the Christian church had spread throughout the whole of the Western Roman Empire as well as destinations in the east as far as India. Nestorian Christians took the good news to Persia and China and many of them were traders. In relation to this, Escobar points out that,

> Commerce in the Eastern part of the Roman Empire, following the trade routes, greatly helped the expansion of Christianity. Christian merchants from Syria and Mesopotamia carried their faith to the places where they established trading colonies… They were the earliest Christian presence in India, many centuries before the Jesuits or William Carey went there.[55]

Especially in the earlier years of the church, during the great persecutions, it is most likely that the majority of 'missionaries' were actually, like Paul, 'tent-makers' in their own professions. Sadly, the spread of the gospel has often been negatively associated with military or political conquests and imperialism – initially in the Roman Empire, and more recently, the British Empire. Missionaries did follow the merchants, soldiers and colonists, but while benefitting from some of their resources, the missionaries' main aim was to share the love of God in the lands to which they went. In addition, some of the other settlers were sincere Christians, who witnessed while they worked in their own professional roles.[56]

Today, once again, and as traditional mission opportunities are decreasing in many countries, 'tent-maker' missionary migrants are discovering new opportunities in many restricted-access countries. This is part of the challenge of Diaspora Mission and specifically for the Nepali church. It is a challenge in which the Filipino Diaspora has set a modern example. While acknowledging that people often migrate from their homelands because their own governments have not given them the opportunities they would wish for, it is still possible to see God's hand for good behind this scattering.[57]

At the same time, back in Nepal, there are also many new opportunities for service and ministry amongst migrants travelling to and fro, their families back in the hills and the many communities of Internally Displaced People[58] (Internal Migrants) in the *Terai*. Already some organisations have begun to take up these challenges. One of the many is the International Nepal Fellowship (INF), which facilitates community programmes in remote villages in western Nepal, and also for Internally Displaced Persons (IDPs) on the *Terai* as well as being involved with safe migration activities at two of the borders with India (Nepalgunj and Mahendranagar). INF also partners the Nepali Pravasi Ekata Sanjaal[xv] (NeMUN), a small NGO, based in Kathmandu. NeMUN provides hospitality, care and advocacy for outgoing and returning migrants from SE Asia and 'Arab' and helps them develop a global network to connect migrant Nepalis wherever they go, especially seeking to link them with Nepali churches in Nepal and fellowships in the diaspora.

[xv] NeMUN = Nepalese Migrant Unity Network

Chapter 3

A MULTIPLICITY OF MIGRANTS

Migrants, Mercenaries & Missionaries

"... I am a foreigner."
~ Ruth 2:10 ESV ~

Migrants come in all shapes and sizes and go by many different names. Apart from IDPs or Internal Migrants, they share one common feature – they have left their own country and gone overseas – or at least they have moved across their national boundary. Most are therefore living in a cross-cultural situation. All are migrants and, the Christians can or should be missionaries, even if part of the reason for their travel is economic or mercenary.

WHO IS A MIGRANT?

"...an alien in a foreign land."
~ Exodus 2:22 NIV ~

While it is clear that migrants are people on the move, we also need to understand the geographical and historical dimensions of their movements. We need to know where they moved from and to, as well as when this movement took place. We also need to discover the reasons why they moved. All this will help us to appreciate the phenomenon of migrants and migration and enable us to enlarge our vision for ministry and mission among different groups of migrants.

Despite some of the scholarly definitions and limitations of the term 'migrant,' in practice and from the perspective of migrant ministry I believe that we must include not only the permanent migrants but also all those who go overseas for work or study, planning to stay for 3 years or longer, and asylum seekers and refugees, who hope to be allowed to stay permanently. Non-Resident Nepalis are another special category of migrants. Technically, Gurkhas are mercenaries although I prefer not to use this term as it is pejorative: they too are migrants. Traditionally, Missionaries are those who have migrated overseas with the gospel. In fact, any Christian going overseas is potentially a Missionary and many Gurkhas have witnessed to their faith. It matters little whether they are labelled as workers, students, professionals, soldiers, asylum seekers or refugees, if they represent Christ and his gospel wherever they go, then they are missionaries.

Christian Migrants = Missionaries?

Usually we think of migrants (like the traditional missionaries) as crossing an international border – moving from their homeland to another country, which may or may not be a neighbouring one. However, we need to broaden our definition to include those who migrate within the boundaries of their own country. Although Nepal is in geographical terms only a small country, this phenomenon of **Internal Migration** is of great importance. Historically, many Newars moved out from Kathmandu in order to develop lines and centres of trade across the country – in places like Pokhara, Tansen and Baglung. In the 1970s, the then government of Nepal encouraged the resettlement of essentially landless people from the hills into certain parts of the *Terai* – like Nawal Parasi. More recently there has been the development of an urban drift in Nepal. Educated (even if not highly educated) young people tend to migrate to the towns to find work, either because they no longer want to be farmers, or because their family no longer has sufficient land to support them. With increasing numbers of professionals working in government service, extended families are split up as the bread-winners, with or without own nuclear family unit, are posted to locations all across the country. The final – and perhaps most worrying – factor has been the effect of the Maoist Peoples' War. Young men in particular, but also whole families, have fled from the hills into the relative safety and anonymity of the towns. Most are uneducated and poor, and they have given rise to communities of internally displaced peoples in places like Nepalgunj. It is estimated that up to 2006, as many as 200,000 Nepali people were displaced in this way during the Maoist insurgency. This is probably a conservative under-estimate.

In 2000, speaking at a global level, Cohen stated that most migration is internal (rural to urban), although some later move on from the towns to other countries.[59] This may have been the case in Nepal prior to the mid-1990s, but since the Maoist insurgency, with a third of the population now working outside the country, it has ceased to be true, although the progressive nature of migration from villages to towns to overseas destinations has definitely been seen in Nepal. Probably the main reason for this is that rural youths are simply not equipped to compete for well-paid jobs in the Kathmandu labour market.[60]

Gugler has described this rural-urban migration as a series of moves that many people make over the period of their lives, starting with temporary migrant labour, followed by the longer-term migration of men, which in turn is followed by migration of their families. Finally, the whole family may either settle permanently in the urban area or return to their own rural community.[61] This is what has happened in Nepal, but with the addition of a further step to overseas migration. As a result, the distinction between internal and overseas migration has become blurred.

In most countries where Nepali migrants are found, they are recognisable as a distinct ethnic group within that country. Where they are able to settle permanently, this distinction tends to disappear gradually as the younger generation intermingles and intermarries with local people and other ethnic groups. This has happened in Burma and in India, and it will probably begin to happen in the UK in the coming years. It is not a feature of the Nepali Diaspora in other parts of Asia where permanent settlement and inter-marriage are generally not possible.

Considering Nepali migrants in India, the situation is further complicated by an historical dimension. The question 'Who is a Nepali migrant in India?' is almost impossible to answer. There are ethnic Nepalis whose families migrated several generations back – mostly to the hill areas. The majority of these people now have Indian citizenship and think of themselves as Indians, although some still speak Nepali. Others have retained more of their Nepali identity like those who have campaigned for an independent Gorkhaland in NW India. Some of these earlier migrants have later internally migrated to the cities of India. Among the more recent migrants, there are two overlapping groups: those who are seasonal migrants and those who have settled long term. But even here the confusion does not end. A few have obtained Indian citizenship; most have not. Some identify as Nepalis and speak Nepali but many others prefer to merge with the surrounding population, particularly in areas where Nepalis are treated in a derogatory manner. They speak Hindi or another local language. And some who have lived in India for many years do eventually return to Nepal.

VOLUNTARY & INVOLUNTARY MIGRANTS

Abraham left Ur to go to the Promised Land 'voluntarily': Daniel left Israel to go to Babylon 'involuntarily'. (Genesis 12:1-4; Daniel 1:3-6)
Paul went on 3 missionary journeys 'voluntarily': he was taken to Rome 'involuntarily'. (Acts 13:1-4; 27:1ff)

Another helpful way of classifying migrants is as voluntary – those who choose to leave their homeland; and involuntary – those who are compelled to leave their homeland. These categories relate loosely to the opportunity-seeking and survival-driven migrants, with different weight attributed to the pull and push factors respectively. Involuntary migrants, by definition, would not leave home if they were given the choice, but in the Nepali context, the distinction is largely academic. If you are poor, with no land, no job, little education and a family to support, no one literally pushes you out of your country, but what other options do you have?

However, there are two categories of Nepali migrants who are clearly compulsory or involuntary.

The **Lhotshampas**[xvi] **(Bhutanese Nepalis)** were compulsorily evicted from their adopted homeland from 1988 onward and forced into refugee camps in eastern Nepal. They were even deprived of their citizenship.

Involuntary Nepali Migrants: Bhutanese Refugees & Trafficked Women.

The other group are those unfortunate **women who are trafficked into sex slavery**, mostly into the cities of India. Often cheated by people they know in the village – and sometimes even by members of their own families – these women are not given a fair choice. They may depart apparently freely, thinking they are going to ordinary jobs from which they can send money back to their families, but soon find out the truth of their situation. Undoubtedly, very few would ever choose this lifestyle if they knew about the brothels in advance.

[xvi] Many Bhutanese Nepalis dislike the term 'Lhotshampas' as it was given them by the oppressive Bhutanese authorities.

TEMPORARY & PERMANENT MIGRANTS

"... a stranger... sojourning with you,
or anyone... living permanently among you,"
~ Numbers 15:14 ESV ~

The other traditional way of categorising migrants depends on their length of stay outside their home country. Those who remain overseas for relatively short periods of time are regarded as temporary migrants and those who fully uproot themselves from home and settle long term in another country are the permanent migrants. However, once again the distinctions are sometimes blurred.

Labour migrants in Asia are by definition – because of the work contracts they are given – temporary migrants. Some do stay only a couple of years but others manage to stay for more than ten years, albeit sometimes illegally. In the UAE, there is currently no limit so long as they can obtain a work permit. And then, if they have sons working in the UAE, they can even remain on into their own retirement – as family dependents. However, in almost all countries where Nepali labour migrants are accepted, they are given no possibility of obtaining permanent residential status.

The one notable exception is, of course, India. With an open border and theoretically at least, no restrictions, Nepalis can settle permanently wherever they wish – and many do so. Over the years, several million Nepalis have done just this and large populations are found particularly in the NE and in the major cities. Even those who settle semi-permanently in

India, but plan eventually to return to their homeland, can – albeit sometimes with difficulty or bribes – obtain various permits and identity (ID) cards that make residence in India a lot less difficult. The other significant difference in migration patterns to India is the possibility of one special kind of temporary migration. Seasonal migration has been followed by many Nepalis from food deficit areas of the Mid-West for many generations.

Although most 'western' countries have recently tightened up on their visa requirements, some of those who go as students or professionals may be given the option to stay on to work and even become naturalised citizens after the requisite period of time has elapsed. However, American green cards or their equivalent in other countries are not easily obtained. Similarly, small numbers of Asylum Seekers have been allowed to stay but many were sent back to Nepal as not fulfilling the stringent requirements of the law. The exception here is the acceptance by several countries – notably USA – of large numbers of the Bhutanese refugees.

REFERENCES FOR SECTION 1

[1] Wilfred Owen, *Transportation and World Development*, 1987:89

[2] Lausanne III 'Cape Town Commitment', 2010

[3] Lorenzo Prencipe in Fisher, William F & Thomas Ponniah (Eds), *Another World is Possible: Popular Alternatives to Globalization at the World Social Forum*, 2003:255

[4] Cindy Perry, "The Nepali Diaspora and the Gospel", *Dharma Deepika,* July-December 2001:35

[5] Andrew Hall, *Himalayan Exodus: Nepalese Migrant Groups,* 1995:132

[6] Ibid 133

[7] "Govt ignoring Nepali migrant labourers." *Himalayan News Service*, 17 Dec 2008 (I think)

[8] Madan K Dahal (Ed), *Impact of Globalization in Nepal,* 2005:6 quoting Thompson, 1997

[9] Enoch Wan in Luis Pantoja Jr., Sadiri Joy B Tira & Enoch Wan (Eds), *Scattered: The Filipino Global Presence*, 2004:110, quoting part of Paragraph 9 of the 1974 Lausanne Covenant

[10] Pantoja et al, 2004:104, quoting Escobar, 2000:34

[11] Pantoja et al 2004:110

[12] *Missiology*, Jan 2003

[13] Wikipedia

[14] Pantoja et al, 2004:23

[15] Ibid 69

[16] Ibid 78-79

[17] Narry F Santos, "Survey of the Diaspora occurrences in the Bible and their contexts in Christian missions" in *Scattered...*, Pantoja et al, 2004:53ff

[18] Pantoja et al, 2004:117 quoting Jehu Hanciles, 2003:149

[19] Ibid quoting Roger Greenway, 1999:554-555

[20] Asian Regional Symposium of the International Labour Organisation (ILO), S Korea, 2006

[21] Darrell Jackson "Europe and the Migrant Experience: Transforming Integration," *Transformation: An International Journal of Holistic Mission Studies,* 2011 28:14 p21, referring to the European Values Survey, 2001

[22] Prencipe in Fisher, 2003:260

[23] Pantoja et al, 2004:107 quoting Escobar 2003:19

[24] William F Hornby & Melvyn Jones, *Studies in Human Geography: An Introduction to Population Geography*, 1980:83ff

[25] Sture Öberg in Wolfgang Lutz, *The Future Population of the World: What can we assume today?* 1996:339
[26] Ibid 344
[27] Jehu Hanciles, "Migration and Mission: Some Implications for the Twenty-first Century Church," *International Bulletin of Missionary Research*, Vol. 27, No 4, Oct 2003:148
[28] Brigitte Suter, *Labour Migration in the United Arab Emirates: Field study on Regular and Irregular Migration in Dubai*, 2005:39 quoting Bimal Gosh, 1998: *Huddled Masses and Uncertain Shores. Insights into Irregular Migration.* International Organization for Migration. 1998:35
[29] Cindy L Perry, *Nepali Around the World*, 1997:16
[30] Dahal (Ed), 2005:156
[31] Josef Gugler (Ed), *The Urbanization of the Third World*, 1988:54
[32] Ibid 36
[33] Suter, 2005:9
[34] Perry, 1997:17
[35] Janak BC, personal communication
[36] "No Data on trafficked nationals," *The Kathmandu Post*, 5 Sep 2013
[37] Nandita Baruah, "Nandita Baruah Examines Realities & New Approaches to Combating Human Trafficking," *Asia Foundation*, 5 Jul 2013
[38] BC Upreti, *The Marginal Migrants (A Study of Nepali emigrants in India)*; 2002:77
[39] Dahal, 2005:38
[40] *Nepal Migration Year Book 2011,* NIDS & NCCR, 2012:20
[41] Dahal, 2005:111
[42] Ibid 2005:10
[43] Hanciles, *IBMR*, Vol. 27, No 4, Oct 2003:147
[44] Michael Lokshin, Mikhail Bontch-Osmolovski & Elena Glinskaya, *Work-Related Migration and Poverty Reduction in Nepal*, 2007:18
[45] David Seddon, Jagannath Adhikari & Ganesh Gurung, *The New Lahures: Foreign Employment and Remittance Economy of Nepal*, 2001:139
[46] *Passage to India*, WFP & NDRI, 2008:16
[47] "Migrant workers burdened by high interest rate," *Ekantipur,* 8 July 2012
[48] *Passage to India*, WFP & NDRI, 2008:13
[49] "Migrant workers burdened by high interest rate," *Ekantipur,* 8 July 2012
[50] Ansie van Rensburg, personal communication
[51] "Nepali gov't to explore potential job sectors, *Xinhua English*, 7 July 2012

[52] Hall, 1995:141

[53] Upreti, BC, 2002:119-120

[54] Information from Focus Annual Report

[55] Samuel Escobar, *A Time for Mission: The Challenge of Global Christianity*, 2003: 41

[56] Escobar, 2003: 48

[57] Pantoja et al, 2004:89

[58] Alastair Seaman, TIN 2005 "A stranger in my own Land", *Today in Nepal*, 2005. There are at least 1 *lakh* IDPs in Nepal.

[59] Robin Cohen & Paul Kennedy, *Global Sociology*, 2000:202

[60] Poertner et al, "Migration in Far West Nepal International Linkages between Internal and International Migration of Rural-to-Urban Migrants, *Critical Asian Studies*, Vol. 43:1, 2011:25

[61] Gugler, 1988:56

SECTION 2

NEPAL & MIGRATION

"But the land that you are going over to possess
is a land of hills and valleys,
which drinks water by the rain from heaven,
a land that the LORD your God cares for.
The eyes of the LORD your God are always upon it,
from the beginning of the year to the end of the year."
~ Deuteronomy ESV 11:11-12 ~

These were the verses through which the founders of one of the major missions, still working in Nepal today, were challenged to serve in this land. If the Lord loves this land of Nepal so much, why is it that so many people are fleeing from it these days? To understand this we need first to take a look back into history and also see how Nepal's migration history is intimately entwined with the history of the Nepali church. Although much of the detail of the origin of Nepal as a nation is lost in the mists of time, it is clear that many of the ancestors of the present day Nepali peoples arrived from lands to the north or south. Today, their exodus, to lands often east and west, is far less obscure and the reasons, as discovered in Chapter 2, have little to do with love for the land. In fact, most would probably still be in living in their beloved hills and valleys if this were a truly viable option.

The other important matter to understand is the legal position of migrants. So before we study the historical dimensions of both in and out migration, it will be helpful to consider the reaction of the UN and the legal position of the Government of Nepal (GoN) with regard to migration.

The UN General Assembly adopted comprehensive international labour standards in its International Convention on Protection of all Migrant Workers and their Families in 1990, but these only came into force on 1 July 2003. Some of the main articles are as follows:

- No arbitrary interference in a migrant's privacy should be allowed (14).
- Migrant workers must have a right to a fair trial (16).
- Migrant workers should be equal with nationals before the law (18).
- No employer should be allowed to confiscate or destroy a migrant worker's passport.
- Foreign workers should enjoy the same conditions as nationals with respect to remuneration, overtime pay, weekly rest, termination of employment relationship and other working conditions (25).

These conditions were meant to apply to both documented and undocumented workers[1] and the Convention has been ratified by many countries. However, the reality is that neither Nepal nor many of the countries to which Nepali migrants go are truly adhering to its terms.

Migrant Rights International (MRI) has summarised this as a vivid description of the plight of many Nepali migrants:

> Migrants often become universal 'scapegoats,' targeted for violence and excluded from legal protections in many places due to their immigration status or nationality. The increased designation of migrants as 'illegal' further aggravates the deprivation of rights entitled to everyone under international human rights law. Historically, little international attention, advocacy, and public education had been devoted to upholding the human rights and dignity of migrants other than refugees, despite the elaboration of international human rights standards for migrants and declarations in international conferences calling for cooperation towards the protection of migrants' rights.[2]

It is not my purpose in this book to provide a comprehensive survey of Nepali Government policy regarding Migration – if you are interested, I suggest you read ***Government Labour Migration in Nepal: An Analysis of Existing Policies and Institutional Mechanisms*** by Bandita Sijapati and Amrita Limbu, published by Himal Books for the Centre for the Study of Labour and Mobility in 2012. This gives an extremely helpful picture of the phenomenon of Nepali Migration and, in particular, the laws which GoN has promulgated in this context. Instead, I want to give a very simple overview, dividing the legislation into four sections.

EARLY LAWS

The first group of laws are those which were promulgated prior to the explosion of out-migration. The **first Foreign Employment Act** was passed in 1985 and amended in

1992/3 and 1998. In general these laws were restrictive, defining destinations to which Nepali citizens could travel and the mechanism (i.e. employment agencies) by which they could get there. Penalties for non-adherence were relatively minimal but in the early days the numbers of migrants were small and this was therefore not a serious issue.

LATER LAWS

The second group of laws are those which have been promulgated since the explosion of out-migration. The **second Foreign Employment Act** was passed in 2007, shortly after the final amendment to the 1st law, and the Foreign Employment Policy was passed in 2012. In addition there were sets of **Foreign Employment Rules** produced in 1999, 2007 and 2008. In general, these laws are far more comprehensive and although they do still legislate concerning manpower agencies and destinations, they also seek to ensure the rights and well-being of the individual migrants. How successful they have been is debatable! The expansion has occurred too rapidly, there has been too much privatisation of manpower agencies, too much corruption with too much laxity in enforcing penalties and therefore too little help and compensation provided to migrants in trouble.

The 2011 Amnesty International (AI) Report[3] revealed the extent to which migrants were still unprotected and frequently deceived despite the 2007 Foreign Employment Act. Employment Contracts were not being given in written form and in Nepali well in advance of departure (p.8). Usually documents are handed over at the airport or just before. Frequently multiple forms, stating significantly different jobs and salary levels, are used, one false one to present at Nepal Immigration and one true one to hand in on arrival at the destination (44ff, 55). There are officially 3 types of placement package[i], but invariably migrants are charged well over the maximum levels set by GoN (p.27) and they are rarely given an (itemised) receipt: this is so the agency can avoid full tax payment (pp.8, 32). GoN does not do enough to prevent trafficking or 'slavery' and does not penalise agencies when they falsify documents (pp. 9, 16). Most migrants have never heard of the Welfare Fund to which official migrants compulsorily contribute Rs. 1,000[ii] Thus it has a huge surplus in hand (pp.7, 86ff). Orientation and medical checks remain unenforced or inadequate (pp.40, 42). Most migrants experience great difficulty in obtaining help while overseas and are also unaware of the procedure for obtaining compensation via the DoFE on return. The time taken for their application to be considered by the Foreign Employment Tribunal is inordinately long (p.77ff). And – whatever laws there are, they still do not cover domestic workers.

BILATERAL AGREEMENTS

The third group of laws are the Bilateral Agreements Nepal has concluded with several countries to which migrants go. To date, in addition to the Treaty of Peace and Friendship,

---

[i] 1. The employer pays for everything (rare), 2. The employer pays the visa and the migrant for everything else. 3. The migrant pays for everything.

[ii] This fund was set up to cover costs of training (for outgoing & returning migrants), compensation and repatriation.

made with India in 1950 (which is not specifically about migrants), there are only 5 others. These are with Qatar (2005), UAE (2007), South Korea (2007), Bahrain (2008) and Japan (2009). It is immediately obvious that there are serious gaps here, especially in relationships with Saudi Arabia and Malaysia, although discussions have been underway with Malaysia for some time.[iii] In addition, not all these bits of legislation are fully binding on both parties and their enforcement has been weak. One important example of injustice is that "the laws of both the origin and destination countries punish the migrant for his/her fake documents and illegal status rather than the recruitment agency/agent."[4]

Laws of both origin and host countries punish migrants rather than recruitment agents.

INTERNATIONAL INSTRUMENTS

The fourth group of laws are the international instruments – the international conventions on migrants, the UN human rights instruments, and the labour standards set by the International Labour Organisation (ILO), one of which I have already mentioned. Some of these have been ratified by Nepal. However, three important instruments have so far not been ratified by Nepal. These are the ICMW (International Convention on Migrant Workers), ILO C97 Migration for

---

[iii] Similar agreements with Jordan, Israel and Lebanon are also under consideration.

Employment and ILO C143 Migrant Workers (Supplementary Provisions). If ratified, they would go a long way towards providing better conditions for Nepali migrants. However, Nepal is reluctant to ratify them, partly because doing so would open up Nepal to provide reciprocal conditions to incoming (mainly Indian) migrants to Nepal. Even if Nepal does ratify them, they will still have little power unless all the countries to which Nepal sends migrants also ratify them. For example, the UAE had not ratified the main ILO convention up to 2005.[5]

Both Nepal and destination countries must ratify these laws for them to be effective.

However, things are slowly changing and hope is on the way. Within Nepal, the development has been as follows:

Although Nepal became an **International Organization for Migration (IOM)** member state only in 2006, since then IOM-Nepal's size and the scope have increased exponentially, covering involvement in the resettlement of Bhutanese Refugees, anti-trafficking measures, border control and migrant health issues. Specifically, IOM works with the Ministry of Labour and Employment (MoLE), and the Foreign Employment Promotion Board (FEPB) to provide technical assistance to the Government of Nepal (GoN) in order to enhance the positive impact of labour migration in Nepal.

The activities include, capacity building training for the government officials, development of services for the migrants and review and reform of the policy. This project aims to contribute to the Government of Nepal's efforts to better manage labour migration processes while preventing irregular migration and hence harnessing the benefits of temporary labour migration. As a result of this project intervention, migrants will be better informed about migration opportunities and procedures and the Ministry can effectively address migration management challenges in the country.

These are important aims and some progress has been made towards fulfilling them. A pilot Migrant Resource Centre (MRC) was established at the FEPB in February 2010 and similar services provided in Jhapa and Chitwan:

Detailed information relating to labour migration for 9 major destinations namely Qatar, Saudi Arabia, South Korea, Lebanon, Japan, Israel, Malaysia, Kuwait and United Arab Emirates was collected and compiled. The centre has been providing individual counselling, e-based guidance and also telephonic guidance to interested aspirant migrants.

Pocket sized information leaflet with basic information on overseas employment was published. The information leaflets are being distributed by the Foreign Employment Promotion Board at the Ministry of Foreign Affairs where the passports are being issued… It is realized that migrants need to be well informed of their rights and obligations prior to departure to the destination countries. 25,000 copies each with country specific information on Qatar, Malaysia, Saudi Arabia, United Arab Emirates and Kuwait was published which is distributed through the Labour Desk at the International Airport and through the NGO partners. An educational video clipping on the basic do's and don'ts of migration was developed and is being displayed through the TV at the departure waiting lounge of the TIA.[iv]

These are impressive achievements, but while all this information is now available, sadly it still does not effectively reach the vast majority of outgoing migrants – or reach them in good time. Services in the airport, for example, are useful but limited as some of the information is given too late to be truly helpful. In addition, outgoing migrants queuing in the airport are probably too excited or nervous to take in all the good advice they are being offered.

One other relevant piece of legislation is the **National Human Rights Commission Act**, signed in January 2013, but it has two potentially serious problems. Its structure and functioning is not autonomous from the government; and a 6 month limit has been set for a case to be filed – this is unrealistic in a country like Nepal and when dealing with issues of psychological trauma.[6]

[iv] Tribhuvan International Airport, Kathmandu.

Chapter 4

IN and OUT MIGRATION

"...I know where you stay and when you come and go..."
~ Isaiah 37:28 NIV ~

Migration describes the movement of people from one place to another in general. Two additional, and more specific, terms are emigration and immigration. Probably I am not the only person to have been confused by these terms as I tried to complete the correct bit of the form in the relevant airport. How much harder is it for those labour migrants who can barely read even the Nepali version of the forms. Very simply, to emigrate means to leave and to immigrate means to arrive. Slightly more technically, we can say that 'emigration' "describes the move relative to the point of departure", whereas 'immigration' "describes the move relative to the destination.[7] However, not all scholars use these clear and simple definitions. Wan seems to almost equate immigration with migration i.e. "just moving to another country,"[8] while Hornby & Jones restrict In and Out Migration to internal flows of people and use Immigration and Emigration only for those who cross international

We emigrate FROM
&
We immigrate TO.

borders.[9] In this book, I am using the terms simply to mean that we emigrate *from* but immigrate *to*. As the actual people flows overlap I am not distinguishing between In Migration and Immigration, or Out Migration and Emigration.

Nowadays, when someone mentions migrants and migration in the Nepali context, we automatically think emigration is meant. However, this is a relatively recent phenomenon in the history of Nepal. In the beginning, before records were kept, the picture was of immigration of various people groups from the north and south into Nepal. Therefore, before we look at out-migration in more detail, I think it may help to set the scene if we first look briefly at this in-migration.

IMMIGRATION
(In Migration)

Although Abraham's family first settled temporarily in Canaan, (Genesis 12:4-9) *it was only in the time of Joshua that the Jews settled there permanently and spread throughout the country and it became Israel – the land of the descendants of Israel/Jacob* (Joshua 1:1-5 & 11:23)

"Nepal is a nation of immigrants. People who crossed the high Himalayan passes… [and]… people from the south… India."[10] Although many of the details of in-migration have never been clearly documented, it is obvious from the racial differences between tribes and castes that the Nepali people are not an ethnically uniform group; nor are they uniformly Nepali language speakers. Dr Perry, in her first chapter, has very adequately dealt with the complex issue of 'Who is a

Nepali?' and her concise historical analysis is an extremely helpful background to understanding Nepal, its people and its diaspora.

Nepal is a nation of immigrants.

The northern hill tribes (Rais, Limbus, Sherpas, Tamangs, Gurungs, Magars etc.), who are Mongolian in their features clearly must have migrated from the north and east into Nepal. This is confirmed by their differing cultures and religious affiliations. That this in-migration occurred in two or three separate waves is substantiated by the differences between the Kirant tribes of the eastern hills, the Sherpas, and the other groups who settled more to the west. In contrast, the Aryans arrived in Nepal from the south and west. They too came in at least two waves – bringing first the Khas and later other Brahmin-Chhetri and 'lower' caste groups at the time of the Mughal rule in India. They are Caucasian in their features and Hindu in their religious affiliation. Even among the Newars, who claim to be the indigenous inhabitants of the Kathmandu Valley, some almost certainly came originally from the north east and later intermarried with other incoming migrants at various times in their history. The diversity of their physical features and the fact that some are Buddhist and others Hindu tends to suggest this.

At the end of the 18th century all these tribes and small kingdoms – about 53 in all – were united into one country of Nepal by King Prithvi Narayan Shah and his successors. At that time, the borders of Nepal briefly extended from the River Sutlej (near Kashmir) to the River Teesta (almost the border of Bhutan) and south as far as Gorakhpur. This partly explains the communities of Nepali peoples living in

Kumaon-Gadhwal (in NW India), those in the Darjeeling hills, Bhutan, Sikkim and the Duars (in NE India) and in some urban centres like Gorakhpur and Lucknow.

Under the succeeding kings of the Shah dynasty all these disparate groups, with their different cultural and religious backgrounds, seemed to be unified within one Nepal. However, with the onset of multi-party democracy, there has also been an upsurge of ethnic awareness. Many of the traditional tribal groups are now identifying themselves as separate from the Brahmin-Chhetri Hindu community in culture, religion and language. At the same time, some of the more recent migrants into the *Terai*, the caste Hindus from North India, are demanding citizenship rights in Nepal.

However, the interesting and exciting thing is that despite these fractures that are appearing in the structure of Nepali society within Nepal, when living and working overseas, many of them seem to disappear. Nepalis in the Diaspora identify themselves as Nepalis as opposed to Bengalis, Indians, Pakistanis, Indonesians, Filipinos, etc. Some of this is undoubtedly national pride but much of the reason for ignoring caste divisions has more to do with practical survival. Within the traditional society of Nepal, high and low (untouchable) castes would never mix, but in the diaspora, where they have to share the same crowded hostel accommodation, this is forced upon them and, amazingly – often to save money – they also cook and eat together. This phenomenon – that when away from their traditional social structures and family pressures, people are far more open to new ideas – is well-known.[11] This is almost certainly one of the factors that has enabled the Gospel to spread with such rapidity through diaspora communities.

EMIGRATION
(Out Migration)

In the time of Joseph, the whole of Jacob's family went to Egypt to escape the famine. (Genesis 12:10) *At the end of the Kingdom period, the Jews were exiled and settled throughout the whole of the Babylonian Empire.* (2 Chronicles 36:20) *In AD 70 the Jewish nation was again scattered this time throughout the whole of the Roman Empire.*

Nepal is a human exporting country.

Today, "…Nepal is considered to be a human exporting country."[12] I believe that it is possible to identify three distinct waves of out-migration from Nepal, although the earlier waves were fairly small and there is a certain degree of time overlap.

FIRST WAVE

The first wave dates back several hundred years and is linked to the spread of Hindu settlement eastwards through India to Sikkim and Bhutan. This is the beginning of many of those Bhutanese of Nepali origin (see p. 201ff).

SECOND WAVE

The second wave had two phases.

The **First Phase** began after the Unification of the country of Nepal by King Prithvi Narayan Shah in 1768-9. The change in political structure from a multitude of mini-states to one unified country, with a large army to support and a high-caste elite to be rewarded, led to changes in land distribution, so that much of the land, originally leased by peasant farmers, was given to the Brahmin-Chhetri aristocracy. This began in the western hills and slowly reduced the ordinary people to subsistence level existence and many even became bonded labourers. Over time, this "cycle of impoverishment and landlessness spread into the central hills, gradually pushing people further and further east, until Nepali ethnics began to spill over into Darjeeling, Sikkim, Bhutan, Assam and beyond."[13] Employed on tea estates, in mines, on construction and in factories of the British Raj, they were the first true Nepali labour migrants.

The **Second Phase** began after the Anglo-Nepali war of 1814-16 when the British army began recruiting Nepalis as mercenaries. At first, Chhetris, Gurungs and Magars, from the west were recruited but later also eastern Rais and Limbus. On their subsequent retirement, many settled in parts of SE Asia, in particular in NW and NE India, and in Burma (which in those days was still part of British India).

These first two waves, and especially the two phases of the second wave, therefore gradually combined to give rise to the 'Gorkhali' communities in India, Burma and Malaya.

As a result of these waves of migration, large numbers of Nepalis were dispersed into communities in the British Empire where there were Christians and churches, and Dr Perry speaks of this early contact, showing its place in the history of Nepali Christianity. Numbers of Nepalis – especially in the NE of India and all along the southern border – accepted Christ, and Nepali churches began to spring up in India. These Nepali Christians, with expatriate missionaries, shared a common burden but only after the revolution of 1950-1, were their descendants able to enter Nepal and begin to share their faith. Thus Diaspora Nepali Christians brought the gospel to their own homeland.

THIRD WAVE

The third wave began in the 1970s, only after modern development started in Nepal. It also has had two phases.

The **First Phase** started when the population began to increase rapidly, which meant that land ownership decreased with each new generation. More opportunities for education sadly did not lead to more jobs but rather to unemployment for those who no longer wished to work in the fields. Young men therefore started to look outside of Nepal for employment and, as a result of this second period of labour migration, Nepali enclaves were established in India, and also in some countries of the Middle East, Europe and North America. However, for the next twenty years relatively few sought work outside Nepal. According to DH Adhikari (Secretary of the Ministry of Labour & Transportation) "the formal procedure of sending locals for foreign employment started in 1986,"[14] but the flood of emigration began only in the mid-1990s.

The flood of Nepali emigration began in the mid-1990s.

When Dr Cindy Perry wrote *Nepali around the World*, in 1997, Nepal was still the only Hindu Kingdom in the world.

HM King Birendra Bir Bikram Shah Dev was still securely on the throne, and Nepal had been endorsed as a Zone of Peace. Politics was a game played only by the elite of Kathmandu and most village people had not yet heard of the Maoists, for the first shots of the Maoist Peoples' War were fired only in February 1996.

It was therefore only in the wake of the terror and turmoil of this escalating civil strife that the **Second Phase** began. Overseas migration soon spiralled out of control. Growing numbers of young men, who had no wish to join the Nepal Army and who were afraid of being recruited by the Maoist insurgents, fled their villages, at first for the towns or the *Terai*, and later began to make their way in ever increasing numbers to SE Asia or the Middle East. Fifteen years on, the peace process was still being discussed, often with violent outbursts. The future of Nepal continues to hang over a precipice and still for many the only bit of stability they can grasp for the sake of their families lies in overseas employment. This is where we are today with still no immediate sign of the flood abating. The net migration rate, according to the Nepal Census of 2011, is estimated at 61 migrants per 100,000 people and the absentee population, of which 87% are males, was shown to have doubled from its rate in 2001, to a figure of almost 2 million. However, that figure almost certainly excludes migrants to India. "About 10% of Nepal's

>2 million Nepali Migrants
61 Migrants per 1 lakh Nepalis
87% Migrants are male
(Nepal National Census, 2011)

26.5 million people are documented as being abroad, but most estimates say double that number could have gone."[15]

My aim in this book is to document this latest wave of Nepali Out-Migration. Some of this has already been done in general terms in the earlier chapters. In subsequent chapters, I give more specific details about the unique conditions in different regions and countries. However, the situation is constantly changing. New laws are being introduced, new destinations for Nepalis are being added, and others removed. New problems are emerging, especially with an increase in female migration. New Nepali fellowships are springing up and new leaders venturing out while others return home. This means that the statistics I quote must be understood as approximations, based on the best available information at the time of writing. This is a problem common to all who try to document a diaspora. Because different counties use different definitions for 'migration' and different methods for counting the numbers of 'migrants,' "even without considering illegal migration, data on official or legal migration are fragmentary."[16] This is so in the Nepali context.

My sincere hope is that the information presented here will inform, but more importantly, that the personal anecdotes and testimonies will challenge you to pray and to become involved in what God is clearly doing in the Nepali Diaspora.

Chapter 5

THE MIGRATION CYCLE

"The LORD will keep your going out and your coming in from this time forth and forevermore."
~ Psalm 121:8 ESV ~

I find it is helpful to think of migration as a cycle with three phases because the problems and needs of the migrants, and the challenges they face are different at different times.

OUTGOING MIGRANTS

"...GO FROM your country and your kindred and your father's house to the land that I will show you."
~ Genesis 12:1 ESV ~

By outgoing migrants, I am not just thinking of someone sitting in a Kathmandu taxi on their way to the airport, but rather of the whole process that leads up to that special moment. It begins when an agent visits the village to promote overseas migration or when a family weighs up all the push and pull factors and comes to the conclusion that one of its members has to find employment overseas for the family to survive. It continues as the would-be migrant processes an application for a passport and decides which country and what type of work s/he can do. It also involves contacting and negotiating with an agent or broker or occasionally a company directly in order to obtain a work contract. The final stage should then be one of training and orientation but in reality this rarely happens. Instead, after maybe several months of this process, finally the migrant arrives in Kathmandu, maybe waits a few days (or sometimes longer) and as soon as s/he receives his/her documents and ticket, s/he is in that taxi and on his/her way.

Preparation

It is therefore clear that becoming an overseas migrant can be a lengthy process, during which important information about migrating in general and orientation to the destination country in particular should be obtained. In fact, most labour migrants leave Nepal with only a very hazy idea of where they are going and what they will be doing and with virtually no concept of the different culture in which they will be living. It is also an expensive process as the family may have to sell jewellery, cattle or land or take out a loan in order to pay the agent. A huge amount of time and money is thus invested in the migrant, which means that most leave Nepal under significant pressure to succeed and earn enough to repay the loans and support the family. If dishonest agents and companies thwart this purpose and the migrant is immediately repatriated (because the job does not, in fact, exist) or is not properly paid for his labour, this can precipitate a major crisis in the family.

Information

As an absolute minimum, outgoing migrants should know the

following facts about their work contract: what exactly the work entails, how the work agreement will be concluded, and if there is a period of probation. They should be aware of the regular working hours, salary scales, overtime arrangements and payments, holiday entitlement and the security situation in the workplace. They should know what conditions may be considered as a breach of contract and what compensation may be awarded in case of injury or death. [17]

Orientation

Outgoing migrants also need good general orientation training and preparation for what will be a very different lifestyle from that to which they have been accustomed in their hill villages. This should also include some teaching about the risks of contracting HIV. [18] Some cross-cultural understanding and basic language skills would also help them to settle more easily in the country of their choice. This is done at least for some workers to Israel and S Korea, but in general, it does not happen. The Nepali Ambassador in Saudi Arabia in 2001 supported this, saying that "Workers should be given at least a few weeks of orientation classes and training before leaving [Nepal]" as he felt this could help them avoid some of the hazards and even perhaps, death.

Pre-departure orientation is very important.

Logistically, such orientation is possible to arrange for those who leave the country legally via TIA, but illegal emigrants and those going to India cannot be reached by the same methods. In the case of migrants to India, the information they need before leaving is similar, but, they also need to know what their labour rights are in India and how they can claim them and also what their rights are at Immigration and Customs so that they are not charged without reason by the Police. They also need to receive advice about the risk behaviours associated with HIV and understand the value of opening a bank account, together receiving with instructions on how to go about doing it. If they are migrating with family, they need to be reminded of the value of education for their children and told how to process the enrolment.[19]

Vocational Training

It is a proven fact that semi-skilled workers do better financially – and socially – than those who have no skills at all. Instead of being general labourers in construction, they may be allotted specific roles in plumbing or electrical installation for example. This means that the provision of basic training in such skills could make a huge difference for many outgoing migrants.

Even semi-skilled workers do better financially than unskilled ones.

In fact, the Foreign Employment Act of 2007 had decreed that skills training should be given but there are too few courses for too many migrants and too many of the organisers simply provide certificates of attendance whether or not the migrants have attended. Furthermore, migrants from remote rural areas cannot afford to travel to Kathmandu to attend trainings and there is no decentralisation of these or other pre-migration procedures.

Slowly, the government is recognising the vital importance of this pre-departure training and orientation. This is partly because of the findings of "a survey conducted by the Foreign Ministry in coordination with the Foreign Employment Board," which showed a link between poor preparation and the high mortality rate among migrants.[20] Sadly, the migrants are not yet aware of this link; they still regard the trainings as unimportant and do not try to attend.

Even some of the essential documentation required for migration is not always provided or obtained in a good way.

The Government of Nepal

The 2007 Act requires citizens pursuing foreign employment to obtain a health check-up before departing, and pay into the Foreign Employment Welfare Fund, which (at least on paper) offers skills training before workers go abroad, emergency financial support while away and job assistance when they return. In addition, it requires foreign employers to offer insurance and orientation training to Nepalese citizens to travel to all the countries the government lists as suitable destinations for Nepalis working abroad.

In July 2008, Nepal was a participant in the Asia Regional Symposium on deployment of workers overseas. Government and non-governmental delegates from most of the involved countries in the region discussed how best they could improve *"dialogue and the management of labour migration so as to benefit both sending and receiving countries and better protect the rights and equal treatment of migrant workers,"* which was the priority that had been identified already in the 14th Asia Regional Meeting in 2006.

Participants agreed on a multilateral approach with responsibility shared between origin and destination countries to promote fair recruitment practices and safe migration for women, develop infrastructure and effective services to migrant workers, and meet the emerging demand for labour and skills training.[21]

In 2011, PS Bhattarai, the then Director of the DoFE reported that the government had formed a high-level task force to reform the migration process and "better protect workers' rights," and in 2012 significant reforms were put in place. These included "a web-based service for both online banking and for filing complaints." As many migrants are not fluent in English and computer literate this is currently of limited value. Nevertheless, in 2012, migrant workers did file over 2,000 complaints, of which about a third were joint or institutional ones submitted by many workers together. However, only about 400 were dealt with.[22] This is therefore only the proverbial 'drop in a bucket' but it is a start. Also, in early 2012, the Committee on Finance and Labour Relations of the Legislature-Parliament directed GoN, in coordination with the Ministry of Foreign Affairs (MoFA), to agree to provide the compensation due to injured migrants and families of migrants who lost their lives while working overseas.[23] Unfortunately, despite these positive measures, Mahato says something which if it is true, is quite shocking:

> … The state's apathy towards the welfare of migrant workers is despicable. The rot starts right at the top. Last week a minister sacked the head of the Foreign Employment Department who was trying to stop kickbacks and punish fraudulent recruiters.[24]

Happily not all officials are like this. In November 2012 there was a conference in Kathmandu concerning the protection and promotion of migrant workers' rights in the Asia Pacific region, attended by National Human Rights Organisations, national and international NGOs, GoN and independent expatriate experts and academics. They produced the 'Kathmandu Resolution 2012' and committed themselves to continuing to work for significant improvements in migrant workers' rights, including ratifying the UN treaties.

Ideally, the Government of Nepal should be aiming for the same sort of negotiated terms for their nationals as has been done for Filipinos overseas [25] i.e. approved government contracts, verified by the overseas embassy and containing all the relevant terms and conditions of their employment; Official Overseas Employment Certificates to prove they are legally processed workers; and adequate insurance coverage with benefits for themselves and their family members.

Overseas Employers

For overseas employers or foreign employment agencies wishing to recruit Nepali workers, there is a set formula for application. They have to submit to the Ministry of Labour in Nepal a Demand Letter (stating the benefits/facilities for the workers), a Power of Attorney (appointing a recruitment agency in Nepal to work on their behalf), a Sample Employment Contract (as will be issued to the workers), a Consular Letter and an Agency Agreement. They must also abide by the rules of their own country, e.g. in Malaysia companies are not allowed to recruit from overseas unless they already employ a certain percentage of local labour.

GoN allows recruiting agencies to send migrant workers to any of the countries on its allowed list, but migrants can process their own applications or go to other countries if they have been able to obtain employment contracts personally. Both routes have their own drawbacks, although some countries only accept recruits coming via the institutional route. Generally, first-time outgoing migrants coming from remote villages have no skill or possibility to negotiate their own work contracts and so heavily depend on agents.

Passports

Before any worker can leave Nepal (with the exception of those going to India) s/he has to obtain a passport and this is neither easy nor cheap, especially for those living in remote village areas. Before AD 2000, passports were only issued in Kathmandu, but now they can be obtained from District Offices. Before, only 5 year passports were issued but now they are given for 10 years. However, Nepali nationals have to pay the highest fee (5,000 Nepali Rupees) and wait the longest time (6 weeks) in the whole of the South Asia Region to obtain a 32-page Machine Readable Passport through ordinary processing. Urgent processing (in 7 days) costs double and very urgent processing (in 72 hours) costs triple this amount. Costs and waiting time are far less in all other SAARC[v] countries and the passport obtained is twice the size. One applicant said "It took me 10 days to obtain a passport in Kathmandu after I paid Rs 10,000," and another complained that he had to stand in a queue for 10 hours despite paying the double rate. Non-Resident Nepalis (NRNs) fare even worse. In the UK, a passport costs 165

[v] South Asian Association for Regional Cooperation.

USD (approx. Rs. 15,000) and is only available after a wait of three months.[26] In addition, Nepal is currently struggling to replace the old handwritten passports (which will become invalid on 15 November 2015) with machine readable ones.[27]

Part of the problem in Nepal is undoubtedly the high volume of passport requests due to the high volume of migrants leaving the country. The Department of Foreign Employment issues 1,500 overseas work permits every day,[28] and the Department of Passport (DoP) issues 1,200 passports each day. In the districts, the District Administration Office (DAO) collects and then sends the passport application forms in batches, which inevitably means delay especially for those who submit their applications just after the previous consignment has been despatched. Thus workers and students (the migrants who can least afford it) have increased costs and hassles as they have to visit the district centre or capital several times.[29] The only way around this is to use an agent.

Every day, GoN issues:
1,200 Passports
1,500 Work Permits

Manpower Agencies

Unfortunately, it is well known that these Manpower Agencies frequently find ways to get around the laws and regulations imposed by GoN and so benefit themselves. They go to the remote villages and recruit those who have no awareness of the reality of overseas labour migration. "They promise people the opportunities to make lots of money, and they believe them," explained Mahendra Pandey, Chair of the

Pravasi Nepali Coordination Committee (PNCC). He also said that "many of the agencies have political links and can act with impunity."[30] In addition, some of the men who run these agencies are so dishonest that after swindling a group of migrants, they just disappear – with the profits.[31] Some make well over half a million USD a day.[32]

The AI Report in 2012 highlighted the extent to which agents recruit dishonestly. In one specific context, Ambassador Pandey stated that "114 agents are mainly responsible for sending 90 percent illegal migrant workers to Saudi Arabia."[33] These same agencies have probably also been recruiting workers for other countries. Others provide fake passports and documents to send Nepali women to Saudi Arabia.[34] Most of the would-be migrants who are cheated in this way are *bona fide* labourers. The scams perpetrated in the student scene are somewhat different, involving the connivance of the 'students'. In mid-2013, the Nepal Central Investigation Bureau exposed a racket "involved in faking student certificates and other documents… [and arrested] … students and operators of eight consultancies and language centres, who had been sending individuals to Japan on student visas illegally," although none were actually planning to study![35]

Most of the problems of migration are related to the recruitment phase.

Preliminary findings of the research conducted in 2012 by the Asia Foundation indicated that most of the problems of migration are related to the recruitment phase, with naïve would-be migrants from remote villages putting their trust in local agents rather than officially registered agencies. This is partly because they are not aware of the dangers and partly because they are offered a quicker service, albeit at a higher cost. The result is a lot of trafficking to disallowed destinations or provision of false documentation, even including fake passports.[36] When women and girls are sent to disallowed destinations, the agents add in extra 'service charges', called 'setting fees,' but which in reality are bribes.

> Women leaving for Gulf countries for employment are forced to pay anything from Rs. 10,000 to 60,000 to immigration officials at the Tribhuvan International Airport [TIA] in Kathmandu… A number of migrant workers interviewed by the Post claimed immigration and 'other officials' at the TIA took bribe through employment agents in return for allowing the workers a 'safe passage.' They said the amount, which the agents refer to as the 'setting fees,' has become almost compulsory for female workers travelling to Gulf countries.[37]

One young woman travelling to Kuwait to work as a domestic help claimed to have paid 1.1 *lakh* (including a setting fee of 10,000) to an agent for a forged passport so she could enter TIA without being stopped by the officials.

Ironically, despite all these problems faced by genuine Nepali migrants, some Bangladeshis have paid exorbitant sums to agents to obtain Nepali passports in East Nepal and so allow them to work (illegally) in Kuwait. (see p.281-2)

Help at Hand

Within Nepal, there are agencies (governmental and private) who can give advice to potential migrants, although many migrants are not fully aware of them.

The **ILO** works with the Ministry of Labour & Transport (**MoLT**), the **Foreign Employment Promotion Board (FEPB)**, various Workers' Organizations and the Nepal Association of Foreign Employment Agencies (**NAFEA**) to raise awareness and strengthen institutional capacity. Since 2007, **IOM-Nepal** has worked closely with the **United Nations (UN)** and also with various Nepali governmental ministries and departments as well as NGOs and private companies to ensure safe migration and help migrants who run into trouble. GoN regularly publishes lists of registered (or blacklisted) Manpower Agencies. The **Ministry of Labour and Employment, Department of Foreign Employment (DoFE)** deals with all the administrative details, whereas the **FEPB** deals with pre-departure orientation and training, which is then run by the **Migrant Resource Centre (MRC)**.[vi] Various reforms in DoFE were carried out in 2012 to try to control the cheating of workers. These included "mandatory verification of migrant workers' document by Nepali mission abroad or by chambers of commerce of concerned countries before giving a final approval," calling visas for those going to Malaysia, and also passport stickers for migrant workers.[38] Some of these organisations[vii] have also produced leaflets giving useful information on destination countries, Embassy addresses and points to know prior to departure.

The **Nepal Institute of Development Studies (NIDS)** conducts research and is also involved in awareness raising

[vi] In practice very few outgoing migrants take up this opportunity.

[vii] In particular, GoN, Ministry of Labour, Employment and Transport, the FEPB, the NRNA and IME Money Transfer.

and empowering local institutions. It publishes many documents including an Annual Migration Report.

The **Pravasi Nepali Coordination Committee (PNCC)** began life as the Pravasi Nepali Sewa Samiti (PNSS) in 1988 in Saudi Arabia but developed into the more global PNCC in 2009. It was established by returnees who understand the issues and are thus able to work for the rights of migrants through advocacy, awareness raising, networking and partnerships. The **Workers' Rehabilitation Centre (WOREC)** promotes safer migration and provides counselling and training, while the **People Forum** is able to provide legal aid services. **Pourakhi,** established in 2003, is particularly concerned with ensuring the rights of female migrants and is involved in counselling, advocacy and training. **Arbeiterwohlfahrt or Workers' Welfare (AWO International)** works with Pourakhi since 2012 in the areas of awareness raising, capacity building, income generation and advocacy. The **National Network on Safe Migration (NNSM)** is particularly involved in women's rights.

The **Nepali Pravasi Ekata Sanjaal (NeMUN)**, formally established in 2010, provides links with Churches and fellowships for outgoing (and returning) Christians. It is also involved in networking, awareness raising, hospitality and helping migrants in medical or legal need.

Christian Migrants

For Christians planning to work overseas, the process and problems are identical but an extra concern is added. Will they find a fellowship in their host country? Will they be able to witness and grow as Christians while they are overseas? Some have waited and searched for a very long time before finding a Nepali language Christian fellowship overseas. On one of my visits to Malaysia, I met one man attending his first Nepali *sangati*[viii] in 6 months. He was so happy. Others, however, are tempted to backslide, partly due to lack of fellowship and partly because of the pressures of work and the unaccustomed 'freedom'.

Ideally home churches in Nepal should be involved in migration – advising members, linking them with Christians overseas and keeping in touch with them while they are away. Sadly, this is not yet reality as most local churches are even more ignorant of migration issues than the outgoing migrants themselves. Remedying this is one of the main aims of the Nepalese Migrant Unity Network (NeMUN).

IN THE DIASPORA

"... sojourners IN A LAND that is not theirs..."
~ Genesis 15:13 ESV ~

Again, when we consider migrants in the diaspora, it spans the whole time from when they alight from the plane in their host country until they embark on their final return flight.

Some labour migrants never get further than the arrivals' hall. Immigration officials discover their false documents and detain them. For the fortunate few, an agent or company comes to their rescue, the documents are corrected and they are able to proceed. The rest are repatriated to Nepal within a couple of days and then face the almost insuperable problem

[viii] Fellowship (meeting).

of getting a refund from their agent.

Some arrivals are left to languish in the airport for up to 2 days before being collected by a representative from their employing company. This is due to inefficiency, lack of care or the simple fact that they arrived just at the beginning of the 2-day weekend break. Inevitably Friday prayers take precedence over meeting migrants! I heard of this happening many times in Qatar and the migrants being marooned without food and drink for the whole time.

Even in the west, I have heard of arriving students, expecting to be met, but who were left to fend for themselves in the vast concourse of Heathrow, not having the vaguest idea of how to get to their destination.

The majority of labour migrants, however, are picked up by their company representative and delivered to their hostel accommodation, and start work within a few days. Most migrants in Malaysia and the Middle East are expected to hand over their passports to their employers. As a temporary measure – for their ID cards to be processed, this is reasonable, but in fact the employers usually retain the passports for the whole time the migrant is in the country. Technically this is outside the law, but they do it to ensure that the migrant continues to work for them and does not run off to another company that offers better conditions. If a migrant does run off and is without a passport, s/he is immediately illegal and liable to be arrested. This issue is compounded as it is possible for the employer in Malaysia to cancel a work permit at will, so rendering the migrant illegal. While the case is being sorted, a migrant can obtain a special pass to stay in Malaysia for up to 3 months, but as it takes at least 6 months to resolve the issues, the migrant is once again denied his/her rights.[39]

Embassies

Overseas embassies are an extension of the care that GoN provides for its migrant citizens. Migrants obtain informal help and advice from fellow migrants, migrant organisations and occasionally from their employers, but the more formal support that can be provided by Nepalese Embassies is very important, especially in any time of crisis. However, because of the rapid growth of the Nepali Diaspora, few host countries have been prepared to deal with the influx of migrants in terms of adequate Embassy support. I have visited one embassy and know these things are true. The premises were too small, there was no adequate waiting area, visitors were excluded during the lunch hour and no help was offered to migrants in completing the complex paperwork that is invariably required before any help is even considered. Many migrants in real trouble, but uneducated and unaware of their rights, are dismissed with flimsy excuses or not seen at all whereas I was dealt with immediately.

Despite the huge numbers of Nepalis working in Gulf countries and Malaysia, in 2011 there were only 28 government staffers working in embassies in these areas[ix] and only a few extra local appointees. The result has been failure to provide proper services.[40] Even basic tasks like translation of documents, passport renewal, recommendation letters and

[ix] Malaysia 5, Saudi 7, UAE 6, Qatar 5, Kuwait 5. The only change noted in 2013 was one extra staffer in Qatar.

company verification, that should only take a few hours, are taking almost three days.

"The Foreign Employment Act 2007 states that the government should appoint a labour attaché in any country where there are more than 5,000 male and 1,000 female migrant workers."[41] Up until 2009 this policy had not been followed, but subsequently more embassy staff have been appointed and consideration given to opening new embassies or consulates. In addition, as part of the DoFE reforms of 2012 it was decided "to connect all the Nepali Embassies to online network… [which] will let the embassies easily verify the status of the workers and coordinate with the department."[42]

One particularly problematic area for embassy staff is dealing with undocumented workers. Because they are undocumented, the embassy has no record of their presence in the country, hence there are difficulties and delay in providing help if such migrants become sick or have an accident. If they are arrested for illegality or crimes, the situation is even more complicated for the embassy to sort out. Periodically GoN and the host country government negotiate an amnesty for all undocumented workers. This helps some in the short-term but is not a long-term solution as more illegal workers continue to arrive.

Surya Nath Mishra, a former Ambassador to Qatar, made it clear that in order for the embassies to deal properly with workers' grievances, and address these together with company management and others, extra staff and skills are essential. For example, the Labour Attaché should have a good understanding of the local labour laws and be able to speak both English and the local language. To achieve this he must be given tenure of at least 3 years. There should also be a minimum of 1 Public Relations Officer for every 1 *lakh* of workers. In addition, the embassy must be equipped to give food and shelter to stranded nationals until their problems can be sorted out.[43] Although there should be at least one government staff member for every 20,000 workers,[44] in 2012, GoN admitted that it did not even have the resources to control the exploitation of Nepali women by Nepalis themselves. In addition, diplomats are often under motivated or not trained in how to negotiate with local officials.[45]

GoN does not have enough overseas embassies or embassy staff to deal with legal migrants, let alone undocumented ones.

Another problem is that some embassies have to oversee the needs of their nationals in several different countries. Until 2013 neither Oman nor Bahrain had a Nepali Embassy or Consulate. Saudi Arabia was looking after affairs in Oman, Yemen, Sudan and Jordan, while Qatar was overseeing Bahrain. In early 2013 there were only 29 Nepal embassies and 3 consulates but in 2012 GoN had "decided to establish additional diplomatic missions in China and three Gulf countries of Oman, Bahrain and Saudi Arabia."[46] The MoFA had also proposed opening diplomatic offices in Bhutan, Afghanistan, Maldives, Spain, Portugal, Italy, Indonesia and Turkey, but to date little action has been taken.

Even if GoN solves its problems of unstaffed embassies, and the large numbers of illegal workers overseas, it still faces the problem of how to care for Nepali citizens who go to countries which have no diplomatic relations with Nepal. The only possible solution has been emphasized by Devkota, executive director of the FEPB, who says that "workers must complete all the paperwork before they leave for their work destination so that the government knows where they are in case of an emergency."[47]

Churches

In India, Nepali migrants often fit easily into Hindi language churches, but in areas where there are many Nepali migrants there are also some Nepali-language churches and fellowships, which are able to reach out to new migrants.

In the west, as migrants are often better-educated and planning to stay long-term, integration into local churches (using local languages or English) is reasonable, but Nepali-medium help as new migrants settle in is much appreciated.

In many of the (Muslim) countries to which Nepali labour migrants go, there are no local churches, although there are some international congregations. Because of the social and religious situation in the Middle East, help from churches is limited, although some of the international congregations have welcomed Nepalis into their membership and helped them establish their own Nepali-language fellowships. In addition, a few professional expatriates from the west have become advocates for the rights of (Nepali) migrants. In contrast, in Malaysia, large numbers of churches and a few NGOs have become deeply involved in migrant ministries – helping Nepalis and other migrant groups with their socio-economic, legal, medical and spiritual needs.

Loneliness and temptations related to alcohol, drugs and sex combine to make a potent source of misery for many migrants, leading to a further downward spiral as they become unable to work and yet, because of these bad habits, have not saved any of their earnings. The fortunate ones are those befriended by Christians, and especially those who commit their own lives to Christ. For many this has been their salvation in both spiritual and physical senses of the word. However, one of the biggest problems for the pastors or leaders of these Diaspora Nepali fellowships is how to disciple their converts. Long working hours, lengthened further by overtime, limit the opportunities for fellowship and teaching to late evening gatherings. In Malaysia, this is compounded by the endemic problem of mugging, as local church people cannot always provide transportation. In the Middle East it is usually too hot to walk and public transport essentially does not exist; and migrant lodgings are often so scattered across the town that even if transportation can be arranged, there is no time for it.

In many places in the Middle East there is no public transport.

RETURNEES

"... who has COME BACK from the country..."
~ Ruth 4:3 ESV ~

Returnees are those migrants who have returned permanently from the diaspora and now settling (or settled) back home. Practically, the term also includes those who have finished one (or more) contract overseas and are back in Nepal but not yet decided whether they will go overseas again. Many of them do go back but largely because the situation at home has not changed for them. Issues relating to returnees begin as their plane lands in Kathmandu and continue until they are fully reintegrated and employed back home.

Even those with little education, return with a broader worldview that makes it hard for them to fit back into village life. Returnees therefore have a special set of problems to solve as they settle back into their homeland, especially if they cannot find local employment. Small children are now teenagers who have never really known their fathers. Some migrants have been away for so long that reintegration is extremely hard and a few have arrived to find that their wives have moved on to alternative partners. In April 2013, *Nepal National* carried a horrifying headline: "Young pregnant woman burnt alive by family in Nepal." Reading between the lines and adding up the dates, it seems this was because she got pregnant while her husband was away in Qatar.[48]

On Arrival

Problems are regularly faced by returnees crossing one of the land borders from India, and migrants are frequently robbed on the road or cheated by Immigration officials. The same problems do not usually occur for those who return by air. However, Thapa reported a horrific story about how a returnee girl was greeted at TIA:

> *19 year old **Sita Rai** (not her real name) spent 4 years working illegally in Saudi Arabia with a false passport and then flew back to Kathmandu in November 2012. On arrival, Immigration officials arrested her for having a*

fake passport. The following day the four men took her to a private lodge, where they raped her and stole her money and belongings. "I was threatened by those government personnel not [to] tell anyone about the incident," she says. When she got home, she initially hid the incident from her family but later returned to Kathmandu and filed a police complaint against the men. When medical examination showed that she was pregnant as a result of the rape, the government provided assistance for her abortion and also compensated her with Rs. 150,000. The officials concerned were dismissed, and the constable who actually committed the rape has been fined and jailed.[49]

More usually the difficulties faced by returnees on arrival are simply re-entry 'culture-shock' and reuniting with their families. Some do not know where to stay – for a reasonable price – in Kathmandu as many carry little money in their pockets. This may be because they have already sent all their salary home or because they have returned under difficult circumstances (direct from jail or detention or seriously ill).

Those who have been invalided home with injuries or a severe medical problem need physical assistance to reach their homes and to obtain any necessary medical treatment.

***Jhabilal** (from Jhapa) sustained an injury to his back due to unauthorised heavy work. His employer neglected to help him and did not allow him to rest and so his medical condition worsened. Kai Lee referred this case to NeMUN, who then contacted his father and guided him through some legal assistance from the Ministry of Labour, and this led to his rescue. In Dec. 2011, Jhabilal arrived back in Nepal—in a wheelchair and needing further medical treatment. NeMUN members met him at the airport in Kathmandu and later, when they* *understood all the facts of his case, the NeMUN board appealed for financial help and this was given by the Government of Nepal. Since then, NeMUN members have kept in touch with the family, who have also suffered a further trauma—as Jhabilal's young wife committed suicide.*

Those who have returned directly from prison or detention, usually without money and without having received recent salary need financial and legal assistance. They need help to access the Report and Investigation Office and process an application for repayment of agency fees or for due compensation. One such was ***Yogendra:***

Yogendra *(from Dang) went to Malaysia with great hopes, but on arrival at the airport, he was immediately detained. Apparently his documents were not in order. He had been cheated by the Manpower Agency in Kathmandu and the Agent in Malaysia. One day later he was sent straight back to Nepal. The Manpower Agency offered to arrange work for him in another country but Yogendra had had enough. He wanted his money back and wanted to go home. The Agency then agreed to send his money to him and so he returned home to Dang... but the money never arrived. However, Yogendra had heard about NeMUN via a church friend of one of the NeMUN staff, and so he returned to Kathmandu and stayed at Mitra Niwas. Devendra Joshi helped him by taking him to the Report and Investigation Office, where together they submitted a report of Yogendra's case. The office called the Manpower Agency, and eventually Yogendra was fully compensated. Without help, Yogendra might have given up or his case could possibly have dragged on for a very long time and maybe not even succeeded.*[50]

Resettlement

The practical problems facing returnees together with the continued difficulty in obtaining employment in Nepal means that within only a couple of months, many migrants are back at TIA, *en route* to another part of the diaspora. The World Bank Nepal Migration Survey in 2009, although only relating to a small sample, showed that more than three-quarters of returnees were interested in going overseas again.[51] Actual figures of outgoing migrants for the first six months of 2010-11 indicated that around half of them were those returning for a second or subsequent contract period.[52] Although this figure may be inflated by the inclusion of some returning from a holiday at home it indicates a serious problem. A lot more still needs to be done to "facilitate the reintegration process of returning migrants."[53] The World Migration Report, 2010, p178 states that "Countries such as… Nepal offer reintegration and skills training." There is little evidence of this, although Pourakhi has given training in organic farming, candle making and handicraft to returning women, such that many are now running their own small businesses. Mahato found that most Nepali women would stay in Nepal if they could earn an extra Rs. 6,000 per month.[54] She concludes that "the long-term solution to

Half of outgoing migrants are returning for another term overseas.

The long-term solution to migration would be to create jobs in Nepal!

migration would be to create jobs within Nepal."

The comments of returnee ladies recorded in *Ekantipur* back this up. Some have received Entrepreneurship Development Training through a programme run by the FEPB with support from UN Women.[55] ***Lalita***, who worked for 1 year in Lebanon but only received 4 months' salary, commented that, "Such trainings are good for women like us but I would like to ask for monetary help in starting a business." ***Man Kumari***, who returned from 2 years of oppression in Kuwait, said, "I want to begin with a small business that can sustain my family." ***Nirmala***, who had worked in Israel, wanted to open a beauty parlour in Nepal instead of going abroad again. "Nobody wants to leave the country willingly," she said. None wanted to return overseas but stressed that training without some capital financial assistance will not really help them. A story from Banke illustrates this:

> ***Nandi*** *joined a self-help group, which had come into being through the community work of INF/Nepal. This enabled her to take a loan to buy some pigs and goats. Later she started a fish cutting and selling business and then opened a vegetable shop. Her "business has proved so successful that she now saves every month, is able to pay for her children to go to school and her husband no longer travels to India to work. Instead he helps Nandi with her ever-expanding business."*[56]

New Christians

New Christians have special reorientation problems to solve. Some face opposition to a newfound Christian faith. Some return full of zeal but with significantly less maturity. Some are determined to go to Bible School, but overlook important prerequisites like settling into a Nepali church and ensuring that their wives and families hear the Gospel and, hopefully, also come to Christ. Some, before originally leaving Nepal, will have been antagonistic to the Christian faith, thus, on their return, a 'Barnabas' is needed to introduce them and assure their local church that they are now brothers in Christ. (Acts 9:26-27)

Often 'a Barnabas' is needed to introduce new believers to a local church in Nepal.

Nepali churches also need to gain further understanding in order to accept these new believers. They have come to Christ in a very different environment and have been nurtured in a very close fellowship that is almost exclusively young and male, with very few families. They have often been transported to and from church and maybe given a meal before or after the service. Hardly surprising then that they often struggle when they encounter the church situation in Nepal and feel it is lacking in the same kind of close fellowship and care.

Chapter 6

TYPES OF MIGRANTS OR MIGRATION

The story of Joseph (Genesis 37-50) *illustrates many of the issues surrounding migration. He was sold into slavery, but made good. He was wrongfully accused and imprisoned. Eventually he was released and obtained a good job. He was able to send support back to his family. Then, when the economic catastrophe in the form of a famine became too great, his family joined him the diaspora in Egypt.*

Migrants come in all shapes and sizes, but may helpfully be divided into two broad categories:

- Ethnic Nepalis living overseas but with local citizenship. This includes the large numbers of (earlier) migrants in India, many of whom no longer think of themselves as migrants, as well as NRNs living in many other lands, who still like to retain strong links with their homeland.
- Nepalis who retain their Nepali citizenship and ultimately return to Nepal. This includes the seasonal and temporary migrants to India as well as labour migrants and many students.

In fact, the situation is far more complex because this

linguistic issue should also be taken into account. Not all Nepali citizens are mother-tongue Nepali speakers, even among those residing within Nepal. Some Sikkimese (Indian) Lepchas are Nepali speakers. Many Gorkhalis in Burma (and Thailand) have largely lost their Nepali language, and can no longer read the Devanagri script.

This confusion about how to define a Nepali and, by extension, a Nepali migrant, clearly affects any statistics of the Nepali Diaspora. When government, scholars or reporters quote figures for migrants they rarely provide any specific definition of 'Nepali migrant'. This is a particular problem in relation to India. When different sources cite figures of 500,000 to 10-12 million Nepalis living in India, it is clear that they cannot all be counting the same people!

A simpler and more practical way is to divide the different groups of Nepalis who go overseas for work into 3 broad categories,[57] although the distinctions between the categories are by no means fixed or clear. The 'skilled' may be only semi-skilled or they may be highly skilled but not professionals in the strict sense of that term.

- Unskilled (75%) – the labourers, cleaners, etc.
- Skilled (23%) – the artisans, technicians, etc.
- Highly skilled (2%) – the professionals.

Everyone knows about the **'brain drain,'** which refers to the exodus of students and professionals from developing countries to 'western' countries. However, this category of Nepali migrants is far outnumbered by the construction, factory and domestic workers now flooding into many Asian and Middle Eastern countries. I have termed this group, the **'brawn drain'**.

A Remittance Economy

Whereas the professionals take their skills out of the country and often do not return, the labour migrants contribute significantly to their country through remittances. Official remittances increased 10-fold in the decade up to 2007/8.[58] In 2009, *The Kathmandu Post* stated that "Remittance sustains 30 pc families" but by 2011 it was saying that "Half of Nepali households have members working abroad." In 2013 the amount sent as remittances was stated as 4.34 billion USD, which was double the amount in 2011.[59] Back in 2009, families benefiting from overseas remittances were on average receiving nearly 3 times the average salary paid in Nepal.[60] However, the level of remittances to Nepal is much lower than that sent home by workers from Bangladesh or the Philippines, and this is because their respective governments have negotiated well on behalf of their migrant workers. Nepali unskilled labourers are now demanding more pay or trying to move to countries like S Korea, which offers higher remuneration.

55% of Nepali households receive remittances from overseas.

By including at least 500,000 undocumented workers, there are now probably around 3 million Nepalis sending back overseas remittances. This works out at just over 4 billion USD sent back to Nepal through official banking channels alone for the 2012-13 fiscal year.[61] Nepal is truly a remittance economy. Without this income, many wonder how the people and the country would survive? Mahato claims that:

> The only reason Nepal hasn't turned into a failed state is because millions of young people from this country are sending money home from India, the Gulf or Malaysia. The latest World Bank survey shows Nepal's poverty rate has declined, the macro-economic situation looks healthy and remittances are pumping money directly into the countryside.[62]

20% of the decline of poverty in Nepal is due to the remittances sent home by labour migrants.

As much as 20% of the decline in poverty in Nepal between 1995 and 2004 may be attributed to labour migration and the remittance inflows from migrants.[63] Without these increased remittances, the level of poverty would have risen, not fallen.

On the other hand, some think that remittances tend to fuel inflation and widen the gap between the rich and the poor.[64]

Remittances make up ~25% of Nepal's GDP

I am not sure that that is the case (yet) in Nepal. However, with remittances contributing a larger proportion to Nepal's GDP than tourism, exports and foreign aid combined, they are certainly a very significant factor in the economy. With the stagnation in Nepal's political development, high levels of pollution in the capital, and continued increase in overseas migration, it is likely that not only the absolute amount of remittances, but its GDP proportion has also increased since these figures were quoted in 2009. Other possible but minor factors for raised levels of remittances include an increasing numbers of migrants using formal (rather than informal) channels for money transfer and a favourable exchange rate for the US Dollar.[65] The real mitigating factor is that the money from remittances actually goes to the families of the migrants rather than getting lost in government funding channels.[x] "The major player in poverty reduction is remittance, as a large portion of it is used for fulfilling the basic needs of families, such as food, clothing and education."[66] In addition, depending on whether they are living in villages or towns, families use up to around 50% of remittances to buy land.[67]

It is easy to assume that the brain drain becomes a permanent loss to Nepal and certainly a large percentage of educated professionals do tend to remain in the west. However, in the long term, there is a degree of 'brain circulation' and even a small **'brain gain'**[xi] as professionals do return, with new skills and a genuine commitment to work in their homeland.

Many factors determine who migrates and to where and for how long.[68] A comprehensive picture emerges when we consider details about several specific kinds of migrants.

NON-RESIDENT NEPALIS

"But our citizenship is in heaven,"
~ Philippians 3:20 ESV ~

According to the Non-Resident Nepali Act 2064 BS (2007), "For practical purposes Nepali citizens living outside South

---

[x] A comment made by participants on The Forum, BBC, 5 June 2011

[xi] Terms coined by participants on The Forum, BBC, 5 June 2011

Asian Association for Regional Cooperation (SAARC) member countries or People of Nepali Origin (PNO) holding foreign nationality other than SAARC nations are considered as NRNs." However, according to Wikipedia, a Non Resident Nepali (NRN) is a person of Nepali descent having the citizenship of other countries and a Nepali citizen living at least two years having any profession or business in any foreign country. It does not include Nepali citizens or citizens of SAARC countries of Nepali descent living in SAARC countries. It further excludes the students and members and staffs of Nepali diplomatic missions staying in any foreign country.

Taking these statements together, it is immediately clear that the definitions are ambiguous regarding NRN citizenship and as to whether labour migrants should be included as NRNs if they are working overseas for at least 2 years. This ambiguity is reflected in the statistics of Nepalis overseas as some figures are clearly only NRNs with foreign nationality who have settled overseas long-term, whereas other statistics seem to include labour migrants.

The Non-Resident Nepali Association (NRNA) was established in October 2003 to unite and bind together the Nepali Diaspora and represent Nepali interests globally, including the possibility of obtaining dual citizenship and its associated rights. The NRNA now has branches in more than 60 countries. In 2009, the NRNA in the UK produced some statistics stating that there were 1,945,000 Nepalis scattered throughout 55 countries. It is not clear whether this figure included labour migrants in some or all of the destinations, although they did say that the vast majority were based in the Middle East and Asia, but it almost certainly excluded India.

NRNs seek to provide a voice for overseas Nepalis, although this only occasionally includes advocacy for labour migrants, probably because their associations are not strong in many of the countries where most of the labour migrants are found. Many of the associations have given generous financial support to medical, educational and other social projects back home in Nepal.

STUDENTS & PROFESSIONALS

Daniel and his friends benefitted from a kind of scholarship education in Babylon, but nevertheless had to face various challenges, not least because of their faith. (Daniel 1, 3, 6)

Nepali Students Overseas
Source: Ministry of Education, 2011

Country	No.	Country	No.
UK	28,667	Rest of Europe	4,489
Australia/NZ	14,076	USA/Canada	6,072
Japan	2,534	S Korea/Thailand Philippines/ Malaysia/Singapore	1,269
India	947	Bangladesh/ Pakistan	1,425
China/HK	852	Russia, etc.	457
Cyprus	1,349	Other Countries	254

Students and professionals are admittedly the elite of the migrants and in general they suffer few of the problems that labour migrants have to face. Those who are fortunate enough to gain entrance to a high standard college find this is invariably their doorway to a good career, whether or not they return to Nepal. These are usually those from rich families or with brilliant academic records, and many of them have found a way not only to study but to stay in the west rather than return to Nepal and invest their skills in their own country. In the case of medical professionals at least, many go, and they stay, because of "low wages, poor motivation, persistent shortages of basic medical supplies, dangerous working conditions, outdated equipment, lack of supervision, and limited career opportunities" back in Nepal.[69]

However, there have been many poor standard institutions that have cheated their students. Some have promised visas that never materialised. Some have advertised educational standards that they do not have. Some have accepted students but made no attempt to meet and greet them on arrival – leaving young students struggling to cope in the airport of a strange new culture with little money and even less understanding of how to find their way around.

As part of her research, Adhikari discovered the following:

> As student visa requirements have become tighter, brokers have started to establish a direct link with higher education colleges, and some have even set up their own colleges in the UK and elsewhere. A common term for these colleges which circulates in Nepal and in the UK is "Hajariya College" or "Visa College" (Thousand Pounds College), and yet they have only been set up to help students renew their student visas—by charging a thousand pounds a year—to forge documents so that a one-year student visa could be renewed, and therefore the migrant could continue to stay and work [not study] in the UK.[70]

Since then, and largely because of this, the UK and other western countries have tightened regulations for student visas: entry for inappropriate courses or to questionable colleges is now no longer possible. This has helped to eliminate some of these pseudo-colleges and it is now much harder for so-called 'students' to gain visas to study at lower levels from which they soon transfer to illegal employment. Unfortunately it has also made it harder for *bona fide* students to obtain visas for genuine degree level courses.

One particular group of professionals to leave Nepal has been the nurses. Nurse migration has occurred since 2000 and by 2008 there were nearly 1,000 Nepali Nurses in the UK alone. Most have used International Educational Consultancies (IECs) to help them prepare all the necessary documentation and attain English language proficiency. However some of these have made offers that 'are too good to be true' and the students have been wrongly advised. Even if they reach a country like the UK successfully, their problems are not at an end. Overseas trained nurses have nowadays, quite reasonably, to successfully complete an Overseas Nurses Programme before they can be registered with the Nursing Midwifery Council, but there is a waiting list and candidates often have a long delay before they can obtain a seat.

> *Adhikari tells of a highly qualified and experienced nurse who took the bad advice of an agency to enter the UK for a NVQ course. She was not met at the airport (as had been promised), her booked accommodation was too expensive and she had to work as a (low-skill) carer for many months until she obtained a seat on the adaptation course.*[71]

GURKHAS

Cornelius, a Roman soldier, had presumably migrated with his regiment from Italy to Israel, where he heard the Gospel from Peter and became a Christian. (Acts 10)

After the Anglo-Nepali war of 1815-16, the British Army, so "impressed by the fighting capacity of the Gurkhas" started to recruit them. "Thus a stream of Nepalese migration to India and other regions began."[72]

Especially for young men from hill tribes, employment in the **British** and **Indian** armed forces remains an attraction.[73] In 2001 there were still more than 50,000[xii] Nepalis in the Indian Army alone.[74] Over the years, the army recruits have tended to come from the same villages and families.[75] Interestingly, labour migration is now most significant from those same hill regions from which the Gurkhas are recruited.[76] However, the benefit to their home villages from army returnees is limited as many have chosen to settle in towns like Kathmandu, Pokhara and Dharan.[77]

Becoming a British Gurkha is still "a great honour and a way to financial security for oneself and one's family."[78] Some 3,000-3,500 Gurkhas are still serving in the British Army, which means that some are still exposed to the dangers of war in countries like Afghanistan and Iraq. Others serve in

Becoming a British Gurkha is still a great honour…

[xii] This figure includes army as well as paramilitary and police personnel.

Singapore and Brunei and large numbers of ex-Gurkhas are valued as security guards in many other countries.

Nowadays there is far more freedom for Gurkhas to hear the Gospel and attend Christian fellowship, but even in the days of restrictions, God worked amongst these soldiers and this accounts for some of the strong churches in East Nepal, as in Dharan. 24 Gurkha soldiers accepted Christ in the UK in the early 1960s and as they were then later posted to Malaysia, HK, Singapore and Brunei, they took the gospel with them.[79]

There are also Nepalis employed in UN peace-keeping forces in several countries around the globe. "As of today [11 July 2013], more than 100,000 Nepali soldiers have worked in the UN's international peace missions since 1950s."[80]

LABOUR MIGRANTS

"So they ruthlessly made the people of Israel work as slaves and made their lives bitter with hard service, in mortar and brick, and in all kinds of work in the field. In all their work they ruthlessly made them work as slaves."
~ Exodus 1:13-14 ESV ~

The latest estimate is that around 2.8 million Nepalis are living as migrants and the vast majority of these are labour migrants, whose aim is to earn an amount sufficient to buy land and build a house as well as to educate their children. This is their insurance for the future but sadly, many find themselves 'back at square one' on their return home.

The fortunate ones may have managed to build their houses and pay the school fees but then they discover that they have nothing left over for day-to-day living costs, and there are still no job opportunities for them at home. It is therefore a sad fact that within a couple of months of their return from overseas, many of these returnees are on their way back to the diaspora. However, there is another – and happier – side to this story. An increasing number of these Nepali migrants have set out to find prosperity but instead, found a Saviour.

It is a fact that two-thirds of Nepali migrants are unskilled and "most of the jobs…fall into the general category... of the '3Ds' (difficult, dirty and dangerous)"[81]. Industrial accidents are frequent, but employers do not always cover migrants with (sufficient) medical insurance. Wages are often lower than they were led to believe and the only way to augment them is to work longer hours – for overtime rates, but in today's financial climate, this is not always possible. Depression is common and so sadly is suicide. Every day 4 dead bodies are returned from the diaspora to Nepal.[82] A breakdown of causes and diaspora locations was given in 2012.[83]

Most jobs are
Dirty
Difficult
Dangerous

Place of Death	No.	Percentage
Malaysia	441	33.5%
Saudi Arabia	350	26.6%
Qatar	306	23.2%
UAE	125	9.5%
Kuwait	21	1.6%
S Korea	9	0.7%
Other	64	4.9%
TOTAL	1,316	100%

Strangely, the absolute figures only account for just over 1 death per day, but the percentages are revealing.

Cause of Death	No.	Percentage
Natural causes	299	22.1%
Suicide	120	8.8%
Murder	100	7.4%
Industrial Accidents	102	7.5%
Road Accidents	185	13.6%
Heart Problems	76	5.6%
Respiratory Problems	292	21.5%
Other Causes	183	13.5%
TOTAL	1,357	100%

Families are often caused further stress as they may have to wait weeks (if not months) to receive back the body of their loved one. Part of the problem is the paperwork involved and part is the high cost of repatriation (anything from 1.5 to 5 *lakh* Rs.). Another problem – this time for officialdom – is that even after the bodies arrive, relatives may delay coming to claim the remains. Up to 2013, there were no morgue facilities at TIA. "The country's only international airport has been using a store room to keep the dead bodies… Let alone an air conditioner, the store lacks even a cooling system. The bodies rotting and foul smell emanating from them have become common in and around the store."[84]

The usual way that labour migrants obtain overseas work is through manpower agents who are, all too often, dishonest. They charge outrageous fees for their services: not less than 50,000 rupees and often a lot more, depending on the country to which they are sending people. Sometimes the migrants reach their destinations, only to discover that their promised job does not even exist. Most spend at least the first year paying off their debts at exorbitant levels of interest, leaving little to send back to their families in Nepal or live on.

"Unskilled foreign contract workers are often exploited ruthlessly and are frequently used as a means to undercut the bargaining power of the characteristically better paid and organized indigenous workers."[85]

In addition, most of this group of migrants are villagers ignorant of or naïve about the affairs of their own country, let alone those of a foreign one. One village lad, when instructed to open a bank account and given a PIN[xiii] number, said, "I find it so hard to remember my PIN: can't we all have the same number?"

UNDOCUMENTED MIGRANTS

"A mixed multitude also went up with them,"
Exodus 12:38

Undocumented is the favoured and umbrella term. There are various categories of undocumented migrants: Asylum Seekers, Refugees, Victims of Ethnic Cleaning and the so-called Illegal Immigrants. Prencipe thus talks about the criminalization of migration: "a crime in which both the source countries and the destination countries are complicit."[86] This definition well describes those Nepali migrants who suffer at the hands of dishonest agents and employers and a government that has rarely negotiated their

---

xiii Personal Identification Number.

rights. Cohen also describes two distinct types of illegal or 'undocumented' migration. One is deliberate illegal entry to another country. The second is overstaying the contract period.[87] Many refugees and asylum seekers come into the first category and many labour migrants into the second. In the Nepali context, I think there is a third type, related to the second but distinct from it. This occurs when migrants flee from workplace violence or other injustices. This makes them in a sense 'doubly illegal'. They are no longer working within the contract they were given; and, in many cases, they are without their passports because these are usually retained by the employers. This third type is frequently not truly the fault of the migrants and they may even find themselves in this situation without understanding its legal consequences. In the same way, some who have become illegal through overstaying their contracts have not done so deliberately but are caught without documents simply because their employers have not renewed their papers in time.

Suter, who conducted research on migrants in UAE, uses yet another term, 'irregular migration', which seems to be almost synonymous with undocumented or illegal migration.[88] She sees this largely as the result of there being more people wanting to migrate than there are legal opportunities for them to do so.[89] This has clearly been a factor for Nepalis who have been banned from certain destinations. Again using her own terms, Suter points out that opportunity-seeking (~voluntary) migrants are much more cautious and will stay home if the risks appear too great. They will not use illegal routes. On the other hand, survival-driven (~involuntary) migrants, driven by economic despair, are more prepared to take risks (even with an illegal route), perhaps because they think they have less to lose and more to gain. They are, by definition, the poorer group and vulnerable to trafficking by unscrupulous agents. If they are caught, they do in fact lose heavily as many have taken loans to enable them to go overseas.[90] Baruah mentioned an important factor:

> …migrants are mostly driven by what they perceive as ease of movement. They rarely weigh their choices against available information on legal or illegal migration. For example, we found that many Nepali migrants are using India as an exit point to circumvent delays or obstacles related to legality of their movement. They find that it is easier and cheaper to exit through India and there are more organized operations that can facilitate extra-legal migration.[91]

In addition, "The risk of exploitation and trafficking increases exponentially in irregular migration, and there is little scope for redress."[92]

Strictly speaking, tourists are not migrants, as they return to their own homes after a relatively short period away. Officially, they do not work or study or attempt to settle in a new place. However, the distinction may sometimes be blurred. It is also well-known that some migrants try to get in at the back door of western countries by applying for tourist visas and then disappearing into the illegal work force.

Asylum Seekers & Refugees

Something that we often forget is that Jesus himself was a refugee for a time in Egypt, when his parents had to flee from the wrath of King Herod. (Matthew 2:13-15a)

An asylum seeker is simply someone seeking to get

recognition for their claims of refugee status.[93] In its narrow and legal sense a refugee is "someone who is fleeing from a real threat of persecution in their country of origin on the grounds of their background or political opinion" but the term can also be used in a more general sense to refer to anyone participating in 'flight migration.[94] This latter sense would then subsume asylum seekers.

The distinction between asylum seekers and refugees in the Nepali context may be illustrated as follows: Individuals who fled for personal safety during the Maoist insurgency were asylum seekers. The Bhutanese Nepalis who became victims of Ethnic Cleansing and were thrust out of their homeland by a ruthless regime were refugees.

Ethnic Cleansing

Over the years many evil dictators from Pharaoh to Hitler and beyond have been involved in acts of genocide or ethnic cleansing. One was Haman, but in this case, God used Mordecai and Esther to foil his plot and save the Jews. (Esther 1:1; 3:6)

In the Nepali context, Ethnic Cleansing refers to "the mass expulsion [of more than 1 *lakh*] of southern Bhutanese of Nepalese origin by the northern Druk majority of Bhutan in 1990."[95] Since 1988, until fairly recently, more than 134,000 Bhutanese Nepalis, deprived of their citizenship rights, were living, mostly in 7 camps, on the eastern border of Nepal.

FEMALE MIGRANTS

The delightful Biblical story, about a young Jewish girl, trafficked as a result of war, but who ends up in a good household, as a maid-servant to Naaman's wife, is in stark contrast to the usual circumstances of modern trafficking or even of female migration in general. (2 Kings 5:2-3)

The World Migration Report for 2010, p.247 states that "Globally, Nepal is the country with the most feminized migrant stock (68.2%)." However, this is clearly a mis-statement probably based on a typing error. Comparing the situation and figures for the years up to 2010 with personal experience, the real figure is far more likely to have been 6.82%.[xiv] The most popular destinations for women migrants are also some of the most dangerous for them.[xv] Nevertheless, the number of female migrants has increased rapidly in the last few years, such that:

~6.82% Nepali Migrants are Women

> ...scholars and advocates are beginning to acknowledge the importance of a gender perspective of migration, examining the roles of women in the labour market or documenting experiences of female migrants in particular ethnic communities or in particular countries, or analysing immigration policies and their effects on female migrants.[96]

[xiv] Similarly, according to *Ekantipur* an Amnesty International report in 2011 "claimed that women constitute 30 percent of the total migrant workers of Nepal although official data puts it at 3 percent."

[xv] They include Kuwait, UAE, Bahrain, Oman, Qatar, & Saudi Arabia in the Gulf; Lebanon & Malaysia as well as Israel & Macau according to the *Nepal Migration Year Book 2011*, NIDS & NCCR, 2012:19

The issue of Female Migration is an emotive one. On the one hand, human rights and gender equality are the priority. On the other hand, protection of female workers is the priority. Personally, I take every possible opportunity to advise strongly against any women going to work as maids in Muslim countries.

Bijaya Rai (founder of Pourakhi) has identified a vitally important issue: "It is despair that forces women to migrate for work. We should be able to create an environment where migration is a choice and not a compulsion."[97]

Trafficking

"Nepal is a source country for men, women and children trafficked for the purposes of sexual exploitation and involuntary servitude. Children are trafficked within the country and to India and the Middle East for commercial sexual exploitation or forced marriage..."[98] "Young girls are sold by poor parents, tricked into fraudulent marriages, or promised employment in towns only to find themselves in brothels."[99] At least until 2007, GoN had done little to combat this problem. Then, in 2007, the Ministry of Labour established a 'safe migration' desk at the airport, but this of course had no effect on the large numbers who were crossing the land border into India. More than 10 years ago, Seddon reckoned "5,000 to 7,000 young Nepalese women [were]... trafficked into India each year"[100] and that there

>2 lakh Nepali girls in Indian brothels

were 40,000 Nepali CSWs[xvi] in each of Mumbai and Calcutta.[101] These figures largely agree with that quoted by Hall of 200,000 girls working in Indian brothels.[102] Not surprisingly, the latest 2010 edition of *Operation World* now puts the figure even higher – at 300,000 – mainly in Mumbai, and says that they are terribly abused; and that possibly 90% of returnees are HIV-positive.[103]

Sadly, one result of this has been a rapid spread of AIDS back in Nepal, but to date "no coherent national plan for AIDS prevention" has been designed. Actually, the single biggest reservoir of HIV/AIDS infection among women in Nepal is not the returned CSWs but village women whose husbands have returned from work outside the country, bringing the infection with them. Although they are usually innocent these women are often rejected by their families and sometimes even blamed for the death of their husbands! However, by 2013, IOM-Nepal had in place a project called 'Trafficking Risk Reduction in Nepal.' Its activities include counselling, business specific training and enterprise development training to help rescued survivors and potential victims attain economic independence.

When we think of trafficking, we automatically think of it in relation to women. However, Bute uncovered some evidence that boys are also trafficked but found little evidence of trafficking in men from Nepal.[104] Nevertheless, if we take a broader definition of trafficking, then it is clear that many Nepali men are trafficked as they are recruited and deployed through deception. There are three inter-related routes of trafficking for Nepali girls.

[xvi] Commercial Sex Workers.

The most commonly known, in the Nepali context, is when young girls are sold into sex slavery in India. There are said to be over 1.2 million children involved in prostitution in India, many of whom are Nepali. Occasionally, and very sadly, it is their own close (male) relatives who engineer this, and not always because of mitigating circumstances of poverty. Sometimes it has involved fraudulent marriage arrangements. More usually it is people from the village or local agents who deceive needy families into sending their girls to work in India, without revealing the true facts. Traditionally, this has happened to many young Tamang girls, who have been enticed from their hill villages, thinking they were going to help out with the family income.

Nowadays, deceptive recruitments are also made of poor and lower caste girls via the carpet factories in Kathmandu. Traffickers take the girls, as unwilling victims, to the Indian border where they are sold to brokers. These middlemen then take the girls to cities like Mumbai where they are sold to brothel owners. The expenses incurred in all this have to be paid off by the girl's subsequent earnings. Once they have reached the brothels of Bombay, it is extremely difficult to rescue these girls, although some Nepali Christians have become involved in rescue ministries. There are now NGOs working at border crossings and they are often able to recognise when a girl is being trafficked across the border and take measures to prevent her from entering India.

The second route is less blatant but does nevertheless still result in many girls being sexually abused. Although the Government of Nepal decreed restrictions on girls going to work in many Muslim countries as maids – largely because of the danger to them of being sexually abused –

unscrupulous agents, even well aware of this danger, circumvent the rules by channelling the girls through India.

The third route is really part of internal migration. Thamel – that tourist 'paradise in the north west corner of Kathmandu – has become 'a little Bangkok' in recent years.

In a rather strange twist of logic, for some women prostitution is now almost a choice. Many women from many different castes and tribes are 'choosing' to get into commercial sex work because there is not enough land or any alternative employment to support the family.[105]

Maids

While it is obviously and increasingly important that a gender perspective is introduced into Nepali migration matters, the issue of women trafficking needs to be kept in proportion. It only relates to a limited number of women affected by migration. Domestic workers in Muslim countries are also at risk, but as they are often there illegally, fear of this status being discovered probably keeps many from reporting bad working conditions or outright abuse.[106] Larger numbers of women are affected by migration as they move passively with their husbands and families to India.

But by far the biggest numbers of women affected by migration are those left behind in the villages caring for children, elderly parents or in-laws and looking after the fields while their menfolk are away.[107] In addition, in some villages up to 90% of the population have moved to towns or gone overseas: "those who have stayed behind are the most vulnerable, such as the elderly and disabled..."[108]

Looking at this issue more positively, an increasing number of women and girls who go overseas now regard themselves as part of the labour market and therefore feel empowered – rather than disempowered – by migration.[xvii] Unfortunately, those who work as housemaids overseas are not covered by the same labour laws that (to some extent) protect construction site, restaurant and factory employees (including women). Only 5% of women get the job and salary that they were promised and a further 25% get something similar, which means that almost three-quarters are badly deceived by the agents.[109] "About 16 per cent of migrant women come home without any income."[110] Not surprising then that Saru Joshi suggests that "instead of favouring emigration, the government should adopt policies that give women rights at home, ensuring equality with men."[111] But rights without accompanying employment opportunities and capital funding will not solve the problem.

> According to a study by the Foreign Nepali Workers Rescue Center (FNWRC), about 90 per cent of all Nepali migrant women are victims of sexual violence and exploitation. The worst cases are in Arab countries where female migrant workers are routinely raped, beaten and not paid. For this reason, the Nepali government limited emigration to the Middle East between 1998 and 2010."[112]

Although this statistic is almost certainly inflated or relates only a specific (but unstated) group of migrants, it does serve to underline a very real problem faced by a certain percentage of women migrants – most of them maids in Muslim countries.

[xvii] Habitat also points out that some women are even empowered through prostitution: a strange way of looking at things!

Despite the effort of GoN to control this problem by setting a ban on female workers going to Gulf countries, huge numbers (one estimate in 2009 put it as high as 200,000) continued to go unofficially and usually via India. After 12 years, the authorities lifted the ban but only 18 months later, in 2012, introduced a new 'over 30 years rule' in the wake of the publicised suicide of a young woman who had been sexually abused in Kuwait. This law proved controversial as some saw it as limiting the rights of women rather than legitimately trying to protect them. Nisha Varia, senior women's rights researcher at Human Rights Watch (HRW) said:

> Nepal is right to be concerned about its migrant domestic workers, but imposing a ban on women under 30 from traveling to the Gulf does not solve the problem and discriminates against young women… A better strategy would be to crack down on abusive recruitment practices, ensure that women migrate with an enforceable contract in hand, and equip embassies to respond quickly to complaints of abuse.[113]

Her 'better strategy' is certainly good but I doubt that it is either realistic or enforceable in the foreseeable future. If it were, then I might have more sympathy with her concern about discrimination. Gayathri suggested something similar:

> Instead of a blanket ban on young women that denies them important employment opportunities, the Nepalese government should work with other labor-sending governments to demand stronger protections for migrant workers in the Gulf… It [HRW] urged the government to improve training of migrant workers, to monitor recruitment agencies rigorously, and to ensure migrant women know where to get help if they need it.[114]

Again, I personally find this suggestion rather naïve in view of all the reports of abuse that come from so many countries. I am even more amazed that Anil Giri should think that, "[the] move by the government of Nepal to lift the ban on women working in Gulf States was an important decision that will help to protect the country's most vulnerable workers."[115] Deliberately allowing women to go and work in situations where there is a high chance of them being abused does not sound like protection to me. It is true that it will probably limit the numbers going illegally and therefore allow the government to know who is working where and so be better able to render assistance when needed. However, I am not convinced that it really indicates true responsibility when GoN has no way of ensuring that the host nations will respect these migrants and give them their rights. I am also left wondering what GoN's stated rationale of "Women above 30 years of age are at low risk of such exploitation"[116] really implies about Nepali ladies!

The government has set the age bar and also introduced provisions for parental consent, etc. to try to dissuade migration, while others have looked at the problem from different perspectives. However, the government still needs to find a way to ensure safe migration and stop trafficking through India. Above all, the government needs to provide alternative jobs for those who would otherwise go overseas, as well as employment for returnees.[117] The government should listen to returnee women:

Sapana is a 26 year-old woman who went to Saudi Arabia in 2007, having paid 700 USD to obtain a baby-sitting job in a Riyadh family:

*On arrival **Sapana** found there was no baby and that she was expected to work as a domestic maid instead. "'The family was one father and two adult sons,' she said, 'I could not understand their language and I was punished every day with a beating.'" For months, her employer and his sons abused her. When she got pregnant, they sent her packing back to Nepal without paying her. In her village, Sapana now works as a seamstress to raise her 2-year-old boy.*[118]

Her conclusion is poignant: "I emigrated to become independent but for women going abroad is too dangerous… They treat us like animals."

Bhawana had a similar experience. She was cheated out of her beautician's job, for which she had deposited more than 1 *lakh* with the agent, and instead sold as a maid. She also says, "I think women should never go for employment abroad. Women are not treated like human beings. Instead, they can do a lot back home if the government supports them."[119]

> ***For women, going abroad is too dangerous.***

Such stories are all too common. Even while writing this chapter, another story of a Nepali maid committing suicide in prison in Kuwait hit the news. To understand this issue in greater depth I recommend you read *Miles Apart: Experience from Foreign Labour Migration*, published jointly by Pourakhi and UNIFEM in 2009 in Kathmandu. It documents the stories of many ladies whose lives have been very significantly affected by their migration experience.

Some attempts are being made to address these issues, both globally and in Nepal. An International Labour Conference, held in Geneva in 2011, identified the specific problems related to domestic workers, who were usually women or girls, and very often migrants. The recommendation of this conference was that all such workers – whether employed in institutions or private homes – should enjoy the same human rights and employment conditions (including official contracts, reasonable working conditions without abuse, regular leave, fair wages, access to medical care when needed etc.) that are (at least in theory) accorded to other categories of workers. The vision of the conference was that each individual country should adopt these recommendations. In fact, there was a follow-up seminar in Kathmandu to discuss these issues, but making recommendations and persuading governments – let alone local independent employers – to abide by them are two very different matters. Even if Nepal wholly embraced this recommendation and more strictly regulated agencies placing female domestics, unless the receiving countries reciprocate, the problems will remain. In the meantime individuals do what they can, but it is not easy. I heard of Nepalis, who had been helping women in trouble by various practical means and through advocacy, who were themselves then threatened by agency workers.

REFERENCES FROM SECTION 2

[1] Brigitte Suter, *Labour Migration in the United Arab Emirates: Filed study on Regular and Irregular Migration in Dubai*, 2005:39

[2] http://www.migrantwatch.org/

[3] *False Promises Exploitation and Forced Labour of Nepalese Migrant Workers*, Amnesty International, 2001

[4] Bandita Sijapati & Amrita Limbu, *Governing Labour Migration in Nepal: An Analysis of Existing Policies and Institutional Mechanisms*, 2012:118

[5] Suter, 2005:39

[6] Pema Abrahams, "New Act a Blow to Human Rights in Nepal," *Asia Foundation,* 14 Mar 2013

[7] The freedictionary.com

[8] Enoch Wan "The Phenomenon of Diaspora: Missiological Implications for Christian Missions, "Diaspora Study" of *Global Missiology*, July, 2012:1

[9] William F Hornby & Melvyn Jones, *Studies in Human Geography: An Introduction to Population Geography*, 1980:83

[10] Jon Burbank, Culture Shock (A Guide to Customs and Etiquette), 1999:29

[11] See Luis Pantoja Jr., Sadiri Joy B Tira & Enoch Wan (Eds), *Scattered: The Filipino Global Presence*, 2004:117 quoting Enoch Wan, Christine D Pohl, "Biblical Issues in Mission and Migration" *Missiology: An International Review* Vol. XXXI Number 1 Jan. 2003 pp 3-15, P Emil Chandran "South Asian Diaspora – Challenges and Opportunities," *Evangelical Missions Quarterly* 10/04 pp 453-4 and Jonathan Ingleby, "Globalisation, Glocalisation and Mission," *Encounter Mission EZine*, Issue 1: August 2004:4

[12] BC Upreti, *The Marginal Migrants (A Study of Nepali emigrants in India)*, 2002:73

[13] Cindy L Perry, *Nepali Around the World*, 1997:16

[14] Lochana Sharma, "Women in Nepal warn of foreign employment exploitation," *Nepal National*, 6 Aug 2011

[15] "No jobs no hope Nepal's workers head to the Gulf and Malaysia," *The Star,* c 28 Oct 2013

[16] Wolfgang Lutz, *The Future Population of the World: What can we assume today?* 1996:298

[17] Susan Thieme et al, "Addressing the Needs of Nepalese Migrant Workers in Nepal and in Delhi, India," *Mountain Research and Development*, Vol. 25, No. 2, May 2005

[18] "Migration & HIV in Nepal," *UNDP*, c Dec 2012

[19] Janak BC, personal communication

[20] "1,357 migrant workers 'died' in 3-and-a-half years," *Ekantipur*, 12 Jan 2012

[21] Regional Symposium on Deployment of Workers Overseas: A Shared Responsibility, *ILO et al*, 15-16 Jul 2008

[22] "Nepali workers rescued over working conditions in Jordan", *Albawaba,* 11 Mar 2013

[23] "House directs for support to deceased migrant workers' kin," *Himalayan Times*, 8 Jan 2012

[24] Rubeena Mahato, "To hell and back", *Nepali Times*, Issue 598, 30 March – 5 April 2012

[25] Dimapilis-Baldos in Pantoja et al, 2004:45

[26] Roshan Sedhai, , "A wait too long in whole of S Asia Nepali passport processing fee is also the highest in region," *Ekantipur*, 5 June 2013

[27] Roshan Sedhai, "Nepali missions in labour nations 'overburdened,'" *The Kathmandu Post*, 22 April 2013

[28] Sedhai, *Ekantipur*, 5 June 2013

[29] Ibid

[30] "Nepali workers rescued over working conditions in Jordan," *Albawaba,* 11 Mar 2013

[31] "An owner of a manpower agency swindled youth two million rupees before fleeing", *Manpower Agency Nepal*, 14 Aug 2010

[32] *False Promises – Exploitation and Forced Labour of Nepalese Migrant Workers*, AI, 2011:6

[33] "114 agents responsible for 90 pc illegal departure of Nepali woman to Saudi Arabia," *Nepal News* 15 May 2013

[34] "Four held for sending Nepali women to Gulf on fake papers." *Calcutta News*, 20 Aug 2012

[35] "Big fake certificate racket busted in Nepal, 15 in police net," *The Kathmandu Post*, 6 June 2013

[36] Nandita Baruah & Shareen Tuladhar, "Nepal's Migrants Boost Economy, But Greater Protection of Rights is Needed", *Asia Foundation*, 19 Dec 2012

[37] "Workers forced to grease TIA officials' palms," *Ekantipur*, 30 Jan 2012

[38] "Changes at DoFE relieve foreign job seekers," *Ekantipur*, 13 May 2012

[39] Information in a Report by Irene Fernandez, director of Tenaganita, 2012

[40] "Nepali missions understaffed: 2.5m workers at receiving end," *Ekantipur*, 26 Jun 2012

[41] "The attaché case – the government has decided to station labour attachés at last", *The Kathmandu Post*, 26 Aug 2009

[42] "Changes at DoFE relieve foreign job seekers," *Ekantipur*, 13 May 2013

[43] Surya Nath Mishra, "Diplomacy for Migrant worker", *Ekantipur,* 30 June 2012

[44] "Nepali missions understaffed: 2.5m workers at receiving end," *Ekantipur, 26 June 2012* quoting Kawari, Director of DoFE

[45] Mahato, *Nepali Times,* 30 March – 5 April 2012

[46] "Nepal to add diplomatic missions in China, Gulf countries *China Daily*, 22 Feb 2013

[47] Ramesh Shrestha, "Nepali migrant workers struck by wanderlust," *Ekantipur*, 14 Dec 2011

[48] "Young pregnant woman burnt alive by family in Nepal", *Nepal National*, 9 Apr 2013

[49] Anu Thapa, "Gang-rape case in Nepal sparks protests," *Top News*, 28 Jun 2013

[50] NeMUN Records, July 2013

[51] Ramesh Shrestha, "Half of Nepali households have member working abroad: Survey", *Kathmandu Post*, 29 June 2011

[52] "Repeat migrant workers account for half of worker departures," *Ekantipur*, 27 Jan 2012

[53] Stanley Johnson, *The Politics of Population: Cairo 1994: The International Conference on Population and Development*, 1994:167

[54] Rubeena Mahato, "Woman Power," *Nepali Times* No. 597, 23-29 March 2012

[55] "Returnee women want to be their own masters," *Ekantipur*, 19 Oct 2012

[56] "A Shy Entrepreneur?" INF *Today in Nepal* No. 224, Jun 2013

[57] *Nepal Migration Year Book 2011*, NIDS & NCCR, 2012:20 with which "Migration & HIV in Nepal," UNDP, c Dec 2012 roughly agrees

[58] *Passage to India*, 2008:4

[59] "No jobs no hope Nepal's workers head to the Gulf and Malaysia," *The Star,* c 28 Oct 2013

[60] "Remittance sustains 30pc of families," *The Kathmandu Post*, 10 Aug 2009

[61] , "Nepali workers rescued over working conditions in Jordan", *Albawaba*, 11 Mar 2013

[62] Mahato, *Nepali Times,* 30 Ma r-5 Apr 2012

[63] Michael Lokshin, Mikhail Bontch-Osmolovski & Elena Glinskaya, *Work-Related Migration and Poverty Reduction in Nepal*, 2007:4

[64] Amador A Remigio in Pantoja et al, 2004:11
[65] Caesar Rana & Suman Lamichane, "A remittance economy", *Boss*, May-June 2009:45
[66] Ibid 47
[67] Ibid 51
[68] Hornby & Jones, 1980:106-7
[69] Omar B Ahmad, "Managing medical migration from poor countries", *British Medical Journal*, 2 July 2005:43
[70] Radha Adhikari in Philippe Ramirez (Ed), "The "dream-trap": brokering, "study abroad" and nurse migration from Nepal to the UK," *European Bulletin of Himalayan Research*, 35-36, Autumn-Spring 2009-10:137
[71] Ibid 133-4
[72] Upreti, BC, 2002:44
[73] Ibid 46
[74] Susanne von der Heide & Thomas Hoffmann (Eds), *Aspects of Migration and Mobility in Nepal*, 2001:173
[75] David Seddon, Jagannath Adhikari & Ganesh Gurung, *The New Lahures: Foreign Employment and Remittance Economy of Nepal*, 2001:67
[76] Ibid 61
[77] Andrew Hall, *Himalayan Exodus: Nepalese Migrant Groups,* 1995:132
[78] *Operation World*, 2010:622
[79] Perry, *Dharma Deepika*, Jul-Dec 2001:42
[80] "Nepal to send peacekeepers to Syria," *Nepal National/IANS*, 11 Jul 2013
[81] Seddon et al, 2001:57
[82] Roshan Sedhain, "Nepal airport facing crisis of too many dead bodies flown in," *The Kathmandu Post*, 26 June 2013
[83] "1,357 migrant workers 'died' in 3-and-a-half yrs," *Ekantipur*, 12 Jan 2012
[84] Sedhain, *The Kathmandu Post*, 26 June 2013
[85] Robin Cohen & Paul Kennedy, *Global Sociology*, 2000:208
[86] Lorenzo Prencipe in William F Fisher & Thomas Ponniah (Eds), *Another World is Possible: Popular Alternatives to Globalization at the World Social Forum*, 2003:255
[87] Cohen, 2000:206-7
[88] Suter, 2005:14
[89] Ibid 14 quoting Gosh,1998:34
[90] Ibid 15 referring to Gosh, 1998:39
[91] Nandita Baruah, "Nandita Baruah Examines Realities & New Approaches to Combating Human Trafficking," *Asia Foundation*, 5 Jun 2013

[92] Nandita Baruah & Srijana Chettri, "As Demand for Migrant Labor Grows, Opportunities for Women Emerge, But Risks Prevail, *Asia Foundation*, 7 Mar 2012

[93] Cohen, 2000:204

[94] Ibid

[95] Wikipedia

[96] Habitat, 2007:1

[97] Mahato, *Nepali Times*, 23-29 Mar 2012

[98] Anon, Nepal: Tier 2

[99] "Migration & HIV in Nepal," UNDP, c Dec 2012

[100] Seddon et al, 2001:114-115

[101] Ibid 38

[102] Hall, 1995:136

[103] *Operation World*, 2010:621

[104] Amanda Bute, *Combating trafficking and caring for victims of trafficking – What could INF/W's role be?* 2006:3

[105] Madan K Dahal (Ed), *Impact of Globalization in Nepal*, 2005:45 quoting Sathi, 1997 and New ERA, 1998

[106] *Consultation on Gender, Migration & Law/Human rights: India, Nepal & Bangladesh*, Jan 2007:2

[107] Dahal (Ed), 2005:38

[108] Kavita Shukla & Michelle Brown, "India: Nepali migrants in need of protection", *Refugees International*, 28 Feb 2007:2

[109] Sharma L, 6 Aug 2011

[110] *Weekly Nepal*, 2 Aug 2011

[111] "Nepali migrant women victims of abuse and exploitation," *Weekly Nepal*, 2 Aug 2011

[112] *Weekly Nepal*, 2 Aug 2011

[113] Amrutha Gayathri, "Nepal urged to revoke ban on young women migrating to Gulf", *IB Times*, 15 August 2012

[114] Ibid

[115] Anil Giri, "Nepal must help to protect women working in the Gulf", *The National*, 16 Dec 2010

[116] "Nepal women banned from Middle East over exploitation," *Armenian News*, 9 Aug 2012

[117] "Returnee Women," *Ekantipur*, 19 Oct 2012

[118] Sharma, 6 Aug 2011

[119] Anjali Subedi, "Migrant workers long for work at home," *Republica*, 28 Dec 2012

SECTION 3

NEPALI DESTINATIONS

"When the Most High gave to the nations their inheritance, when he divided mankind, he fixed the borders of the peoples according to the number of the sons of God."
~ Deuteronomy 32:8 ESV ~

The New 'Lahures'

Among the earliest, and the best-known, to venture beyond the borders of Nepal were the soldiers who joined the British Army in Lahore. "The old Lahures fought bravely in foreign armies and helped establish a name for Nepal. Our resilient boys who work hard as migrant labourers and send money home are doing the same thing, so are the intellectual Lahures who sell their skills internationally."[1]

Labour Migrants - The New 'Lahures'

Prior to the 19th century, there were more Nepalis in Tibet than in any other country outside Nepal.[2] During the (British) 'colonial era' Nepalis were sometimes sent to places like Fiji, Natal, British Guiana and Trinidad as part of the indentured labour force.[3] Therefore, although Nepal was essentially a closed land until 1950, "for around 200 years, men (and to a lesser extent women) from Nepal have been leaving their homes in Nepal to seek their living abroad…."[4]

Until 1981 almost all Nepalis who left their homeland went to India.[5] By 1997, more than 40% of overseas Nepalis were in Hong Kong (the majority), Singapore and Brunei, although there were also significant populations in the UK and Japan.[6] These were mostly the descendants of the 'old Lahures.' The great exodus of the 'new Lahures' only began to the Middle East (Bahrain) in the 1980s and Malaysia in 2001.

Nepal Census figures present an interesting, even if not fully comprehensive, picture of Nepali migration:

Date	Nepalis Overseas		Comments
	No.	%*	
1952/4	198,130	2.3%	Mostly from the hills
1961	328,480	3.4%	
1971			No appropriate data
1981	402,977	2.7%	
1991	660,000	<3%	78% in India but > 71,000 elsewhere
2001	762,181	3%	77% in India
2011	1,921,494	7%	

The census figures, unlike many others, include migrants to India, and so give a truer picture. However, from studying the census data, it seems that the figures quoted for migration are actually the numbers of absentees from Nepal at the time of each census. In 1971, there was really no appropriate migration data and only in 1991 was there an attempt to separate migration to India and elsewhere. In addition, even the census data is probably under-counted, because where whole families have migrated there would have been no one left to provide census information!

*The percentage is that of the total population. It stayed relatively static at around 2-3% until recently, when it shot up to 7.2%, and if all migrants (including internal relocations) are counted, it would rise further to 20%.[7] If the calculation is made instead as the percentage of the active labour force, it would be approximately double. However, In the FY 2012/13, only around 2% of the total working population left the country, but this is probably exclusive of those travelling to India as it was not a census figure.[8]

The most interesting comparison of numbers that I have discovered was given by the Minister for Labour and Transport in 2001. He cited figures of those going abroad through formal channels (excluding India) of 12,000 migrants in 1997/8 compared with 127,675 in 2001. However, others have suggested that these numbers are out by a factor of 10, on the basis of a calculation of 1.15 million migrants in 1996/7.[9] Baruah & Chettri suggest an increase from 55,000 in 2000 to 294,000 in 2010.[10] Perhaps the most important thing to note is the trend rather than the absolute numbers and this has shown a year on year increase from <50,000 in 1998/99 to >350,000 in 2011/12 (both figures excluding India) according to NIDS.[11] Female migration has only been significant since 2007/8.[12]

Everyone also agrees that out-migration from Nepal exploded

between 1993 and 2006, even if the figures quoted (from less than 4,000 to almost 2 *lakh.*[13]) are gross underestimates.

By October 2011, the estimates begin to assume a greater degree of reality for migrants leaving for all destinations, excluding India.[14]

Nepali Date	Date	Nepalis Overseas
2064/5 BS	~2007/8	1,239,661
2067/8 BS	~2010/11	2,108,436

In the decade 2000 to 2010 the numbers of official work permits granted by the government increased from less than 10,000 per annum to over 100,000 per annum.[15]

Every day 900 Nepalis receive permission to work abroad.

Nowadays, "According to the Department of Foreign Employment (DoFE), an average of 900 people… receive final approval from the government to work abroad every day…"[16] The cumulative figures, based on the numbers of work permits issued up to 2010/11 were:

The Gulf	Malaysia	Elsewhere
13.2 *lakh*	6.8 *lakh*	10.5 *lakh*

The official final figure for the total population of Nepal at the time of the 2011 Nepal Census was 26,494,504. Around the time of this census, it was estimated that a third of all Nepalis were living outside the borders of Nepal. In terms of figures, with a population of nearly 27 million in Nepal, there must therefore be a further 12-13 million living outside Nepal. After excluding the 10 million or so Nepalis who are in India[i], this means there are probably at least 2 (and maybe as many as 3) million Nepali migrants working elsewhere overseas. This agrees well with the officially stated figure of 2.8%. At least 6.8% of these migrants are women.[ii]

By 2013, Nepalis had reached around 130 of the countries of the world. Of these, 107[iii] were officially 'allowed destinations' authorised by the Government of Nepal, although in some of these, only a handful of Nepalis are domiciled. However, although at least one country, Iraq, was 'disallowed', Nepalis are still known to be living and working there. Of the remaining 20 or so countries, about half may be regarded as 'safe' and the other half as potentially dangerous. They are countries like Afghanistan, Libya, Egypt, Somalia, Mali, Sudan, and Congo, where there have been recent wars or where there is still a war zone. This clearly poses a challenge to Nepali embassies around the world as to how they can effectively care for their citizens in such situations.

12-13 million Nepali Migrants
(including those in India)
Nepalis in > 130 countries
Most countries are in the 10/40 window

Another interesting fact about Nepali destinations is that

[i] It is impossible to give an accurate figure for Nepali migrants in India. See below and also Chapter 7.

[ii] Other sources suggest a figure of around 3%. That is probably too low now as increasing numbers of women and girls are finding their way into the Diaspora.

[iii] 108, if India is included.

around one third of the countries to which Nepalis travel are situated in the 10-40 window.[iv] Many of these are where the majority of the Nepali labour migrants end up; countries like Qatar, UAE, Saudi Arabia and Malaysia which are Muslim states. This poses a challenge to the Nepali Christians working in the Diaspora as to how they live, work and witness in a Muslim environment, for this is not a situation that more than a few from some *Terai* Districts have previously experienced.

Top 5 destinations:
Qatar
Malaysia
Saudi Arabia
UAE
Kuwait

On the occasion of International Migrants Day in December 2012, it was reported that, "Qatar, Malaysia, Saudi Arabia, the UAE, and Kuwait are the top five labor destination countries with the highest number of Nepali migrant workers…"[17]

Despite every effort to obtain accurate estimates of Nepali populations in different countries, this has proved virtually impossible. This is a problem that everyone recognises. Ramesh Badal (Legal Advisor, GFONT) said, "Migrant records are confusing. We keep records of those who go abroad but there is no record of returnees. We calculate the remittance they bring in but don't have any account of how much we [sic] have spent to go abroad."[18] Overall I have found that the most helpful figures – although not official and still subject to error – are the ones provided by personal

[iv] The 10/40 Window refers to the area of North Africa, the Middle East and Asia situated approximately between 10 and 40 degrees north of the equator. Countries in this area have the highest level of socioeconomic challenges and the least access to the Christian message and Christian resources.

informants. Apart from these, the main sources that I have used are:

Operation World – which only speaks of the Nepali Diaspora as a whole and migrants in general under each country, without specifying their origins, except to distinguish Asians from others.

Wikipedia – which is notoriously incomplete and essentially based on multiple personal postings. This means it may be really up-to-date in some cases but hopelessly inadequate or out-of-date in others.

Joshua Project – which is not easy to navigate to discover facts about Nepalis in general, as they are categorised under several different names and also under castes and tribes or languages spoken. Only in a handful of countries do their figures tally with those from other sources.[v]

Finishing the Task – which only provides data on unreached people groups. Excluding the deaf, which are not relevant in this context, they mention 20 groups of whom half do have Christian witness within the country. It is quite possible that many individuals among the 50% unreached may be in the diaspora and within reach of a Nepali fellowship. Just a simple count of how many Nepali Districts are represented at any one diaspora fellowship – sometimes more than 20 – gives great hope for this.

---

[v] Myanmar, HK and USA are probably accurate. Bhutan, Malaysia & UAE are probably under-estimates and Australia is a gross over-estimation.

As already noted, Nepalis abroad are often very open to the Gospel: many more so than they would be at home in Nepal. Numerous churches have been established among Nepali migrants, even in restricted access nations. Some details of these are included in the Regional and Country surveys that follow.

Nepalis abroad are often very open to the Gospel.

REGIONS

"And he made from one man every nation of mankind to live on all the face of the earth, having determined allotted periods and the boundaries of their dwelling place..."
~ Acts 17:26 ESV ~

It is helpful to categorise Nepali migrants nowadays according to the three different parts of the world to which they go. These three regions are India, Asia (both SE Asia and the Middle East) and the 'West', including Australia and New Zealand. While these locations are geographically discrete, there is some overlap in areas and also in the types of migrants reaching them. Predominantly, however, students and professionals travel to the 'West' while labour migrants go to various destinations in Asia. Also, the flows are not exclusively in one direction. "A large number [of Nepalis]… go to India in search of work and a large number of Indian workers come to Nepal for the same." [19]

In the following three chapters, first a general overview of Nepali migration to the region is given. This is then followed by details of specific counties, or, in the case of India, of states and specific cities or centres of Nepali migration.

COUNTRIES

"... the provinces from India to Ethiopia, 127 provinces, to each province in its own script and to each people in its own language,"
~ Esther 8:9 ESV ~

I have tried to describe the situation of Nepali migrants in as many countries as possible. First, I categorised them by the three main areas mentioned above. Then, I sub-divided them under a number of headings which aim to keep together countries with relatively similar situations for Nepali migrants. This system works well for those areas and countries where many Nepalis are found, but in the other areas – such as Africa, Central and South America and Central/Eastern Asia – it breaks down as these countries do not fit into any specific bloc and there is only minimal data available. Where I have been able to discover the figures, I have given the total numbers of Nepalis in a country and details of any Nepali Christian fellowships or churches. In addition, I have tried to add personal anecdotes to illustrate the problems and joys in the diaspora.

Stating figures for numbers of migrants I have discovered is a very inexact science. Those I have given, therefore, are the best possible guesses at the end of 2013. In India, where most migrants are located, there are several confusing issues. Movement back and forth across the open land border is not recorded. When sources give numbers of Nepalis it may not be clear whether this refers to Nepali speakers, Nepali citizens living in India or Indian citizens of Nepali ethnic origin. Even in other countries, the statistics are never wholly accurate even when available. One reason is that the numbers are continually fluctuating. Another important reason is the presence of large numbers of illegal immigrants in Malaysia and the Middle East particularly. What is known from figures published by the Government of Nepal is that every day between 1,000 and 1,500 Nepalis leave from TIA (the airport in Kathmandu) for work overseas.[vi] However, these are only the legal emigrants, travelling to destinations other than India, for "the number of Nepalis going for foreign employment is counted as per the work permit issued by the department... the statistics of aspirants through India illegally [often to restricted destinations] is unknown."[20] On the other hand, these figures may well be confounded by those coming and going on holiday as well as migrants returning overseas for subsequent tours of duty.

Every day, 1,000-1,500 Nepalis leave from the airport for work overseas

Different sources give widely differing statistics for the numbers of counties in which Nepalis are found and for the numbers of Nepalis in these different countries. For example: Wikipedia mentions 26 countries and the INF website 34, but they are not all the same countries! Together they total 41 different locations around the globe – presumably the most common. Although the July 2011

[vi] In 2009, the figures were 700-800 (Truslé in Ramirez, *EBHR*, 2009-10:16)

DoFE list contained 107 countries (excluding India) where Nepalis may go to work, GoN statistical records of monthly departures mention 117 countries to which Nepalis have recently travelled. In fact, in just the first 4 months of the FY 2011-12 a total of 72 Nepalis had already left for 16 different unlisted countries.[21] This trend is particularly marked in the hospitality, security, medicine and engineering sectors.

Ramesh Shrestha described this phenomenon in a comment I find strange in view of what we have already discovered about movements of Nepalis over the last two centuries:

> Nepalis are not known for globetrotting tendencies, but with employment trends favouring migrant labour, they seem to have been struck by wanderlust. These Himalayan landlubbers are now setting sail for exotic destinations attracted by unprecedented job opportunities… You will find Nepali workers in the far corners of the New World.[22]

And again, "Adventurous job seekers are heading for destinations not on the government's permitted list. And bewildered officials at the Department of Foreign Employment (DoFE) are dashing for their atlases for a refresher course in geography."[23] While this development clearly has potential benefits for the individual workers who qualify for better paid jobs, it also raises issues of security for the Government of Nepal. Unless this category of workers complete and submit the relevant paperwork before departure, the Government will not know where they are and if any emergency arises, rescue would be very difficult.

In this context, it is an interesting exercise to compare the countries to which Nepalis travel with the countries in which Nepal maintains an Embassy or Consulate.

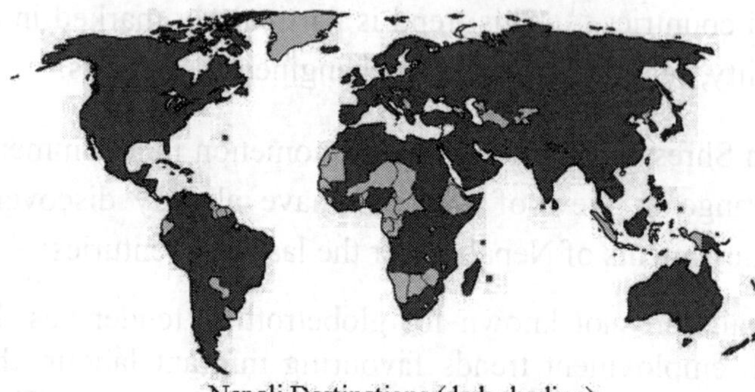

Nepali Destinations (dark shading)

WORLD COVERAGE in 2012

Nepali Diplomatic Missions (dark shading)

On the following pages, I have included 3 tables:
The first shows where Nepali diplomatic missions were situated in 2013.

Nepali Diplomatic Missions (2012)			
INDIA & Nearby	INDIA	New Delhi	Embassy
		Kolkata	Consulate
	SRI LANKA	Colombo	Embassy
MIDDLE EAST*	ISRAEL	Tel Aviv	Embassy
	KUWAIT	Kuwait City	Embassy
	QATAR	Doha	Embassy
	SAUDI ARABIA	Riyadh	Embassy
	UAE	Abu Dhabi	Embassy
AFRICA	EGYPT	Cairo	Embassy
	S AFRICA	Pretoria	Embassy
SE ASIA	JAPAN	Tokyo	Embassy
	S KOREA	Seoul	Embassy
	MALAYSIA	Kuala Lumpur	Embassy
	MYANMAR	Yangon	Embassy
	THAILAND	Bangkok	Embassy
The Rest of ASIA	BANGLADESH	Dhaka	Embassy
	CHINA	Beijing	Embassy
		Hong Kong	Consulate
		Lhasa	Consulate
	PAKISTAN	Islamabad	Embassy
EUROPE	BELGIUM	Brussels	Embassy
	DENMARK	Copenhagen	Embassy
	FRANCE	Paris	Embassy
	GERMANY	Berlin	Embassy
	RUSSIA	Moscow	Embassy
	UK	London	Embassy
AMERICAS	BRAZIL	Brasilia	Embassy
	CANADA	Ottawa	Embassy
	USA	Washington DC	Embassy
OCEANIA	AUSTRALIA	Canberra	Embassy

*Oman added in 2013

The other two tables summarise Nepali destinations. One is a list of destinations for which the Government of Nepal has given permission for Nepalis to travel; the other is of the extra countries to which Nepalis have been known to travel.

Government of Nepal Allowed List of Countries (2013)					
1	Afghanistan	2	Albania	3	Algeria
4	Argentina	5	Armenia	6	Australia
7	Austria	8	Azerbaijan	9	Bahrain
10	Bangladesh	11	Belarus	12	Belgium
13	Bolivia	14	Bosnia Herze Govina	15	Brazil
16	Brunei Darussalam	17	Bulgaria	18	Canada
19	Chile	20	China	21	Columbia
22	Cambodia	23	Costa Rica	24	Croatia
25	Cuba	26	Cyprus	27	Czech Republic
28	Denmark	29	Egypt	30	Estonia
31	Fiji	32	Finland	33	France
34	Germany	35	GB / UK	36	Greece
37	Guano ?	38	Holy See	39	HK
40	Hungary	41	Iceland	42	Indonesia
43	Iran	44	~~Iraq~~	45	Ireland
46	Israel	47	Italy	48	Japan
49	Jordan	50	Kazakhstan	51	Kenya
52	Kosovo	53	Kuwait	54	Laos PDR
55	Latvia	56	Lebanon	57	Libya
58	Luxemburg	59	Macau	60	Malaysia
61	Maldives	62	Malta	63	Macedonia
64	Mexico	65	Moldova	66	Mongolia
67	Mauritius	68	Morocco	69	Mozambique
70	Myanmar	71	Netherlands	72	New Zealand
73	Nicaragua	74	Nigeria	75	Norway
76	Oman	77	Pakistan	78	Panama
79	Peru	80	Poland	81	Portugal
82	Qatar	83	S Korea	84	Slovakia
85	Rumania	86	Russia	87	Saipan
88	Saudi Arabia	89	Singapore	90	Slovenia
91	S Africa	92	Spain	93	Sri Lanka
94	Sweden	95	Switzerland	96	Seychelles
97	Tanzania	98	Thailand	99	The Philippines
100	Tunisia	101	Turkey	102	Uganda
103	Ukraine	104	UAE	105	USA
106	Venezuela	107	Vietnam	108	Zambia

Countries not on the GoN Allowed List					
109	India	See p.162ff			
110	Angola	111	Bermuda	112	Bhutan
113	Burundi	114	Central African Republic	115	Cayman Islands
116	Congo	117	Djibouti	118	Ghana
119	Guatemala	120	Guinea	121	Haiti
122	Jamaica	123	Liberia	124	Madagascar
125	Malawi	126	Mali	127	Palau
128	PNG	129	Somalia	130	Sudan
131	Uzbekistan	132	W Indies	133	Yemen

Even this extra list may not be comprehensive

Note

In the following pages, countries which are NOT on the Government of Nepal's allowed list are marked with an asterisk after their name.

India has an asterisk, as it is not on the list, but the situation is different. Nepalis are clearly allowed to go to India but it seems that the Foreign Employment Act does not cover India and therefore India does not appear on the GoN allowed list.

Estimates of total Nepali populations in specific countries, although not guaranteed as fully accurate, do hopefully represent in general terms, the overall size of the Nepali Diaspora in these different countries.

Chapter 7

INDIA*

(plus Bhutan, Sri Lanka & The Maldives)

"... INDIA..."
~ Esther 1:1 ESV ~

By far the largest number of Nepali migrants is found in India. The biggest concentrations are in the hilly regions of the north-east and north-west as well as in the big cities. This is because most of the earliest Nepali migrants went to Bengal and Assam, with some also in Bihar, Orissa, Himachal Pradesh and the United Province as well as Sikkim. It is also because the large number of Nepalis who were recruited into the Indian armed forces settled around cantonment areas, Dehradun, Ranchi, etc.[24] Perry says that "by the late 1800s there were Gurkha settlements near the regimental homes in the Kangra Valley, Dharmsala, Bakloh, Abbottabad, Dehradun, Almora, Pithoragarh, Shillong and even Maymyo in Burma."[25]

Most (78%) of Nepali migrants are in India.

After 1950, Nepalis also began to move to the industrialised areas,[26] but, until two decades ago, Nepalis working in cities were mostly confined to Mumbai (called Bombay until 1996), Kolkata (called Calcutta until 2001) and New Delhi.

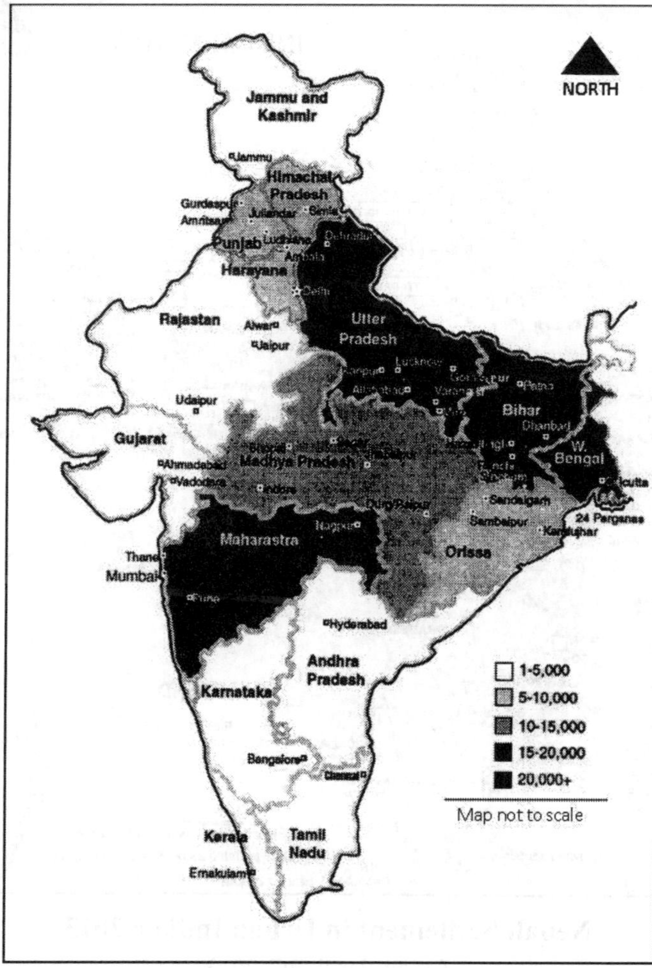

Nepali Settlement in Urban India c mid-1990s

Credit: Perry, 1997:302

Nowadays there are huge Nepali populations in all the major Indian cities. This change is illustrated by comparing Dr. Perry's map with one recently produced by Janak BC:

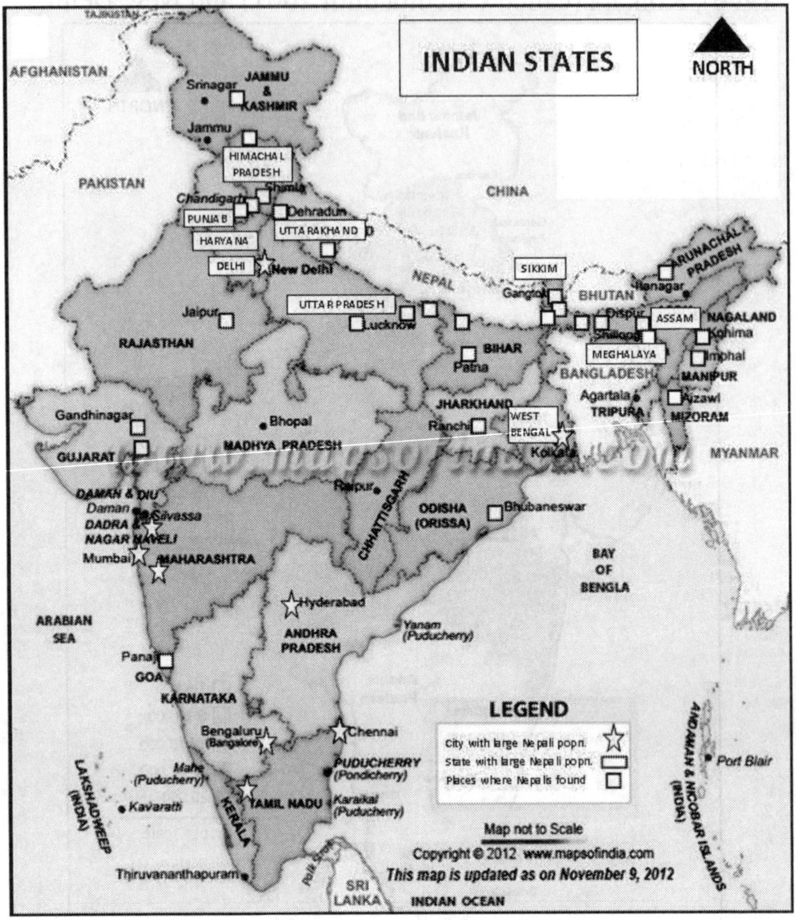

Nepali Settlement in Urban India c 2013

Credit: Janak BC, 2013

New Delhi	7 *lakh*	Mumbai	7 *lakh*
Chennai	5-6 *lakh*	Bangalore	5-6 *lakh*
Kolkata	7 *lakh*	Hyderabad	5 *lakh*

In the 1991 Nepal Census 89.2% of all Nepali migrants (i.e. absentees in the census) who had gone to India, >80% were in just four states: Uttar Pradesh, (including Uttarakhand), Bihar, Assam and West Bengal.[27] These figures date from before the Maoist insurgency and the mass exodus from Nepal. By 2004, the picture had changed completely, and there were maybe 200 Nepalis crossing the border into India every hour.

The Government has no record of the hundreds of thousands of Nepalis known to be working in India.

Back in 1995, numbers for people of Nepali origin settled in India varied between 2 and 6 million.[vii] [28] Today's figure is quite likely to be double that, but no one really knows. Even a Government officer himself "admitted that the government has no record of the hundreds of thousands of Nepalis known to be working in India."[29] 3.3 million people from at least 24 people groups in India claim to speak Nepali as their mother tongue;[30] many are probably descendants of earlier generations of migrants. Attitudes among such Nepali Indians vary. Some Nepali speakers still tend to identify as Nepali ethnics, but many of these from the Darjeeling area, the largest Nepali ethnic enclave in India, identify both as Gorkhas and as Indians and still campaign for a separate Gorkhaland state. Perhaps the majority are now fully integrated as Indian citizens.

During the time of the British Raj in India, hillsmen, often labelled 'Pahadiyas' were invited by the British into the NE

[vii] It is also estimated that there are 5.5 million Indians living in Nepal.

hills, where their work was initially to clear the hills and jungles so that Darjeeling, Sikkim, the Bhutan Duars and the Assam hills could be developed. Subsequently, many remained to work as wood-cutters, herdsmen, dairymen, plantation labourers, coolies, watchmen, and cooks.

In the later period also, most Nepali migrants continued to be pulled towards the NE and NW (Darjeeling) – for two reasons. They had a close affinity with the Nepali speaking groups recruited into the British army, who were mainly based in that region. There were also many employment opportunities in the tea gardens and other agricultural work. Push factors at that time included the grinding poverty and the increasingly repressive regime in Nepal.

In the 1920s and 1930s large numbers of Nepalis went to India; and during the 2nd World War many were recruited into the army in India. At the time of Indian Independence, many of the Gurkha regiments were absorbed into the Indian Army, and in 2007, still around 50,000 Nepalis were serving in the Indian Army.[31]

During the 1960s large numbers of Nepalis were welcomed into India to work as household-level security guards, although numbers declined in the following decades, partly due to political and security issues.[32] Nevertheless the Nepal Institute for Development Studies (NIDS) calculated that in 1997 there were at least 750,000 Nepalis working in the private sector in India.

As the Indian economy grew, it led to opportunities and access for migrants all across the country. The increased demand for workers in Indian cities coincided with the increased desire for Nepalis to find employment outside Nepal, but preferably nearby.[viii] As a result, migrant populations in many cities in India increased enormously. Some research in 2005 suggested that between 6 *lakh* and 1.3 million Nepali men migrate to India for seasonal or longer term work, of whom 4 *lakh* alone were going to Mumbai.[33] Jha and Seddon believe that "there is hardly any village or town on the Nepalese side of the border from where the people do not migrate to India in certain seasons in search of employment..."[34]

In the time of the Maoist insurgency, a further wave of Nepalis left for India, often taking their families with them, but although there are more migrant families in India than elsewhere in Asia, this is still not the common practice.

Perhaps because of Nepali links with the British rulers – in the time of the Indian Mutiny (1857) and during the Indian independence struggle, there remains a heritage of some distrust even though the 1950 treaty gave both Indians and Nepalis the freedom to travel to, and work and settle in each other's countries. The fact that a significant number of Nepalis chose to migrate to the hills of Sikkim perhaps aggravated these feelings. In reality, some Nepalis as well as some Indians, usually those living on the *Terai* – on one or other side of the border – have managed to acquire (unofficial / illegal) dual citizenship!

[viii] Although many of the more recent Nepali immigrants in India went to flee from the Maoist threat in their own country, India has its own Maoist problems – in the so-called 'Red Corridor' which stretches from the border of Nepal as far as Andra Pradesh.

In the Overseas Development Institute (ODI) Background Note of November 2011, concerning cross-border mobility between Nepal and India, Samuels et al reported on a survey conducted among Nepali migrants living in Delhi and Mumbai and returnees and their families in the FW Nepal Districts of Kanchanpur and Achham. Much of this can be extrapolated to migrants from other parts of Nepal, who go to India[ix] but some is specific to people from the remote hills.

Types of Migrants to India

> ***Most recent Nepali migrant men in India are uneducated and unskilled.***

The vast majority of Nepali migrants in India are relatively uneducated men who take up labouring or other unskilled work. For example, men from the Far Western hills of Nepal have a tradition of seasonal (and also more permanent) migration dating back for several generations – initially because they lived in a food deficit area and latterly because of the threats of the Maoists. In Indian cities, the majority of men are employed in restaurants, or in roadside *dhabas,*[x] as watchmen or in factories. Many other Nepali migrants, especially those in the rural areas of the NW states, are employed as rickshaw-pullers, coolies/porters or stone-workers or involved in agricultural work. In the NE, Nepalis have worked in the mines. Women who work outside their

---

[ix] Much of the statistical information in the following paragraphs is taken from Fiona Samuels et al, "Vulnerabilities of movement: cross border mobility between India, Nepal and Bangladesh," *Overseas Development Institute Background Note*, November 2011

[x] Small roadside food stalls.

homes usually work as house-servants; only a few work in factories. One good thing is that most migrants can get work – if they want it – all through the year. Other migrants have more prestigious work. A few semi-skilled migrants have found work as drivers and others as security guards, although these jobs are becoming harder to get as school certificates of education are now being requested. Some – because of their educational level – are able to compete for professional employment, or work in call centres. A few have even been employed in the Indian Government Service.

There are many Nepalis who go to India to study. Bangalore and Chennai (called Madras until 1996) especially are favourites for Nursing students, and Delhi for those training to be Chartered Accountants. Degree level courses in Indian Colleges and Universities are sometimes perceived as better than many in Nepal and are usually significantly cheaper than the alternatives in the west. For Christians wishing to study theology – in English medium – India has been a popular destination. There are now over 1,000 Bible Schools and over 100 degree level seminaries in India.[35] Yet others try and join the Indian Army. Janak BC has recorded the unsuccessful story of a lad called ***Akhil:***

> *I finished 12th standard in Nawal Parasi. I came to Delhi in March of 2009. I thought of joining the Nepal Army but didn't because of the political crisis. My friend came to India before me and got a job in the Indian Army. He told me that I would have to work for one of the officers for about a year and then the officer could easily help me in getting recruited into the army. I came to Delhi and started to work for one of the officers. It's almost a year now but the officer has not given me any hope for army recruitment. It seems that he is not interested in my life.*

I worked for him for nearly 11 months, without a single penny, hoping that he will give me the job. But he says that he cannot do anything unless I work for him for another year. All my hope is gone. I lost one year. I think I will have to go back to my country. I will join a college and resume my study.

There are also significant numbers of migrants who try to use India as a stepping off platform to western destinations. This has given opportunity to dishonest agents who traffic people to the Middle East or dupe others into thinking they will be sent to places like Australia, Canada or New Zealand.[36]

Characteristics of Migrants to India

More men than women work as migrants in India, and about 60% of men migrate on their own, even if they are married. However, their families may subsequently join them. With the obvious exception of those women who are trafficked, usually women migrate to be with their families.

Many Nepali women who migrate to India go to live with their families.

The average age of migrants is just under 30, with most migrants first going to India between the ages of 16 and 20, although sometimes even younger boys go.

Particularly those who migrate from the remote hill villages of western Nepal are uneducated. Of the survey group 1/3 to 1/2 had never attended school. Other male migrants to India are usually literate. Students are in a separate category.

The Ease of Migration to India

It is much easier for Nepalis to travel to India than any other country. Agents and visas are not needed. There is an open border and much smaller costs are involved – about 2,500 compared with around 90,000 Nepali Rupees for other countries[37] Migrants usually choose to go to the place where their own kin group has already migrated.[38] Almost all travel in groups and go overland by bus and train. For travel to NW India the two main crossing points are Mahendra Nagar/Gadda Chauki (in the Far West and Nepalgunj (in the Mid-West). For other Indian destinations, the crossing place is more likely to be Bhairawa/Sunauli (or perhaps Nepalgunj/Rupaidiya or Birgunj/Raxaul, but the choice is mainly based on which point is nearer to their home in Nepal. Since the completion of the East-West highway up to the western border, migrants prefer to travel through Nepal as far as possible.[39] Those going from Eastern Nepal to work in NE India, usually cross at Kakarbhitta.

Seasonal Migration

Partly because of the nearness and the relative ease of travel, seasonal migration is possible. Men can work in India for half a year and return to celebrate their festivals and cultivate their own fields in Nepal for the other half of the year. Records of land border crossings confirm this by showing peaks that coincide with these fluctuations in the agricultural and festival year. The usual dates given are from *Mongsir* to *Baisakh* and again from *Asar* to *Asoj*.[xi] Poignantly, there is a local Jumli saying that "If a migrant doesn't return in time for

[xi] This translates as approximately Nov to Apr and July to Sept.

sowing, he may as well be dead."[40] In fact it is more likely that his family will die.

Migration to India & HIV

It might be thought that this frequent coming and going would not lead to the breakup of families in the same way that longer absence in other countries can do. This may be true for many but it overlooks one other serious issue. With more frequent travelling through India, the migrants are more likely to be exposed to sexual temptations and the risk of HIV infection. This has now become the main route of transfer of HIV/AIDS into remote hill villages – through the male migrants to their families. According to the survey, around 13% of the migrants were having sex with partners other than their spouses; 6% of it unprotected.

Single biggest source of HIV in Nepali women is male returnees from India.

Although many migrants had heard of HIV/AIDS, their knowledge was far from accurate and their practices, in terms of condom use, inconsistent. Horrific statistics are emerging:

- 15% had no knowledge of HIV.[41]
- 27% of returnees to the FW and MW had had sex with a sex worker while in India.[42]
- 1.5% of migrants who have spent 3 months to 3 years in India are infected with HIV.[43]
- 41% of HIV cases in Nepal are among labour migrants.[44]
- 12,000 new HIV infections occurred among labour migrants in 2011.[45]

A sad – but all too typical – story appeared in the INF/Nepal Annual Report for 2011-12:

> ***Kabita*** *was married at 16 and soon pregnant. Her husband went to work in India, but soon died of AIDS, although Kabita did not know the diagnosis. His family blamed her and chased her out of the house. Only when she needed a blood transfusion after her delivery did she discover that she was also HIV positive. In due course she joined a local church, whose pastor referred her to INF Paluwa for counselling, etc. Initially devastated, she has now decided to live for her daughter's sake.*

Nepali Migrants living in India

Some migrants feel that in India they will be able to obtain more nutritious food, find better educational opportunities for their children and also better health services. However, these benefits are by no means universal or guaranteed, and many have difficulty in accessing them. Unless both parents work, they often cannot earn enough to pay for such benefits, but if they both work, their children may not get adequate home care or schooling. Many also have difficulties in enrolling their children in local schools because of a bias against the Nepali community. And even if the children do get seats in school, they frequently struggle because the medium of teaching is Hindi. This is a problem in the cities and, to a certain extent, in the NW, but not for those who work in the NE hills as Nepali is the *lingua franca* in much of the area.

Earnings and remittances

Because around 80% of families are heavily – if not totally – dependent on the remittances the wage-earners are able to send back home, one of the main factors that influences migration is the perceived better employment opportunities with higher wages. Reality is another story. Almost all migrants are paid monthly and in cash, but for the sort of work they are able to do, salaries are not high, and this is the main reason why many take a second job or their spouses need to work. In 2002, most only managed to save 8-16,000 Nepali Rupees to take home after 4-5 months' work.[46] Even in 2010, most labourers earned only 1,000-3,000 Indian Rupees per month.[47] Low wages also explain why migrants change jobs frequently, always looking for one with a slightly higher level of remuneration. They will even move to another town if they think there are better employment opportunities. This again has a negative effect on their children's schooling. It also makes it difficult for NGOs or churches to develop any consistent outreach programmes.

Most of the male migrants do send money back to their families, although a few drink their wages or otherwise squander them. In the past, sending money back to Nepal was problematic as there was no system of bank transfer available to them. Only those with more formal employment were allowed to open bank accounts. As a result, they used to accumulate their wages and hand-carry the cash back over the border to Nepal. As thieves knew this happened, many were robbed *en route*. Others entrusted their hard-earned wages to a friend but sometimes these 'friends' made off with the money. Yet others used an informal

> ***Only recently has a reliable remittance transfer been established from India.***

system of money transfer, known as *hundi*.[xii] Nowadays increasing numbers use banks or official remittance agencies, although only 10% of those in the ODI survey said they did.

Cultural Issues, Living & Working Conditions

It is much easier for Nepalis to adapt to life in India because of the similar cultural heritage. However, this does not necessarily ensure their acceptance in the destination communities. Most Nepalis working in India either live with their families or share rented accommodation with fellow labourers. Depending on location, up to one half live in slums. Although they may have electricity, they usually have to share toilets and have a limited water supply. Many are discriminated against by their landlords, who tend to cut off their electricity, and deny them basic amenities while still charging them higher rents than they do from local Indians.

Work conditions are also far from desirable, and unskilled workers, like watchmen, have no formal contracts and thus no formal rights under Indian law. They get paid a pittance and are frequently denied paid leave. When an industrial accident occurs or some other tragedy – like the bomb blast in a bakery in Pune in 2010 – local authorities and even officials from the Nepal Embassy are not always helpful.[48] There is little provision for medical insurance or provident fund. Part of the reason for problems is ironically that India

---

[xii] A *hundi* is a traditional form of money transfer that evolved on the Indian subcontinent. It is a completely trust-based arrangement, with no written record maintained. It also has no formal legal status. The client pays a sum of money to a broker in the country in which he is working. This broker then sends an order to another broker in the country to which the client wishes to send his money. This second broker then hands over the money to the beneficiary.

is not included in the list of 107 countries for which the 2007 Foreign Employment Act is in force.

Indian Brothels & other forms of trafficking

Although this is not the central concern of this book, trafficking of women into Indian brothels is a significant and serious issue, which needs to be tackled both in Nepal and in India. The women usually end up in one of the major cities – Mumbai, Kolkata, Delhi, Lucknow, Varanasi (Banares), Agra, Kanpur, Chennai or Bangalore – where their working conditions are both degrading and dangerous because they are exposed to both physical violence and HIV infection.[49] One of these ladies explains:

> *I am from Achham. I got married in my early teens. My husband brought me to Mumbai. In fact, he told me that he works in the city and life is easier in the city than in the village. He introduced me to his aunt but she was not his real aunt (but the pimp) and the next day he left the house and the aunt showed me her real colours, forcing me to engage in the business which was not even in my dream and imagination. I didn't have any other option. I had no chance to escape at all!*[50]

Rai tells a similar story about ***'Sita'*** from Banke, who was tricked into marriage and then sold to a brothel in Delhi. Only after a year of hell did she manage to escape and return home. Eventually, with legal help she brought a case against Prakash and he is now serving 20 years in jail.[51]

Various figures are quoted but probably the most believable is between 2 and 4 *lakh* Nepali girls forced to work as

CSWs[xiii] in India. In 2011, Maiti Nepal reckoned 15,000 were being trafficked each year, although that included those being sent to the Middle East. Daywalka research in 2009 revealed a 43% HIV positive rate among such women.[xiv]

43% of Nepali CSWs in India are HIV positive.

Perhaps an even sadder fact is that often victims rescued from prostitution are not accepted back into their families or communities. They are seen as 'debased' and so suffer twice over. However, maybe 75% do eventually return to their villages.[52] Gautam tells us a sad story with a happy ending about a trafficked Tamang girl from Sindhupalchok:

> *When* ***Charimaya*** *was only 16, she was drugged and abducted from her village, taken to Gorakhpur and then sold into sex slavery in a brothel in Mumbai for 50,000 Indian Rupees.*[xv] *For nearly two years, she was forced to work there until rescued by the police in 1996. However, although repatriated to her village, "she wasn't allowed to attend social functions, and her family members refused to eat the food she cooked." She said, "My relatives and people from the village told me I should have died and not returned." Nevertheless, Charimaya refused to let that deter her and determined to fight against trafficking and joined Shakti Samuha where she worked for many years, and in June 2011, she was awarded the Hero Acting to End Modern-Day Slavery*

[xiii] Commercial Sex Workers

[xiv] In 2000, *Family Health International* quoted an even more horrifying statistic of 73% positive for FSWs who had worked in Mumbai.

[xv] In the *Kathmandu Post* of 3 Jan 2006, Mathema noted that Nepali girls were being sold for up to 100,000 Indian Rupees.

Award by Hilary Clinton. She also won a legal suit against her abductors. And – against everyone's predictions, a Tamang man fell in love with her and now they are happily married with a family.[53]

An internal INF publication in 2012, recorded an even happier – and earlier solution – for one young girl:

*INF Migration Support staff noticed 18 year old **S** in a rickshaw heading for the Indian border in Nepalgunj. Because she looked innocent and yet fearful, their suspicions were raised. They stopped the rickshaw and took her to their office for a chat. It transpired that the man she was supposed to be with, who at first she said was her brother, was someone who had lured her with a marriage proposal and exciting prospects in Delhi. The INF staff took the couple to the border police and then contacted her parents who were shocked and immediately came to the border. Later, S thanked the migration support staff saying, "If the Migrant Counselling Centre was not there, I would have been trafficked and sold into a brothel. My life was in danger but now I'm perfectly safe."*

A related issue, concerns the treatment or safety of female migrants in India. During the early months of 2013 there was a flurry of articles in the press about Nepali women – at least two of them students – and also some small children, who had been raped in various Indian cities.

Not all women who are 'trafficked' are sent to brothels: many are simply used as slave labour. ***Raji*** was lured to India at 16 years of age, with promises of a well-paid job as a domestic help, but then found she had to work on building sites:

When we felt weak and couldn't work, they would beat us with metal rods... It was very hard... We had to carry bricks; not just one or two, lots of bricks ... you had to put the basket on your head. After that, they would put more than 20 bricks in it at one time. We carried them up two floors. We had to work from 6am to 7pm. We were given food twice a day. Rice, and potato in soup, and the rice was old. We were hungry. We'd been told we would get 180 rupees [£1.37] a day. But they gave me 100 rupees just one time. We slept in the house that was being built... we just slept on the ground on thin bedcovers. Once, we tried to escape at night, but they found us and beat us.[54]

Other Problems

When questioned about the problems they face as migrants, around half mention loneliness and shortage of money. Loneliness is particularly common among the men, who cope by watching TV and films, listening to the radio, smoking, chewing *pan*[xvi] and chatting with friends and/or families. More than a quarter of the men admitted to drinking alcohol. 10-13% each confessed to using drugs, having heterosexual sex (presumably extra-marital) and homosexual sex – activities that decrease their funds further and which can be detrimental to their health. Women migrants seem not to have these problems or indulge in such doubtful solutions. However, the families back home in Nepal certainly suffer from shortage of funds and loneliness while the menfolk are away.

Half the migrants admit to being lonely.

Other problems faced by some migrants include discrimination and a perceived fear of violence and

[xvi] Betel nut.

harassment; even a fear of being imprisoned. Especially 'lower castes' working in menial jobs may be discriminated against in their workplace. For example, they are sometimes denied work-related benefits like membership of trade unions or provident fund. For this reason, those who can, try to hide their Nepali origins by speaking Hindi and not admitting to their citizenship. They do not like to be called 'Bahadur' or 'Gorkha' which they consider derogatory, although these terms in fact reflect their strength and value as security guards and have a link back to the brave Nepalis who joined the Indian Army.[xvii] A Nepali even murdered a fellow rickshaw-*wallah*[xviii] in Mumbai simply because he teased him and called him 'Yeh Nepali'.[55] Other Indians, however, appreciate the hard working Nepali migrants and employers often trust the Nepalis with the goods they carry.

Sometimes political crises in India adversely affect Nepali migrants. In the wake of the terrorist attacks in Mumbai in 2008, government authorities ruled that hotels and lodges should not register any foreign nationals (including Nepalis) who could not produce a photo ID card. Many Nepalis in Lucknow for work or with their families for medical treatment were caught by surprise and affected by this.[56] Similarly, because many Nepalis look similar to north-eastern tribal people, some migrants in India felt threatened in 2012 during the violence that erupted in Mumbai, Lucknow and Allahabad as retaliation against NE Indians for the alleged atrocities on Muslims in Assam.

Despite all this, the Indian government is officially very

[xvii] However, sometimes 'Bahadur' is deliberately corrupted to 'bandar' meaning 'monkey'.

[xviii] Man or person. Used here to mean the man who pulls a rickshaw.

generous to Nepali migrants. It welcomes them and allows them to live and work in India. However, there are no specific laws which really deal with migrants' rights: the 1950 Treaty of Peace and Friendship between the Government of India and the Government of Nepal states:

> Article 6: Each Government undertakes, in token of the neighbourly friendship between India and Nepal, to give to the nationals of the other, in its territory, national treatment with regard to participation in industrial and economic development of such territory and to the grant of concessions and contracts, relating to such development.
>
> Article 7: The Governments of India and Nepal agree to grant, on a reciprocal basis, to the nationals of one country in the territories of the other the same privileges in the matter of residence, ownership of property, participation in trade and commerce, movement and other privileges of a similar nature.

It thus ensures Nepali citizens the right to travel, carry on trade and seek employment, as well as access education and health services in India. It also allows for the purchase of land and property in India and so means that Nepalis can stay there long term with their families. However, it has not been exercised well and articles No. 6 and 7 make migration both tacit and ambiguous. As a result many migrants are unaware of their rights. Nepalis can legally obtain ration cards, driving licences and PAN cards but only if their landlord or the

Indian government is officially very generous to Nepali migrants.

company they work for make the recommendations but nowadays landlords tend not to do this. In addition, there is a decentralized system so that every state has different laws about this. There are many Nepalis who have also managed to obtain election cards, Adhar cards and finally passports, but this latter has often been done illegally by giving bribes. Another informant suggested most Nepalis can obtain the ID and even Adhar cards legally, as without them, getting rations, travelling and opening a bank account would be almost impossible.

However, Bhattrai scathingly said that in practice, "despite the legal rhetoric, the Indian state treats the Nepali laborers as rights-less, non-citizens... docile cheap laborers."[57] This is perhaps too sweeping a statement. At least, educated migrants or those who have grown up in India in earlier generations usually do not have these same problems: they are well accepted and themselves speak well of both Nepal and India.[58] My remarks thus mainly concern labour migrants.

Crossing the border

One of the major problems for migrants travelling to and from India is the border crossing. "Money can travel and prosper. Poor people cannot… For them the border-crossing… is far more difficult"[59] even though to enter India they do not need visas. Only a few report problems while crossing out from Nepal to India, but huge numbers complain of serious harassment on their re-entry into Nepal.

Some of the outgoing difficulties are experienced by men who travel with their wives. In one way this is good as it indicates that officials at the border are trying to stop women trafficking. However, sometimes this is done very rudely.

On the other hand, many returnees complain of verbal, physical and even sexual abuse by the border police and others while they are crossing back into Nepal. Part of the reason is that the border guards know very well that returnees usually carry their accumulated wages in cash and are also bringing back household gifts for their families.[xix] Indian customs and border patrols frequently demand bribes, as do their counterparts on the Nepal side. I was told that some Nepal Police pay large amounts to obtain a posting to the border patrol as they know that within a couple of years they can make a huge profit in bribes.

Re-crossing the border back into Nepal is one of the migrants' biggest problems.

The other serious problem at the border is that there are also unscrupulous common thieves at work. Their *modus operandi* is well known but often naïve returnees are not aware of it. They befriend a returnee, usually between the Indian and Nepali border posts, and offer them food or drink. This is heavily drugged and soon the migrant falls unconscious. Some migrants have even died as a result. The thieves then quickly steal everything the man has – including most of his clothes – and leave him lying by the side of the road. Some onlookers just assume the man is drunk and ignore him. Others know and turn a blind eye. Yet others,

[xix] Bahadur et al, 2002, suggested that many migrants now buy their household goods at Nepali shops at the road-head, largely because these shops may have given them a loan on their way to India.

like the Good Samaritan in Jesus' parable, stop and help. "Among the Nepali workers returning from India, every day 1 was robbed in the bus park in Rupaidiya."[60] However, a campaign was initiated in the Far West, where both Indian and Nepali authorities gave out warnings in the bus park. It was apparently successful in decreasing the number of robberies,[61] but probably needs to be repeated continually if this problem is truly to be eradicated.

Because of the reciprocal terms of residence in each other's countries in the 1950 Friendship Treaty, there can, by definition, be no Nepali asylum seekers in India. This means that any who have fled to India have to fend for themselves.

INDIAN STATES

There are 28 Indian States and 7 Union Territories. Although Nepalis are found throughout India, they are more likely to be found in large numbers in some states than others, i.e. the NE and NW States and also the major cities. Migration to the Himalayan regions (including much of West Bengal) is different from city migration, not least because it includes areas that were once briefly part of the territory of Nepal.

Research has shown that there are definite linkages between some Districts in Nepal and some towns in India. This is due to the tendency for Nepalis to migrate to those places where they already know friends or family. For example:[62]

Nepali District	**Destinations in India**
Achham	Mumbai, Bhopal, Indur, Delhi, Madras, Gujurat, Jaipur, Andra Pradesh & Madhya Pradesh
Baitadi	Indian Army
Bajhang	Bangalore
Bajura	Delhi
Doti	Mumbai, Gujurat
Kalikot, Dailekh, Humla, Jumla, Bajura	NW Hills
Surkhet	Simla, Kullu, Kumaon-Gadhwal, Ladakh, Punjab

According to the Joshua Project, there are about 26 people groups who speak Nepali but as they do not link them together as one Nepali group, it is very difficult to state any figures.[xx] However, by 2005, Satish Chhetri had discovered at least 5,000 Nepalis in each of 17 major Indian cities: 800,000 in

[xx] Operation World mentions only 24 groups – see page 147.

Mumbai alone.[xxi] Apart from the NE, where many states have a majority Nepali population, there were then at least 2.8 million Nepalis in India. Since then, the figures have undoubtedly increased.[xxii] Sikkim state is about 75% Nepali, and Darjeeling district in West Bengal is 60% Nepali.[63]

Nepali Churches and Fellowships

The Nepali church started in the Nepali Diaspora in India. Prior to 1952, expatriate missionaries and their Nepali converts, especially those in the NE corner of India, prayed for Nepal to open up to the Gospel. It was Nepali migrant believers who first reached out to fellow migrants in India and later in Nepal. In her book, Dr. Cindy Perry has documented this exciting story and also told of how Nepalis reached the four corners of India. My aim is to update, rather than duplicate, this information. Those who are interested should therefore refer to ***Nepali around the World,*** first published by EKTA Books in Kathmandu in 1997, to get the fuller historical perspective.

No one knows how many Nepali Christians there are in India.

A new wave of migrants entered India at the end of the 20th century, and churches in Nepal and India became more aware of the need and opportunities among them.

[xxi] Information from the Nepali Diaspora networking meeting, Kathmandu, 9 Nov 2005, but see below.

[xxii] This figure probably refers only to relatively recent migrants who still fully identify as Nepalis.

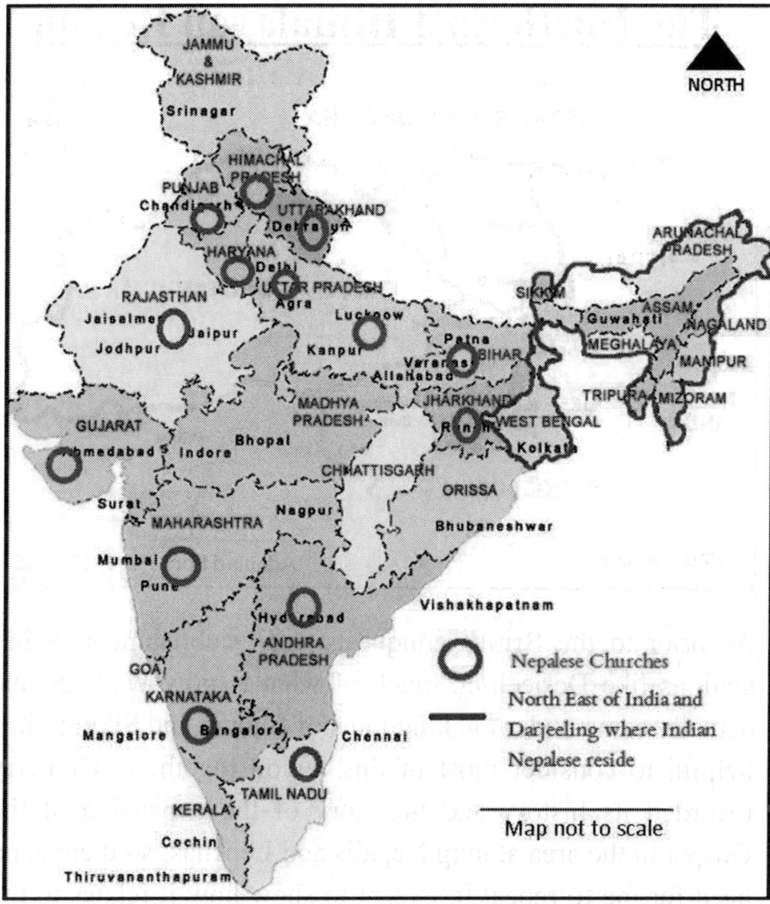

Locations of the Main Nepali Churches in India

Credit: Janak BC, c 2013

However, it is impossible to state any realistic number for Nepali Christians in India. This is for the same reasons as the total population of 'Nepalis' in India is unknown but also importantly because many Nepalis join Hindi or multilingual churches rather than exclusively Nepali language Fellowships. Most of my estimates are therefore of Nepali Fellowships in the NE, NW and in cities.

The North East Himalayan Region

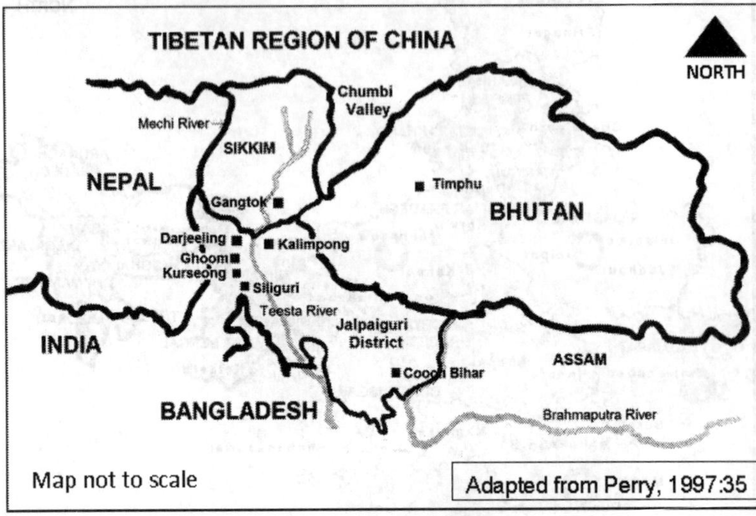

As prior to the British conquests and establishment of hill stations like Darjeeling, much of what is now West Bengal actually came under the kingdoms of Bhutan and Sikkim, it is helpful to consider most of this region together. Dr Perry recorded its history and the story of the expansion of the Gospel in the area among Nepalis and Lepchas; so there is no need for me to repeat it, except to show how it relates to the current status of Nepali migrants in the NE of India.

"Nepali migration to Northeast India… began in the 1820s and still continues."[64] In the middle of the 19th century, when Jung Bahadur Rana was Prime Minister, it was the loss of land and state taxation that pushed people out from the hills and British India accepted them. The trend continued even into the post-colonial period in India, partly because of the family and social networks that many Nepalis had developed with NE India. During the Maoist insurgency in

Nepal, a fresh wave of migration occurred. The village areas of Eastern Nepal are somewhat better off economically than those in the Far West, but there is still a tradition of migration to India and a long association with Darjeeling, Kalimpong and Sikkim. These towns and the cities of Bihar and W. Bengal, remain favoured destinations for Nepali migrants.[65]

Due to past links with the Gurkha regiments, Nepali settlers in these states often refer to themselves as 'Gorkhas', as they do also in Burma and Singapore. The Gorkha National Liberation Front (GNLF) hit the news in 1986-8 with its demands for a separate Gorkhaland territory, the Nepali language (or 'Gorkha *bhasa*') to be accepted as an official Indian language, liberal entitlement to Indian citizenship, separate Nepali regiments in the Indian Army, and abolition of parts of the 1950 India-Nepal Treaty. Most of these concessions were never granted but the Darjeeling Hill Council was set up to have executive control over agriculture, health and tourism. Even today the issue is not settled.

Nepali Churches in the North East

Churches in the NE of India were very involved in the early days of the Nepali church. 'Padre' Ganga Prasad Pradhan was minister of St Columba's Church in Darjeeling but also an official translator with the British and Foreign Bible Society. A revised edition of his Nepali Bible of 1914 was the one in the hands of the church at the time Nepal opened up to the Gospel. Nepali and Lepcha Missionaries, especially from Darjeeling, Kalimpong and Sikkim, together with overseas missionaries, were among those who planted the first fellowships inside Nepal when it began to open up in the early 1950s. In the little town of Mirik, in the Darjeeling hills, the very first Bible School in Nepali medium was established in the 1950s – at which time, due to the political situation inside Nepal – it was impossible for such training to be offered in country. DHBS[xxiii] trained many of the early Nepali leaders. Nepali Fellowships in Indian cities were often pioneered by Indian Nepalis who moved from the NE, although more recently there has been an increasing number of Nepalis coming from Nepal as missionaries. Many migrants who have accepted Christ in India have started churches back home after their return to Nepal.[66]

In India there have always been many denominations – both international and home-grown, despite the development of the Church of North India (CNI) and the United Church of North India (UCNI). In contrast, in Nepal, there was essentially no denominationalism until after 1990, this having been a deliberate policy of the early Nepali and expatriate missionaries. Thus, while in Nepal there was relatively little conflict over issues of adult believers' baptism by immersion and charismatic manifestations; these have sometimes been a problem in the Indian Nepali-speaking churches. For Nepali Christians who migrated to India in the later part of the 20th century, this may have seemed strange. My own experience from the late 1990s indicates that while some, mostly the independent churches, were growing rapidly, others had apparently lost some of their original evangelistic and missionary fervour and even become quite legalistic.

WEST BENGAL (Kolkata)

This is the largest state in the region and today Nepalis make

---

[xxiii] Darjeeling Hills Bible School

up a significant proportion of the population (c 5 *lakh*), and Nepali is one of the official languages. "In Darjeeling, where there was said to be barely a hundred inhabitants when the territory was granted to the East India Company by the Raja of Sikkim in 1835, there are now perhaps 700,000 ethnic Nepalese – 60 per cent of the population in 1995."[67] Many had migrated from the area around Darjeeling.

Nepali Fellowships

The NE corner of the state was the early centre of Nepali mission. From **Darjeeling** and **Kalimpong**, missionaries and local Nepali believers (a former generation of Nepali migrants) began to reach out to fellow Nepalis throughout the District of Darjeeling. Those were also the bases for outreach on into 'Assam', Sikkim and Bhutan as well as the Duars area and around Siliguri. Today there are many Nepali medium churches and a host of Bible Colleges and Schools.

Although we associate the name of Calcutta with the early mission of William Carey and his efforts to produce a Nepali Bible around the turn of the 19th century, the first real outreach to Nepalis in **Kolkata** was in 1916-17 by Nepali ethnics from Darjeeling. A small fellowship was formed in 1928,[68] but from then until the 1970s there was little growth or outreach. The total number of Nepali Christians in the city is ~3,000 in 10 churches[69], and, according to Ps. Dilip Chhetri, there are around 200 members in the AoG church alone.

The 'Seven sister states' (to which Sikkim has now been added), in the NE hills were all, with the exception of Manipur and Tripura, originally part of Assam. Since Partition, they have been linked to the rest of India by just a small strip (the 'Siliguri Corridor') of West Bengal.

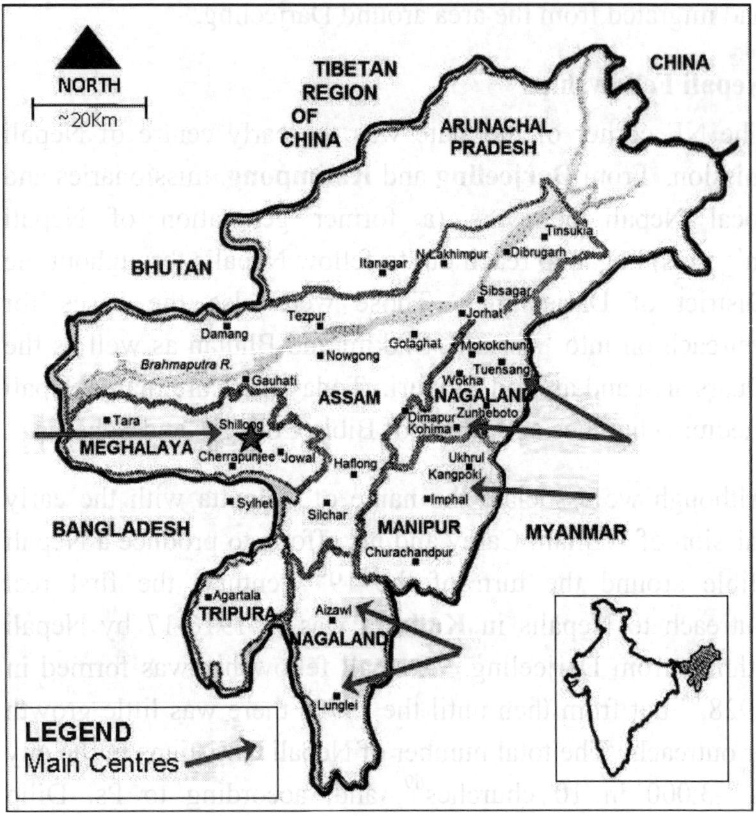

The Seven Sister States of the NE

Adapted from Perry, 1997:175

ASSAM (Guwahati) & MEGHALAYA (Shillong)

Until Meghalaya attained statehood in 1972 these states were originally one and Assam subsumed 5 of the present-day NE states. Meghalaya is home to mainly three hill tribes: the Khasi, the Jaintia and Garo while modern Assam encompasses the Brahmaputra Valley. Both states have significant Nepali populations. By 1961, Nepali-speakers were the second-largest non-indigenous group of settlers in the Khasi-Jaintia hills, and their numbers had doubled in Meghalaya by 1981.[70] Nepali migrants to the area came in a series of waves: first the Gurkha soldiers recruited by the British to defend the Eastern frontier; then skilled and unskilled labourers who came to work in plantations, coalmines and oilfields from the middle of the 19th century; and finally the Nepali *Gwalas* (dairy farmers) who came at the end of the 19th century. During the 2nd World War this region was a recruiting ground for the Gurkha army and after the war some soldiers returned. Later many Nepalis were forced to leave and returned to Nepal in the wake of racial tensions with Muslim immigrants. Over the years, many Nepalis have continued to trickle into this area to work in the Assam Rifles in Shillong, Indian Oil Corporations in Duliajan and the Assam Oil Corporation in Digboi. However, in 2010, over 15,000 of the Nepali speaking community (who at that time constituted 2.6% of the population of Meghalaya) were deprived of some of their political rights. They were displaced from Meghalaya and had to take refuge in Assam and the adjoining hilly regions.[71] Today the official census figure is 80,000 but in reality there are probably >2 *lakh* Nepalis in the state.

Nepali Fellowships

Early outreach from Kalimpong targeted 'Assam', especially its hill areas, Bhutan and also the Duars. According to Perry:

> It was in the Khasi hills, not only where the oldest Nepali settlements in NE India are found, but also where missions have the longest history in NE India, that the Nepali of NE India first began to respond to Christianity.[72]

One of the earliest Nepali churches, the Nepal Christian Fellowship, is situated in **Shillong**, now the capital of Meghalaya. Before Nepal opened up, the missionaries of the Nepali Evangelistic Band used to spend the hot season in Shillong and the cooler season on the Nepal border in Nautanwa. Significant expansion of Nepali work in the hills around Shillong only occurred in the 1990s,[73] although since the 1970s, there have been Nepali churches in the Bengal Duars (now Jalpaiguri District) and the Assam Duars (Kokrajhar, Barpeti, Nalbari and Darrang Districts). One of the earliest Nepali congregations was established in Jaigaon (just over the border into India from Phuntsoling, Bhutan).[74] At the beginning of the 21st century, there were 42 Nepali churches in Assam and 12 in Meghalaya, mostly around Shillong.[75] Today, there may be as many as 60-70 churches in Assam and 50-60 for >2,000 Christians in Meghalaya.[xxiv] Other sources give smaller numbers, perhaps indicating that many Nepalis attend bilingual churches.[xxv]

MIZORAM (Aizawl) & NAGALAND (Kohima)

Mizoram, which includes the Mizo and Lushai hill tracts became a state of India, separate from Assam, in 1972, whereas Nagaland, covering the Naga hill tracts had already achieved statehood in 1963/4. Nepali Gurkhas probably only

[xxiv] Ps. Dilip Chhetri, personal communication.
[xxv] Ps. Hemanta Kaphle & Ps. Prahbat Thapa, personal communication.

reached Mizoram at the very end of the 19th century and initially settled in the north around Aizawl, whereas they had begun to settle in the Naga hills around Kohima some 20 years earlier.[76] By 1961 Nepalis were the largest non-indigenous group in Nagaland and by 1981, they were the largest non-indigenous group in Mizoram.[77] Today there are around 150,000, most of whom are believers.[78]

Nepali Fellowships

In Mizoram the Nepalis settled in the north, around Aizawl; and in the south, around Lunglei, where they came into contact with Presbyterian and Baptist missionaries respectively.[79] By the beginning of the 21st century there were already 7 Nepali Fellowships in Aizawl:[80] today, according to BK Thulung, there are 2 Presbyterian churches, 5 preaching points and 7 Fellowships in Jong fai, Sai ya and Longtlai, the churches having more than 20 members each. There is also a Nepali Baptist church in Lunglei and a church for the Assam Rifles, Aizawl, with over 60 regular attendees.

The first four Nepali churches in Nagaland were established in the 1970s in Kohima, Mokokchung, Wokha and Dimapur, and by the beginning of the 21st century this number had increased to 60.81 Today Rudra Ramauli says there are 48 All Gorkha Baptist Churches with 5 associate churches, another 5 in Peren and also 2 churches of the Nepali Christian Fellowship.

Both of these states are now very largely Christianized and both have, in more recent years, sent missionaries to Nepal. In the 1980s before the explosion of Bible Training Institutions in Kathmandu, several pastors received their theological training at the Baptist College in Kohima.

ARUNACHAL PRADESH (Itanagar)

Arunachal Pradesh became a separate Indian state in 1987. The most remote and wild area of the NE, it was largely ignored by the British.[82] Most Nepalis still work in the jungle felling trees. Others are domiciled in and around Ziro.

Nepali Fellowships

Until the 1980s Arunachal Pradesh was barely reached by Christian mission, but by the beginning of the 21st century there were 2 or 3 Nepali churches:[83] one in Itanagar, another nearby and a third in the far north in Tinsukia plus some scattered believers.[84] For a time the Apatani Baptist Church provided leadership for the Nepali ministry and a new Nepali church was built in Ziro in around 2005, although they still lacked their own Nepali pastor/evangelist. Outreach teams have ministered in the Nepali communities. In 2005, they prayed for two girls tormented by evil spirits and 12 others accepted Christ. According to Ps. Dilip Chhetri by 2013 there were 20-25 churches in the state.

MANIPUR (Imphal)

A princely state under British rule from 1891, Manipur became a state of the Republic of India in 1972. Nepalis in Manipur, as in so many of the areas of the NE and Burma, prefer to be called Gorkhas, as although their roots go back to Nepal, they see themselves as Nepali-speaking Indians. The first Nepali settlers probably came to Manipur in 1824, recruited by the British to help the king of Manipur defeat the Burmese who were then ruling his land, but this led to British overlordship rather than independence for Manipur! Others arrived around 1880 and again in 1917 with the Assam

Rifles. After the 2nd World War other contingents arrived via Singapore and then with the Indian National Army. Finally, a small group of Gorkhas came with the Nepali wife of the last Manipur king and established the Manipur Rifles (later Police). Few have come since then. The main areas of Nepali settlement in Manipur include Maram, Irang and Kangpokpi in the Senapati district as well as Pukhao and Serou. The 1961 census of India showed Nepalis were the largest non-indigenous group in Manipur. In 1990, it was said that there were about 45,000 Nepalis in Manipur, but the real figure now is probably nearer 1 *lakh*.[85] Most Nepalis still live in the north[86] and work in the army or in agriculture.

Nepali Fellowships

Although there were probably individual Nepali Christians in Manipur even from 1915, the first Nepali Fellowship was only established in Imphal in 1974.[87] By the start of the 21st century there were 45 Nepali churches mostly in the hill districts,[88] and now there may be 5,000 Nepali Christians. However, compared to adjacent NE states, Manipur society is more Hindu and often hostile to Christians.[89]

TRIPURA (capital **Argatala)** was also a princely state under British rule, but became part of the Republic of India in 1972. There are few Nepali settlers: it is a strongly Hindu area and as far as I know, there are no Nepali fellowships.

SIKKIM (Gangtok)

Sikkim has been an Indian state since 1975: before that it was an independent monarchy, albeit under the suzerainty of Britain for a period in the 19th-20th centuries. Hall states that in "1901 [Sikkim] had a population of about 60,000 – almost entirely made up of the Lepcha tribe and the Buddhist Bhotiyas,"[90] but by 1995 population was about 400,000 and three-quarters Nepalese in origin.[91] Perry reckoned that even in 1891 Nepalis were 65% of the population of Sikkim.[92] Today, of the total population of almost 5 *lakh*, maybe 60% are Nepali and 30% Lepcha. Nepali is the *lingua franca*.[93] While most Nepalis are Hindus about 15% are Buddhists.

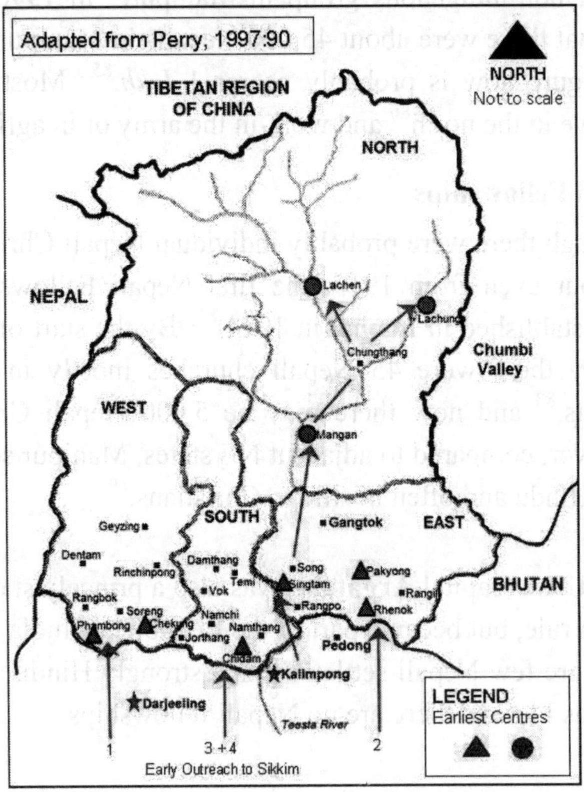

Nepali Fellowships

According to Perry, there were two early mission ventures into Sikkim – one targeting the southern areas of the three more southerly districts and the other venturing much further north towards Lachen and Lachung.[94] Since then, many Buddhist Lepchas have turned to Christ and today they are the largest group of Christians in Sikkim. The total Christian population of Sikkim is now around 14% and the church is growing fast.[95] Almost every village has a church. The migrant groups are the ones most responsive to the gospel. Most conversions are in the Nepali and Lepcha communities.

The North West Himalayan Region

Uttarakhand and Himachal Pradesh are situated in the NW hills – geographically a western continuation of Nepal. The whole area is 'the land of the gods' containing many of the most holy of Hindu pilgrimage sites. It is also part of the wild North-West Frontier and a tourist destination. The Indo-Asian News Service reported on 6 Jan 2013 that 3 Nepali truck drivers raped a tourist near Manali.

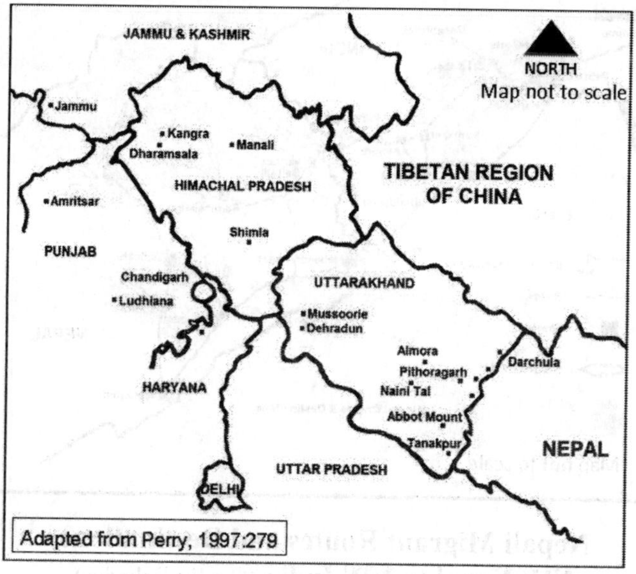

UTTARAKHAND (Dehradun)

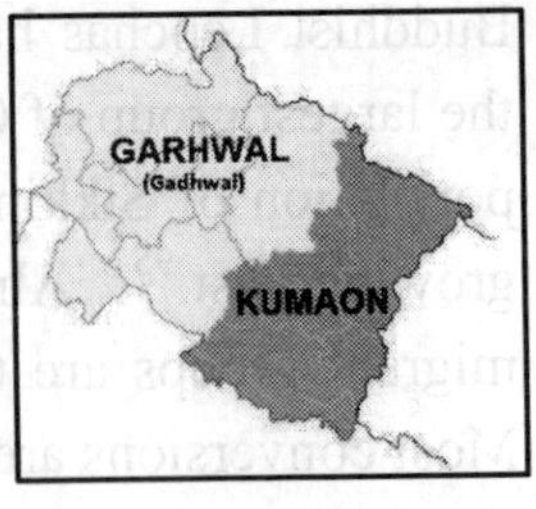

Uttarakhand (formerly part of Uttaranchal until c 2010) is the eastern state, on Nepal's western border. It consists of two major administrative divisions: hilly Kumaon, in the east, and mountainous Garhwal in the west.

The people and the languages of this whole region are similar to those of Nepal – unsurprising, as the region was conquered by Nepal at the end of the 18th century and part of Nepal until the Anglo-Nepali War of 1814-16. Thus, some of the earliest settlement of Nepalis in Almora, Nainital and Dehradun dates from that time, and there is a close affinity between the people of Uttarakhand and Nepalis from FW Nepal.

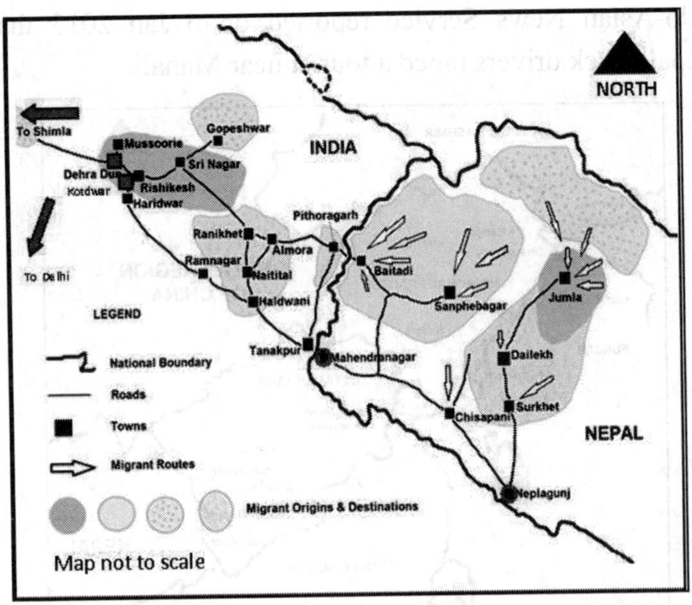

Nepali Migrant Routes and Destinations
NW Nepal to NW India (Credit: Bahadur)

In 2010, there were more than 100-150 Nepali families living in Mussorie alone. A further link is with the famous Kumaon regiment of the Indian Army. More recently, Pithoragarh, Bageswari, and Gadhwal Masourri have become the chosen destinations for seasonal migrants from Far West Nepal.

Bahadur described some horrific work conditions in 2002:

> A huge dam is being built in Tehri for a hydro-electricity plant. Many Nepali migrants are doing labouring work. If they work inside the hill, blasting and removing stones, they receive Indian Rupees 35 per hour because of the danger involved. They sign in when they start work and if they haven't signed out at 18.30 hr. they are assumed dead. Before they start working at the dam site they sign a paper that if dying at the site their bodies will be thrown in the river.[96]

Nepali Fellowships:

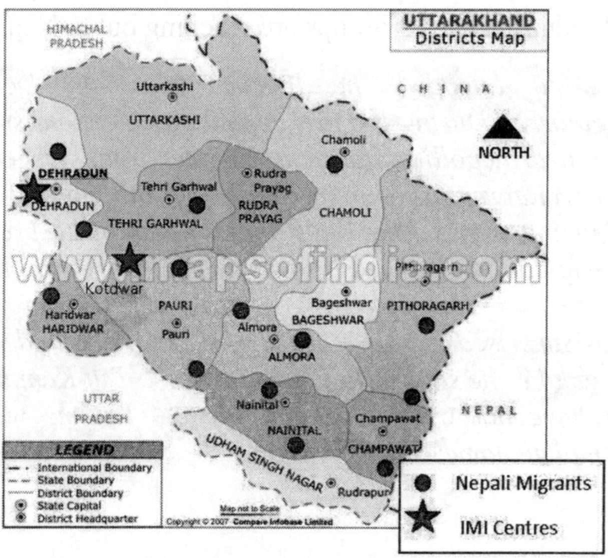

In 2002, a local Nepali Indian pastor said, "there is no Nepali work among the migrants [in his part of NW India] because of the quick adjustment to Indian culture when settled 5-10 years. Many don't speak Nepali and don't celebrate Nepali festivals."[97] Bahadur also found no churches reaching out to the needs of migrants. A few expressed interest but said they did not have the time to do so. This is a real contrast with the situation in NE India.[xxvi] However, ten years on there is quite significant Nepali outreach in these same areas.

In **Dehradun**, perhaps the first outreach to Nepalis was done in the 1970s by TB Limbu from Sikkim, but only at the end of the 1980s, when Ps. Nicanor Tamang arrived, having been exiled from Nepal, did Nepali work really begin.[98] There are now 5-6 fellowships and c 1,000 Nepali Christians. Most churches are multi-language but one is specifically Nepali medium. Some other individuals also have links to Nepali ministry. There are several Bible Colleges, which are attended by a few Nepali students. In **Mussorie** (just north of Dehradun) at least 3 groups are reaching out to Nepalis.

> ***Kamala*** *attended the literacy class in Dehradun regularly. During the last community election, she went to a nearby polling station to cast her vote. Surprisingly, her relative was the in-charge of the polling booth. Thinking that he knew all about Kamala, he brought a stamp pad and pushed it towards her. In return, Kamala said, "Could you please give me a pen?" Her relative was surprised but gave her a pen. After she had written, 'Kamala,' he said, "Now, you can go." But Kamala said, "I have not written my full name. Let me write my complete name, 'Kamala Devi.'"*[99]

[xxvi] Perry, 1997:358, notes a big difference between NW and NE India in this respect.

This incident boosted her confidence. She is thankful to the people who had worked behind the scene. "I am proud that I can read and write. Now I can see," she says.

***Sunil** is a young lad who has attended the tuition class in Dehradun. He is now studying in Class 8, but when he joined the centre he was a very shy and quiet person. Sunil and his parents are happy because he has got admission in a new English medium school which is not easy to get. They said, "Though we both are uneducated (Sunil's mother Bhumisara has joined the adult literacy class), we are happy that we can send our child to a better school." They want to say 'Thank you' to teachers and other people who encouraged and gave them moral support.*[100]

In **Kotdwar** there is one Nepali Fellowship, led by Ps. Narendra (a missionary from NIM Gyaneshwar in Nepal); and also some Methodist work. In **Haridwar** there is also a Nepali Fellowship. In **Pithoragarh** (very near the Nepali border) a Nepali Fellowship is led by Ps. Simon Nepali. There are probably also many smaller groups.

HIMACHAL PRADESH (Shimla)

Himachal Pradesh is the more western of the two states and lies between Uttarakhand and Kashmir. It was the western limit of Nepali territorial expansion at the end of the 18th century. At that time, the Nepalis annexed both Shimla and Sirmour, thus, like Uttarakhand, it was briefly part of Greater Nepal. There are most likely families whose ancestors migrated at that time and stayed. Nepalis work around Shimla – in the town area and also in apple orchards to the north, as well as in the extreme north-east in Rekong Peo.

Nepali Fellowships

There are 3 main groups who work in the state capital, **Shimla.** There is a very active Nepali ministry carried out under the auspices of a local NGO, Manav Kalyan Sabba (MKS), based in Shimla and Ps. Vijay Koirala has pioneered a lot of Nepali outreach in the area.[101] According to Ps. Ram Singh Rana, they now have 12 churches and 40 daughter churches, situated in their main centres of Manali, Mashobra, Chail, Rohru, Rampur, Solon, Parwanoo, Rekong Peo and Rishikesh (in Uttarakhand).

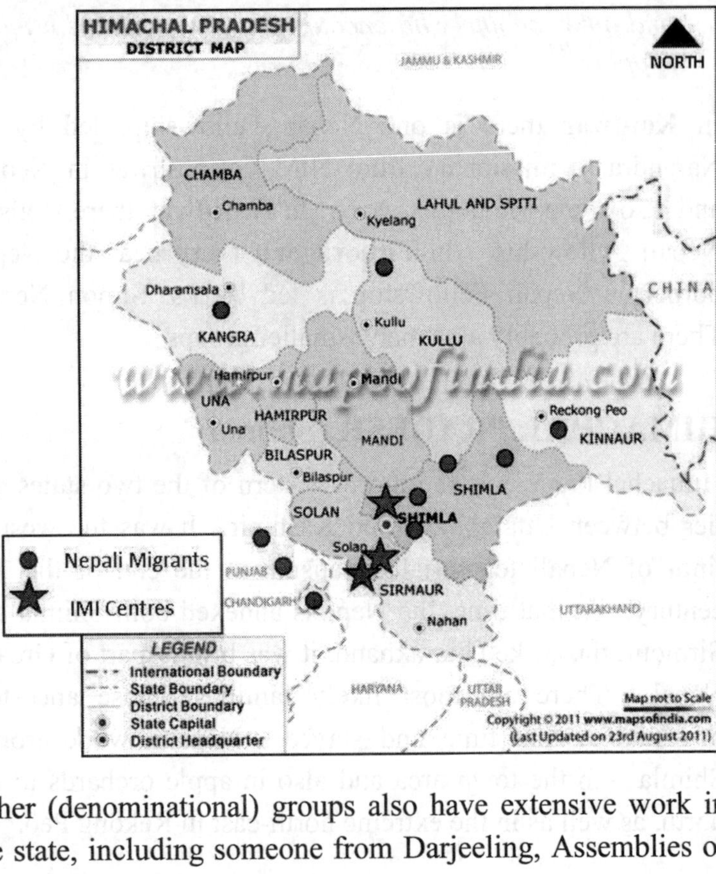

Other (denominational) groups also have extensive work in the state, including someone from Darjeeling, Assemblies of

God, Friends Mission Prayer Band, the Southern Baptists, and Gospel for Asia, which has around 80 churches. However, most of these, except the groups in the remote areas, are Hindi medium and not exclusively Nepali fellowships.[102] In the whole state there may be more than 5,000 Nepali Christians.[xxvii]

In the far NW corner of India is one other state where there are Nepali migrants, albeit far fewer than in the two states nearer to Nepal.

JAMMU–KASHMIR (Jammu & Srinagar)

An unusual state as its 3 geographical regions are Hindu, Muslim and Buddhist respectively, and probably most of the Nepalis are settled in the northern hilly part of the state. There are approximately 25,000 Nepali migrants in Ladakh, who have come from both the east and west of Nepal and for the usual economic and political reasons. According to Hem Raj Kafle,[103] the Nepalis in Kashmir are in danger of losing their Nepali-ness. There are many broken families and children with no real care-givers. Many migrants are seasonal. Some rotate between Nepal and Ladakh; others work in Kashmir for one season and when they have earned enough money to reach the Middle East, they leave to earn more money. Restaurant workers tend to rotate between Ladakh (in the summer/monsoon), Goa (in the winter) and Nepal (in the spring and autumn). The permanent migrants are rather different. Many men work in construction and if they do well, they can become contractors but increasingly

[xxvii] Some current leaders in Himachal Pradesh are Harak Singh & Kamal (Shimla), Vijay Koirala (Manali) and Hari (Parwanoo).

they are finding better jobs in the booming trekking industry. In Leh there are many female domestic workers and also some children who have effectively been sold for their whole lives as household slaves. Riek[104] mentions one family where a Nepali man, fighting with his wife, set her on fire. After she died, he sold the 2 older children to a Ladakhi family. In Ladakh, most Nepali migrants are involved in road construction work – a never-ending task, such that the workers are always on the move and live in tents by the side of the road, and their children miss out on schooling, ending up doing the same work as their parents, but they are also at high risk for trafficking. Again Riek has a sad story:

> *During the winter 'off-season' when families have difficulty feeding all their members, a man arrived offering "Good job for girls". 14 year old **Muna** was sold to him and her parents were later told she was doing well in Kuwait, but no one knows if that is really true.*

In the area near to the Chinese and Pakistan border, there are many army camps, (Nubra valley, Kardung La, etc.) where some Nepalis have been able to get well-paid jobs. However, the Indian soldiers also use Nepali women as prostitutes.

Nepali Fellowships

There are at least two groups working with Nepalis in the state. According to Riek, there has been a growing Nepali church in **Leh** since around 2008. It is officially under the local Moravian Church but has separate Nepali language services led by a Ps. Ghaman, a Nepali from Gorkha. It is however a transit-church with approximately 50-80 believers. There are also house fellowships in 6 nearby villages (Shey, Spituk, Skalzangling, Nimu, Mato, Sabu).

It is very difficult for the church to reach out to the seasonal migrants as their working hours and times in Ladakh are so erratic. However, there is a children's hostel 'Himali Mitra' and literacy programmes running in connection with the church, which have been a great opportunity for the Christians – both teachers and participants – to share with and help other women. Mina's story is an encouraging one:

> ***Mina*** *was born into a migrant family in Manali. When her parents split up, she left school and worked to support the family. When she herself got married, her husband turned out to be a drinker just like her father and step-father. Then she got to know some Christians and accepted Christ. A few years later, her husband did the same. Now they run a hostel for more than 50 Nepali migrant children.*

To the south of Nepal are two states that have long had an association with Nepal. They share a long common border with Nepal and part of their territory was almost certainly part of Greater Nepal for a short while.

UTTAR PRADESH (Lucknow) & BIHAR (Patna)

In the days of Greater Nepal, the southern border may have extended for a while as far as Gorakhpur. Lucknow was one of the main towns involved in the Indian Mutiny and Gorkhali troops served with the British at that time. Links between Nepal and UP / Bihar are strongly bound up with the Gurkhas – their recruitment and pension camps. In the west (UP) these centres were in Gorakhpur and Nautanwa while in the west (Bihar) they were in Purnea, Darbhanga and Laheria

Sarai.[105] There are also longstanding marriage and family ties across the border. In addition, pilgrims and labour migrants have travelled via Nautanwa or Raxaul to visit or work in one of these states or to get to the railheads at Gorakhpur or Mirzaffapur and reach destinations further afield in India. Many Nepalis still travel to Gorakhpur for pilgrimage and medical treatment but from 2005 Indian security checks – looking for Maoists – in the city made it an unfriendly place for Nepalis. The largest number of (mostly high caste Hindu) Nepalis settled in Varanasi/Banares[106] and today many Nepalis work in the factories.

Nepali Fellowships

This part of N India is strongly Hindu, hence both local and Nepali outreach has always been rather limited. Of special significance, however, are the border towns of **Nautanwa** (UP) and **Raxaul** (Bihar). The former was the base of the early NEB work before the group were able to go into Pokhara and the latter is the site of the Duncan Hospital. In both places there was significant early outreach to Nepalis, especially those travelling to and from Nepal, as was also the case in **Rupaidiya**, just over the border from Nepalgunj in MW Nepal. Further south were the Nurseries in **Gorakhpur** and literature work in **Motihari.** All were centres from which the praying members of the Nepal Border Fellowship had their eyes fixed firmly on Nepal itself.

Today there are still Nepali fellowships in most of these centres: **Lucknow** (led by Ps. Rolly Singh), **Rampur** (led by Ps. Man Bahadur Sijali), **Kanpur** (led by Ps. Ezekiel Joshua & Dipendra from Surkhet), **Bareilly**, **Banares, Gorakhpur** and **Patna.** Ps. Ramesh Chhetri works in Bihar.

OTHER STATES & INDIAN CITIES

WEST BENGAL (Kolkata)

In the northern area there is just one large metropolis, **Kolkata** in W Bengal (see p.172ff.), but it is different from the other Indian cities, being situated in a state where Nepali outreach is longstanding and where, at least in Darjeeling District, there is a large Nepali-speaking population.

PUNJAB & HARYANA (Chandigarh & also Ludhiana)

According to Perry, many earlier Nepali migrants went to Himachal Pradesh but later moved on to Punjab and Haryana – to places like Ambala, Gurdaspur, Amritsar, Firozpur and Jullundar.[107] In Rajpur (like Sonipat and Panipat, relatively near Delhi) there are some Nepali families and many of the men work in the local factories, but a lot of them have drink problems – sleeping rough on the road and fighting. Those in Chandigarh also earn good money but again there is an alcohol problem. Some college girls are living loose with 'big' friends. Other Nepalis are educated professionals.

Nepali Fellowships

In **Chandigarh** there are 3 main groups working with Nepalis. According to Ps. Daniel Pathak, in the city alone, there are more than 14 churches and approximately 700-800 Nepali Christians.

In **Ludhiana** there is a big Nepali group, and also, in various other parts of Haryana like Panipat and Sonipat, there are several fellowships.

DELHI & NCR (National Capital Regions)

Especially since the start of the Maoist insurgency in Nepal, large numbers of Nepalis have migrated to Delhi. The most recent estimate suggests a figure of around 7 *lakh*.[xxviii] There are two reasons why Delhi is the favourite destination for many Nepali migrants, especially those from the western hills of Nepal. The first is because Delhi is the nearest Indian city to the Nepal border (only 507 km away), and it is easier to reach Delhi than any other major city in India. The second reason is related to urbanization and the recent industrialization of the city, which has opened up many opportunities for work for semi-literate Nepalis. However, because central Delhi itself has little industrial advancement, many migrants tend to move out to adjoining cities, such as Noida, Gurgaon, Panipat, Sonipat and even to Chandigarh and Jaipur. A man from Doti explains why he is in Delhi:

> *Why should I stay in Nepal? I can't support my family. The harvest is not good at all. Our family is from a poor background. My father can't work like before. I tried to find some jobs in Nepal but couldn't find anything except in politics. There are more political leaders than workers! I am happy here. At least, I easily get paid at the end of the month. I can see a better future here in Delhi than in Nepal.*[108]

Janak BC says that some Nepali entrepreneurs have set up *momo*[xxix] stalls, as these Nepali snacks are very popular in Delhi. However, the vendors are continually cheated by the local people who charge them for occupying a small site

---

[xxviii] This is a huge increase. In 1995, one survey found 32,000, while in 2001, Suter et al estimated there were 50-60,000.

[xxix] Tibetan-style dumplings.

close to a shop or on the roadside. For example, if they are located outside a shop, they have to pay 2,000-3,000 Indian Rupees per month to the shopkeeper even if he does not own that shop. "The large majority of new arrivals end up living in illegal squatter colonies that grow into slums, mostly lacking water, electricity, sewage and legal status."[109] There may be 3,000 such slums in Delhi, many hosting large numbers of Nepalis.

Nepali Fellowships

The beginning of the Nepali fellowships in Delhi seems to have been multi-focal, with various ethnic Nepalis (with Indian citizenship) coming to Delhi sometimes for work but also with a burden to share the Gospel among other Nepali people. One of the earliest was Ps. ML Tamang, who originally worked in the Indian Navy. He was transferred to Delhi in 1984 and started the first Nepali Congregation at Uttam Nagar.[xxx] Pradeep Pradhan "migrated to Delhi from Darjeeling in 1987 specifically for full-time Nepali-focused Christian work in conjunction with the Delhi Bible Institute (DBI)."[110] He, along with Nagendra Kumar and Sasir Adhikari of Kalimpong, began to contact other Nepali/Lepcha Christians who were also living in the city. It seems that as a result of this, a group started to meet together. According to Nagendra, the Nepali fellowship was begun in June 1987 at the Free Church in Connaught Place and Pradeep became the pastor. Others, like Satish Chettri and Umanand Gaire, have also made a significant contribution to the history of the Nepali church in New Delhi.

From these small beginnings, there are now about 35

[xxx] Personal communication from ML Tamang via Janak BC.

churches and 150 house fellowships scattered across the city. The total number of Nepali believers attending Nepali-language churches is around 3,000. Many others attend Hindi or other language services.[xxxi] Training and church planting are seen as their biggest needs. Holistic mission, as a practical demonstration of Christ's love, is a powerful way to reach especially the slum-dwellers.[111]

United Nepali Churches Association (UNCA)

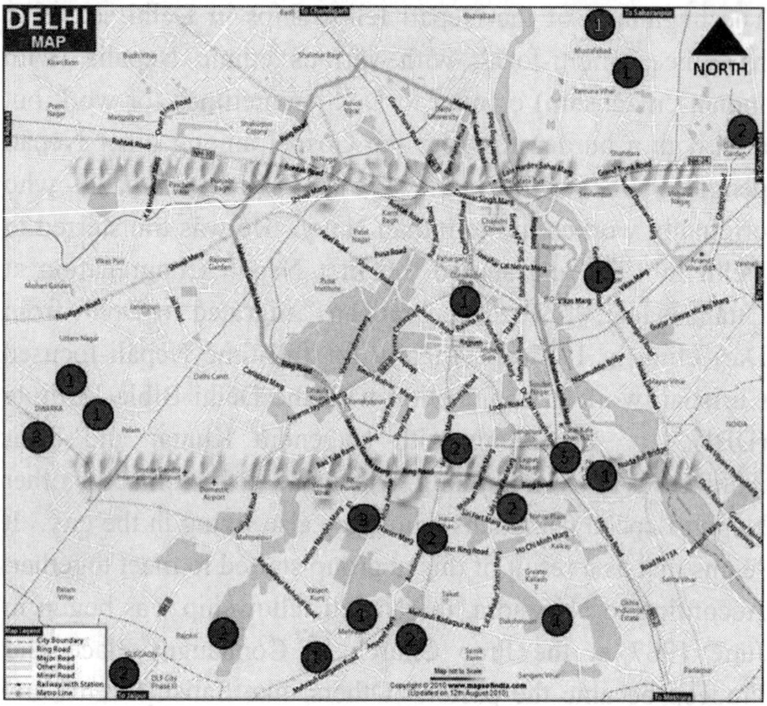

Approximate Distribution of Nepali Churches in Delhi
(Credit: UNCA but scale too small to show accurately)

[xxxi] Personal communication from Ps. Umanand Gaire via Janak BC.

UNCA is an association of the Nepali speaking churches in Delhi and NCR regions. In 2002, a few Nepali pastors began to come together for prayer. Slowly, leaders from other Nepali speaking churches in the area joined them and in 2005, when they decided to structure the association, ML Tamang became the first president, and served from 2005 to 2006. Since 2012, Ps. Umanand Gaire has been the chair.

The main objective of UNCA is to bring the Nepali churches under one umbrella, display their unity and so enrich the ministry among the Nepalis. UNCA has therefore subsequently emerged as a platform for the Nepali speaking churches in Delhi. It organises different programmes for women, children and youth, as well as various trainings for the Nepali church leaders. Around 33 churches/fellowships are officially linked with UNCA, but, for a variety of reasons, there are other fellowships not (yet) linked.

Apart from the big cities, there are relatively few Nepalis living and working in the southern half of India. This may be because of the greater distance needed to travel and the corresponding greater expense to reach the area, plus the fact that Hindi (which most Nepalis can pick up easily) is not widely spoken in the south. Nevertheless it seems that Nepalis are more welcomed in South India than elsewhere. People in Chennai are particularly friendly and helpful. For Christians, there is also the attraction of the many Bible Colleges, especially in Kerala.

ANDRA PRADESH (Hyderabad)

There has been large-scale immigration from all over India to the modern, fast-growing city of Hyderabad. This has included Nepalis coming from northern India as well directly from Nepal. It is estimated that there may be as many as 5 *lakh* Nepalis living in Hyderabad.

Nepali Fellowships

In **Hyderabad** there are at least 2 Nepali churches and around 500 Nepali Christians. One fellowship is led by Dr. Ps. Hem Sagar Rasaily, who has been instrumental in reaching the Nepali migrants.

KARNATAKA (Bangalore)

Estimates of the number of Nepalis in Bangalore vary between 5 and 8 *lakh*. An interesting fact noted by Upreti is that "The emigrants from Bajhang district of Far Western Nepal find their way to Bangalore alone in India."[112] Others also reckon that "Bajhang survives on the basis of remittances from Bangalore"[113]

Nepali Fellowships

In **Bangalore** city alone there are at least 8 Nepali churches and around 2-3,000 Nepali Christians. There is a very active work amongst the Nepali population in the city. Basant Prakash, a faculty member of Southern Asia Bible College, has been involved in outreach and also runs a Nepali church. Similarly, All People Nepali Church has been growing under the leadership of OB Timothy Thapa, who is a missionary from NIM Gyaneshwar church in Kathmandu.

MAHARASHTRA (Mumbai)

The Nepali population in Mumbai is around 7 *lakh*. Mumbai, despite its distance from Nepal, is one of the oldest destinations for Nepali migrants, even before New Delhi. People from the Mid and Far Western hills, especially from Achham, Jumla, Humla, and Bajura came to Bombay (as it then was) to sell their herbal medicines (*jadi-buti*). Later, some found employment in the diamond factories, and later still, as the city's infrastructure boomed, more avenues for migrants opened up. Nowadays migrants still come from these districts and also from Doti, Kailali, Syangja, Gulmi and Nuwakot. Those from Humla and Jumla tend to come only when it is very cold back home i.e. for the 5 months November to March. Mumbai is popular as it not only offers more work in factories and construction than Delhi and Chennai, but also more all-round opportunities to Nepalis of all levels of skill and education. Many work in restaurants; as watchmen or in car washes. On average, Nepalis in Mumbai earn around 11,000 Indian Rupees a month. Some Nepalis are office workers or have their own businesses. A few have even been elected as local politicians. Two Nepali language newspapers are published in Mumbai.

Nepali Fellowships

The first Nepali church in **Mumbai** was established in 1980. A small Nepali church was formed in Mumbai during the mid-1980s in Andheri, but it has not seen such growth as has occurred in Delhi. In May 2007, Ps. Abhay Sharma started the Everest Christian Fellowship, which is the only government registered Nepali church to date. According to pastors Peter Rai and Abhay Sharma there are now around 8-10 Nepali fellowships, some of which are independent while others are linked to mainline churches in the city. There are between 4,500 and 5,000 Nepali believers in the greater Mumbai area and also around 100 mission or full time Nepali workers in ministry there. With almost half the 2 *lakh* sex workers in Mumbai being Nepali, it is unsurprising that one of the main ministries of the churches is concerned with anti-trafficking. Manna Prayer House, a new ministry, is concentrating especially on helping women and children alongside its church planting activities.

Pune (previously Poona) is the second city of the state of Maharashtra. There are said to be around 2 *lakh* of Nepalis living there. Pune has at least 3 Nepali churches and a Nepali Christian population of maybe 1,000, although more than 20,000 Nepalis have been reached through Gospel tracts, other programmes and personal evangelism. Poona Nepali Sangati is led by Ps. Pradip Bajracharya, who is a missionary from NIM Gyaneshwar Church in Kathmandu. The other pastors are Ps. Sunil (Daniel) Bhutia from Bhutan, who ministers to some Nepalis in a mixed congregation in Masih Sangati, and Ps. Milan Sasankar. There are usually a few Nepali students attending Union Bible Seminary (UBS), who get involved in Nepali ministry. Exact numbers of Nepali Christians are not known as many attend Hindi or Marathi services and a lot of students go to English-speaking churches.

In **Nasik** it is estimated that there may be as many as 2 *lakh* Nepalis, but I have not heard of any Nepali fellowships. In **Nagpur** there are at least 2 Nepali churches.

TAMIL NADU (Chennai)

The estimated Nepali population of Chennai is >2 *lakh* (maybe 5-6 *lakh*). Between 1931 and 1951 the city grew rapidly due to a huge influx of refugees from Burma and Sri Lanka. Nepalis only started arriving after this.[114] Nepali ethnics come from Darjeeling, Sikkim and Nepal itself, and most work in the service sector. Nowadays migrants move back and forth between Bangalore to Chennai, partly because the cities are closely linked, being only 6 hours apart.

Nepali Fellowships

According to Perry, there was a small Nepali fellowship in **Chennai** (known as Madras until August 1996) in the early 1980's started by a converted Buddhist, although he then moved on.[115] After that, Nepali Christians coming to the city tended to join other language churches. Even today, most of the Nepali students still go to English medium churches as they like the exposure to that language. There are thus only 2 specifically Nepali Fellowships: Chennai Christian Fellowship, started in 2004 by Ps. OC Lepcha in Anna Nagar, and Chennai Nepali Word of Life Fellowship in Nungambakkam, started in 2010 by Ps. Raju Tamang. There are >20,000 Nepali Christians, but most live too far away to attend a Nepali church, although some attend one of the 30+ cell groups. Outreach is through personal friendship evangelism and cultural events.

In **Coimbatore,** where there may be another 1 *lakh* of Nepalis, there is at least one known Nepali church in the city.

It is estimated that they are around 3 *lakh* Nepalis living and working in **GUJERAT.** Many work in the cloth and other factories around Ahmedabad. There is one Nepali church in the capital, **Gandhinagar,** served by Ps. Govind with about 300-350 believers. There is also a fellowship in **Ahmedabad**.

The Nepali population of **RAJASTAN** is only about 60,000. In **Jaipur**, the capital, there are 2 Nepali fellowships, including an Assembly of God church that ministers to the Nepali community. According to the Assembly of God pastor, Vinod Aryal, there are about 300-400 believers. Other pastors are Mohan and Amosh.

Although I have no figures for numbers of Nepalis living in **JHARKHAND,** there is at least one Nepali fellowship meeting in **Ranchi**, the capital.

I have been unable to discover any information about Nepalis in **CHATTISGARH** (capital **Raipur**), but do know that the economy in **MADHYA PRADESH** (capital **Bhopal**) is growing and therefore it has recently begun to attract a lot of migrant workers. Some may be Christians.

Although **GOA** (capital **Panaji**) has not traditionally been a Nepali destination, it seems to have recently become popular, with many job opportunities connected with the tourism industry, especially in Panaji.

In **ORISSA** (capital **Bhubaneswar**) one of the units of the Orissa Armed Police has 1,500 Gorkhalis. I do not know whether any of them are Christians.

In **KERALA** (capital **Trivandrum**), I have not heard of any Nepali fellowships. This is interesting considering that a significant number of Indian missionaries to Nepal have come from this state.

ASIAN COUNTRIES (Near India)

There is one country each in the NE and off the SE and SW coasts of India which are included here. Only in the north, however, in Bhutan, is there a significant Nepali presence.

BHUTAN*

STATISTICS	
Total Nepali Population	>2 *lakh*
No. of Nepali Fellowships	See below
No. of Nepali Christians	? 1,800

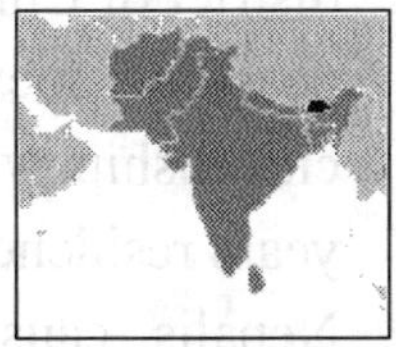

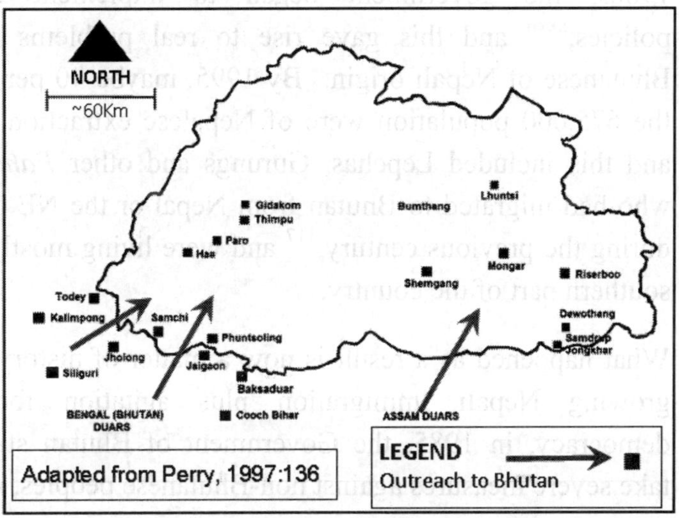

Adapted from Perry, 1997:136

Unlike Sikkim, Bhutan has retained its status as an independent kingdom. However, it is helpful to consider it in this section on India because it is situated geographically close to the NE Indian States.

According to the Joshua Project "Bhutanese society had three main groups: the Bhotia of Tibet, which includes the Bhutanese; the Sharchop, or Eastern Bhotia; and the Nepalese. There are also various other smaller tribes." In fact, until the Indo-Bhutanese War of 1864, after which the Nepalis started settling in large numbers in Bhutan, there were only the two main groups. Some of the earliest Nepalis to visit / settle in Bhutan went to the more low-lying SW part of the country in the 1870s to quarry lime and to the SE district of Chirang to tap the rubber trees. Initially there was peaceful coexistence between these groups and in 1958 citizenship was granted to all settlers who could prove 10 years residence. However, increased migration, especially of Nepalis, caused concern to the rulers of Bhutan, so in the 1980s, the government began to implement racialist policies,[xxxii] and this gave rise to real problems for the Bhutanese of Nepali origin. By 1995, maybe 40 per cent of the 675,000 population were of Nepalese extraction,"[116][xxxiii] and this included Lepchas, Gurungs and other *Paharis,*[xxxiv] who had migrated to Bhutan from Nepal or the NE of India during the previous century,[117] and were living mostly in the southern part of the country.

What happened as a result is now a matter of history. With growing Nepali immigration plus agitation for more democracy, in 1985, the Government of Bhutan started to take severe measures against non-Bhutanese peoples, and this

---

[xxxii] Laws were introduced enforcing the wearing of national dress, usage of the Dzonka language and harmonization of Hindu practices within Buddhism.

[xxxiii] Bhutanese authorities tended to quote a figure of 20% in line with their desire to minimise the number of Nepalis in Bhutan.

[xxxiv] Hillsmen.

eventually led to what was effectively ethnic cleansing. First, two discriminatory laws were passed – the Marriage Act of 1977 (enforced 1988) and the Citizenship Act of 1985: these aimed to reduce the number of 'Lhotshampas' in Bhutan. In particular they changed the definition of citizenship. "Since the Act was given a retrospective implementation of 1958, all children born of a marriage between a Bhutanese father and a non-Bhutanese mother, between 1958 to 1988 were declared non-citizens and labelled 'illegal' and 'economic migrants.'"[118] Citizenship was granted only by registration to those who were included in the census as permanent residents prior to 1958. In addition, only documents dated specifically in 1958 were accepted as proof and not those with earlier dates! The category of citizenship by birth was no longer considered valid. However, citizenship by registration was virtually impossible for the Nepalis to prove as there were no records prior to the first census of 1981! Those who did not comply were declared 'illegal immigrants'. This led to protests and demonstrations in 1990/1. Those who criticised the government or fled the country were deemed to have forfeited their citizenship. Others were systematically harassed and restricted until they also left.

Thus the Bhutanese Buddhist majority suppressed Nepali culture and language, committed acts of violence against people and property, took away citizen rights and expelled around 150,000 Nepali Bhutanese (whom, they called 'Lhotshampas'). From 1989/90 onwards, a steady stream of refugees began to leave Bhutan, the number reaching 10,000 a month by 1992. Indian authorities, "unwilling to permit anything that would cause King Jigme discomfort, herded them into trucks and drove them to the Nepali border town of

Kakarbhitta."[119] Then, with the help of UNHCR, "the refugee population was eventually moved to camps built in Beldangi, Khundunabari, Timai, Goldhap and Sanischare in Jhapa and Morang Districts."[120] One interesting side effect of this was that "many poor, border-dwelling Nepalis claimed to be refugees in order to receive aid, and within a year, the camps' population grew to more than 100,000, according to UNHCR."[121]

Then for nearly 20 years, most of these people lived in refugee camps run by UNHCR in south-eastern Nepal. A few managed to move and live independently in Nepal, about 25,000 settled in India, and a few emigrated to the west. In March 2001, there were almost 1 *lakh* Bhutanese refugees living in 7 refugee camps in Eastern Nepal. From 1993 until 2007 there were 15 unsuccessful rounds of ministerial level talks between Kathmandu and Thimphu.[122] At one point, the Nepal authorities cut the refugees' kerosene rations and gave them coal briquettes but to start the fire they needed wood and were not allowed to collect it. Funds for higher education were also cut. The refugees said, "We were being told to stand on our own feet, but we are not allowed to work."[123] All this increased the tension in the camps – especially among the younger men.

Until 2007 most were still hoping for repatriation but gradually they gave up that hope and turned towards the offer of resettlement in the west. However, rumours spread about conditions in the west – that they would be put in camps, etc. and so feelings about resettlement remained ambivalent. "One elderly man said 'We want to go back to Bhutan. If we can't do that, we would rather stay here in Nepal,'[124] but an elderly woman with more spirit said, "In America they say that we'll be made into fish feed. Well, let us be fish feed rather than stay here, where we don't have firewood to feed ourselves."[125] In addition, a few Nepalese Nepalis tried to cash in on this offer of settlement in America by pretending to be Bhutanese Nepali refugees! At last, in March 2008, a multiyear resettlement to third countries including the United States, Canada, Australia, New Zealand, Denmark, Norway and Germany began and by 2013 was virtually complete. Already, in 2009, more than 20,000 had left the camps and by 2010 the figure had reached 40,000. By 2013, the majority (at least 60,000) of these 'Lhotshampa' refugees had been resettled in America, mostly in Texas, New York, Georgia, Arizona, Pennsylvania and California. Australia had resettled around 5,000 while there may be another 1,000 or more in Europe (notably Netherlands, Norway, Austria, Denmark and the UK).

Still some (maybe as many as 25,000) remain in the camps. 13,000 do not want resettlement and are still vainly hoping for repatriation, but they are not the only ones still affected by this tragedy. "The effect of refugee resettlement has forced [Nepali] business persons to search for other alternatives," as there are no longer enough people in the Beldangi area to support their businesses that grew up to serve the refugees."[126] Yet others – who presumably fulfilled the stringent citizenship conditions – are still living in Bhutan, but numbers are difficult to state. In addition, some Nepalis continue to travel to Bhutan for work although there is even a bias against people like this. Not long ago, a Nepali Engineer was jailed in Bhutan on apparently false corruption charges.[127] I therefore find it strange that in 2012 the Nepal

MoFA was considering opening a diplomatic office in Bhutan,[128] or maybe that is exactly why it is needed.

Nepali Fellowships

According to Perry, Christian influence only began to spread over the border from Darjeeling and Kalimpong into Bhutan at the end of the 19th century, despite the fact that William Carey's son tried to establish a 'Bhootan' mission at the very beginning of the century.[129] Once Nepalis began to migrate to Bhutan, they tended to settle in the southern part of the country, which was the easiest area geographically to reach. The Nepalis – both domiciled and temporary migrant workers – proved more responsive to the gospel than the indigenous Bhutias.[130] By 1964 there were already 13 centres where Nepali-Lepcha Christians gathered but in the 1970s and 1980s some Christians began to be persecuted for their faith.[131] Today – after the expulsion of most of the Nepali ethnics, there may be as many as 1,800 scattered Christians left who worship in around 300 'mini' house fellowships. but accurate information is difficult to discover as due to persecution, many Christians do not reveal themselves openly.[132]

Other Nepalis who had settled on the Indian side of the border, in places like Jaigaon, in the Bengal and Assam Duars were also reached by the Gospel and there are Nepali-speaking fellowships in the area today.

During the existence of the refugee camps, a work of God occurred there too. For details of what has happened since, especially among those resettled in the USA (see p.456ff).

SRI LANKA

STATISTICS	
Total Nepali Population	200
No. of Nepali Fellowships	Nil
No. of Nepali Christians	?

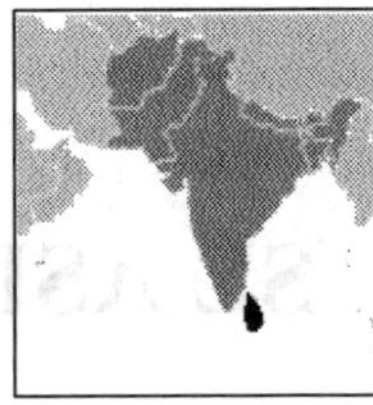

There may be 200 Nepalis in Sri Lanka, but I am not aware of any exclusively Nepali language fellowships in the country.

The MALDIVES

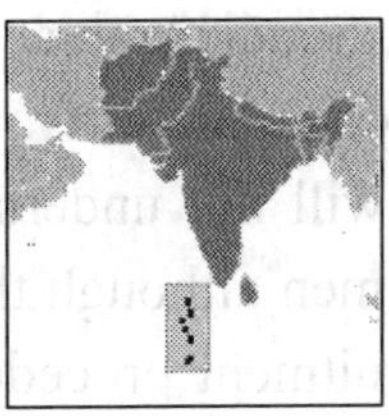

STATISTICS	
Total Nepali Population	400
No. of Nepali Fellowships	Nil
No. of Nepali Christians	?

There may be 400 Nepalis in the Maldives or even more as in 2012, GoN was considering whether it would open a diplomatic office in the Maldives.[133] Most are employed as guards. Like Saudi Arabia, the Muslim government of the Maldives does not allow any Christian gatherings. Due to small numbers and religious restrictions, it is doubtful if there are any Nepali Fellowships in the islands.

Chapter 8

SE ASIA & THE MIDDLE EAST

"Therefore in the EAST give glory to the LORD;
in the COASTLANDS OF THE SEA, give glory to the name of the LORD, the God of Israel.
~ Isaiah 24:15 ~

By 2013, the official estimate for Nepalis working overseas (excluding India) was around 2.8 million, of whom the greatest number were in SE Asia and the Middle East. Most are employed in construction work, factories, security or domestic work in Malaysia, Qatar, UAE, Saudi Arabia, and Kuwait. The work is frequently '3D' (difficult, dirty, and dangerous), the sort of work that locals will not undertake. The majority of the migrants are (young) men although there are increasing numbers of women. Recruitment procedures and problems faced by migrants are similar for the two destinations, but from a Christian perspective, there are several significant differences.

Manpower Agencies

In order to obtain an employment contract and a worker's visa, and make all the other necessary arrangements, would-be migrants to Malaysia and 'Arab' are generally forced to use the services of manpower recruitment agencies. The fees they charge for these services represent a substantial level of profit for the agencies and an equally substantial level of hardship for the migrants and their families, such that a large percentage arrive overseas already saddled with a huge burden of debt. Amnesty International (AI) claimed that 90% of the migrants they interviewed in their survey had been cheated by these manpower agencies with regard to their contracts. As their survey sample was only 150, it seems this figure is probably inflated by some factors. One of these may be the naivety of workers from remote villages, who do not understand their contracts and could easily be misled by obscure, but not technically fraudulent, wording. Nevertheless AI has highlighted a hugely important issue.

Most migrants are cheated by the Management Agencies.

Working Conditions

There is also a lot of truth, but possibly again some exaggeration, in another comment from the AI survey: The "majority of migrant workers are not given salary as per their contract, [are] forced to work without a rest day, [and] are locked up and physically abused."[134] While many are certainly given less salary than they expected and denied legitimate weekly days off, and some are physically ill-treated, it may be an over-statement to say *the majority* are locked up and physically abused.

SE Asia and the Middle East, the main hosts of the current bulk of labour migrants, provide only limited contracts, and do not offer any hope for long-term permanent settlement.

Not only is the ultimate chance of citizenship denied to them, but also "migrant workers in Asia are just viewed as tools imported to ensure that their foreign-labor dependent economies thrive… Such workers were readily discarded once they have outlived their usefulness."[135] The medieval *kafala* system (see p. 218), still practised in many Middle East countries, is perhaps the most potent proof of this condemnation.

Most migrants are treated as 'tools'.

Salary and the Nepal Government

The Nepal Government has so far not negotiated sufficiently, as Bal Bahadur Tamang, Chairman of the Nepal Association of Foreign Employment Agencies (NAFEA) implied in 2013 when he admitted that unskilled labourers from other countries, like the Philippines and Bangladesh, were being paid at higher rates than Nepalis for the same work. This is because their governments have agreed better deals for them. Migrants are therefore often paid only the absolute minimum an employer can get away with without actually breaking the law. The combination of dishonest manpower agencies and inactivity of the government were the main factors that apparently led to the riots of 2004 in protest against the death of 12 Nepalis killed in Iraq. The complaint was that the government had neither ensured that migrants were sent safely to allowed destinations nor, when problems arose, done enough to bring them home safely. However, since

Most migrants are paid the absolute minimum.

then GoN has begun to take steps to rectify this situation and in early 2013, a significant increase in the basic pay was announced for workers in Malaysia. Tamang cited this as a good example of progress, although many unscrupulous employers have managed to find ways around it, leaving workers only minimally better off (see p.317).

Contracts

Information about their placements and details of work contracts are often given to migrants either in English or in a local language, like Arabic. In both cases, it means that outgoing migrants are unaware of the true conditions of their contracts and they usually have no idea to where they are being sent. This language problem could easily be solved by enforcing the ruling that all contracts must be given with a Nepali translation. The geographical aspect of the problem is less easy to solve. Most migrants have little concept of Malaysia or the Middle East and so even if told where they are being sent, the place name means nothing to them. I met one lad on the plane from Doha, on his way home to Kathmandu, who still did not know where he had been working. I asked him how long he had been in Doha and he told me he had not been there at all. I therefore assumed he had been working outside the city in one of the outlying industrial estates, but when I was helping him fill in his immigration form, it was clear he had been in Doha for the last umpteen months! Giving country-specific orientation prior to departure would help here.

Labour contracts have not been provided in Nepali.

Orientation (or lack of it!)

It is unrealistic to expect most migrants to learn anything more than the rudiments of the local language before leaving Nepal, but even a few simple phrases would help. Other general and cultural matters could profitably be addressed in short orientation training courses. Officially, the Government does run courses but few outgoing migrants take advantage of them. Most migrants still leave TIA in complete ignorance of the land to which they are going.

Most migrants get no real orientation.

Employers

Outgoing migrants are usually led to believe that the company which is going to employ them will arrange for them to be met at their destination airport. Although this is usually so, it does not always happen, and it does not always do so smoothly. Fortunate migrants are met on arrival and provided transport to their hostels and settled in work within a few days. Others are kept waiting in the airport arrivals hall for several hours or even longer. I have heard tales of those who have been kept waiting in the airport – without any arrangements for food and drink – for days.

Most employers care little for their workers.

Costs

The costs involved in reaching SE Asia or the Gulf are so

much higher than going to India because the migrants have to travel by air and because of the huge fees the agents charge them. Most migrants, therefore, find they have to work for at least one year before they start making a profit over and above their initial outlay.

Most migrants have to work at least 1 year before they make a profit.

Students

Although the majority of Nepalis in this region are labour migrants, there are also some students. As with India, some Asian countries, like China, S. Korea, Japan, the Philippines and Malaysia, offer university level courses that are generally less expensive and for which entrance is easier to obtain than their equivalent in the west. The drawback is that students often have to spend their first year learning a new language before they can start their courses properly.

Most college courses are cheaper than in the 'West'.

THE MIDDLE EAST

(& Other Muslim Countries)

"He turns a desert into pools of water,
a parched land into springs of water."
~ Psalm 107:35 ~

This part of the diaspora is generally known as 'Arab' by most Nepalis. In fact, the Middle East (ME) is a huge and rather disparate area, which in practice includes not only the Gulf States of the Arabian peninsula, where most Nepalis are found, but also North African and West Asian counties from the Mediterranean to Iran. Geographically, it also includes Israel, but migration conditions are different as it is the only unequivocally non-Muslim country in the region. That almost all the others are officially Muslim nations is a significant factor in determining working conditions and provision of religious freedom. The Gulf States and Israel are some of the most popular destinations for Nepalis. The type of work, the restrictions and the problems are essentially the same in all the Muslim countries, although magnified in the Gulf States because of the huge numbers of migrants involved. Israel is obviously rather different and generally a lot safer, especially for female migrants. Other African and a few other Asian countries are listed at the end of this section, although they host few Nepalis and the living and working conditions are sometimes rather different.

Labour migrants generally face the same problems in the ME and Malaysia, but some are more serious in 'Arab'.

> Hundreds of women emigrated for work to Kuwait, Iraq, Afghanistan and other Islamic countries, and have not been heard from for years. Those who succeed in returning home shows signs of physical exhaustion, injuries and are often infected with AIDS.[136]

Despite efforts by GoN to control the numbers of women going to work in these areas, they still go. Over 80,000 women leave Nepal each year for work and the majority end up in places like Saudi Arabia and Kuwait, where they have been led to believe the job opportunities are better.[137]

GULF STATES

At one time it was thought that the Persian Gulf was hosting 87% of all documented Nepali migrant workers,[138] but in view of the statistics emerging from SE Asia, particularly Malaysia, this proportion must have dropped significantly. However, there are fluctuations in the numbers of migrants going to different regions or countries. This is usually because of local cut-backs, or because another region is offering better paid jobs.[139]

In the Gulf petrol is cheaper than water!

Total numbers of Nepalis in the Gulf are approximately 1.5 million, but this includes more than 5 main destinations. The wealth of the GCC countries is almost exclusively dependent on oil revenues. If and when this non-renewable source eventually starts to dry up, it is likely that migration will also begin to decrease,[140] although hopefully the employment market in Nepal will have improved long before then.

'Trafficking' of Women to the Gulf

According to The Department of Labour, in 2012 there were more than 2 *lakh* Nepali women[xxxv] working in the Gulf, of whom only 4% had legal work permits.[141] This is despite the fact that earlier in 2012, GoN had set a minimum age of 30 years for girls to work as housemaids in the Gulf. Saru Joshi Shrestha of UN Women, explained what happens:

Only 4% Nepali women working in the Gulf have legal work permits.

> 'Brokers are taking advantage of the information gap and are trafficking women to the Gulf through visit visas.' More than 3,200 Nepali women have been intercepted at New Delhi Airport in the last few months after the government requested Indian authorities to stop Nepali women transiting there to go to the Gulf on visitor visas. Immigration officials at New Delhi airport told *Nepali Times* they intercept up to five Nepali women every day on forged passports or visas.[142]

90% of women travelling illegally to restricted destinations go via India and until recently almost all went through Delhi, but Mumbai and Chennai are now also being used. This demonstrates how difficult it is for GoN to close all the loopholes. A shortage of air tickets on the Gulf route and an exorbitant price hike from 22,000 to between 32,000 and

Most illegal WMWs travel via India.

[xxxv] In 2011 Pourakhi gave an incomplete country breakdown as follows: 70,000 in Saudi, 30,000 in Kuwait, 14,000 in Israel and 15,000 in Lebanon, but did not mention Oman, Qatar and Emirates.

almost Rs. 50,000 as compared with only Rs. 20,000 on the Delhi route in 2013 recently made it even harder for GoN to clamp down on travel via India.[143] Nevertheless, in an attempt "to curb cases of abuse, women wishing to work abroad must now receive prior approval from the department of labour." In addition, the government is also trying "to enforce mandatory registration and documentation programmes at Nepal's missions in Saudi Arabia, Qatar, Kuwait and the UAE."[144] Baruah and Chettri point out that women who migrate through irregular channels have no recourse to compensation, partly because it is not possible to trace the dishonest brokers they use.[145]

Medical Problems

In 2005 at least 5 Nepalis died every week in the Gulf.[146] This works out at 270 a year, of which the majority occurred in Qatar. The list of main causes is salutary:

- 50% Heart Attack
- 25% Road Accidents
- 15% Industrial Accidents
- 10% Suicide

Heart attacks are most likely precipitated by the stress of enduring long hours working physically hard in very high temperatures. I was told that there is a rule that outside (construction) workers should not be expected to work if the temperature goes above 50 degrees. However, some employers fix the public thermometers so that the gauge never reads above 50. Industrial accidents are often due to

Hard work in high temperatures is a recipe for tragedy.

lack of safety measures in the workplace. Road accidents happen because men from remote hill villages are unused to traffic, especially when it drives on the right! Suicides are the result of a combination of physical, mental and financial stresses. Murder was not included in this list, but it is also an important cause of death. As many workers are not fully medically insured very few families get compensation.

The *Kafala* System

In the Arab Gulf States there is a system called *kafala*,[xxxvi] which is officially a sponsorship system used to monitor the migrants who come to work in the construction industry or as domestic helpers. Human Rights Watch (HRW) has denounced *kafala* as an opportunity for exploitation of employees by employers, who have little fear of any legal repercussions. Although the system has already been abolished in some places (like Bahrain), it continues in Saudi and Qatar, where thousands of migrant workers are abused by their employers "in ways such as non-payment of wages, forced confinement in [their] workplace, confiscation of passports, excessive work hours with little rest, physical and sexual abuse, and forced labor including trafficking."[147] The Nepalese Embassy in Saudi

The kafala system is really a kind of slavery.

[xxxvi] According to the *kafala* system, all unskilled labourers must have an in-country sponsor, who is usually their employer, who becomes responsible for their visa and legal status. In practice this gives the employer almost complete control over the migrants because "the employer must grant explicit permission before the worker can enter Saudi Arabia, transfer employment, or leave the country."

Arabia claims that about 70,000 to 80,000 Nepalis are caught in this trap. This is probably an under-estimate as the situation is usually worse for the women in domestic employment. According to HRW, the system is clearly incompatible with Article 13 of the Universal Declaration of Human Rights. In fact, "some abusive employers exploit the *kafala* system and force domestic workers to continue working against their will and forbid them from returning to their countries of origin". Others are refused necessary medical treatment. Some employers even feel entitled to exert 'ownership' over their domestic workers. This in turn leads to slavery-like conditions, such that some women have "thought they were being bought and sold,"[xxxvii] and to all practical intents and purposes, they were!

Social Restrictions

All across the Middle East (and in Malaysia) migrants are restricted from integrating in the socio-economic sphere.[148] Rules are not the same or as strict everywhere, but include:

- No job; no residence (usually) – thus families are rarely able to stay together.
- No legal access to housing, social benefits or medical care.
- No right to appeal in respect to their migrant status.
- Deportation is allowed at any time by a simple decree
- Not allowed to own property.
- Not allowed to join Trade Unions.
- Restricted access to social benefits.
- No right to naturalization/citizenship.

[xxxvii] See Bina's testimony on page 279.

Detention & Imprisonment

Another horrifying set of statistics concerns Nepalis who are in prison, where they face harsh treatment and poor food as well as suffering from the extreme heat. In 2012, there were nearly 300 Nepali migrants in police custody facing criminal charges as well as around 900 in detention centres in Saudi, UAE and Qatar.[149] The crimes they are charged with include drug abuse, forgery and counterfeiting, as well as abduction, rape, and murder and quite a number are caught largely because they are unaware of the laws. In addition, nearly 80,000 illegal workers were trapped in Saudi, waiting for exit visas to be processed by their employers.

Nepal Embassies

In February 2013, at last "the government approved proposals to open a… consulate office in Jeddah of Saudi Arabia and two residential embassies in Oman and Bahrain."[150] Previously Saudi looked after Oman and Qatar looked after Bahrain.

Women in Gulf Countries

Women working in Muslim countries, especially those employed as maids in the Gulf, are particularly vulnerable to exploitation and injustice. That this is a very serious problem is illustrated by many stories from many countries. One Tamang woman was

Maids working in Muslim countries are particularly vulnerable to exploitation, injustice and violence.

apparently even tortured by her employers in Saudi until she agreed to convert to Islam.

Between 2009 and 2011, the UN carried out a study on women in Gulf countries. The findings from this 1-2 year period showed that many Women Migrant Workers (WMWs) in those states were facing different forms of violence:

- 2,820 WMWs were rescued from different Gulf countries in miserable conditions.
- 111 Nepali WMWs were imprisoned, and due to the mental and physical exploitation…
- 415 Nepali WMWs lost their mental balance.[xxxviii]
- 86 women returned home pregnant.
- 32 returned home along with the children [conceived] from the foreign employers.
- 80 WMWs committed suicide.[xxxix]
- 31 went missing.

The obvious conclusion is that these countries are not safe for female migrants. Saru Joshi, of UN Women, suggested that the solution was for GoN "to end [gender] discriminatory practices that force women migrants to resort to underground ways to reach the Gulf countries and face the greater risk of exploitation in the foreign land." Allowing women and girls to migrate legally, however, will not solve the problem or keep the women safe, for legal migrants also suffer from exploitation, even if not to the same extent as illegal ones. Allowing women to go legally may mean that GoN has a record of all who go, and can better help those who do get into trouble, but it will

---

[xxxviii] Another report, by Anil Giri, in *The National*, in Dec 2010 suggested that only 33% return home healthy and of the 67% with medical problems, almost all have some kind of psychiatric illness.

[xxxix] This tragedy is continuing and increasing. The *Nepal News* in Oct 2012 said that 82 had committed suicide in the preceding 18 months.

surely open the door for greater numbers to go and inevitably, for greater numbers to be abused.

Nepali Fellowships

Despite all these problems God has been working mightily in many of these countries and – with the exception of Saudi – there are vibrant Christian fellowships in almost all major centres. Because of the rules about the meeting of Christian congregations, these are usually quite large but there are only one or two in each country. Because full-time pastoring is not an option, there is a need for mature lay leadership and/or pastors who are willing to be 'tentmakers'. In some places, the migrants themselves arrange to bring back supplies of Nepali Christian resources after their visits home: in other places and where there are far fewer Christians this is a problem. Running training seminars is difficult despite the migrants being keen to learn – for two main reasons. Due to long working hours with a shift system, seminars can only be held late in the evening. Arranging transport for migrants living across a hugely scattered area is logistically almost impossible. As in much of the Asian diaspora, there is a need for greater input into the smaller numbers of female migrants.

Seminars can only be arranged late at night after long working shifts.

The first Nepali church was established in the Gulf in Bahrain in 1993 (fellowship began in 1986). Since then fellowships have sprung up in Kuwait, Qatar and in 3 of the 7 UAEs. Gatherings are not permitted in Saudi Arabia.

QATAR

STATISTICS	
Total Nepali Population	*5 lakh*
No. of Nepali Fellowships	~5
No. of Nepali Christians	>3,000

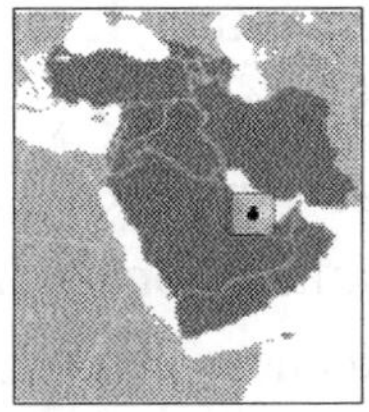

The State of Qatar is situated on a small peninsula, jutting into the middle of the Persian Gulf. It is near Bahrain, but linked by land with Saudi Arabia. An absolute and hereditary emirate since the mid-19th century, it was a British Protectorate until 1971. Originally one of the poorest Gulf

States, dependent on pearl fishing, today it is now possibly the richest country in the world. Huge oil and gas[xl] reserves were discovered in 1940 and this has led to unprecedented economic development. Its per capita GDP in 2013 was 88,314 USD (compared with 1,300 USD for Nepal). Qatar has invested heavily in infrastructure and welcomes multinationals in an attempt to make the country a major business centre. It is a Sunni Muslim country, with freedom only for Christians to meet in registered premises. Foreign workers make up over 90% of the total population, far outnumbering the native Qataris.

Nepali migrant workers are about 16% of the total population of Qatar. In 2013 there were nearly 500,000 Nepalis working in the country, coming from almost all districts of Nepal. Two years earlier, it was estimated that around 1 *lakh* of Nepalis go to Qatar each year and that the country vies with Malaysia to be the most popular Nepali destination. According to former Ambassador Mishra, 90% of these workers were arriving with irregular documents, i.e. they were essentially illegal, and this was largely due to Nepali agents in Qatar issuing them with fake visas.[151] However, from May 2012, the Ambassador started a process of verification of all workers' personal details through the embassy and in liaison with the employing companies.

Most migrants live and work in Doha but there is also an Industrial Estate at Al Khawr (Al Khor) where many work. The vast majority live in labour camps situated in the middle of their factory area. Official working hours are 8 hours per day, 6 days a week, but overtime is also possible and

---

[xl] Qatar has the third-largest reserves of natural gas in the world.

employers do not always adhere to the rules. Of all the Gulf States, Qatar employs the most Nepalis, who are the preferred nationality to do most of the unskilled labouring and construction jobs. A few (maybe 100) have executive jobs – in engineering, accountancy, and the hotel and travel industry. The women usually work as cleaners or housemaids. The former are slightly better off as they live in groups in hostels rather than being isolated in private homes. Many – if not most – are cheated and have no redress, but some manage to fight back. In 2011, five girls decided to fight against being made to do work extra to that stipulated in their contracts. They managed to flee to the Nepal Embassy and were eventually vindicated and compensated.[152]

The *kafala* system is still in force in Qatar, such that most of the migrants are essentially there as 'forced labour'. HRW notes that they "cannot change jobs, leave the country, get a driver's license, rent a home or open a checking account without the permission [their] employer." Foreign workers are 'modern-day slaves' owned by their Qatari 'masters'. However, they put up with being called 'dogs' and 'monkeys, "because 900-1,200 Qatar riyal ($250-$330) a month was far more than they could get at home."[153]

Girls working in Qatar and those men working in outlying areas have little freedom, but many do get Fridays off, when they are able to congregate in the city centre – in an area now known as 'Nepali Chowk' and enjoy *momos* or *daal-bhat*[xli] in one of the several Nepali restaurants, such as Nepali Bhansa Ghar, Sagarmatha, Himalayan Restaurant, Samsara or Nepali

---

[xli] Traditional Nepali meal of lentils and rice.

Chowk, and read the Qatari versions of the *Kantipur* and *Rajdhani* newspapers.[154]

One of the problems faced by all migrant workers is how to handle their money. An innovative scheme – the Qtel Mobile Money service – was launched in Qatar in 2011. It "provides a 24/7 facility to transfer funds instantly to… 18 major banks in Nepal." Users can also withdraw cash from a Qatar National Bank without an ATM card or even an account.[155]

In 2006/7 I was told that about 60-65% of workers in Qatar were not being paid a reasonable wage. In 2012, the basic minimum salary listed by the Ministry of Labour & Transport was between Rs. 15-25,000 (approx. 220 USD) for non-skilled and semi-skilled workers. The salary they were offered appeared good in Nepali terms, but no one told them about the high cost of living in Qatar. One way for migrants to supplement their income is to obtain a second job, but for most this is not an option. In early 2013, the Nepal Embassy in Qatar was discussing the possibility of Qatar raising the minimum above Rs. 25,000, but were hesitating because when the Government of the Philippines tried to raise the basic rate for their domestic workers over Rs. 30,000 (400 USD) the Government of Qatar imposed a temporary ban on Filipino maids.[156]

Most of the jobs offered are for non-skilled labourers. The general rule is that those who migrate without skills, stay in very low-level jobs. However, because the factors that have pushed Nepalis out of their country are basically the same for graduates, there are many educated men working as labourers in Qatar. If, because their ability is noticed, they are offered a better job, commensurate with their skills and training, when they ask for release from their current job, their original sponsor's representative may blackmail them, by threatening to expose them to the sponsor. They are given only the choice of continuing to work in a low-level job for the sponsor or get a ticket home to Nepal.[157] However, usually those who arrive with skills do get better jobs and better pay, and even a few of those who start with minimal skills do occasionally manage to increase these and improve their position overseas. Bruslé relates the story of "a young boy who arrived as a cleaner. He saved some money to take his driving licence (more than six months' salary) and now, as a driver, he is earning more than twice what… cleaners earn."[158] In 2013, however, after a joint meeting between Qatari and Nepali government officials, it seems that some high-skilled jobs may be offered to suitably qualified Nepalis and a general improvement made in conditions relating to other migrant workers in Qatar.[159]

As in all the Gulf States, deaths of Nepali workers are all too common (~200 pa), the main cause, according to the former Nepali Ambassador, Mishra, is stress related to cheating and the poor living and working conditions. The heat, especially for construction workers, is another major contributing cause, leading to heart attacks and kidney failure. Nepali construction workers have the overall highest suicide rate in Qatar.[160] "In the 12 months to July [2013] the [foreign employment] board paid about $1,500 in compensation each to 726 families whose relatives died abroad," but it was admitted that many more were never compensated.[161]

In September 2013, the Guardian newspaper published a horrific article on the Internet accompanied by a heart-rending video about Qatar. Pattisson highlighted "exploitation and abuses that amount to modern-day slavery, as defined by the International Labour Organisation, during a building binge paving the way for [the FIFA World Cup in] 2022."[162] He reported dreadful conditions of forced labour under the *kafala* system, including confiscation of passports and non-issuance of ID cards effectively rendering the migrants illegal aliens, non-payment of salary for months on end, squalid hostel accommodation, and denial of food – and even water – to outside construction workers in the gruelling Middle Eastern climate. He claimed that migrants were dying from heart conditions and accidents at the rate of almost one a day. "The overall picture is of one of the richest nations exploiting one of the poorest to get ready for the world's most popular sporting tournament."[163] Maya Kumari Sharma, Nepali Ambassador to Qatar, used hard language to describe the emirate and Umesh Upadhyaya, General Secretary of the General Federation of Nepalese Trade Unions said:

One of the richest countries in the world exploiting one of the poorest!

> Everyone is talking about the effect of Qatar's extreme heat on a few hundred footballers… but they are ignoring the hardships, blood and sweat of thousands of migrant workers, who will be building the World Cup stadiums in shifts that can last eight times the length of a football match.[164]

Even as I write, discussions are still ongoing, even raging, between FIFA, construction companies and the Qatari government as to how to solve these problems for migrants as well as footballers. Although AI never claimed that all migrants were treated so badly, the response of the Undersecretary of the Ministry of Labour was to say:

> This is an effort to undermine Qatar and an attempt to spoil its hosting of the 2022 World Cup, a conspiracy driven entirely by political motivations. There was a search for indirect excuses to achieve this goal, among them the releasing of false reports not linked to the facts around the situation of the workforce in Qatar.[165]

This was not an isolated comment. The head of the Doha Bank also said something similar when interviewed on the BBC World Service. What I found especially disturbing was the comment in the report that the 'sponsorship' system cannot be cancelled otherwise the employees might 'escape' (p.97): the kind of language that reinforces the imagery of slavery. AI discovered that among government officials, there was a general tendency to downplay the scale of the abuse. While many admitted that there may be isolated or individual cases of exploitation they insisted that 'there are no significant wider problems to be addressed.'[166] In addition, it became clear that it is not just individual employers (some of whom are multinationals) who are involved in the abuses but that there are systematic problems in the regulation of migrant employment in Qatar. Sometimes sub-contractors cannot pay workers because they themselves have not been paid. Responsibility rests with all employers but also with the Qatari and Nepal governments and manpower agents in Nepal. In particular, AI recommended that the 'sponsorship' (*kafala*) and NOC (no objection letters needed to change employment) systems should be abolished. It is only fair to add that instances of help to migrants by Qatari nationals were also documented.[167] However, I wept as I read the report: a man whose wedding was called off because he could not get home in advance (p.21), families evicted because no money was sent home to pay the rent (p.21), migrants living in squalid conditions sometimes with no AC or lighting although nearby the new stadia were ablaze with lights (p.22, 47ff), non-payment of salaries and no salary during work stoppages (p.41), 2 days' salary cut for one day's missed work but no overtime paid (p.31), migrants (undocumented through no fault of their own) who dare not go out in case they are arrested (p.36)… And they cannot 'escape' because they are frequently refused exit permits or these are only granted if they falsely sign to say they have received all salary. Then they even have to pay a fine and purchase their own air tickets (pp.39, 98-101).

> "The Gulf countries should recognise the crucial role foreign workers play in their economies and take measures to ensure that their rights are fully respected," said Brad Adams, Asia director at Human Rights Watch. "South Asian governments should join forces to press for reforms to end the terrible abuses against migrant workers that have gone on for far too long."[168]

Most Nepalis have little idea of the conditions of life and the laws in their destination country. In 2012 a Nepali worker was sentenced to 3 years in jail and fined nearly 5 million Rs. for carrying drugs into the country. In fact he was carrying a couple of handfuls of *bhang* (cannabis seeds) back from Nepal for a relative working in Qatar. In Nepal, *bhang* is not illegal but used for making a homemade pickle. He was granted bail but I never discovered the final outcome of his appeal.[169] He was perhaps fortunate that he was travelling to Qatar and not Malaysia, where there is a death penalty for carrying drugs! I heard another sad story of a young man in Qatar who tried to stand up for the rights of his fellow workers, but as a result he was fired from his job and had to pay his own air fare back to Nepal.[170]

Many interesting headlines come from places like Qatar. A happy one was, "Nepali wins 1 million dollars [87m Rs.] in Qatar Duty Free lottery."[171] A far less happy one was, "Accused of insulting Islam Nepali teacher fired, detained in Qatar."[172] Dorje Gurung had apparently responded to students who were continually harassing him for his Mongolian (Chinese-like) appearance and asked them to refrain from stereotyping people. A little later, as the harassment continued, he responded in English, saying, "How would you like it if all of you were stereotyped as terrorists." This was misinterpreted as categorising all Muslims as terrorists and when a student reported it to his father, Gurung was arrested and sacked from his post less than a month before his contract was due to end. He subsequently spent almost 2 weeks in jail with a group of other Nepalis, at least one of whom had been there for over two years. None seemed to be receiving help from the Embassy,[xlii] but perhaps because he was a skilled teacher, Dorje did get help and eventually the charges were dropped, he was released and able to return to Nepal. Had they been sustained, he would have faced 7 years in jail. Once back in Nepal and reunited with his family, he declared that he was staying put. He had had enough of travelling. He had

---

[xlii] In June 2013, *Nepal News* ran a story about a Nepali in Qatar whom the current Ambassador had tried to deport apparently because he wrote an article against her and the lack of consular services for migrants.

worked in many countries and always received respect – except for this one incident in Qatar.

Nepali Fellowships

Today, in Qatar there are huge numbers of Nepali Christians. The latest estimate given by one of the ex-migrant Christian leaders is 3,000 in 2013.[xliii] The beginnings of this vibrant fellowship have been well-recorded by Philip Pacle in Chapter 21 of *Scattered*... 'Filipino-Nepali Connections.[173]

> In the late 1996, three Nepali Christians found their way to a country with religious intolerance. Hungry and longing for the Word of God to feed their soul, these Nepalese searched for Christian fellowship. They came to know Jay, who offered a room at his place for them to have fellowship. Later their group increased in number so that the tiny room could no longer accommodate them. They moved to another room in Street No. 1. There were eight who studied the Bible and fellowshipped with one another…
>
> When the evangelism group of QICM[xliv] extended into the industrial area, they met another Nepalese named Sanji. It was at this meeting that the Filipino-Nepalese fellowship became a reality…
>
> Other Nepali believers came to Christ and were baptized at this fellowship on Street No. 1. However, there were many adversities and trials to be experienced. The tiny group was evicted from Street No. 1, and so it became difficult to meet as a group. But this handful of faithful servants of the Lord did not stop. They moved out towards 'wilderness' and exercised their faith in the 'open field', hiding behind sand dunes and avoiding getting

---

[xliii] It is estimated that in 2006 there were 300-400 Nepali Christians, but by 2008/9 this figure had already increased to 1,200.

[xliv] Qatar International Christian Ministries.

caught by the authorities. They memorized verses in their meetings as they opted not to bring Bible for security reasons. They prayed quietly and did as if they were whispering with each other so that they won't be suspected of doing anything 'illegal'.

In the early days, Nepali believers met in the sand dunes.

The Lord continued to teach and build these Nepalese. The Holy Spirit continued to move and show signs that they had to do something for harvest. It was early 1997 when some of these Nepali brothers came forward to seek the helping hand and fellowship from QICM.

The Nepali brothers were praying for a larger place for worship and God answered their prayers. God touched the heart of QICM leaders to allow them to use the adjacent place which was built just a few weeks earlier. There they met weekly. It was during this time that the name 'QICM Nepal Chapter' was formed and became part of the church (QICM).

As the number of believers grew and some brothers missed the chance to join the weekly fellowship due to the distance of their accommodation and work place from their new meeting place, the Lord allowed them to move back to Street No. 1 with a bigger place of worship. On August 13, 1997, the Nepali Christian Congregation, QNCF[xlv] was born.

Over the next couple of years, QICM and QNCF had to move twice more.

QICM and QNCF finally got its new worship house on Street No. 4 which was offered for lease with a minimal fee by a Korean businessman. A new 4x4 van was later provided by QICM for its continued support to QNCF

[xlv] Qatar Nepali Christian Fellowship.

evangelism and other ministry purposes. The Lord is blessing QNCF. It has produced very faithful servants who are instrumental in nurturing QNCF leaders and members as well as making the church a strong foundation. Some members have gone on to seminary for theological training.

As well as the help and support of the international congregation and especially of the Filipinos, one of the reasons for this massive growth of the Nepali church in Qatar is attributed to the work of the Spirit bringing unity. They used to have an annual all-night prayer vigil even though it meant going to work the next morning not having slept at all. God has blessed through all this. On at least one occasion they were able to show the Jesus film in one of the labour camps: miraculously the CID arrived just after they had packed up! In May 2009, 48 people were baptised in one group at Umm Said beach: a record for Qatar Nepali Christian Ministries (QNCM), although there are usually over 30 each time.

48 Nepalis baptized in one group.

As in all Middle East countries, worship services are held on Fridays (or sometimes Thursday evenings) but the membership fluctuates as old migrants return home and new groups arrive. Nowadays there are 3 main Nepali speaking fellowships. One is the fellowship led by Ps. Bijaya Nepali and another is led by Ps. Manohar Upadhaya (with links with S Indian Kerala Christians). Probably the largest is QNCM which has 4 branch fellowships: One is in Mansura in Doha city, another in the nearby Doha industrial area, a third is in the Al Khor Industrial Estate (about 1 hours' drive from the capital) and the newest in Sailiyah (north Doha). There is another smaller group at Umm Said, about 50 km outside Doha, and a much smaller group, mainly of girls, in Duhail, near the Atlantic University, where they work as cleaners. Nowadays the two groups in Doha meet in the same premises but at different times. The ministry is growing very rapidly, and in addition to the main week-end fellowships, there are at least 20 cell groups in hostels. A few Nepalis also attend the English-speaking international churches.

In 2006, there were virtually no ladies able to attend fellowships because of strict supervision in their hostels, and also because women do not go out on their own in Doha and men driving women, who are not close family members, can be arrested. However, the situation had improved by 2009 and at least 35 were by then attending the Mansura church, although the increase was partly due to a growing number of women working in Qatar.

As in many Arab countries, any authorised church with its own building shares its premises with many congregations. The International Church in Mansura has English, Tagalog (Filipino) and Nepali services. Partly because of the huge growth, especially in the Nepali group, and partly due to local rules on numbers allowed to attend Christian meetings, they had to divide into several sections and meet at different times. Until about 2010, this system worked well in rented accommodation in the city. Then the rules began to be more strictly enforced and churches were told they could only meet in buildings constructed on separate land allocated to them by the government. As the Nepali congregation and the Church as a whole had no international registration as a recognised denomination, they were not able to purchase land, which was exorbitantly expensive anyway. To date this situation has not been finally resolved.

Due to the rules of Muslim government and society, there are many challenges for both church members and leaders. There are no full-time pastors: all have secular jobs and work long hours as well as being involved in the Nepali church. However, partly because the fellowships are large, the leadership can be strong as leaders can work together and support each other. One of the leaders expressed how much the Lord had taught him during his time in Qatar. They experienced the Holy Spirit working amongst them but then persecution started. Thus, since 2009 most of the older and more experienced leaders have completed their contracts and left or been required to leave the country.[xlvi] A serious accusation was made against the church in around 2010 and as a result they had to stop taking up offerings. Another less serious, but still significant problem is that of providing appropriate transport for migrants from all across the city to attend fellowship. Usually big buses are hired for the town fellowship but this is not necessary in the Industrial Estate where the meetings are held in some otherwise unused property or in hostels. Finding time to arrange training seminars is also a concern for the leadership. Despite all this, they have produced an album "Voice of the Desert" and distribute a bi-monthly newsletter.

Since 2009, many of the experienced leaders have had to leave Qatar.

[xlvi] Mainly for this reason, I have not mentioned the names of current or recent leaders, or of informants.

Many Nepali workers (and even their families back in Nepal) have come to Christ through fellow migrants, who were Christian believers, and showed the love of God in practical ways. One leader shared this story with me:

> *When he heard of a group of 20 Nepalis in a desperate situation, he and a church friend visited them. They had one room with no beds: they had to sleep on the floor; a kitchen and just one shared bathroom. For 6 months they worked, all the time expecting their salary but it never came and so they stopped working. They had no money for rations or medicines and no ID cards to attend the hospital when they got sick. The Christians took them food supplies, prayed for those who were sick (who were then healed) and gave them money to go to the labour court. They asked why the Christians were doing all this and the reply was 'because of the love of Jesus'. As a result they came to the church and accepted Christ. Eventually they were able to return to Nepal and again the church helped by giving them money for the bus fare to reach their villages.*

UNITED ARAB EMIRATES

STATISTICS	
Total Nepali Population	3 *lakh*
No. of Nepali Fellowships	11
No. of Nepali Christians	1-1,500

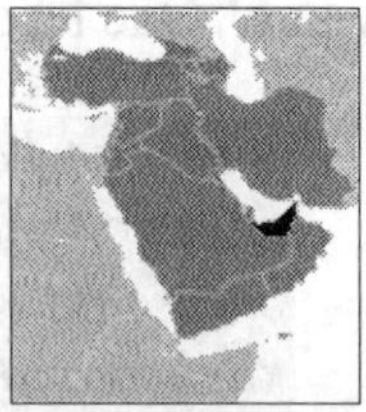

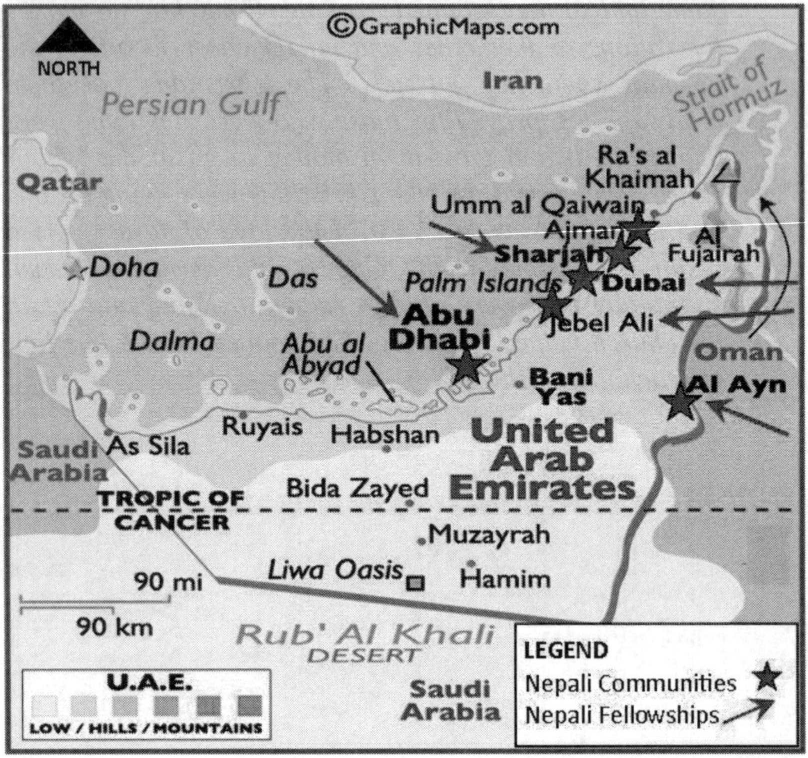

The United Arab Emirates were formerly known as the Trucial States, because of the 19th century truce that was made between the local sheikhs and the United Kingdom. They were then under British protection for about a century.

Originally, these desert countries were poor and depended mostly on the pearl industry but then in the 1960s, the discovery of oil changed everything. It led to extraordinary wealth and development. "In 1971, the six states of Abu Zaby, 'Ajman, Al Fujayrah, Ash Shariqah, Dubayy, and Umm al Qaywayn merged to form the United Arab Emirates (UAE). They were then joined in 1972 by Ra's al Khaymah."[174] Now UAE is a federation of these seven states, all ruled by their own emirs, but having one national president. Overall there is stable government and a rapidly growing tourism industry. They share either land or sea borders with Saudi Arabia, Oman, Qatar and Iran.

In the past, illegal immigrants mostly from Iran, Pakistan and India used to enter the UAE, travelling by boat and landing in the hilly part of the east coast.[175] Since the mid-1990s, this route has largely been closed and so never used by Nepalis. Throughout the Emirates there are huge numbers of migrants: one report suggested that migrants (of all nationalities) outnumber Emiratis by about 6 to 1! Many are illegal although new visit visa regulations were introduced in 2008 to try to deal with this problem. Nepalis started going to the UAE in the mid-1990s but there were relatively few migrants before 2000. The first batches, mostly ex-police and army men who knew already how to handle weapons, tended to go to Abu Dhabi to join the police & security.

According to the Nepal Embassy, in July 2012, there were around 160,000 Nepalis in the UAE, of whom 60% lived in the northern Emirates, i.e. the majority live and work in the conurbations of Abu Dhabi and Dubai, while the rest are found scattered in the other Emirates. This was probably an under-estimate: the real figure in 2013 is about 3 *lakh*. An indication of the size of the Nepali migrant population in the UAE is seen by the fact that "the UAE and Nepal have signed an air service agreement allowing its state-run carriers to operate up to 70 flights a week between the countries."[176]

Employment law in the UAE as of 2005 was quite complex.[177] Nowadays companies must employ a minimum quota of local staff before the government will allow them to request expatriates. Prospective workers must have a sponsor, who should process an employment visa for them. Workers can also originally and legally arrive in the country on a visit visa, but in order to stay long term, they must change this into an employment visa, and obtain a residence permit, and to get this, migrants must pass the medical test within 30-60 days. Only then will they get medical insurance. There are also agents who act as sponsors for those who do not fulfil the conditions for a visa, but this is essentially illegal. Change of visa cannot officially be done inside the country, so there are other agents who organize short trips to Kish Island (off the coast of Iran), or sometimes, for double the price, arrange a circular air trip without actually landing outside the UAE! In such cases, if the sponsor stays the same he usually pays the costs, but if a new work sponsor (and it is not easy to change sponsors) takes over, he will pay but then deduct the cost from the worker's salary. In fact, according to the law, an employer is supposed to bear all visa and permit-related costs, provide an air ticket back to the home country for each annual (or more usually, 2 yearly) leave and also at the end of the contract. These regulations are often bypassed and also, most employers illegally retain the worker's passports.

Two good things about the UAE are that it "offers vast

opportunities to high-skilled as well as low-skilled foreign workers"[178] and that the punishments for irregular workers are relatively small. This is probably why even those coming from less desperate situations in Nepal are prepared to put up with the conditions of illegality in UAE when the potential rewards are so much more. However, there are also other factors at work. It is not possible to get an exit visa without a passport and a sponsor's approval. Those who have some sort of social network are better able to survive as irregulars and of those low-level workers who do get into trouble, most do not take their case to the courts because it is too expensive. This puts an extra burden on the embassy. For local companies, hiring an illegal and paying the subsequent fine may even be cheaper than the costs of doing it through legal channels. In addition, the government has tended to announce an amnesty for illegals approximately every 5 years.[179] There is yet another reason why the UAE is a popular choice for migrants. They see the Emirates as a stepping stone for onward emigration to Australia, Canada and the USA. Many reckon that they stand a better chance of obtaining a visa by being in Dubai rather than in their home country.[180]

There are good opportunities for skilled workers in UAE.

The laws pertaining to migrants in the UAE are generally good and in theory guarantee reasonable working conditions. Maximum working hours should be 48 a week (article 65) with a few careful exceptions. All except daily-paid labourers should normally have a weekly day off on a Friday, and if required to work then be given a day off in lieu or

150% payment. After a probationary period of 6 months, workers should be allowed 15 days of paid sick leave followed by 30 days of half pay and any subsequent time as non-paid leave. (article 83) An employer can summarily dismiss a worker but only under certain limited conditions (article 120). A worker can leave his employment without notice if his employer fails to fulfil the contract or acts contrary to the law or if the employer assaults the worker (article 121). Unfortunately, as in so many countries, companies often manage to find ways around these rules.

It is still mainly Nepalis who fill the security jobs in UAE and especially they are recruited for the jobs near the Sheiks (as these rulers prefer to trust outsiders with this responsibility). As a result, some Nepalis are also posted to UAE Embassies overseas (e.g. Korea, Jordan, Qatar, etc.) and they also accompany the sheiks when they travel overseas, though not usually to Europe. Nowadays, however, since many more Nepalis have travelled to the UAE, the proportion working in security (including police and prison guards) has dropped to about 10% while about 70% are labourers, who work extremely hard for long hours in the stifling heat. Of the remaining 20%, about half work in malls and the other half work in a variety of other jobs, like the growing tourism industry. There are also a few professionals. For the 10 years that there was a ban on Nepali girls working as maids in the Gulf, the numbers of ladies was relatively small and those who went, did so illegally. Once the ban was lifted in 2010, large numbers applied for these posts and some measures have been taken to make the conditions better. Dipak Adhikari, deputy chief of mission in the Nepal Embassy in Abu Dhabi, said:

> We have recommended that the sponsor provides a financial guarantee and a written undertaking.... to ensure that they pay salaries on time and also allow them [i.e. the maids] to travel to Nepal in case of a death or serious illness in their family.[181]

The Nepal embassy has also drawn up a list of recommendations in relation to this. These include enforcing a minimum wage, stipulating work hours, providing medical insurance, provision of food by the sponsor and making background checks on sponsors. As a result, all UAE residents who wish to employ a Nepali maid now have to apply through the Embassy. According to the Nepali Ambassador, Dhananjay Jha, they have to submit documents including their marriage certificates and family status, make a deposit of 5,000 Emirati Dirhams and promise to pay a fixed minimum wage of 900 Dirhams a month, as well as providing food and accommodation. Jha also pointed out that in fact "many employers treated their maids well and sometimes the maids were at fault." Where problems arise, the Embassy contacts the employer and tries to settle the issue harmoniously. The Embassy also distinguishes between those Nepalis who are in jail as undocumented (often innocently or ignorantly) and those who have actually committed a crime, although even the latter are usually only 'petty criminals'. They can help genuine cases but have to leave the law-breakers to serve their sentences.[182]

With salary levels directly related to nationality, gender and religion, Asian labour migrants are regarded as at 'the bottom of the pile.'[183] The basic salary for labourers is 650 Dirhams from which 150-200 is deducted for food. However, labourers can earn at least 900 with overtime. An experienced security guard can earn 4,000 Dirhams a month (90,000 Rs.) and I heard of a clerical worker who was getting around 15,000 Dirhams a month (around 3.5 *lakh* rupees). However, according to one informant, most migrants are paid about half the salary of locals whereas many of them actually do twice the amount of work![184] 4,000 Dirhams for a taxi driver might sound good, but to receive that they have to work to set targets. A migrant from Pokhara explained to me how it works. His target is to earn 15,000 Dirhams in fares a month. If he reaches this, he gets 24% (4-4,500 Dirhams) but if he misses the target even by just a few Dirhams, the boss cuts his salary drastically i.e. by 300-500 Dirhams. Officially he can take a holiday on Fridays but in fact if he does not work most Fridays he may not reach his target. Consequently, he works very hard for 3 weeks and only when he is sure of reaching the target does he take the final Friday off.

Asian labour migrants are 'bottom of the pile' salary-wise.

Almost all the migrants are men although those (professionals) who earn over 4,000 Emirati Dirhams per month (i.e. Rs. 80-90,000) can arrange to bring over their families. However, schooling is expensive and the overall cost of living in the UAE is very high. Food is relatively cheap, but accommodation, especially in Abu Dhabi, is horrendously expensive. I have been told that one small room costs at least 2,500 Dirhams per month and most rooms now are around 3,000

Cost of Living in UAE is very high.

(Rs. 60,000). Thus a whole flat (and not a particularly big one) would cost 1.5 – 2 *lakh* rupees a month! Most Nepalis, at least in Abu Dhabi, therefore share flats. Even with 5 families in one flat they are still paying Rs. 40-50,000 each. They are given good salaries but have very high expenses: and so are indirectly cheated. In the end, therefore, most do not have their families with them.

Single construction workers are given free dormitory (bunk-bed) accommodation by their companies. These are known as 'labour camps'. Suter is very scathing about them:

> In my opinion, labour camps often bear a resemblance to prisons. It has been reported to me that it is not uncommon that up to ten men share one small room. Furthermore, some construction companies that work in three shifts around the clock let their workers share the same bed with two other shift workers.[185]

This is something I have heard about and seen in other places too. Thus both living and working conditions can be very severe and the migrants have little control over them.

The UAE is unusual among destinations for Nepali labour migrants, as theoretically they can stay as long as they want – so long as their contracts are renewed. They are also given one extra month after the expiry of their job and contract before they have to leave the country. There is the possibility for high-level migrant entrepreneurs to open their own companies, except that they can only do this with a local partner, which inevitably leads to a syphoning off of much of the profit.[186] However, there is very little chance to get citizenship, and even if migrants do succeed in getting citizenship by naturalization, they still do not qualify for the same social benefits[xlvii] as nationals by birth.[187]

Everyone must have medical insurance as part of their work contract, but for the unskilled workers, earning less than 5,000 Dirhams the level provided is not really sufficient. In 2011, Migrant Rights reported on recent research conducted at the UAE University, which showed that 25% of migrants were clinically depressed.[xlviii]

The UAE is one of the slightly less strict Gulf States and expatriates can meet and share their faith (with other non-Muslim migrants) discreetly. "The church has [almost certainly] been allowed such freedoms because of the work of a Christian hospital in Al Ain, which improved child mortality dramatically including the successful birth of a son to Sheikh Zayed, ruler of the UAE, from 1971 to 2004." However, Christians are restricted from proselytising, and "arrests, imprisonment and deportation still occur for those who evangelize or distribute Christian literature unwisely."[188] Domestic workers, maids especially, "have unique access and witness to their Gulf Arab employers, despite frequently enduring difficult conditions."[189]

There are 4 Anglican clergy in the UAE and, according to one of them, Rev Andy Thompson, they have special privileges and are respected by the Muslims, who view them rather like their own religious leaders, as people of great

---

xlvii These benefits include provision of free education from primary school to university, free health care, free water and electricity, and low-cost housing.

xlviii The study also revealed that >6% entertain suicidal thoughts and 2.5% actually attempt suicide.

authority.[xlix] They can therefore have a very big influence and are often able to develop good relationships with senior government officials. Largely because of this, Rev. Thompson has been able to become an advocate for migrants in the Middle East. He told me about a project to use the type of recorders that the Bible Society has developed for scripture readings to give advice to migrants about the laws of the country. He was working on a project to produce material in all the main migrant languages and hoped the government would give him assistance because he could tell them, "Your laws are good, but migrants need to be aware of them." Most of the laws relating to work conditions of migrants are generally good even if not always implemented by companies. Also the migrants do not know their rights. Rev. Thompson also told me that several embassies run shelters for runaway abused maids. He was not aware that the Nepal Embassy does this, but then there are relatively few Nepali maids in UAE compared with those of other nationalities.

> ***The laws in UAE are essentially good, but migrants need to know them.***

Before the Nepal Embassy was established in UAE, a government official used to visit from time to time from Saudi in order to conduct the diplomatic business. In the beginning it was the Nepali Christians who would give assistance to those in need and even when the embassy was set up, the staff still looked to the Christians for advice as

[xlix] There is also one Anglican clergyman in each of Kuwait, Bahrain, Saudi, Qatar & Oman.

well as to other organisations. As representative of the Nepali Fellowship, when Youbaraj left Emirates, he was presented with an appreciation certificate for their help.

Nepali Fellowships

There are active and growing Nepali fellowships in 3 of the 7 emirates. In all there are 11 Nepali congregations. Compared with Malaysia, the overall number of believers is similar (about 1,500) but the fellowships are far fewer and larger. This is because of the rule that Christians must only meet in designated premises in certain areas. Each church building therefore hosts many different congregations. The Nepalis rent a room for 2 hours each week and sometimes for extra meetings, but the timing is extremely strict. As the earlier language group is leaving, so the Nepalis are entering and fixing up their sound system. Precisely 2 hours later, the next language group is waiting at the door.

Every year, since 2005, the Christian groups for all the Emirates have joined together for a combined conference, alternating their venue in the different Emirates as far as possible. It began like this… Around 2002, more and more Nepalis started to arrive in the UAE and among them, many Christians, for most of whom there was no nearby church or fellowship. So, 180 Nepali believers from 5 emirates came together for the first time on 4 November 2005, for the 1st Emirates Nepali Christian Unity Conference at Christ Church, Jebal Ali, Dubai.[1] This resulted in the formation of the Emirates Nepali Christian Association (ENCA), whose leaders were drawn from four Nepali churches – Abu Dhabi, Al Ain, Dubai and Sharjah. Youbaraj Rai (from Abu Dhabi)

[1] There were 300 by the time of the 2nd Conference the following year.

was the visionary behind this and the main aim of the partnership was to "mobilize missions and plant wholistic churches and community development among the Nepali Diaspora in the UAE, Gulf region and eventually in other nations." They also planned to be involved in quality training and equipping, sponsorship of Bible Students, construction of community / worship centres and establish the Frontier Management & Communication Center (for mission-training-mobilization) in Kathmandu. After some difficulties in Dubai in 2007, the organisation was reconstituted as the Nepali Overseas Christian Fellowship (NOCF).[li] NOCF organises a joint annual gathering for members of all the UAE fellowships, to which overseas (Nepali) speakers are invited. At the 5th gathering in 2011, pastors, elders and deacons were anointed. NOCF also produces its own 3-monthly magazine, called *'Marudhan'* (Oasis). In 2012 NOCF-Nepal was formed as a link group. It is led by Titus Rai, one of the former Nepali leaders in the UAE. Together these two organisations are trying to make a bridge of relationships, fellowship and prayer between churches, organisations, businesses, pastors and other individuals in UAE and Nepal.

The Nepali church in the UAE has grown very rapidly and there are some mature leaders, but all are tentmakers. It has not been possible for a Nepali to go as a full-time pastor. However, there are full-time pastors (Indian or other expatriates) working with the registered churches, but they have to give proof of formal theological qualifications before

---

[li] To date there have been five Presidents of NOCF-UAE: 1. Youbaraj Rai (Abu Dhabi), 2. Kumar Lama (Dubai), 3. Ramesh Lama (Sharjah),. Shyam Gurung (Abu Dhabi) and 5. Peter Gurung (Al Ain).

the government will consider giving them a visa. As in other Middle Eastern countries, arranging transportation for Nepalis scattered across each Emirate is a real problem. Unsurprisingly, petrol is cheaper than water and several Nepali leaders have their own or company vehicles. Arranging seminars and teaching sessions is not easy but some from Al Ain did ITEEN[lii] studies under the tutelage of Tawa from Sharjah and BM Rai from Abu Dhabi.

ABU DHABI

Abu Dhabi is the largest of the Emirates. The city of Abu Dhabi lies on an island and it is the seat of the federal government of the UAE and the largest city in the country.

Nepali Fellowships

The Nepali work started in Abu Dhabi in 2000/1 when Youbaraj Rai, Gopal (Paul) Rai and Ram Lal BK came looking for Christian fellowship. Almost the first thing they did was to hold an outreach meeting on Christmas Day 2001: 85 non-Christians attended and some accepted Christ. Initially the Nepalis were linked with the registered Evangelical Church under the leadership of Daniel Grimmer, an Indian pastor, and the services were combined (with translation). Later a small (15-20) Nepali fellowship began before the English service. By 2009 there were 50-100 members. Then, on 14 August 2009, the Nepali group became an independent fellowship with the name of **New Revival Nepali Church (NRNC)**. Because of the restrictions on meetings in the Middle East, they had

[lii] Institute for Theological Education Extension, Nepal.

problems finding a meeting place. At first they met in a school hall and then a restaurant but now they rent a room from the Brethren Church Centre in Mussafah in one of the labour camp areas. Unfortunately this is located 40 km from town and rents and transport costs remain a problem. Nevertheless the church continues to support various people or groups in need back in Nepal as well as giving towards Bible College students and church building projects. Since independence, the church has grown rapidly and by 2012, attendance was up to 300 for special events. There had been 32 baptisms since 2007 and in 2009 alone there were 50. In 2009 the first group of leaders were anointed: the second group in 2011.[liii]

NRNC also runs several house fellowships, which are a blessing for those unable to attend the weekly worship services. One group meets in the Mission Centre and another in the open air (due to lack of a room) at the ICAD Camp. Other groups meet at Abu Al-Abyad Camp, 110 km away near the coast, at China Camp, 70 km away, and at Sahama Fabric Camp, 50 km away. There is a weekly prayer fellowship in Sabiya. There is a ladies group in Kalifa City A and a monthly ladies fellowship in the Mission Centre in Abu Dhabi town. They have also run ITEEN courses. In 2011, NRNC, inspired by Amrit Pun in Abu Dhabi, set up a Skype Online fellowship. Nowadays it functions each evening at 10pm and more than 250 people from 21 countries[liv] participate in one of three groups. They are able

---

[liii] The Nepali leaders in 2012-13 were Shyam Gurung (Snr Pastor), Som KC & BM Rai (Pastors), DB Gajmer & Sunil Thapa Magar (Elders) and Gopal Pulami & Ratan Mahatara (Deacons).

[liv] 1. UAE, 2. Qatar, 3. Saudi Arabia, 4. Kuwait, 5. Bahrain, 6. Iraq, 7. Afghanistan, 8. Israel, 9. Lebanon, 10. UK, 11. USA, 12. Malaysia,

to pray for each other, preach and teach and some have even accepted the Lord through this medium.

There are 3 main Nepali fellowships in Abu Dhabi plus 2 smaller groups in Medina Jayat and Rouis. Some Nepalis may also attend other churches. The Evangelical Church (ECC) of Abu Dhabi has a ministry to labour camp migrants. Crossroads is a group for young singles that works with FAMM (For All Mankind Movement) to collect and distribute 'compassion kits', which are simple, inexpensive and effective boxes of hygiene items used as a tool to share the Gospel. This is done through compassion kit parties when challenging Bible stories are also related.

AL AIN

Although considered separately here, Al Ain is not a separate Emirate: it is actually the 2nd city in Abu Dhabi Emirate; a beautiful – and even green – oasis city, situated on the border of Oman. Here TEAM Mission established their hospital in the early 1960s, when there was nothing but the oasis in the middle of the desert. By 2013 there were more ladies in Al Ain than in any other Middle East country (even Kuwait). There are Pakistani, Indian and Bengali ladies but also Nepalis, many who work as maids or as school cleaners.

Nepali Fellowships

There is one Nepali Fellowship in Al Ain, which meets inside the Oasis Hospital compound. Total membership is about 20

---

13. France, 14. Korea, 15. Nepal, 16. Belgium, 17. HK, 18. Switzerland, 19. India, 20. Italy, 21. Denmark. (NRNC Smarika 2001-2012)

with a regular weekly attendance of 12-15. Most of the Christian Nepalis in Al Ain work in labour (construction), but there are also some in security, a few work in a mall or coffee shop, others in Oasis Hospital and a small number in offices. There are also quite a number of maids, many of whom are illegal. The problems they face are common to migrant groups across the whole area. Labourers often do not get a regular day off: others work a shift system. They do get 1 month's holiday per year but only about 12 separated days apart from that. Only those working in the hospital get time off at Christmas and Easter. Minimum wages for labourers are low (600-1,000 Dirhams per month). Some companies pay for them to go home once every one or two years but others have to pay themselves if they want to spend their leave in Nepal. Only if they earn at least 2,000 Dirhams they can manage this.

The relative degree of freedom for Christians in Al Ain is due to the heritage of the Oasis Hospital. From those early days – when there was no other medical assistance available for rich or poor in the area, the staff built up extremely good relationships with the local ruling sheiks, such that it is accepted as a Christian hospital, with a chaplain and the church is built on the same compound.

> ***The relative freedom for Christians in Al Ain is due to the heritage of the Oasis Hospital.***

The Nepali fellowship had a dual beginning. Nepalis started to arrive in Al Ain in 1998 but there were no Christians until around 2003. While Gyanshyam (Peter) Gurung was studying hotel management in Kathmandu, a friend took him to Gyaneshwar church a few times but he did not understand until a fellow Gurung shared her testimony at a house fellowship. But then he left for work in the UAE. Shortly after this, Simon Moktan, a member of Gyaneshwar, also went to UAE and a mutual friend, who knew Gyanshyam, asked him to take a Bible for him. Simon originally planned to be in Abu Dhabi but was soon shifted to Al Ain where he shared a room with Gyanshyam and not long after that he led Gyanshyam to accept Christ. Together they started looking for a fellowship and eventually joined the English medium Filipino group at All Nations Full Gospel Ministry (ANFGM). Gradually others joined them and they began to pray about establishing an independent Nepali group. As the result of a split in the mother church in Abu Dhabi, some of the ANFGM group moved out to a hotel. The Nepalis began to meet in Simon's room, but this was not satisfactory because their numbers were increasing and they were surrounded by Muslim neighbours who might well complain. At this time, they met with Ps Stan from Oasis Hospital.

The other origin was with Ps. Stan and his wife, Carol, and a Nepali, James. Stan often went for walks around a local construction site, and there he met a couple of Nepalis, whom he invited back to chat. At that time, James, a Christian Nepali, who had previously been in Malaysia, arrived in the UAE to work in security for a Sheikh. He started looking for fellowship and claimed that an Indian Engineer had told him there was a Nepali outreach in the hospital. No one knew who this man was and some suggested that perhaps he was an angel! Carol heard about this and before long James joined

Stan on Friday evenings and together they shared with Nepalis, showing the Jesus film. The two original Nepali contacts accepted Christ at this time (c 2008) and so did a lady called Akriti. After Stan returned from home leave in 2009, this small group started outreach in the labour camp and also felt the need to start a fellowship in the hospital. This was about the time they met with Simon and Kishor, Peter, Rabin and Jacob, whom Simon had led to the Lord. When Khem Raj, from the labour camp, was transferred to Dubai, he asked Simon's group to help Ps. Stan.

After this, the two groups joined forces and Ps. Stan arranged for them to meet in the hospital, where still today they rent a room. Out of this was born the **Nepal Bible Sangati (NBS).** Not long after this, God brought about another amazing link. Dr. Siemans and his wife, Dorothy (ex-Nepal missionaries), came on a 6 week visit, and so were able to help NBS get started. By 2012, NBS had a team of Nepali leaders.[lv] Although total numbers of believers in the area may be as many as 50+, the regular attendance in 2011 was <25 with just 5-6 ladies. There are also two small house fellowships. Ps. Stan helps the Nepali leaders with preparation. Baptisms take place in the swimming pool! One limitation is the lack of festivals when they can arrange special meetings.

> ***Kishor*** *was one of the early migrant workers in Al Ain and one of the earliest to accept Christ there. Born into an unhappy home in Dharan, in which his father had 4 wives, he got himself into a lot of trouble – drinking, smoking, using pan, etc. He was also much into Tae*

[lv] The leaders were Simon (Rajendra) Dhakal, Peter (Gyanshyam) Gurung, Kishor Shrestha and his son-in-law, Ajay Shrestha, Sanjay (Mahesh) Rasaily and Bishnu Tamang.

Kwondo and training fighters. He moved between many jobs but eventually arrived in the UAE in the 3rd batch around 1999 to take up a security post. 5 years later he accepted Christ and his life was turned around.

Akriti is married to Mahesh and they have a small child. The whole family is in Al Ain. She currently works as the in-charge of the housekeeping department of Oasis Hospital. She tells her own story:

I was brought up in a strict Hindu family, but did not find it any benefit. When I first arrived in Al Ain, I worked in security but after 3 years, because they saw I did good work, I was invited onto the staff of Oasis Hospital. The atmosphere there was so good and happy. One person gave me a Bible and another kept asking me which religion I followed. By this time, all I could say was, "I don't know," but the question challenged me to search and find out. Then, one of the expatriate sisters befriended me and explained the gospel. After some time, I "turned from idols to the living God." (1 Thess. 1:9) As a Hindu, I had worshipped many idols but had had bad experiences. Now I discovered that Jesus could help me: he gave me assurance that he loved me and that I was his child. I felt God was with me (something I had not experienced in Hinduism) and that he was listening to me. Now I know the living God; I am his child. Before I had chosen idols but now I know Jesus has chosen me. Now I belong to him and want to follow him.

Peter (Gyanshyam) has also shared his testimony:

To date, ***Peter*** *is the only real Christian in his family. As a Gurung, Peter's father longed for him to join the British Gurkhas, but this did not work out and he ended up studying hotel management in Kathmandu. His first application to work in UAE was also unsuccessful but* *eventually he got a job with another company and that is how he arrived in Al Ain. On his first visit back home in 2005, he was too afraid to speak of his conversion but later, after hearing that two uncles had died young, he became fearful for his father and witnessed boldly. His parents believed but because of lack of fellowship and pressure from the community they soon backslid. Also in 2005, he met Ronnie, a Filipino also working in Al Ain, and in 2008 they were married and visited Nepal together. At first Peter's parents were unhappy about him marrying a non-Nepali but were won over by the love and care Ronnie showed them, although they have tried to pressurize Peter to take a second wife as to date Peter and Ronnie have no children.*

One interesting fact is that NBS, Al Ain supports a sister church in Nakkhu Dobato, Christko Jagriti Mandali, pastored by Tilak Thapa.

DUBAI

Dubai is the second largest emirate but the most populous. It is the foremost city of the Dubai-Sharjah-Ajman metropolis.

Nepalis live scattered over a wide area extending from Dubai to Jebal Ali to Sharjah. They are mostly men who work long hours in construction, but also an increasing number of maids. Both groups are abused and many reports of this have appeared in the Nepal press over the years:

One Tamang man said that although he and his friends had worked 12 hours a day, after their first 2 months, they then received no pay for four months straight.[190]

***Bhawana** was thrilled to have landed a beautician's job* *in Dubai for a salary of Rs. 30,000. When she got there, she discovered that in fact her agent had sold her as a maid to a rich family, and only after 18 months did she manage to escape.*[191]

***SM** said she had been sold for 8,000 Dirhams but the wife of her sponsor used to say to her, "I will cut your hands. You don't know how to clean the house." They even made her eat their leftover food, "They threw food in front of me."*[192]

***SP** said that although she was paid regularly her sponsoring family used abusive language and mistreated her. "I used to go to bed at 1am and wake up by 4 am to prepare the children for school."*[193]

***RT** was illegally sold to her employer for 7,000 Dirhams. She then worked for 16 months without receiving a single penny! When she asked about this, she was told it was being sent directly to Nepal, but of course it wasn't. When she arrived at the Embassy shelter she was 'out of her mind'. To add further insult to injury, her sponsor demanded repayment of the original 7,000 Dirhams!*[194]

Nepali Fellowships

In Dubai there are four Nepali fellowships which cater for Nepalis from Ra's al Khaimah as well. The widely scattered nature of the Nepali population in this Emirate makes transportation very difficult and largely determines which fellowship group the believers are able to attend. The bigger group, of about 100 (some said 2-300), meets in the **International Church in Jebal Ali**. The other main group is called the **Dubai Nepali Christian Fellowship (DNCF),** which has its own leadership team.[lvi] They are about 35-50 in number and they meet informally in a building rented by a Korean Christian group, linked with Cana Missions and the late Daniel Grimmer.

SHARJAH

Sharjah is the third largest emirate by area, and closely linked with Dubai and Ajman.

Most Nepalis in Sharjah work in construction companies and therefore live in labour camps. A few work in security, as drivers or in hotels. Only a few have really good jobs. The ladies work in hotels as waitresses, in offices, teaching, etc. Conditions are similar to those elsewhere in UAE and other Gulf countries.

Security, Hotel and Mall staff get one day off a week but not always on a Friday. Construction workers are usually not given a regular day off, but if work is slack then they have half day holidays. Although the law says they should have a day off, the companies simply do not give it to them. Most workers get an annual holiday and in some jobs their companies pay for them to return to Nepal for about 2 months. Others have to pay for themselves as they only get a holiday travel allowance every 2 years.

Labourers are provided with free accommodation but get only a basic salary of 700 Dirhams. In order to raise this to 1,200-1,500 they all try to work as much overtime as possible. Drivers get 1,700-3,500, but those in even more

[lvi] Their leaders are Jiwan Thapa, Ramesh Tamang, Heman Rai and Bimal Pradhan.

skilled jobs can earn over 4,000 Dirhams per month. As in other Emirates they can bring their families (meaning wives and children) but only if the man is earning over 4-5,000 Dirhams. Rent is quite expensive – maybe 1,500 pm for a basic 2 room flat with bathroom and kitchen. Better accommodation costs up to 45,000 Dirhams a month. Migrants can continue working (if they get a contract) in UAE until a retirement age of 60 years. Then they have to return to Nepal unless they have children working in UAE. In that case, they can stay on as 'dependents'. Marriage is theoretically possible but does not seem to happen with locals.

Families can join the worker but only if he earns at least 4,000 Dirhams.

Nepali Fellowships

There are more Nepali believers in Sharjah than in the other Emirates. However, there is only one Nepali fellowship. This began in Sharjah around 1999, when Ramesh Lama came to Sharjah from Bahrain with a vision to start a Nepali fellowship in the UAE. He met others, including Prem Thapa and a couple from India. They had all come primarily for work but Ramesh came because he believed God told him to come. Later, in 2003, Titus Rai joined the team. Initially, they met in Harold's house (one of the Indians) but after a year they moved to the **Good Shepherd Church (GSC)**, which meets in St Martin's. At first they attended the English service at GSC but then also ran Nepali meetings. The Nepali fellowship was officially started in the GSC hall on 7 July 2000 with a few Indians and some Nepalis.

Sometime later, there was a big split in GSC and so now the English section is very small but the Nepali fellowship has grown greatly, with 110-150 attending each week and up to 220-250 for a special event like Christmas. They need to hire four buses to transport all the Nepalis to the service.[lvii] The numbers of ladies working in Sharjah has increased and so has the number coming to church: now up to 35 attend and there is a monthly ladies' fellowship at Ps. Netra's residence. Because of the spread-out nature of the Nepali population in Sharjah, the 6 house groups are particularly valuable for those who cannot (regularly) get to the Friday worship service. They are held in Al Quoz, Sonapur, Ajman, Airport area, Sharjah city area and in Rolle. There is also a small (10-11 member) ladies' fellowship.

One of the main problems in Sharjah is getting a hall in which to meet. Meeting in an unauthorized place can lead to trouble, but sometimes they can and do meet in people's houses or even in company rooms if the company gives permission. Strictly speaking the house groups are illegal.

The Sharjah group has some relationships with the Nepali fellowship in Dubai but nothing formal, except for the annual meeting.

> ***Paul Tamang*** *comes from a Lama family in Nuwakot. He was a seeking Buddhist/Hindu and did a lot of puja.*[lviii] *He went to India, where he was told that if he bathed in the Jamuna River he would receive peace and salvation. In fact it was filthy and he got sick! When he returned to*

[lvii] The leaders are BB Gurung, Netra Bohora, JB Limbu and a group of 12 Elders (including Beg Bahadur Magar) and Deacons. Ramesh and Titus are no longer in UAE.

[lviii] Ritual Hindu worship.

Nepal, a relative invited him to church. He went along and was so touched by the worship and word that he immediately asked the pastor for baptism. In fact he only received the Lord the next day when he went to a Christian funeral, but after that he was baptized and immediately started to witness. Only 20 days later he left for Qatar, trusting that the Lord would show him a Christian fellowship. Because he straightaway began to witness in his workplace, his Hindu colleagues told him about another Christian and so he found fellowship within a couple of weeks! He has continued to grow in the Lord. Back in Nepal, he married the daughter of a pastor and then came to the UAE.[195]

AJMAN

Ajman, surrounded on 3 sides by Sharjah and linked with Dubai, is the smallest emirate by area.

Nepali Fellowships

Fellowship-wise, Ajman is combined with Sharjah as it is very close. One of the house groups meets in Ajman, but there is no separate Nepali fellowship there.

Ra's Al Khaimah, Fujeirah & Umm Al Quain

These three small emirates are situated near to the Straits of Hormuz, although Umm Al Quain has coastline only on the Gulf of Oman and not on the Persian Gulf.

Although there are fewer Nepalis in these emirates, they still face the same problems and harassment.

One typical case is of a lady who came to Ra's Al Khaimah to earn money to support the education of her younger siblings:

> ***BL** arrived in Ra's Al Khaimah seven months ago. She... was inappropriately touched by the sons of her sponsors. "When the parents were out, they banged on my maids-room door asking for sexual favours... They touched my body parts. The boys were a big problem so I decided to leave. When I found nobody was at home I packed my belongings and escaped. I took a taxi and came straight to the embassy."*[196]

She stayed 2 months in the embassy's safe house, but to add insult to injury, when the embassy approached the sponsor, he demanded 6,000 Dirhams to cancel her visa, because he had originally paid the agent 7,000 for her.

Ahmad recorded an all too familiar story from Fujeirah:

> ***SC,** 26 year old, said, "I was also meted out with bad treatment and no proper food and sleep, so I fled and sheltered at the mission."*[197]

To date there are no Nepali Fellowships in these 3 Emirates.

SAUDI ARABIA

STATISTICS	
Total Nepali Population	5 *lakh*
No. of Nepali Fellowships	Nil
No. of Nepali Christians	unknown

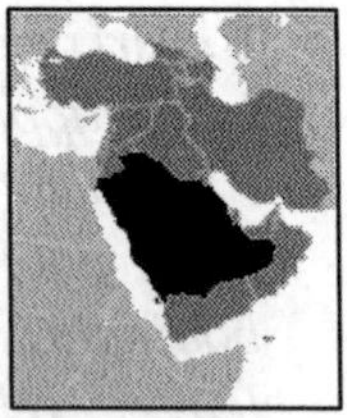

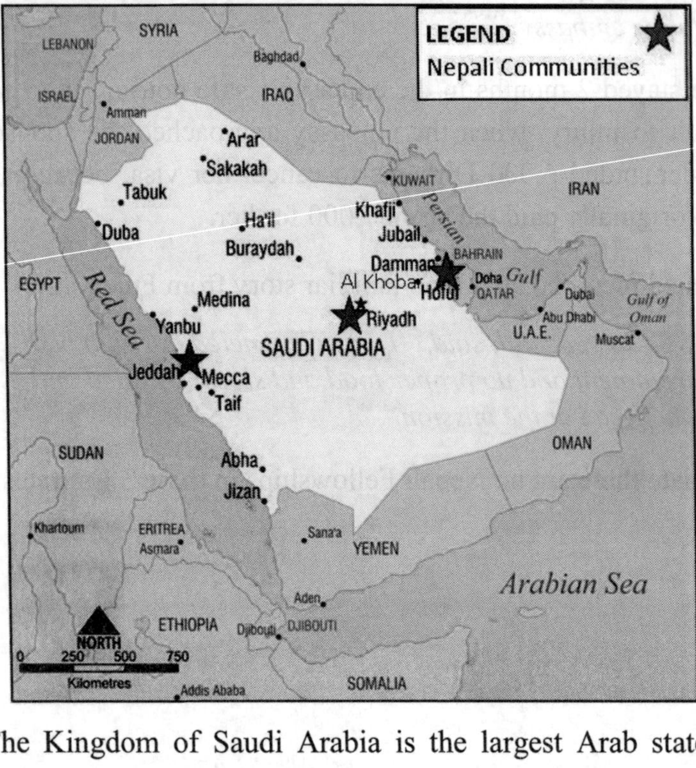

The Kingdom of Saudi Arabia is the largest Arab state in western Asia with a landmass that occupies the vast majority of the Arabian peninsula. It was founded as an absolute monarchy in 1932 by Ibn Saud and it is probably the strictest of all the Sunni Muslim countries. Oil was first discovered in 1938 but it was not until the 1980s that the country started to receive full income from this. Only then did economic development begin in earnest and this led to the need for migrant workers in the construction industry, for example.

There are an estimated 500,000 Nepalis working in Saudi Arabia according to the MoFA (2012). As many as 80-100,000 are illegal: perhaps more. Most are men and they are working as skilled and semi-skilled labourers in the Riyadh and Jeddah areas. However, there are also at least 70,000 Nepali women mostly working as housemaids.[lix] These women are all illegal as there is an official GoN ban on young women going to Saudi. However, in the Amnesty International report, Katuwal, President of Foreign Employment Agencies, Nepal (FEAN) asked pointedly, "How did 80,000 women reach Saudi, a country banned for female workers?" implying that GoN was as much to blame as the manpower agencies for allowing people to circumvent the rules. On the other hand, in mid-2012, Ambassador Pandey said that "The embassy has been traveling across Saudi Arabia in its campaign to raise awareness. We have [also] been providing orientation to workers so that they will not stay here illegally."[198] Then, in May 2013, after one year of investigation, the Ambassador revealed that 114 agents had been exposed as responsible for sending 90% of the illegal workers to Saudi. Their names had already been forwarded to GoN so that legal action on

How did 80,000 women reach Saudi, a country banned for female workers?

[lix] Wikipedia gave a figure of only 10,000, but I believe the 70,000 suggested by Pourakhi is more likely.

charges of human trafficking could be pursued. At that time Pandey estimated that 70,000 male and 50,000 female Nepali migrants were in Saudi illegally.[199] The one bright note in his report was that he claimed that of the 300 ladies working legally as maids, none had suffered problems.

One way of dealing with the problem of undocumented workers is to offer them an amnesty. This was done by the Saudi government in 2011, and then again in early 2013, an Amnesty from May until July was announced in *The Kathmandu Post* saying that, "Saudi Arabia has formally asked the Nepali mission in Riyadh to facilitate its citizens either to correct their legal status or move out of the country without facing punishment."[200] Under the terms of the Amnesty, runaway workers, including domestic workers, who had valid passports could become legal by changing their sponsor through the labour office. Those without passports would be issued with travel documents and exit visas but expected to leave the country. By 19 May 13,000 Nepali workers had taken up this offer.

The *kafala* system (see p.218) is still practised in Saudi Arabia. Consequently, one informant opined that Nepali girls should be thoroughly dissuaded from working in the Riyadh and Jeddah areas, but it could perhaps be safe in Al Khobar (in the east, near Bahrain). There are so many tragic stories of young women who have suffered during their time in Saudi that only a couple can be included here:

> *Forced to work as a maid rather than a nanny, "One month into the job, **[B]** says her employer's unmarried son raped her, with the help of three other men." Later, things got even worse. "Once, the elder son called me in*

his room and asked me to sit on his bed... I refused because I was just a domestic helper there. But he forcefully pulled me to the bed, and I kept on crying for help, but no one came to my rescue. Despite using all his [force, when] he still couldn't get control over me, he hit me with a box on my head. I became unconscious." While unconscious she was raped. This happened repeatedly, sometimes after she had been drugged in her food and sometimes just by using masculine force.[201]

Another young woman, ***Manju***, developed uterine prolapse due to the heavy manual labour she was forced into, while ***Sanam***, who had applied for a job in a beauty parlour, instead found herself trying to cook every day for a family of 48.

Men working in Saudi also face many problems, albeit not as many or as horrific as do the women. One young man has been in custody for more than 2 years—simply because he was a witness (not even a suspect) in a murder case.

Despite the figures given of deaths among migrant workers in Gulf countries (see p.108), it seems these may be under-estimates at least in relation to Saudi. In July 2012, the Nepal Press reported that 25-30 Nepalis die there every month.[202][lx] A total of 3,200 have died since 1978 (when the embassy was first opened). Nepali Ambassador, Pandey, opined that although the deaths are officially attributed to the causes as listed on p.109, in fact there are also a significant number of natural cause deaths and many are due to alcohol, but not recorded as such because alcohol is illegal in Saudi. Even when a migrant has died, the trouble for their family does not end there. Ghimire, Charge d'Affaires in 2011, explained why.

[lx] A report in onwuhk.wordpress.com in March 2011 quoted a figure of 200 per month: I hope this was a misprint!

13 documents in Urdu and English are required before an 'exit visa' is issued to allow the Nepali Embassy to fly the body back home. The death may have occurred 3,000 km from Riyadh. Thus, the process can take up to 8 months, especially if the workers were illegal and previously unknown to the Embassy. The MoFA in Kathmandu receives on average one complaint / claim every day from families, but few are compensated by Saudi officialdom and then only in amounts between 600 and 25,000 Saudi Riyals (max. 7 *lakh* Rs).

Returning a dead body to Nepal can take up to 8 months.

Not only for Nepalis, but for all foreigners, especially those in unskilled or semi-skilled roles, life in Saudi is extremely restrictive socially. I have met young Nepali girls returning from Saudi via Doha, still swathed from head to toe in black. All ladies have to wear the *abiyah*[lxi] in Saudi. Even if they have not been abused, they will have had no social life during their time in the country. They will almost certainly have been totally restricted to the house and compound in which they work, not allowed out on their own and denied access to fellow Nepalis (even those working for neighbouring families) with whom they might have made friends.

All ladies must wear an abiyah.

Nepali Fellowships

Officially there are no fellowships, though scattered believers

[lxi] All-covering garment worn by Muslim women.

try to encourage each other and even meet together. There is also absolutely no religious freedom at all. There are apparently new laws introduced almost every day in Saudi and so many are imprisoned for breaking laws they did not know existed. Unlike in most of the other Gulf countries, there is no provision made even for one shared Christian meeting place, but some expatriates do manage to meet informally in each other's houses. Some Nepalis have recently done this, although meeting together is risky. There are two types of police – the ordinary police and the *Muttawa* or religious police. These men know where the house churches are but generally do not do anything unless there is a report submitted. *Operation World* describes it like this:

> Christian expatriates live under strict surveillance; even meeting in homes as a group of believers is forbidden. Those caught can be subjected to humiliating beatings, imprisonment, expulsion and even execution. This is particularly so for Asian Christians who are often the most effective witnesses and whose governments have the least international influence.[203]

In addition, Bibles and other Christian resources are banned.

BAHRAIN

STATISTICS	
Total Nepali Population	~33,000
No. of Nepali Fellowships	1
No. of Nepali Christians	>150

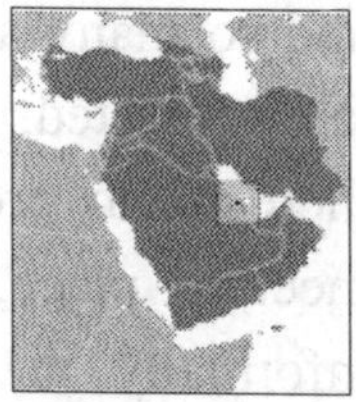

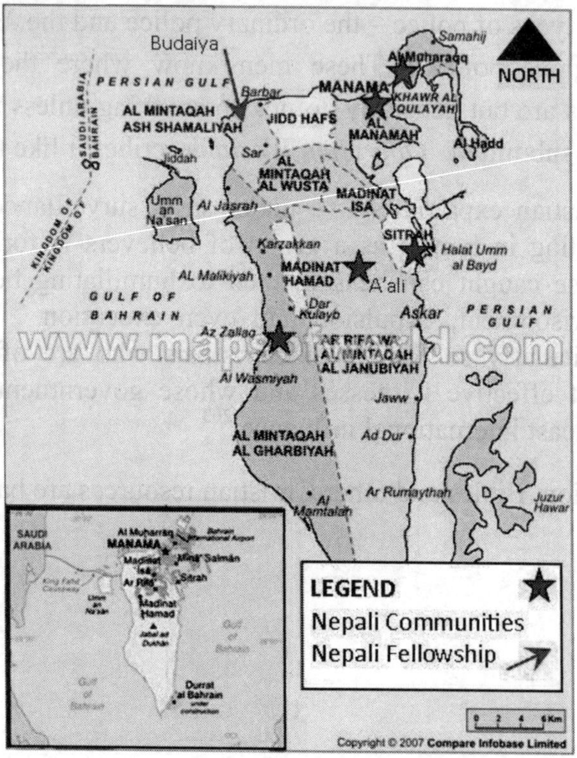

The Kingdom of Bahrain is an archipelago in the Persian Gulf, close to Qatar and linked to the Saudi Arabian mainland by the King Fahd Causeway. Formerly a Protectorate of the UK, it gained its independence in 1971.

Oil was discovered in 1932 and this led to unprecedented economic development. Bahrain is unusual among the Arab Gulf states as it is 2/3 Shi'a and 1/3 Sunni Muslim but the government is Sunni. The Shi'as have some links with Iran. It is less strict than its close neighbour, Saudi Arabia.

In 2013 there were around 33,000 Nepalis in Bahrain, according to official sources at the time of inauguration of the Nepal Embassy in September.[204] Diplomatic ties had first been established in 1977 but until recently, the Saudi Embassy had covered Nepali affairs in Bahrain.

Most migrants work as labourers, maids, in factories or security (but not in the police). There are few girls. Some men cross the bridge each day to work in Saudi, which they prefer, as although conditions in Bahrain are far from ideal, they are much better than in Saudi. The employers of those who work in Bahrain do not take away the workers' passports, so they are free. The working conditions are also much better here than in the UAE. The law regarding employment is similar to that in Abu Dhabi but rent is cheaper. There are no labour camps, so workers have to rent rooms, but they can share. There are no high rise apartments in Bahrain – only villas, each with a maid's room and a driver's room attached. Those who work there get their lodging free but are only paid 40-60 Bahraini Dinars (approx. 10-15,000 Rs.). Most also have to buy their own food from this, although Christian families often provide food. Those who work as labourers or in schools get one day off a week

Living & working in Bahrain is better than in most other Gulf countries.

on a Friday: those in other jobs work shifts and so do not get a regular day off. The annual leave entitlement is 2 months in 2 years but it depends on the company whether the workers actually get it. The companies are supposed to pay for them to return to Nepal but usually this payment is made only to those at higher levels. Locals get a week at the end of Ramadan but Nepalis only get 1 day. There is also another holiday at the end of Dec/Jan and some have 2-3 days off at Id. On the whole, Nepalis like it in Bahrain. Workers can stay as long as they want – depending on their having a job in a company. This could be 10-15 years. They are supposed to retire at 65 but this also depends on whom they know in the ministry. Company visas via agents are available for men only, and nowadays all visas are obtained online. There are no 'free' visas in Bahrain. All have to be paid for, and even these have been curtailed because of the recent problems. The system works in this way: a local man can have 5 maids working in his house and so he can get 5 visas. So he keeps 2 and the other 3 then work outside, but he has no responsibility for them.

Partly in the wake of recent problems in Bahrain, which shook the locals, there has been talk of changes. There has been an as yet unsuccessful attempt to amalgamate all the Middle East (mostly Sunni Muslim) Arab Countries (GCC = Gulf Cooperation Council) so that they can unite against (Shiite) Iran. Another possibility discussed was stopping all visas for Indians, Sri Lankans and Nepalis while accepting Bangladeshis, Chinese and N Koreans instead, because they could pay them less!

Nepali Fellowships

Bahrain has more freedom for Christians than other Gulf countries. Christian congregations are free to register, worship and allow their premises to be used by different groups of Christians. There is a Bible Society shop and even street preaching is allowed![205]

The Nepali fellowship in Bahrain began in 1986, linked with the National Evangelical Church (NEC) English language congregation. Various (professional) expatriates used to meet regularly for Bible studies and the children were looked after by one of the (Sri Lankan) maids. This girl accepted Christ and then started inviting her friends, among whom were some Nepalis. The group became known as the Budaiya Bible Fellowship. It grew and received help from some of the professionals, who ensured that everything taught or said during the Bible study was translated into Urdu, Nepali, Hindi, and Sinhala and sometimes into Tamil, and Malayalam. The leaders of each language group came an hour earlier so that they could understand the study first in their own language. One evening the group specifically prayed that the Lord would bless the Nepali group and establish a Nepali Church. They agreed it should be located in the NEC premises which was more accessible.

Later in 1986, Phillip Rai, who was working for Alwadi Transport, took the leadership and he led the Nepali group for many years, while the group continued to meet in Budaiya. After the Friday Bible Study and snacks, those with cars drove the others home to Aali, Muharraq, Sitra, Manama and other locations on the Island. Later, the group moved to another expatriate home. The husband led the Bible studies and the wife taught English to those interested to learn. When they left, the group moved again – to a house on the NEC premises. All this time the numbers were growing, and there were several baptisms (in swimming pools) each year. For the Nepali group transport problems remained, but the Holy Trinity (or Navy) Chapel helped with the funds. At this time, God planted the desire in their hearts to pray for the first Nepali Church in Bahrain. They prayed week after week for God's guidance and eventually an advisory board for the Nepali Church was formed with members from various different denominations. NEC then offered the use of their fellowship hall. It was given freely but the Nepali group was challenged to raise 10 Dinars monthly. Thus the first Nepali Church in Bahrain was dedicated in January 1993. For the first few years, membership was around 40 and the word was shared in Hindi. A joint Nepali-Indian committee was set up and one of the Indians, who had worked in Nepal and could speak Nepali, began to share the word in Nepali once a month. Several Christian leaders from Nepal visited and gave specific teaching. More than half a dozen new members were baptized each year.

By 2000, the numbers had further increased, including some from Zallaq. A 15-seater bus was bought with locally raised gifts and the church buildings were extended. At that time the Nepali Church managed to contribute 75 Dinars monthly while the English Language Congregation helped them with the rest. In 2010 further transport was arranged for those living in the south. The board was all Nepali with Man Thapa as the leader who trained up 4 or 5 others. They have even partly supported members to go for Bible Training.

As of 2012, there were 150 members in the Bahrain Nepali Church. The Nepali Assembly is basically independent but under the English Language Congregation (ELC) of the National Evangelical Church (NEC) in Bahrain as it is dependent on the NEC for a meeting room. An Indian doctor from Hyderabad is overseeing the assembly as they do not have a pastor of their own, nor is there any possibility for them to have a full-time Nepali pastor. Members work all over the Kingdom of Bahrain (and some in Saudi), thus transport remains a problem, although one Nepali brother uses his old van to collect members from different places and bring them to the church every Friday. The hall rent had again risen to Bahraini Dinars 45 per week (approx. 125 USD), which is almost all their offerings, and because of this the Nepalis had to cut down from 3 to 2 hours usage. Many of the Nepalis would like to be fully separate from the NEC as they feel that would facilitate their outreach vision better. However, the Assembly is not a registered body and therefore not legally recognized. Other problems are that they have no pastor and are short of funds. In 2012, largely because of time and funding constraints, there was no regular Bible study going on. One person, who can speak Hindi, used to hold Bible Studies (given in English and translated by Kailash) in her home, but this was a difficult venue for the Nepalis as it was near the border with Saudi.

KUWAIT

STATISTICS	
Total Nepali Population	40-65,000
No. of Nepali Fellowships	3
No. of Nepali Christians	600-700

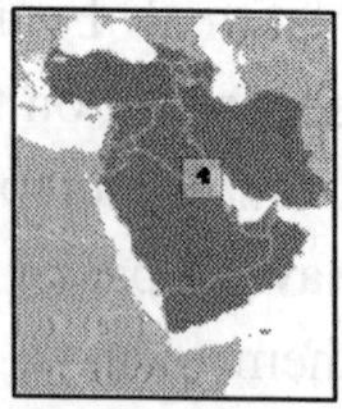

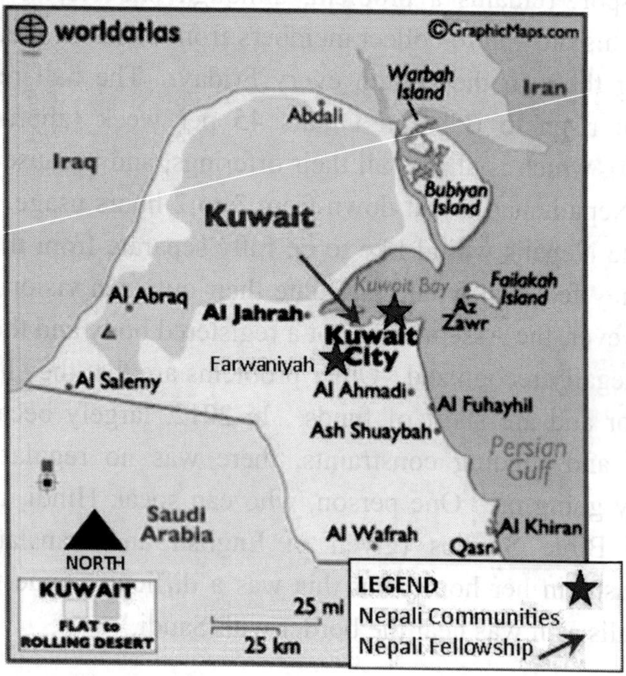

Kuwait is a small Arab state, situated at the head of the Persian Gulf. It gained its independence from the UK in 1961 and is now a Constitutional Monarchy. Oil was discovered in the 1930s and this has led, as elsewhere in the Middle East, to unprecedented economic growth. The state religion is Islam: 70%, including the king, are Sunnis; and 30% are Shi'ites, who have links with Iran. Like Bahrain, there is a significant degree of religious freedom and there are even some Christian Kuwaiti citizens.

According to Wikipedia, there are 40,000 Nepalis residing in Kuwait, mostly in Kuwait City and Farwaniyah. Other sources suggest figures of 52,000 or even 65,000. Uniquely, the majority are (female) domestic helpers, although until 2010 there had been a ban on such workers except for those taking up Government contracts. This was lifted when the new embassy was opened.

Around 75% Nepalis in Kuwait are maids.

Men are frequently cheated out of their wages and find it hard to survive, but life is often far worse for the women. Officially they have no GoN permission to work in Kuwait and so they are open to victimization and abuse (both physical and sexual). Only a few succeed in earning the high salaries they dreamt of. Despite the high numbers who end up on the doorstep of the Nepal Embassy, describing their inhumane working conditions, their employing families are rarely investigated or punished. The women are repatriated to Nepal and a new batch of innocents replaces them.

There are countless stories of Nepali women trapped in domestic employment in Kuwait, desperate to get out and yet with little hope or help:

> ***Manika*** *worked in Kuwait for 18 months, almost daily facing abuse and exploitation. Whenever she requested*

her salary, she was locked in the toilet for 3-4 days without food. Eventually she managed to escape to the Nepal Embassy, but then, because her passport was not genuine, her employers filed a case against her. After several weeks of imprisonment, she was ultimately repatriated with the help of the embassy.[206]

The press has reported on several groups of runaway housemaids.[207] Approximately 150 had recently been returned to Nepal but more than 100 were still having their papers processed by the Embassy. There has been a steady stream of such women presenting at the embassy ever since it opened in 2010. Before that, the situation was far worse for these abused women. Some were driven to the extreme of suicide, and Kani Sherpa's death in 1998 led to the ban on women going to the Gulf. The ban was removed in 2007, but even now suicides still occur when the women become really desperate. Just two of the many examples are as follows: a maid who hung herself in the house of her sponsor in December 2012 and a woman who committed suicide in her cell at the Central Jail in May 2013.

Maiti Nepal published the story of Ramkumari (not her real name) in 2007:

***Ramkumari** was often physically abused; compelled to work 20 hours a day, and had to eat their leftover foods. Intolerably, after 9 days of stay she managed to run away from the house and went to the agent office in Kuwait. Even there she was abused by the staff and was impelled to brothel [sic].*[208]

In the end, she and a Filipino friend, who had also been abused, managed to escape and then, with the help of her brother, another migrant and Maiti Nepal, Ramkumari returned safely to Nepal. As well as innumerable cases of sexual abuse within the house where they work, women are not safe on the roads. In February 2013, 3 Bangladeshi migrant workers raped a Nepali woman.[209] A different story from October 2012 is also worth noting. A young Kuwaiti man was discovered kissing a Nepali woman in his car. The woman confessed she had been paid to please him.[210]

Bina's story is only unusual in that it had a happy ending:

> *Sometimes things happen to us that we never think will or that we do not want to happen. This is what happened to me...*
> *In Asoj 2067 (July 2010), I left Nepal and flew to Kuwait, with the aim of earning a lot of money. I thought that I would be able to earn well and that what I hoped for would come to pass. When we arrived at Kuwait, an agent came to fetch me. He put me in his vehicle and we set off. As we went along the road I saw that the people were dressed so differently. I began to wonder how I would ever work with people like this? Then we arrived at the office and he took me inside. There were a lot of ladies there—young and older. Some were Nepali and some Indian. I was told to sit down. I was shocked. I did not know anyone, I could not speak this new language and the clothing!*
> *After a little while, some very fat and tall men, dressed in Arab clothing, arrived. They looked at us all and for those they liked, they gave the agent money and took them away. Remembering my dream of what it would be like here, I thought this was dreadful. They were selling people just like we sell animals in Nepal. When I thought that they were going to put a price on me and sell me like this I cried and cried. I had had this great dream of earning a lot of money and now I saw this happening. I realised I had made a mistake [coming here] but there*

was no easy way to return to Nepal. I just had to do what I was told.

The next day, a man bought me and took me to the bazaar. Four hours later, an Arab man and his wife came, and after looking at me carefully, took money out of their bag and gave it to the agent. The agent said, "Sister, now you must go and work in their house." The Arab lady signed that I should go and so I followed her. She also signed that I should get into their vehicle. In one hour, we arrived at their house.

Because I did not know the language, everything was done by signs. However, I tried hard to learn some of the language. I had to do a lot of work. I only got 2-3 hours' sleep at nights. For about 5-6 months I worked like this and then I got a fever. Even though I had a fever, I was made to work and if I didn't then they told me off. I was in a foreign country where I couldn't speak. Although I was sick, I worked for 5 months. Then my legs stopped working and I couldn't walk. I thought I was going to die. Then I said to them, "I can't work, please send me back to Nepal." But they did not want to do that and instead, took me to the Government Hospital, where I got some treatment but did not get better. In fact I got weaker. At that time I had no plans, but was able to use the phone secretly. I said to my husband, "I am ill, I can't work and they won't send me home."

The rules in the house were very strict. I was supervised in everything. I was not able to speak to anyone. I did not have a mobile of my own to use. When I asked them to call on my behalf they took no notice. I got even more worried. Then one day I was able to ask a visitor to let me call my husband, and, by God's grace, this happened. Anyway somehow there then came an opportunity for me to be repatriated to Nepal. After that, my husband contacted folks in NeMUN and they began to try to help me. Also, because this was a Christian organisation, they prayed a lot for me. I am also a Christian and my *regular prayer was that I would be able to return to Nepal. Today I give thanks—to God, for his grace and to NeMUN for their prayers. Because of these, I returned successfully to Nepal on 15th Pous 2068 (Jan 2012).*

I have realised that my desire to go overseas to earn lots of money was a mistake. When I think of the problems I had in Kuwait, in a country where I could not even speak, I realise that it is better to earn less at home in Nepal. There are many other Nepalis suffering in that country. Some have even lost their lives. Others have returned home disabled.

So—rejoice in your own family, society and country.

Over 80% of the workers who seek help from the embassy are 'illegal'. The embassy said that in a four-month period in 2011 it issued over 3,500 travel documents.[211]

In March 2011, the horrific story of 50 men abandoned in the desert emerged:

All had arrived in Kuwait with only visit visas. After they asked their employer to give them valid documents, including the driving license and work permits, "they were ferried in a bus to the desert". Homnath, one of the group, said, "They have left us at a house without anything. There is no food and there is no water." A Nepali organization provided them with a one-time meal: the nearest settlement is two-hours walk away, but who would walk in the heat![212]

There is another side to illegal workers in Kuwait that only indirectly involves Nepalis. Since Bangladeshis are restricted from working in Kuwait, they have evolved a system for getting there: they travel on their own Bangladeshi passports with a tourist visa via Dubai to Saudi, where they 'lose' their own passports, buy Nepali passports off an agent and then enter Kuwait as if they were Nepalis. However, all Nepalis who reach Kuwait now have to go to the embassy for a police report before they are issued with a work permit. This is where many Bangladeshis have been uncovered and arrested.

Kuwait has experienced religious freedom ever since it formally became the State of Kuwait in 1961, and this is enshrined in its constitution. "The one restriction that Kuwait makes upon the Christian community is that it does not proselytize."[213] Kuwait is more tolerant of other faiths than many Middle Eastern countries, and this is largely because foreigners make up the majority of the workforce,[214] and because of the positive heritage of the early (medical) missionaries. Interestingly, much of the child-raising is left to the foreign maids and nannies. The Filipinos have seen this as a mission opportunity, but in view of the high level of abuse, I wonder if the cost may not be too high?

Nepali Fellowships

Like many other Middle Eastern Arab states, there are few churches allowed. The one Evangelical Church compound in Kuwait hosts 60 different congregations or 20,000 Christians. The Nepalis have 3 fellowships of their own, pastored by Agam Limbu, who first went to Kuwait in 1998, but became pastor only in 2001. He reckons that today there are 6-700 Christians.

OMAN

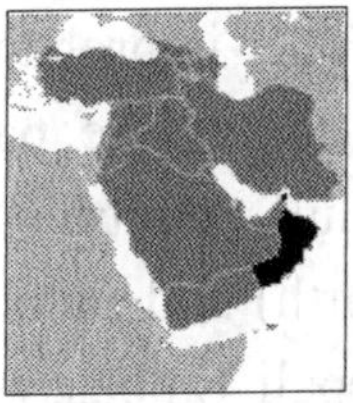

STATISTICS	
Total Nepali Population	~40,000
No. of Nepali Fellowships	?2
No. of Nepali Christians	? <50

The Sultanate of Oman is situated at the SE tip of the Arabian peninsula. Unlike most other Arab states, it was never part of the British Empire and is still an absolute monarchy. Most Omanis are Muslim; over half of them are Ibadis and of the rest, most are Sunni, making the country somewhat different from all the other Gulf States. Christian congregations are allowed but must be registered.

There are estimated to be a total of only 40,000 Nepalis in the country, of whom just under half are documented, but there is also an active NRN association. In contrast to the other Arab countries there are relatively large numbers of ladies, despite the fact that women are officially banned. This is probably due to illegal trafficking and the fact that maids are paid significantly more in Oman than in other Gulf countries.[215] The two main centres are Muscat (in the north) and Salalah (in the south). Until 2013 there was no Nepali Embassy in the country but then GoN agreed to work towards opening a residential embassy in Muscat by the end of the year.

Many of the men work on road construction projects 35 or 80 km distant from Salalah. Others in the capital are professionals. They have no problem in travelling on their own, except for the distance. Those who can, often go to central park on their day off. All the girls are maids in the homes of Omanis, who do not usually give them a weekly day off. Some get a day off a fortnight; others only once a month. Many are not allowed (nor is it advisable for them) to go out on their own, except perhaps to visit nearby houses, although some are not allowed to do even that. I heard that many of these girls are 'ruined', which probably meant they had been abused or allowed themselves to be.

Nepali Fellowships

There are 4 centres for international Christian worship in Oman but to date only 2 specific Nepali fellowships. In Muscat, the Oman Nepali Christian Fellowship (ONCF), currently a dynamic house fellowship, has 12-15 members but is expecting to move to a hall in the Protestant Church of Oman (PCO) in 2014.[216] Mainly due to distance other Nepali Christians attend other churches. Total numbers are therefore not known. In the south – in Salalah, where a large number of girls work, there is a small group of up to 30 Nepalis, mostly maids. They meet at the English Speaking Congregation (ESC). This is on the official church compound where all the churches are situated and so is legal. Other meetings are technically illegal. ESC even has a Bible Society bookshop which can supply Nepali Bibles – fortunate as some Christian girls arrive without bringing one. Sadly it has no other Nepali literature, even hymnbooks. Some sponsors let the girls go to church or to special (Christian) activities as, for example, at Christmas. Other sponsors only let girls who claim to be Christians go to such meetings because that is apparently the law. I met one girl who lied about this in order to attend but was still not given permission. Because the men live so far away from Salalah, they cannot get back to their hostels in the evenings after a meeting. Even to attend in the daytime, if they get a weekly day off, is difficult as there is a paucity of transport.

Partly because of the preponderance of girls and partly because they are working as maids, the Salalah Nepali fellowship has specific leadership problems. One man I met in 2008/9 was a coordinator rather than a leader. Many of the ladies can only attend sporadically (when they are given permission by their sponsors). Most are young and not well educated, therefore communication with leaders of the English congregation is limited. In 2008/9 there was a Hindi-speaking couple working in Salalah, but they may have now returned to India. Nevertheless, the fellowship is growing slowly. A few girls had believed while in Oman and one girl accepted the Lord after the Christmas meeting when I was there.

OTHER MIDDLE EASTERN & MEDITERRANEAN COUNTRIES

YEMEN*

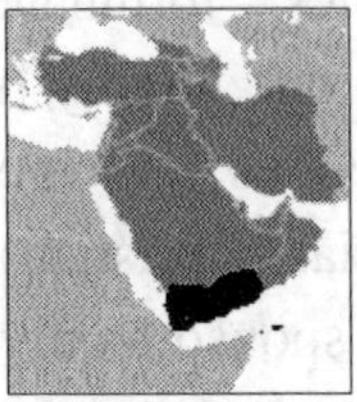

The Republic of Yemen, strictly speaking, is not a Persian Gulf State but it occupies the SW tip of the Arabian peninsula, adjoining Oman and many islands. It is one of the oldest civilizations in the Middle East and tradition holds that the Queen of Sheba came from Oman. Nowadays, however, it is the poorest of the Arab nations as it has minimal oil resources and a lot of its population are tribals. The majority of the people are Muslim, about 50:50 Sunni and Shi'a with a small Sunni majority, but there are also a few indigenous Christians. There is a degree of religious freedom but no possibility to proselytise.

I have not discovered any information about resident Nepali workers or any Nepali Christians.

IRAQ* – Not allowed

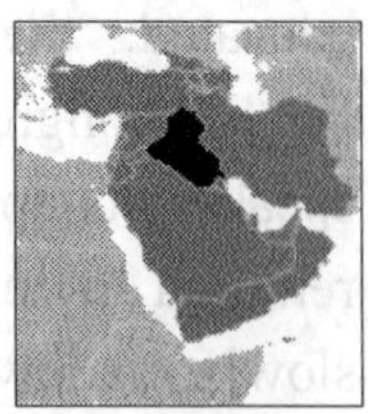

Iraq is a large republic in the Middle East, situated largely in the area that used to be known as Mesopotamia. It was home to many ancient civilizations. Previously part of the British Mandate, it gained its independence in 1932. Although a monarchy had been established in 1921, it became a republic in 1958. The state religion is Islam and of its adherents, 2/3 are Shi'a and 1/3 Sunni (including the rulers). There are a few, but rapidly dwindling numbers, of native Christians.

Iraq is the one country on the GoN list which had been clearly disallowed to Nepali migrants. This came about because during the war in Iraq, and after 12 Nepalis were assassinated in 2004, GoN imposed a ban on further workers going there. However, Nepalis still continued to find their way into Iraq, tempted by the relatively high salary they could earn, despite the very definite risks.

In August 2010, GoN finally decided to lift the ban for the sake of the 30,000 Nepali workers in Iraq, who were likely to lose their jobs because the US Central Command had decided to insist that contractors should remove workers who were there illegally. It is not clear whether Nepalis are now allowed to go to Iraq for other jobs.

I know there are Nepali Christians in Iraq but have no knowledge of any fellowships.

JORDAN

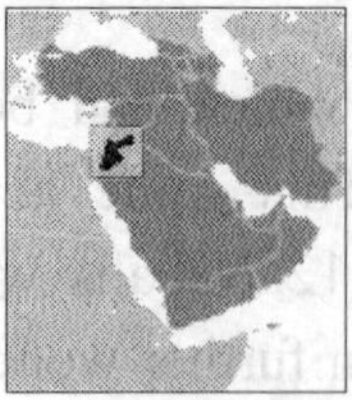

STATISTICS	
Total Nepali Population	4-5,000
No. of Nepali Fellowships	1
No. of Nepali Christians	~100

Jordan became an independent state in 1946 and the Hashemite Kingdom of Jordan was fully established in 1949. It has some oil and gas reserves but these have not been really developed. It is a Muslim state with a dwindling minority indigenous Christian population, and limited religious freedom – to worship but not proselytise.

It is estimated there are 4-5,000 Nepalis working in Jordan. Many work in the garment industry and around 100 are employed in the Royal Palace. In early 2013, the story of five women working in a Jordanian garment factory came out. They claimed to have been 'exploited, ill-treated and harassed by their employers and local youths'. A larger group of 100 women were also wanting to return to Nepal, but the Nepali Ambassador to Saudi Arabia, Udaya Raj Pandey, said that "Our embassy was not even informed of the presence of Nepali women in the Jordanian industry. Earlier, the government would provide work approvals only after verification from us, but they did not consult us in this case." In fact, they had all got to Jordan 'legally' through the SCC employment agency, having paid Rs. 40-50,000 each, and then felt cheated as the manpower company had promised them a salary of Rs. 22,000 but they were only getting just over half of that despite working an 18-hour day and being without proper food and lodging. Although the spokesman for the manpower company claimed that the women were exaggerating the situation, he set things in motion to bring the women home.[217] By March, the women had been safely repatriated by the Government under pressure from and through the efforts of the Women's Rights Protection Alliance, who paid for their passage home. Subsequently, the Pravasi Nepali Coordination Committee (PNCC) has filed complaints on their behalf against SCC.[218]

Nepali Fellowships

Until 3 years ago, when they heard of the Indian fellowship, in Mafraq led by Abraham Mani, some Nepalis from the Al Dulayil area used to go to an Arab church in nearby Zarka. Nowadays there is an active multilingual group of Indians and Sri Lankans as well as Nepalis, who meet in Mafraq, 80 km northeast of the capital, Amman, and at the junction between two industrial zones, Irbid and Al Dulayil. Ps. Nour generously allows them to use the premises of the CAMA church. Some Nepalis arrive without their personal Bibles, thinking that this is not permitted, but in fact limited Christian literature is available. The Nepalis have even established a 6-member gospel band called 'Nepali Chautari'. Roopa Abraham tells of the beginning of the fellowship:

> *A Nepali brother named Yogin used to go to the Arab church but longed to attend a gathering where he could pray and worship in a language he understood. Then, one day in 2010, as he passed by his dormitory, he overheard an Indian brother named Kiran talking on the phone and sharing the gospel with someone in Hindi, which Yogin understood. He waited for this brother to*

finish talking and introduced himself. This led Kiran to invite Yogin to the Friday fellowship, and that was the beginning of a few Nepalis attending this meeting. Slowly the word spread and other believing Nepalis began attending and also inviting their friends and roommates.[219]

Nowadays, there is a weekly attendance of about 30-50, including enquirers, and the church arranges a private bus for them as it is a 60 km round trip from their factories. In fact it is quite a sacrifice for them to come as they have so little free time with 12-14 hour working days Saturday to Thursday and only one day off. To spend 6 hours (including travel) coming to the fellowship really shows their commitment. During the week, Mohan Bahadur Baiju leads a small fellowship for 5 brothers most evenings in their hostel, helping them understand the Bible and reach out to their friends as well as praying. Each year a small group of new believers are baptised. This takes place in the River Jordan, close to where Jesus himself baptised. ***Pan Bahadur***, one of the first Nepalis to accept Christ in Jordan tells his story:

I am from a Hindu family and have a wife and three children and I used to worry about responsibilities back in Nepal and so would drink heavily to overcome the sadness in my heart. Sometimes I drank so heavily that I would vomit and make a mess in my room and would not be conscious of my surroundings. At those times, Mohan and his friends treated me with love, cleaned my vomit, patiently took care of me and gave me good advice. I wondered why they should do this in spite of my shameful behaviour and so they introduced me to Jesus. Finally I accepted him and the same day I stopped drinking. Now I have joy and peace and am praying for all my family in Nepal to put their trust in him.

LEBANON

STATISTICS	
Total Nepali Population	>8,000
No. of Nepali Fellowships	?
No. of Nepali Christians	10-15

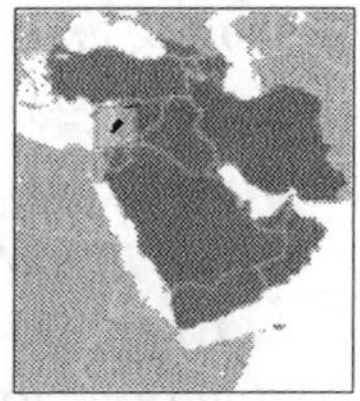

One of the oldest civilizations in the world, the Lebanese Republic is situated on the Eastern Mediterranean coast, bordering Israel and Syria. It gained its independence from France in 1943. Earlier it was mainly a Christian country but today the population is approximately 1/3 Christian to 2/3 Muslim, with about equal numbers of Sunnis and Shi'ites. There is a large degree of religious freedom with all groups having to be represented in the government.

One source suggests that in 2012 there were 8,032 Nepalis in Lebanon, but this was the official figure for legal migrants and many others are undocumented and there illegally. Pokharel gave a figure of 17,000 of whom 95% are women. As in so many of the Middle Eastern countries, "Lack of adequate legal documents and illegal migration are the main reasons behind Nepali women's miserable condition in… Lebanon," according to one migrant rights activist, Renu Rajbhandari.[220]

In late 2011, Arpana Adhikari revealed the horrific story of a lady called ***Pabitra,*** who had gone to Lebanon to earn money to support her other-abled husband:

> *Working as a domestic, she immediately faced problems and abuse. Interestingly, all through the account her*

employer is referred to as her 'owner'. On one occasion Pabitra worked for two weeks without food. After 6 months of this kind of drudgery and no salary, she locked herself in her room and asked for her salary. As a result they gave her just half of what she was due. It seems that in this case, the biggest problem was a cruel female 'owner'. One day Pabitra heard this woman planning to kill her, but the very next day the owner's husband and daughter took her to the airport and immediately sent her back to Nepal, but without paying her salary![221]

According to Pokharel[222], Lebanese recruiting agencies and employers often choose to hire Nepali ladies as domestic workers as it is easier to cheat these women because the Embassy or Consulate does not scrutinize or contest their contracts. However, there is now a new Standard Unified Contract, approved by the Lebanese government, although many agencies have not yet started to use this.

Right across the Middle East, domestic workers especially are viewed as inferior beings and exploited. Pokharel reckons that about 70% are badly treated in Lebanon. Common complaints include "non-payment or delayed payment of their wages,[lxii] the forced confinement to the workplace, having no days off, working outrageously long days, sometimes 17 plus hours a day and verbal and physical abuse" as well as sometimes being "sexually abused by their employers or their employer's friends."[223] All this has led to a high rate of suicides as "these women feel lied to and trapped with no way of escape." Some women have died in escape attempts, but it is just labelled suicide and the matter not fully investigated. And so the abuse continues.

[lxii] Nepali domestic workers are promised a wage of 150 USD per month but often receive no more than 125.

In Lebanon, members of the NRNA have been active on the behalf of abused migrant domestic workers. They have provided transportation and translation as needed, food (while workers are in Beirut's Immigration Jail and not fed), and – in liaison with the Nepal Embassy – arranged for the bodies of those murdered or who committed suicide to be sent back to Nepal. In the same way, Caritas, who has also been advocating on behalf of these domestic workers, runs a safe house to where abused women can flee, but sadly most migrants are unaware of this provision.

Similarly, the situation for Nepali soldiers working in war-torn areas of the Middle East is always hazardous. Even though Lebanon is not currently one of the most dangerous of postings, a Nepali soldier working for the United Nations Interim Force in Lebanon (UNIFIL) died in May 2013.[224]

Nepali Fellowships

There are a few Nepali Christians and there used to be a small Bible Study group. Currently there is no fellowship.

SYRIA

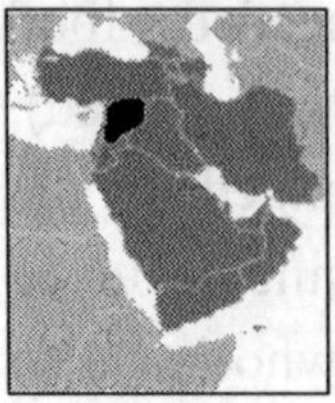

Damascus, the capital of the Syrian Arab Republic is the oldest continuously inhabited city in the world. After the 1st World War, Syria became a French Mandate, but gained its independence in 1946. It does have oil reserves but these seem to be declining. It is a Muslim country with a small number of indigenous Christians. The majority are Sunni Muslims but the rulers (up to 2013) were Shi'a Alawites. There has been, up to now, a degree of religious freedom. In view of the political struggle and violence in the country at the time of writing, no one knows what the future will hold.

I have not found evidence that Nepalis have been working in Syria as labour migrants. However, in July 2013, *Nepal National* reported that GoN had "decided to send Nepali peacekeepers under the UN flag to Syria to help in the establishment of peace and order." MP Ghimire (Minister for Foreign Affairs) informed that 130 Nepali Army personnel would be deployed in July and a further 130 in September 2013.[225]

ISRAEL

STATISTICS	
Total Nepali Population	7,000
No. of Nepali Fellowships	? <5
No. of Nepali Christians	c 100

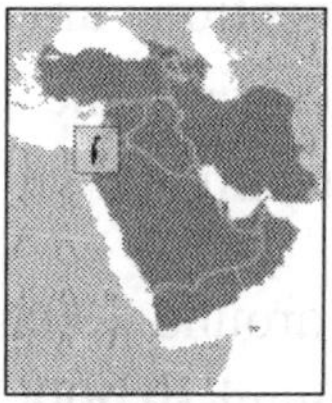

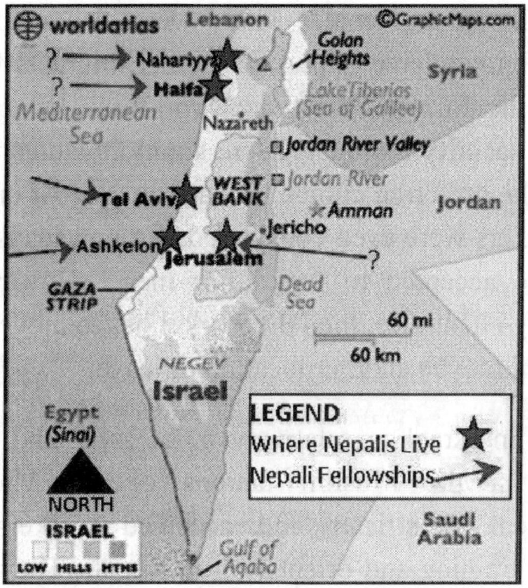

The State of Israel was established after the 2nd World War, in 1948, as a homeland for Jews who had survived the holocaust. It is now democratically ruled as the only Jewish state in the world. However, it is totally surrounded by Islamic countries, except where it borders the Mediterranean Sea. The country's borders are quite different from those of Israel in Old or New Testament times and in three places (the Gaza Strip, the West Bank and the Golan Heights) these borders are disputed by the Palestinians. 75% of the population are Jews, though not all practise their religion. There is a high degree of religious freedom. Israel is thus an exception among the Middle Eastern / North African countries: the only one that is not wholly or significantly Muslim and very restrictive for Christians.

In around 2008-10 the numbers of Nepalis in Israel peaked to around 30,000, but have now dropped to about 7,000 as many have moved on to different parts of Europe or the USA or returned home to Nepal. There were also many illegals. Nepali migrants have (along with other migrants from Asia) replaced the former Palestinian workforce, which was cut down for security reasons. There are more ladies in Israel as they are the preferred choice for care givers. At one time, no male workers were even considered, but nowadays male care givers are accepted to look after men. However, if the employing client dies, then the worker has to move to another family and maybe another location or leave.

Working in Israel is relatively a lot safer and nicer than working in the Muslim nations of the Middle East. Recruitment is stricter and accepted workers have to complete training and orientation in Nepal. They are taught the basics of Hebrew, Kosher cookery, how to be caregivers and other facts of life in Israel. The down-side is that the fees that manpower agents demand for organizing placements in Israel are therefore much greater. Even some years ago it was 4 *lakh* but is now 10 *lakh*. Also, the Israeli Government is cracking down on any illegal workers and, at one time, stopped requesting workers from Nepal, apparently because the Nepali Government had paid no heed to repeated Israeli requests.[226] Nevertheless, in general Nepali (and Filipino) workers are liked in Israel.

Although the care givers do work on their own in homes, this work is not to the same degree difficult or dangerous as in the Muslim countries. One reason is that there are two systems: if the client has a family, then the caregiver can live out while if there are no family members in the house, the caregiver is expected to live in. Most are given a weekly day off or overtime payment in lieu of this. The family covers for the day off. There is also a much greater freedom of social life in Israel. Even days off can be flexible as they are allowed to get a friend to cover if they want to change the time. However, one Nepali migrant caregiver, employed in the home of a senior Israeli minister, said she had been verbally abused and sometimes denied meals or days off. These claims were denied although this is not the first time this minister's wife has been accused of abusing her domestic staff and leading an extravagant lifestyle at the expense of her husband's business donors."[227] Sad, and politically convoluted as this story obviously is, the interesting thing is that it is the only one I have found about this kind of treatment of migrants in Israel in comparison with the dozens – hundreds – from Muslim nations.

In July 2013, news of an advanced agricultural training scheme in the Negev of Israel for a total of 200 Nepali students, who were "selected through lottery and interviews from among the family members of Small Farmers Agriculture Cooperatives (SFACLs) associated with the Small Farmers Development Bank." On return, they will be expected to apply and share their knowledge.[228]

Nepali Fellowships

Israel is a Jewish state but there are many different kinds of

Jews – from the very orthodox to the secular and also some Messianic Jews. Although open preaching is frowned on, there is significant religious freedom for the migrants. They do have a weekly day off, although not necessarily at the time when there is a Nepali fellowship. The first Nepali Fellowship – **United Nepali Church** – in Israel was established by Ps. Jonathan Sunuwar in a park near the central bus station in Tel Aviv. Later, this group split up and in 2009 Jonathan had to move to the north. While in Nahariya, he started another fellowship: now he is in Haifa. It is not clear whether these two groups are still meeting. Another leader, who is now in charge of the Tel Aviv church is Ps. Maya. With a majority of female members it is good to have a female leader.

At one time there may have been as many as 5 Nepali fellowships in the country, but fewer now with fewer migrants. All are small and they meet on a Saturday or Sunday morning. The biggest is in Tel Aviv, established around 7 years ago in 2006 and with a membership of up to 80. Ps. Daulat was in the Tel Aviv church for a while but then left to start his own fellowship. Nowadays, although still based in Tel Aviv, he is involved in leading tour groups all over Israel but not, as far as I know, in leading a regular fellowship. There was at least one group in Jerusalem, led for a while by Ps. Binod. He came to Israel around 2008 but in 2012 he was sent back to Nepal by the government due to his illegal status. This group has not continued. The small group (6-10) in Ashkelon seems to be separate from the others and run by a local Israeli Yeshua believer, Orel (Thulo Dai), who opens his home for their meetings. At first they had no musicians but then Bijay Rai began to play his guitar and was able to set up a choir group. Bijay also told me about the tour groups which he, like Daulat, used to lead. They were an amazing opportunity for outreach among their fellow Nepali migrants. On their days off, the group would visit some of the historic sites in the Holy Land and Bijay would be able to explain from his knowledge of the Bible, the significance of these places and maybe even lead a short time of worship. Baptisms are unique as they are held at the River Jordan. Migrants can arrange special programmes at the times of Nepali festivals. While numbers are nothing like those in the Arab countries or Malaysia, the Lord is working and migrants have reported several miracles.

> ***Maya*** *was working in Israel but over a period of time she slowly began to go lose her sight and eventually became effectively blind. Because of this she was about to be sent back to Nepal, but at this time she found herself living in the same apartment as the church in Tel Aviv. Ps. Binod witnessed to her and prayed for her – and she was healed and believed.*[229]

> *Ps Binod also prayed for a couple who had been married for 9 years, but had no children. They believed and later had a son.*

With relatively small numbers and the need for workers to move to another place if their assignment comes to an end, leadership is not always easy.

AFRICAN COUNTRIES

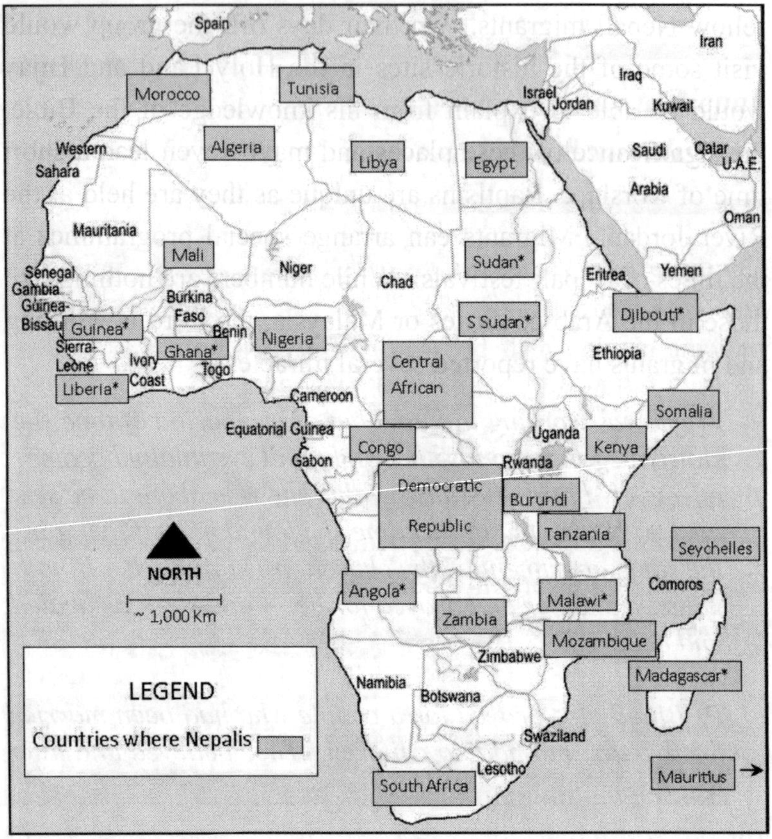

Nepali migrants are known to have travelled to all the countries marked on the map but no details of numbers or of Nepali Christians or fellowships are available for most of these.

Nepali labour migrants have worked in most ***North African Islamic countries****, whose economies largely depend on oil revenues, but not in such numbers as in the Gulf States. Since the 'Arab Spring' numbers have declined dramatically.*

The State of **LIBYA** gained its independence from Allied occupation in 1951 and was then a kingdom until 1969. From 1969 until 2011 it was the 'Great Socialist People's Libyan Arab Jamahiriya'. Oil was discovered in 1959 and in the 1970s the economy grew dramatically. It is a Muslim country and most people follow Sunni Islam, but there is also a small indigenous Christian population.

According to the MoFA just over 3,000 Nepali migrant workers were based in Libya at the time of the Libyan Civil War in 2011/12. Most were employed as construction or industrial labourers in Tripoli, Misrata, Derna and Benghazi. By the end of March 2012, the last 125 Nepali workers were on their way home via Tunisia. Others had already left via Egypt or Tunisia, but many had spent several months languishing in camps, suffering poor conditions and food shortages. These were all the workers known to GoN but the Government expressed concern that there might have been other Nepali nationals in Libya 'on personal work.'[230]

The Government of Nepal had only opened up Libya as an allowed destination for migrants in 2009, when 2 years later workers had to be repatriated, but by August 2012, the FEPB was considering reopening Libya (and other banned countries), saying, "In view of a growing number of Nepali job-aspirants visiting those countries illegally via India, we have decided to open those countries for Nepali workers if we find the countries safe."[231]

Many migrants to Libya and other parts of N Africa choose these destinations because they are jumping off points to reach Europe. However, I have not heard any specific stories of Nepalis entering Europe this way.

There is limited religious freedom but few Christians and I am unaware of any Nepali Fellowships in Libya.

*Nepali migrants have reached many **Sub-Saharan African countries**, although many of these countries are not on the GoN allowed list. I have not discovered any statistics.*

Inevitably, Nepali soldiers, serving with the Gurkhas or the UN Peacekeeping Forces around the world, in countries like the **CENTRAL AFRICAN REPUBLIC*** do occasionally get injured or killed. This is an occupational hazard, but others travelling independently to non-allowed destinations to work in dangerous projects, also face the same risks.

> ***KB** was employed with MIs Jaguar Overseas and involved in the construction of a cement plant in Bangui, the capital of the Central African Republic. He was inadvertently killed by French troops guarding the airport in the war-torn country.*[232]

During the colonial era, some Nepalis were shipped to Natal as indentured labour.[lxiii] It was then not until the 1980s that Nepalis really started to travel to **SOUTH AFRICA**. Today there are still only a few living in the country: maybe 150, based mainly in and around Pretoria and Johannesburg. They are nearly all professionals.

A story from 2012 illustrates several of the problems faced by workers who travel to non-allowed destinations, using the services of unscrupulous agents. A group of 20 Nepali workers was recently rescued from **MADAGASCAR***.

[lxiii] Perry, 2001:36

They had paid Rs. 300,000 each to an agent to obtain what they thought would be well-paid employment in a hotel. What exactly happened to their job and salary is not clear, but when they could no longer afford to pay their food and accommodation bills, the hotel owner cut off the supply of water and power to their rooms. As Nepal does not have any bilateral agreement with Madagascar, the Nepal Embassies in Egypt and S Africa were called in to help. Eventually the S African Embassy was able – and not for the first time – to help the stranded Nepalis. A post script to this story is that at the time of writing the article, *Ekantipur* was able to report that one of the agents had been arrested.[233]

Nepalis have been permitted to work in **MAURITIUS** since 2009, although some may have arrived as indentured labourers in the 19th century. According to the Ministry of Labour & Transport there may currently be around 500 Nepalis working there, mainly in the sugarcane industry and tourism. They are based around Port Louis and Petit Raffray (Goodlands). Like migrants elsewhere, they usually have to take out loans to pay the agents who arrange the work for them. In addition, at least some groups are housed in broken down and crowded dormitories and grossly underpaid. In March 2011, a group of Nepali and Bangladeshi workers went on strike, protesting a monthly food allowance of only Rs. 600 and the fact that their quarters had not been supplied with domestic water for over 3 months.

WESTERN & CENTRAL ASIAN COUNTRIES

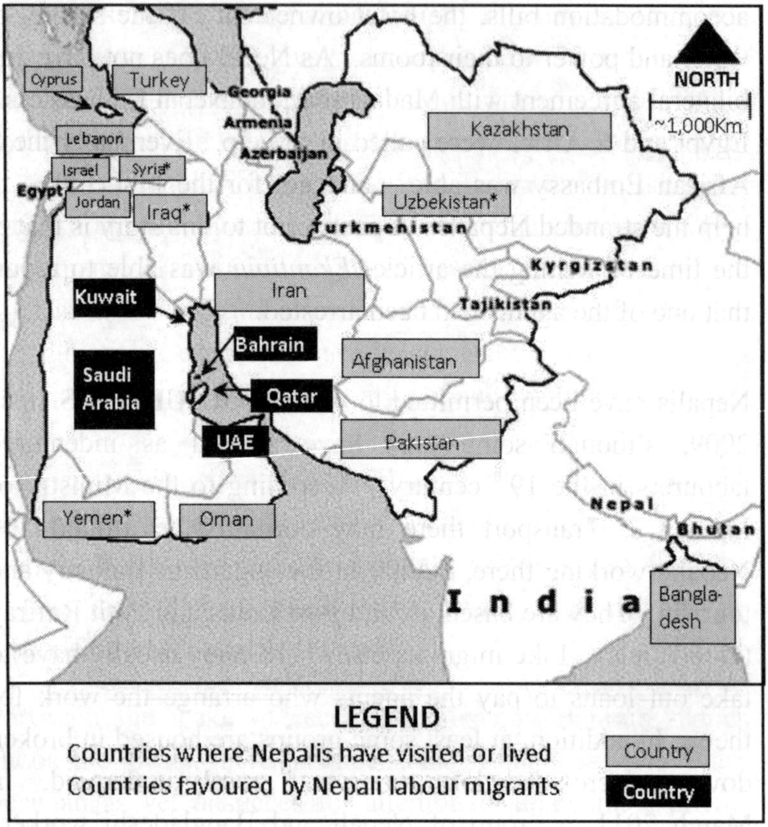

Nepali migrants are known to have travelled to all the countries marked on the map but apart from the Gulf and Mediterranean countries already described in detail, few details of numbers or of any Nepali Christians or fellowships are available.

AFGHANISTAN

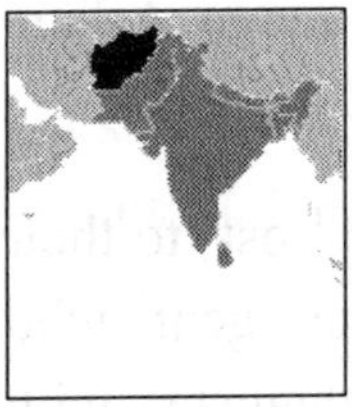

In 2008, there were still British Gurkhas serving in Helmand Province. Otherwise, the situation regarding Nepali migrants and Afghanistan is confusing. In the wake of the assassination of 12 Nepalis in Iraq in 2004, Afghanistan was banned for Nepali workers (apart from serving soldiers) for some time, and certainly at the height of the Afghan war in 2007, Nepalis were officially not permitted to go there for work. When the country was reopened and under what conditions is not clear. Nevertheless, by 2011 there were around 15-20,000 illegal Nepali workers based in Afghanistan.[234] Respectable Manpower Agencies at that time understood that Afghanistan was still a banned country and refused to try to process work permits. In fact, the Government of Nepal did issue 4,286 work permits for security jobs, but most Manpower Agents were unaware of this. However, unscrupulous brokers based in Nepal, Delhi and Dubai established a trafficking racket to entice Nepalis to Afghanistan by arranging 15-day visas from India. Many ended up in Afghani jails while others returned home from Dubai, having lost the money they paid in fees (sometimes as much as Rs. 250,000). Just a few of the fortunate ones (maybe 10%) eventually managed to find legal employment and earn good money, although the risk of living in Afghanistan was considerable. According to the Nepal Embassy in Islamabad, most "get caught in Kandahar and are sent to jail… Nobody knows how many Nepalis are in Afghan jails. We issue travel documents for their release and return to home only when we are informed."[235] Part of the problem is that there is no Nepal Embassy in Afghanistan and monitoring this situation from Pakistan is complex and difficult. All liaison has to be done through the ICRC[lxiv] in Kabul. However, in 2012 the Ministry of Foreign Affairs proposed opening a diplomatic office in Afghanistan.[236]

The sad thing is that many of these workers are 'lost' to their families. There is a story about some manpower agents who had taken a group of 10 Nepali workers to Afghanistan with promises of lucrative jobs. These jobs never materialized; instead the workers were locked up by the agent in Bagram for 10 months, until, "upon a formal request from the MoFA, the IOM and the Interior Ministry of Afghanistan rescued the workers, while the Nepali Embassy in Pakistan arranged the travel documents for them."[237]

Nevertheless, in August of the same year (2012) the GoN considered reopening Afghanistan to workers other than those working in security and employed through UN agencies, and the British and American embassies there. In 2013 there was still a partial ban in place, but workers continued to go through non-official channels. For them, the situation can be particularly dangerous, but even for legally authorized workers the risks are high. Four Nepali guards were among a group killed as the result of a Taliban suicide bomber blowing up a truck at the NATO[lxv] compound.[238]

It is estimated that 20-30,000 Nepalis work in the various US and NATO bases in Afghanistan. Their minimum salary is 600 USD and the average figure is 1,000 USD a month. In addition they also receive various other perquisites. However, when the Nepal Government started restricting

[lxiv] International Committee of the Red Cross (& Crescent)
[lxv] North Atlantic Treaty Organisation.

Nepali workers leaving TIA for various labour destinations on 'visit visas' in October 2012, this caused a significant problem for this group of legal workers. Because of the unique way in which they are transported to Afghanistan, it is not possible for them to acquire 'work visas' from the Afghanistan authorities, but they have to travel on 'visit visas' as far as the Gulf. Therefore, this new action by the GoN, which was legitimately designed to stop dishonest manpower agents abusing 'visit visas', meant that these workers faced a dilemma as to whether they could return home for a holiday at Desai and still get back to their work. This illustrates some of the complexities faced by GoN in dealing with the issue of illegal migration.

Although situated on the north-eastern side of the Persian Gulf, **IRAN** is not usually included in 'Arab' – the largely Sunni Islamic countries to the south east where most Nepali labour migrants go. It is the stronghold of Shi'ite Islam. I am unaware of any Nepali Fellowships in the country.

The estimate for Nepalis domiciled in **PAKISTAN** is given by the Joshua Project as around 1,000. Most are located in Lahore and Islamabad. There are two main groups. Those who have been there for many years are thought to be descendants of Nepalese Gurkhas who served in the Punjab Army.[lxvi] However, Aryal wrote in 2008 that "Lahoris do not

[lxvi] It is said that some Nepali commanders and about 200 troops joined the Punjab Army of Ranjit Singh to fight against the British in the Anglo-Nepali war of 1814-16. Because they were stationed in Lahore, they became known as Lahures. After the war, the British began to recruit such brave soldiers into their own army and then they started to be known as Gurkhas.

know who the Lahures are, and don't even remember that Gurkha soldiers used to be brought here in the last century to fight in Afghanistan."[239] The second group are more recent migrants from Nepal – mostly doctors and medical students. In all, approximately 200 are pursuing various medical courses. There are 70 students in Punjab State alone.

According to the Joshua Project, it is estimated that there are around 1,200 Nepalis living in **BANGLADESH**, but no known Christians among them. They are said to be the descendants of Nepalis who left Nepal in the 1950s, plus a number of international students studying in Dhaka. This includes about 300 at the University of Science and Technology in Chatgaun.

SE ASIA

(& the Rest of Asia)

"... went on his journey and came to the land of the people of the EAST."
~ Genesis 29:1 ESV ~

THE MALAYSIAN PENINSULA

PENINSULAR MALAYSIA FELLOWSHIPS

KEDAH (c 6) PENANG (c 7) PERAK (2) PAHANG (? 1) SELANGOR (>30)
NEGERI SEMBILAN (? 4) MELAKA (1) JOHOR (>22)

SINGAPORE FELLOWSHIPS (4)

MALAYSIA

STATISTICS	
Total Nepali Population	700,000
No. of Nepali Fellowships	80-90
No. of Nepali Christians	>1,500

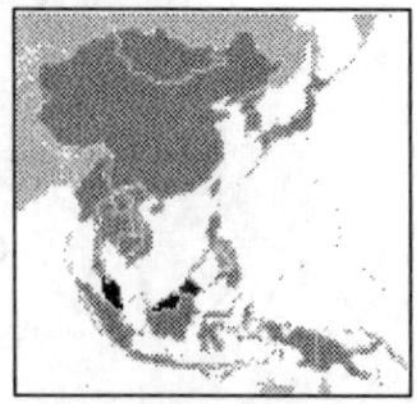

Although Nepalis had already started travelling to Malaysia in the late 1990s, the country was only officially opened for labour migration in February 2001.[240] The latest (2013) estimate for numbers of Nepalis in Malaysia is around 7 *lakh*.[lxvii] According to Kosh Raj Dahal, on average 300 Nepalis travel *to* Malaysia and another return *from* Malaysia every day. In addition to the migrant workers, there are also maybe 1,500 Gorkhalis or ex-Gurkha families who stayed on in Malaysia after the 2nd World War. In 1957, after Independence, some joined the Royal Ranger Regiment of the Malayan armed forces; others became security guards. Most have become integrated with the local population and lost much of their Nepali language. The numbers of labour migrants fluctuate and a drop was noticed in 2009 when the Malaysian government temporarily stopped recruiting for the manufacturing and service sectors. The vast majority of Nepalis live in peninsular or West Malaysia and are labour migrants, working mostly in factories, or on construction although in the Cameron Highlands and the north some do

---

[lxvii] As usual, estimates vary greatly: figures of 4.5 and 5 *lakh* were quoted in 2012. This may have been just the numbers of documented workers! In 2009, the number was said to be 3 *lakh*.

work in agriculture. Some are employed in the service sector, as in the tourist hotels and restaurants of Penang.[lxviii] Others work in supermarkets. The most popular, and slightly better paid, work is that of security guards, although this was blocked from 2009-2012. Most are (young) men but there are growing numbers of ladies, who generally work in factories and are not allowed to work as maids.

Most Nepalis in Malaysia are male labour migrants.

Many migrants do not know the local Malaysian labour laws and so can easily be cheated by dishonest agents or employers. There are two kinds of agents. One is an agent who arranges employment with a single employer. Any worker who leaves that employment automatically becomes illegal. The other is an Outsourcing Agent and he himself is the actual employer and can therefore arrange work with different individuals or companies and he can move the workers around. However, a worker must only work in the sector for which he/she has been granted a work permit. In order to obtain a Work Permit, a worker must pass the FOMEMA medical test initially (and then annually) and have

[lxviii] According to *Ekantipur* (29 Dec 2011) Malaysia opened up 10 sectors (croupier, mining, mangrove wood, café and catering, restaurant, fast food, grass cutting, newspaper vendor, house and vehicle cleaners and auto workshop workers) and 11 sub-sectors (scrap metal, cargo handling, welfare home, spa and reflexology, hotel, golf caddy, laundry, barber, goldsmith, wholesale and retail and textile business) for migrants, who previously were only allowed in production, construction, agriculture, plantation and service sectors.

a signed employment contract.[lxix] A contract is usually given for 3 years but the Work Permit for only one year and so needs to be renewed annually. All workers must always carry an Identity Card or their passport. It is the responsibility of the employer to process the work permit / ID card and also to provide the compulsory Compensation Scheme card for illness or accident, but workers are also expected to buy other medical insurance themselves. They can join a Trade Union but not become officials in it.

However, the one thing they cannot do is to marry a local Muslim. If they do, they have to convert to Islam. Of course, no one can stop them marrying a fellow Nepali although the official registration is not easy. I heard about the first Nepali Christian 'wedding' in Malaysia in 2009:

> It was only arranged at the last minute. The bride asked my friend to come for some blessing service for them, but when she enquired as to whether this was a wedding, the answer was "I think so." As my friend was on the bus on Sunday morning, the bride called again saying, "*Didi*[lxx] come quick, they want to start at 11am and I have no female *saathi.*[lxxi] My friend thus arrived after the service had begun and had no time to change from her jeans before escorting the bride to the front of the church! Still – it was a good chance to show the Nepali community the real meaning of a Christian wedding![241]

Generally the Government of Malaysia recognises a need for migrant workers and grants them some rights, including:

- 1 complete day of rest each week

[lxix] Some dishonest agents issue two contracts which do not contain the same terms. This is illegal.

[lxx] Older sister.

[lxxi] Friend

- 10 paid public holidays per year
- Paid annual leave of 8-16 days per year, depending on the length of service with that company.
- Proper overtime payments when working on a day off or for more than 8 hours in one day.[lxxii]

At the same time, migrant workers are not liked. According to one informant they are victims of profiling (targeted by enforcement officers), stereotyping, exploitation and of insufficient or incongruous government policies. I was told that on 16 February, 2010, the news announced that "our Home Ministry is devising a mechanism that would enable the authorities to monitor *each and every foreigner* from the moment they enter the country till the day they leave. [The] Home minister… said the ultimate purpose was *to create an environment where foreigners without legal status would feel afraid and threatened and prepare to leave the country immediately.*"

In August 2011 there was an amnesty and undocumented workers were allowed to register or return home without legal proceedings against them. Many took advantage of this: maybe as many as 6,000 were able to return to Nepal and 25,000 were legalised for work in Malaysia.[242] However, "many [immigrants] were persuaded by their employers that they would not run into any kind of legal action, even if they ignored the amnesty."[243] They thus paid no attention to the opportunity and assumed nothing would happen to them. And, for two years, almost nothing did! Then, probably partly due to economic problems in the country, in August

---

[lxxii] Domestic workers do not have the same rights as others do, but as Nepalis are not employed as maids in Malaysia, this is currently not an issue.

2013, the Malaysian Government announced a 3 month crackdown on illegal migrant workers. Parajuli commented that, "More than 65 thousand Nepalese migrant workers risk arrest and deportation from Malaysia... Nepal fears for its citizens and has asked for a period of time to allow migrants to be regularized."[244] However, the operation went ahead as from 1 Sept 2013. It is described as "the largest nationwide crackdown on unwanted foreigners in the country," involving "150 officers from the Immigration Department, police, Armed Forces, Rela, Civil Defence, National Registration Department [and dogs]."[245] Within the first two days, there were 40 raids.[246] Although undoubtedly the migrants, who will be deported immediately, are those who will suffer the most, and often through no real fault of their own, "Saravana added that... local employers can be fined up to 50,000 ringgit ($15,213) or face jail time of up to five-years or six strokes of the *rotan* (cane), or all three."[247]

Workers can become illegal by moving to employment outside that specified in their contract or by overstaying in the country. Both the Police and the volunteer RELA[lxxiii] workers can question migrants and ask to see their documents, but workers can only be arrested if the documents are not with them or are not in order and if the Police give an adequate reason for the arrest. Workers can also be arrested if their employer lodges a complaint or makes an accusation about them. This happened with one man. His boss accused him of stealing 5kg of noodles, he was arrested and spent 2 years in jail for a crime he had not committed. Not knowing Bahasa Malaysia and having no lawyer or translator, he had no way to defend himself.[248] Such unfair treatment by

[lxxiii] Ikatan Relawan Rakyat or Malaysian Volunteer Corps.

employers is not rare, but it is innocent migrants who pay the price for their employers' inefficiency or lack of care. Police who arrest and interview migrants often treat them 'like dirt'.

Workers need to obtain a Check-out Memo (COM) from their employer before leaving Malaysia. They can resign before the end of their contract but may be penalised financially for so doing and have to purchase their own air tickets home. If workers are ill-treated, sexually harassed, or unfairly retrenched or dismissed, they must report this and are then entitled to a court hearing. However, this takes time and they can only remain on in Malaysia if they manage to get a Special Pass to do so.

In practice, the conditions under which they work are essentially the same as in the Middle East: the jobs are invariably dirty, difficult and dangerous and hostels are usually locally rented flats or apartments in which large numbers of workers are squashed together. The first time I was told about the system of sharing one bed between the night and day shift workers I was horrified. This is scrimping on costs at the expense of workers' rights and health. Agents and employers frequently cheat the workers. Employers keep hold of the workers' passports and often do not renew their papers on time. Many do not get regular days off. Some get short holidays at the two main Malaysian religious festivals – Chinese New Year and Hariraya (the end of Ramadan) but migrants are invariably given less time off than locals. They do not usually get time off to celebrate

Beds are often shared between day & night shift workers.

their own (Hindu) festivals. Migrants need to work long hours of overtime (OT) in order to earn a decent salary and have enough to send back to their families. They therefore have suffered during the financial crisis years as employers have cut back on OT. Paid holidays back in Nepal after at least two years are also the exception rather than the rule.

There is a disturbing story of 13 workers stranded in Malaysia, not given their due remuneration and asked to do work that was not included in their contracts. But that was not all. The extra work included cleaning vessels used for storing chemicals and the health of several has been significantly affected by this.[249] Another unpleasant bit of news was of the Nepali who "slipped into a 10-feet deep chemical tank in JYC International Company, where he used to work as a cleaner."[250]

Sometimes, issues are exaggerated or the local press may express bias against foreign workers. For example, the local DCP in Johor commented after some riot that was blown out of all proportion, "If these foreign workers want to come here and find a good job with a good pay then they must also respect Malaysia's laws."[251] He also said, "Earlier this month the police also arrested more than 100 Nepalis for holding an illegal protest demanding their wages," but in fact the workers were simply demanding implementation of the basic salary rise (see below). At other times, it seems that Nepali workers have gone too far in their protests, despite a certain amount of justification. In early 2013, a group of workers in KL rioted, trashing furniture from their apartment, because their employer made them redundant after only a few weeks of work and then kept them waiting for several months for repatriation with only 2 months compensation.[252]

In May 2012, Malaysia's Prime Minister announced a monthly basic salary rise from 540 Malaysian Ringgits to 900 Ringgits (800 for those in E. Malaysia), but it was not immediately given to all workers. In fact, Nepalis in Johor state held a protest sit-in because they were not included.[253] This big rise sounds like a great advance, as it seemed that the migrants would immediately draw around Rs. 24,000 instead of Rs. 15,000 However, for many it was simply the cause of more hassles. Such a major rise all at once put a lot of pressure of employers who had been anyway struggling through the financial crisis. The majority therefore found ways to reduce their increased payments. Many removed various allowances, such as the food allowance and pay in lieu of holidays worked. They changed to a 3-shift system instead of 2 shifts and OT. And the levy[lxxiv], which had been payable by the migrants up to 2009 and then by the employers from 2009-2013, was once again made chargeable to the migrants. As a result most migrants were no better off than before and some were even worse off because they had no way through OT to increase their salary. However, some business owners, like Margaret Chong, who runs a small laundry, are far more understanding of the migrants' situation. She reported that she did not intend to pass on the levy to her workers. "I will pay. I want my workers to have peace of mind," she said.[254]

Part of the problem is that there has been no effective Memorandum of Understanding between the governments of Malaysia and Nepal concerning the terms and conditions for

---

[lxxiv] The levy may be regarded as a sort of tax levied on the non-tax paying migrants for use of Malaysian public facilities for which Malaysian national tax-payers have to pay.

Nepali migrant workers. However, in June 2013, Tika Bhandari, director of Nepal's FEPB, said that GoN was trying again to sign a comprehensive MoU with Malaysia, covering areas of workers' health management, wages, insurance, social security, etc. However, one point of dispute between the two sides was that the Malaysians proposed direct recruitment of workers from Nepal, boycotting Nepali manpower agencies, while the Nepalis wanted direct recruitment but within the limit of the Nepali laws and the Foreign Employment Act.[255]

There is no real MoU between Nepal & Malaysia.

In addition, life insurance covers only workers who lose their lives actually on the job, while, in reality, many other deaths (e.g. heart attacks and suicides) are indirectly due to harsh and stressful work conditions. One source reckons that 50 Nepalis die each year in Malaysia,[256] but another informant gave a much higher figure (>200 per year since 2005) and attributed most of them to medical conditions and a lack of effective training and pre-departure orientation.[257] The breakdown was as follows:

- 394 (25%) Chronic[lxxv] medical conditions (Tuberculosis, Gastritis, Pneumonia, Renal Failure and Myocardial Ischaemia)
- 144 (9%) Road Accidents
- 169 (10.5%) Suicides
- 227 (14%) Industrial Accidents
- 662 (41.5%) Other Causes (incl. murder, natural causes & stress)

[lxxv] It is not strictly accurate to call Pneumonia or heart attacks (MI) chronic conditions.

As the correspondent points out, this high percentage of deaths from medical conditions raises important questions about the health certification issued to Nepali migrant workers by authorised health centres.[lxxvi] Industrial accidents reflect a lack of proper training and probably also a lack of safety measures in the workplace.

> ***Krishna*** *suffered a work related accident in Malaysia that left him quadriplegic—unable to move from his neck downwards. He was then sent back to Nepal but faces the rest of his life as severely disabled.*

> ***Laxman*** *was involved in a road traffic accident. He was hit by a motorcycle helmet thrown at him while riding his bicycle. He sustained brain damage that led to coma and required surgery. In time he recovered and returned to light duties and eventually went home to Nepal.*

In July 2013, "one Nepali was killed and two others were injured after a rock hit them following an explosion at a quarry some 500 m away."[258]

The headline, "Cheated migrant workers return home empty handed"[259] describes what is a frequent experience of Nepali migrants. Seven Nepalis from Myagdi had to borrow money from their friends to get back to Nepal because of the unfair treatment by their agent and employer. We read this same kind of story over and over again. A friend tells of a group of cleaners at her university who were denied their full pay "because of administrative rules and regulations and a faulty computerised attendance system." Many other Nepalis have allowed themselves to be trapped by temptingly lucrative

[lxxvi] A small random survey showed a significant number of health certificates were fake.

pyramidal schemes like DXN and Unity Life only to discover that they simply do not work for the majority.

However, there are some significant differences and life is generally freer than in 'Arab'. Migrants, especially the men, can come and go in their spare time. There is reasonable public transport and the temperature – although hot all the year round – is nothing like that in most Gulf states. Malaysia is officially a Muslim country, but because of the mixed local population (with many Indians and Chinese) the enforcement of Muslim practices is far less strict. Non-Muslim girls are not expected to cover their heads; Chinese girls frequently wear shorts. However, mugging is endemic, which means that it is not safe even for small groups of young men to walk home in the evenings.

Xavier, of the NGO, Penang Office for Human Development (POHD), relates a common tale. ***Jivan*** entered Malaysia legally and found his job in a restaurant. However…

> *The agent and employer did not bother to apply for a Work Permit although levy payments were deducted every month from his salary. He was also not regularly paid for his work. When Jivan insisted on a work permit and his outstanding salaries, he was beaten up by the manager, robbed of the little cash [he] had as well as his handphone and thrown out of his hostel.*

Eventually Jivan heard about POHD: they helped him make a police report and saved him from being arrested by the immigration authorities. The Labour Department set a trial date for mid-December, but the Immigration Department, despite knowing the facts, insisted that he leave the country in early December – before the hearing, which therefore allowed the employer to escape prosecution.

The US State Department 'Trafficking in Persons Report 2009' blacklisted Malaysia and described the country's treatment of migrant labourers in scathing terms:

> Some migrant workers are victimised by their employers, employment agents, or traffickers who supply migrant labourers and victims of sex trafficking. Some victims suffer conditions including physical and sexual abuse, forced drug use, debt bondage, non-payment of wages, threats, confinement, and withholding of travel documents to restrict their freedom of movement… the government continue[s] to condone the confiscation of passports by employers, while employers passed the government's 'immigration levy' on to the low-skilled migrant workers, which facilitated debt bondage.

From time to time the press gives accounts of Nepalis in jail in Malaysia. Some are there because they have broken the law and been convicted of robbery, assault, murder or drug-related crimes. Others are there for undocumented entry to the country, which is not always their own fault. Once they have completed their sentences, they are allowed to return to Nepal, but have to pay their own air fares, but there is generally a backlog of unfortunates who remain in detention simply because they do not have the money for a ticket home.

The earliest Nepali workers to seek employment in Malaysia often travelled via Thailand or Singapore, and so often encountered problems at the border. Nowadays this is not necessary, but still some migrants arrive at Kuala Lumpur International Airport (KLIA) without correct documentation and are immediately arrested. This is usually due to cheating by the agents but the naivety of the migrants is also a factor.

Large numbers of illegal migrants work in Malaysia – for the same reasons as elsewhere. Most are those whose agents or employers have not provided them with the correct documents or not renewed their work visas in time, but also many who have overstayed their visas deliberately, having found a job with better pay outside of the official contract system. In 2011, the Nepal Ambassador, Dr Rishi Adhikari told me that there were 25,000 illegals, but this was almost certainly an under-estimate.[lxxvii] At that time a 3-week amnesty was announced, during which time, undocumented workers could either leave the country without being arrested or make arrangements to stay on legally. Some charges (for over-staying and for levy) were required and also everyone was required to go through biometrics (finger-printing). For some this was a great opportunity but I heard later that it was far from successful in reducing the number of undocumented workers. What happened was that the agents doing the biometrics, did them and took the fees but never sent the results to the embassy.

Most illegal workers have been cheated by agents or employers.

Nepali Fellowships

The first Nepali Christians in Malaysia were among the British Gurkhas serving there in the 1960s,[260] but then there

[lxxvii] It must have been an under-estimate as Giri reported in the *Kathmandu Post* in Dec 2012 that 8,000 had decided to return to Nepal while 25,000 were planning to stay on in Malaysia.

was a gap of many years before the labour migrants started to arrive. Since then, God has been working amazingly amongst the Nepali migrants in Malaysia. The latest estimate for the number of fellowships stands at around 80-90.[lxxviii] When I first visited Malaysia in around 2005-6 the number was only about 50 and probably only a couple of the leaders were able to work full time. By 2013 the numbers of fellowships and full-time pastors had grown considerably, although some of the original leaders had already returned to Nepal. Some pastors were able to work on outsourced visas and others had jobs courtesy of sympathetic factory owners. A few have worked as part-time pastors while continuing their theological studies at one of the colleges, although most found this very hard and it is also not ideal for the migrants as their P/T pastors are only available at the week-ends.

Almost without exception, all the Nepali fellowships are linked with local Malaysian churches. In some towns, individual churches each host their own relatively small Nepali fellowships. In other places, a group of churches or various denominations, have joined together to be involved in migrant ministry, which includes one church in the group hosting a fellowship. This joint ministry has benefitted the unity of the churches as well as helped the Nepalis and other migrant groups. This link with local

All Malaysian Nepali Fellowships are linked with local churches.

[lxxviii] It is impossible to state a fixed accurate number as it fluctuates. Migrants come and go. Sometimes meetings are centralised and at other times, decentralised into several smaller groups.

churches is usually a strong and positive feature of the Nepali migrant work in the country. Church members (ethnic Chinese or Indian Malaysian Christians) support the ministry with provision of meeting rooms, transportation, food, medical clinics, language, computer and music classes etc. However, with a couple of notable exceptions, few Malaysians have learnt Nepali,[lxxix] so real communication is not possible. Just occasionally the national leadership in these churches has tried to control the Nepali group to an unreasonable extent. This seems to be partly due to lack of understanding about the Nepali Church in Nepal.

One Nepali pastor, Kosh Raj Dahal, is a relatively independent tentmaker. He has registered the Kairos Reconciliation & Migrant Services (KRAMS) under a company called MarketPlace Venture, with its main work in Kajang, where he established a church in June 2013, but which also reaches out to Nepalis in Kuala Lumpur, Klang, Kuala Tringanno and Johor Bahru. His aims are to "Evangelize, Edify, Equip and Empower Nepalese in order to Exalt the name of the Lord." He has recorded the story of ***Kra*** who attended a leadership training:

> *I was a nominal Christian before. When I received this leadership training, I realized that I am not even a nominal one. Now, I commit myself, that I will make disciples even I am uneducated, I will encourage people to study Bible seriously and prayerfully which will transform communities.*[261]

Monika, also found Christ through this ministry: her story is poignant, and illustrates some of the severe pressures that

[lxxix] The majority of Indian Malaysians are Tamil speakers.

migrants face when separated from their families:

> ***Monika*** *came to Malaysia with a dream to fulfil all the needs of her family and make them happy by earning money, but like so many others was disappointed with the poor treatment and low remuneration she received from her company. Nevertheless she worked faithfully. Then one day a phone call 'destroyed her heart' as she heard that her beloved husband had died back in Nepal. This so affected her that she was taken to hospital and even for a month she was desperately lonely and unable to eat and think properly. The company refused to give her leave to spend time with her grieving family. Then, as the wound was just beginning to heal, she heard that her mother had died. This second tragedy left her so shocked, puzzled and depressed that she 'decided to go with her lovely husband and mother taking poison'. She bought the poison and hid it until there was an opportunity to take it one Sunday morning. That very day 'one brother from KRAMS came and forcefully brought her to KRAMS where Ps. Kosh preached a message from John 3:16.' She says, "The message entered into my body like water entering into a heap of sand... I got satisfied... and realized that there is a God... AND, I received Jesus Christ as my saviour and the Lord..."*[262]

Almost all the Nepali fellowships – either on their own or in groups, regularly arrange outreach celebrations especially at festival times. Some of these have seen spectacular fruit:

- At a Christmas Day celebration in Penang in 2005, of the 268 who attended, 47 accepted the Lord and a further 118 were interested to know more about Christ.
- In Ipoh, in 2006, 110 Nepalis attended an evangelistic meeting and 25 accepted Christ.

- In Klang, also in 2006, 320 attended an Easter celebration and 20 accepted the Lord, while 200 attended another evangelistic meeting and 20 accepted Christ.

One of the needs of these rapidly growing Christian fellowships is for Bibles. Even some young believers from Christian families in Nepal arrive in Malaysia without a Bible. However, getting Christian literature into Malaysia is not always easy. Sometimes Nepalis hand-carrying Bibles back from Nepal have been charged excessive rates of duty by Muslim customs officials. As a western 'tourist' however I was able to freight a consignment of Christian books with very minimal charges imposed. Perhaps when the officials discovered that they could not read a word of them they decided they could not be subversive to the local population!

> *A friend tells the lovely tale of security guards asking for something to read to help them cope with the overnight boredom. All she had were Bible story books and New Testaments to give them!*[263]

Among the local churches involved in migrant ministry, several distinct groups have emerged, although their geographical boundaries overlap and in some cases the group is interdenominational while in others it runs along denominational lines. In the Klang Valley / Kuala Lumpur conurbation there are many Nepali fellowships associated with a variety of different churches, and several networks.

Probably the first Nepali Christian to go to Malaysia with ministry in view was Uttam GC. He visited in 1999 to explore the possibilities and in 2000 moved there as a secular student at what is now UCSI University. He met various Malaysian Christians, including the Dean of the College and members of an FGA (Full Gospel Assembly) church who had a desire to reach out to Nepali migrants and start a church. Several denominational groups asked him to work with them but he felt called to a different style of mission. After some time Uttam met Franklin Karong and together they started a couple of fellowships – one near a factory where there were many Nepalis and one in a restaurant in town; and these soon grew. It was Uttam who challenged the folks in Klang (see below) to make their ministry interdenominational and seek for a Nepali pastor, and because of that Ps. Pasang David came. Uttam also worked on developing local partnerships with churches and factory owners. With a Nepali evangelist from Nepal and practical help (accommodation, transport, food and finance) the original ministry grew and meetings began to be held in 1st Baptist Church, Petaling Jaya.

The first group to emerge as an actual network was the **Malaysian Sangati Network (MSN)**. This began as something very informal in around 2001, when the flood of Nepali migrants to Malaysia was just beginning. Franklin Karong was the main facilitator and he was joined by Kelvin Yong, and Joo Tatt. They helped 3 Nepali fellowships in the KL area (Balakong, Sri Petaling and Bukit Bintang) get started and encouraged Uttam GC as their Nepali leader while he was still studying at University. By 2003, this had become more formalised and other groups, like DUMC[lxxx], River of Life, Brickfield Tamil Methodist, and Kajang AoG, in different parts of the Klang Valley, had come into being. From 2004, they organised regular holiday Bible camps and evangelistic meetings, which still continue under the

[lxxx] Damansara Uttama Methodist Church.

chairmanship of Soong Wai Ming from FGA Damansara.[lxxxi]

When Franklin and Sapana (née Basyal) joined Asian Outreach (AO), MSN became an AO partner. In 2005, they decided to establish a drop-in centre for migrants near the Central Market in KL, and as Sapana got more involved it became exclusively a *Samajik Sewa Kendra*[lxxxii] for Nepali migrants. Sapana ran this for about 2 years and helped many Nepalis with legal problems. It was then taken over by Andrew Ng and Michael Moey; the name was changed to **Shalom Centre** and the work expanded to help migrants of other nationalities. Tika Ram worked with Sapana for about a year and then left to minister at the Nepali fellowship at KL Wesley Methodist Church.[lxxxiii] In the meantime Sapana had gone to Nepal, but later, Buddhi Khadka was involved and again the ministry was mainly directed to Nepalis. However, in 2011 the centre was closed.

Around 2004/5 Andrew Ng (from Klang), Eric Chia (from Penang) and James Wong (already active in MSN) joined together to form **Outreach to Foreigners (O_2F).** Franklin was also later involved. This was a broader ministry to all nationalities of migrants in Malaysia. In 2005, it was formalised and a group of Malaysians made a historic visit to Nepal – to meet Nepali church leaders and see how they could work together. This was the time that Heike and I personally became involved. Later, this ministry was

---

[lxxxi] Recent Nepali leaders in these fellowships include Raj Kumar Gautam (St Mary's), Lalu Paudel (Sg Buloh), Karpa Tamang & Akkal Lama (Serdang/Rawang/Nilai/Seremban), Phurke Tamang (Segambut)

[lxxxii] Social Service Centre

[lxxxiii] He was followed in 2011 at KL Wesley by Isai Rai, an MBS student. Another student, Yakub Rai, will follow Isai from the end of 2013.

formally registered as **Mobilisation Network (MNSB)** and it continued until 2013, when another new entity was formed, called **Malaysian Nepali Ministers' Network (MN²)**. In retrospect, it seems that perhaps the smaller, local networks have overall been more active and effective.

In 2007, Franklin and Sapana, who were members of 1st (now Pantai) Baptist Church, PJ were involved with two Nepali fellowships. Shirley Tan organised one at the Luther House and Sapana led the other in Sungai Way Christian Church. The Lutherans had got involved by giving IT and English lessons to Nepali migrants, some of whom started to attend the English church services. Shirley then started a small Nepali fellowship in her house in January 2006 and it grew rapidly. Franklin and Sapana introduced Shirley to Santosh Basnet and later Prakash Basyal, both MBS[lxxxiv] students, who were able to give Nepali help. They also had a vision to draw these groups together and eventually that happened and the meeting place was fixed in 1st Baptist Church. Thus this group became the **Migrant Ministry Partnership (MMP),** and in 2011 it established a second fellowship in Shah Alam.

In Klang town, a large group of churches from various denominations joined together to form **Migrant Ministry Klang (MMK)**, which supports several migrant language ministries, including Nepali. Andrew Ng, its inspiration and founder, calls it 'mission at our doorstep'. The work began in 2002 after 2 Nepalis – Chandra and Tulman – walked into Klang Chinese Methodist Church looking for fellowship. From that grew a central weekly fellowship and several preaching stations that gradually became full fellowships.

[lxxxiv] Malaysian Bible Seminary.

Within a couple of years 200 migrants were attending on Sundays and in 5 years, around 400. English, Computer, and Music teaching were offered, and also a Nepali Library. In 2008, they produced a CD called '*Mero Eota Chahana*' (My one desire). The central Nepali group meets in the Tamil Methodist Church in Klang although since around 2011 it has been decentralised into at least 9 smaller ones - to make transportation easier and also to encourage more to become involved in leadership roles.[lxxxv]

The MMK twice monthly migrant medical clinics have been much appreciated. Many workers have no access to medical advice or treatment in their companies and attending an outside clinic means taking time off and is expensive. Until the local doctors learned enough simple Nepali and understood how Nepalis present their symptoms, Heike Priebe, ex-Nepal missionary and student at UCSI University, used to interpret for them. This was good as many of their problems were worries rather than real physical illnesses. They just needed to chat in Nepali with someone who understood and could explain to the doctor. In 2010 she was asked to translate for another doctor running a first aid course for a small group of Nepalis in KL. Her translation was much appreciated, especially as Heike could explain the new concepts in the Nepali context. She had been praying about how to also share the gospel with this group and so when the doctor showed a slide about the 'Good Samaritan' principle, this was the answer and she was able to explain this and read the story from the Nepali Bible to them. Then, in the

---

[lxxxv] The main leaders have included Pasang (David) Sherpa and Dhan Shrestha as well as those who have led the small groups. There has also been one lady, Arati Thapalia, studying at MBS.

afternoon, after the teaching on heart attacks, she was able to introduce the well-known Nepali tract called the 'Heart of Man'. After the training they took all the copies she had.[264]

The Christian friendship, prayer and support when one of the migrants has been seriously ill has often powerfully witnessed to God's love: Such is ***Yuvaraj's*** testimony:

> *Less than a month after arriving in Malaysia, Yuvaraj was struck down with a severe disease which left him totally paralysed and with a tracheostomy on a ventilator. He was told he had muscular dystrophy*[lxxxvi] *and that the prognosis was bleak. Over the months his condition deteriorated until the only movement he had left was in his eyes. At one point he was even pronounced dead. However, some of the Christians from Klang regularly visited him in hospital. Yuvaraj said later, "I just knew that they prayed for me and gave me some words of encouragement and hope... I was so much touched by their love and concern for me." They also provided him with booklets and tapes and through these he heard the Gospel and began to wonder if Christ could perform the same sort of amazing miracle he had done in the Bible. And he did! Suddenly one day the Nepali pastor received a phone call from Yuvaraj himself saying that he was now again able to speak and move his hands and from then on he slowly recovered the use of both arms and legs. After almost 2 years in hospital, Yuvaraj returned home to Nepal and has been a great witness to his family and community. As he himself said, "I was dead, but now I live for Christ."*

The (Tamil) **Methodist Missionary Movement (MMM)** has links with Nepali fellowships in the KL area as well as

[lxxxvi] In retrospect, almost certainly the correct diagnosis was Guillain-Barré Syndrome.

Ipoh.[lxxxvii] In 2007, 14 of their churches were involved in migrant ministry. They have produced two CDs called '*Pariwartan*' (Transformation) and '*Asha*' (Hope).

In the north, centred in Penang, is the **Love Penang Network (LPN)** which is an interdenominational group of churches, anchored by Fettes Park Baptist Church. The Nepali Sangati Penang meets at *Sancho Mitra* (True Friend) and runs the work on the island[lxxxviii] as well as on the mainland (Perai) and also has strong links also with Valdor, Alor Setar and other small fellowships in Kedah.[lxxxix] The 'full-time' Nepali leaders are all working on social visas.[xc] Their former founder/leader was Kai Lee Wong, a Chinese Malaysian who worked for some years in Nepal, and Subash Pradhan, a Bible College student, was involved with her near the beginning. This group has been particularly blessed and also used in advocacy amongst needy migrants. In 2009 alone, Kai Lee spoke of helping at least "60 Nepalis in case handling especially detention cases, permit and wage problems and [says that] many were led to trust in Jesus to deliver them from their troubles even though they did not personally accept Christ as their Lord and Saviour." The Penang team have many stories of individual migrants they have been privileged to help, but one is particularly sad:

> *While doing outreach, some of the Penang team met **Jit***

[lxxxvii] The recent leader in Ipoh was Surya Natasa.

[lxxxviii] Fellowships are situated in Georgetown, Bayan Point, Ayer Itam, Batu Feringgi & Batu Maung.

[lxxxix] These include Alor Setar, Kuala Kedah, Jitra, Gurun, Sungai Pettani & Kulim.

[xc] In recent years they have included Kishor & Letty Rana, Chandan Pun, Anil Lama, and Rabin & Gita Bogati apart from the leaders of the local scattered groups.

***Bahadur**, a migrant who had been undocumented for the last 4 years and who was now extremely thin and weak. After praying for him, they enlisted Kai Lee's help, who in turn found a helpful Chinese doctor. The diagnosis (perforated bowel due to TB) indicated urgent surgery but he was too sick to have it, and he died that very night. All the team could then do was to liaise with all the authorities and help raise funds to repatriate his body.*

For a while also the Penang group was also supported by another Nepali leader, Ashok Ghimire, who was able to help them understand ministry in a Muslim environment, something much needed in the Malaysian context.

In the south, in the large state of Johor, there is the interdenominational **Johor Nepali Christian Fellowship, Malaysia (JNCFM)** which is more a group of Nepali fellowships than local churches, but several local leaders (like Sister Chew and Ps. Sunil Abraham) are also involved with them. In fact, the beginning of the Nepali work in the south of Malaysia is linked with what God had also started to do in Singapore. Some of the earliest groups to be established were in Batu Pahat and Pekan Nanas.

Ps. Freddie Ho (retired from the Bible College in Singapore) used to visit Batu Pahat at least once a month and invited Solomon Adhikari to join him. They met 2 Christian brothers. At the first Nepali service in June 2003, there were 2 believers and 3 non-believers at the beginning: by the end of the service there were 5 believers! Seeing the great need and opportunity, Solomon committed himself to visit once a month and did so for many years and still goes occasionally. Kiran Das and Khadga (James) Magar also used to visit from Singapore. God multiplied the numbers so much that it became clear a Nepali pastor was needed on site. Indra Thapa served until around 2011 and now (in 2013) James Tamang is in Batu Pahat. They have received great help and support from several local people from Girija Grace Presbyterian Church like Mr & Mrs Loh and Mr & Mrs Cho. Their providing English lessons in the church on a Sunday evening led on to fellowship meetings. By 2013 there were over 200 Nepali Christians in Batu Pahat with an average Sunday attendance of more than 60. To date >250 Nepalis have accepted Christ through this ministry.

In 2006, Ps. James (Power) Tamang (then working in Johor) met with Solomon Adhikari (from Singapore) in a Nepali restaurant near City Square in JB to discuss the possibility of having occasional combined services. After this idea was shared with Sr. Chew and Ps. Sunil Abraham (on the Malaysian side) and Kiran Das (a Bible College student in Singapore) and the result was the establishment of the Johor Nepali Christian Fellowship, Malaysia (JNCFM) at the Chinese New Year Camp in 2007. After that and for several years, both Kiran and Solomon used to visit Johor regularly to help with training camps and special programmes. However, two local Malaysians, Scott Ang and Roger Wong, were instrumental in establishing the Tampoi fellowship.

The southern group now includes Johor Bahru town and surrounding areas[xci], Batu Pahat, Kluang and Muar but, not

---

[xci] These include Ps. John (Aita Singh) Titung (in Tampoi, JB town, Jayamass, Perlin Sutera, & Kulai), Ps. Rohn Pakhrin (in Pekan Nanas & Gelang Patah), Ps. Santalal Dong (in Kota Tinggi & Johor Jaya (ex Desa Cemerlang), Ps. Dawa Sherpa (in Senai & Skudai), Ps. James Tamang (in Batu Pahat), Ps. Bhakta Yonghang (in Kluang, Simpang Renggam, Endau, & Kahang), Mr David Limbu (in Kota Putri), Mr. Rabi Hamal (in Pasir Gudang) and Mr. Silas Lopchan (in

Malacca although some groups in the KL area (Serdang, Rawang, Nilai & Seremban) even further away, are linked with them. 9 pastors are based in Johor as well as other (lay) leaders. Only since 2013, has Malacca had a designated leader, Dipak Shrestha, an MBS student: before that some other leaders used to visit from time to time. By 2013 there were probably at least 22 Nepali fellowships in Johor State alone. The Johor Nepali pastors meet together regularly with several Malaysians and plan for joint celebrations and/or outreach meetings at festival times or seminars by visiting speakers. In particular, they run 3-day training camps during Malaysia's two long holidays – Chinese New Year (CNY) and Hariraya. They also produce a magazine called '*Muktiko Sandesh'* (Message of Salvation).

Nepali churches in Nepal practise believers' baptism by immersion, although only a relatively small number are formally Baptist churches. This practice arose largely because of the inter-denominational nature of mission in Nepal, but perhaps more, because of the high cost of becoming a Christian in the early years (1952-1990) in Nepal. One informant told me of the difficulty this caused initially in one Presbyterian Church in Malaysia. Only after lengthy discussions between the church and the Nepali leaders was it agreed that the Nepalis should have freedom to continue their traditional practice.

Muar) with Amrit Tamang. Other recent pastors/leaders include Indra Thapa (Batu Pahat), Rajan Nagarkoti (Pasir Gudang) and Bedu Khanal (Muar).

SINGAPORE

STATISTICS	
Total Nepali Population	15-20,000
No. of Nepali Fellowships	4
No. of Nepali Christians	>100

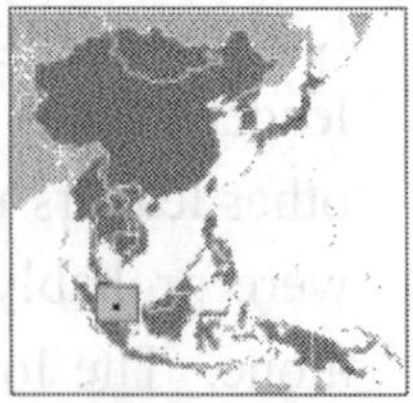

The history of Nepali migration to Singapore is tied in with the history of Nepalis in India, Burma, and Malaysia and the events during and shortly after the 2nd World War. During the war, as the Japanese invaded Malaya, the British forces, among whom were some Gurkha troops, gradually retreated to Singapore. Throughout the Japanese Occupation (1942-45) the Gurkha troops became famous for their fighting skills, bravery and absolute loyalty to the British.

Then, when Indian Independence was declared in 1949, and the various Gurkha battalions were divided between the British and Indian Armies, those who were allocated to the British Army were transferred to other British colonies like Malaya and Singapore. They were used to help counter the increasing communist threat, and subsequently (between 1950 & 1964) were deployed as a neutral force to quell race riots between Malays, Chinese and Indians. From then on, and largely because of their impartiality in a multiracial state, the Gurkha Contingent became established as the Singapore government's anti-riot police squad. Some were even enlisted as wardens for Changi Prison in 1978. Even today the Gurkhas still function as a specialist force, assisting the police in guarding Singapore against terrorism.

Recent estimates suggest that there are about 15-20,000 Nepalis in Singapore, but this includes some who have come from India. There are also some illegals, although the Government of Singapore is better able to control this problem than the governments of many other larger nations. There may be around 5-6,000 Nepali Gurkhas living in their 19 hectare camp in Mount Vernon. This is a well serviced and self-contained community. The Gurkhas are long-term but still temporary migrants as they are committed to return immediately to Nepal at the end of their 20-year service contracts. The law also precludes them intermarrying with locals and even discourages integration in Singaporean society, so the Gurkha camp is in effect a small Nepali ghetto into which foreigners (including Singaporeans) cannot enter without permission. Ironically this is actually a plus factor for them as the Singapore Government therefore allows them to be accompanied by their families. Even back in Nepal, ex-Singapore Gurkhas often congregate together because of their shared memories. Some have established manpower agencies to recruit retired Gurkhas for security work in countries like Brunei, Hong Kong, Afghanistan, and Iraq.

Although migrant workers now make up a third of Singapore's workforce, apart from the Gurkhas, the number of Nepalis is relatively few compared with some other SE Asian nations. Most of the ethnic Nepali domestic workers have come from Darjeeling and Sikkim. Foreign maids have an important socio-economic role in Singapore society because most couples need to work to cope with the high cost of living and because of the rapidly aging population, but they are frequently exploited by their agents and employers. However, this is more related to excessively long working hours rather than the abuses common in Muslim countries. In 2013, the Singapore Government introduced a new law, making a weekly day off for maids mandatory, but this has upset some Chinese employers who themselves work exceptionally hard, and so want a relaxing day off themselves: rather than having to do their housework. They also want to know where their maids are 100% of the time!

Nepali Fellowships

To my knowledge, there were no Nepali churches in Singapore until the late 1990s despite the longstanding presence of the Gurkhas and individual Christian Gurkhas who, from the 1960s, were sometimes able to worship in English congregations.[265] When Solomon Adhikari arrived in 1994 he therefore attended an English-speaking service, as presumably any Christian Gurkhas and some Bible College students had been doing. Only in March 2001 did discussions begin about starting a Nepali Fellowship. The initiative came from Hom Tamang, then a Bible College student. He and his wife, Ps. Ezakio and his wife, who was also a Bible College student, and Solomon met and discussed the issue. Then on 1 April they held the first service at Zion Church, MacPherson Road, with the help of Brother Santon, Sr. Genny Goh and Ps. Stephen Goh. Ps. Ezakio was the first leader, followed by James Khadga Magar and then Solomon, when the 3 students left after completing their studies. For some years also Brother Jiang helped – until he started to assist the Nepali fellowship in Malacca, Malaysia.

In 1998, Kris went to work in Singapore: 4 years later, he and his wife, Sangita, and their daughter, Nisha, accepted Christ and were baptised in December 2002 in the Elim Church.

Then, in January 2005, Kris, together with Senior Ps. Peter, started a morning Nepali Fellowship in **Crown of Glory Church (COGC)** in Lavender. Kris and his family, Peter, and a Sister, Muna Samuel, were at the first meeting. Kiran Das, Ram Buddhathoki (both Bible College students) and Solomon assisted in COGC for some years. Eventually, however, both students returned to Nepal, but between 2007 and 2011 Solomon was an elder in COGC with Kris.

According to Solomon, who has been involved in various ways right from the beginning, the development happened like this: A fellowship started at Elim Church but after some years closed; and another fellowship started at History Maker Church but that too later ceased. Sometime during this period, Ps. Prem Tamang (another Bible College student) together with friends started the City Hall Fellowship. Sr. Mina Tamang took this over when Prem returned to Nepal. Later, Sisters Anita, and Lilu Lepcha joined the leadership.

Up until 2010, COGC was meeting in factory premises, but then URA (a Government body) asked COGC to move out from the factory. In addition, some Gurkha families from the '*camp*' felt it is unsafe to attend services there. At this time, Bartley Church opened its doors to the Nepali group and **Bartley Nepali Christian Fellowship, Singapore (BNCFS)** began in July 2010 with the blessing of Ps. Ricky, the senior pastor of COGC, although some of the Nepali members stayed with COGC. In January 2012, Solomon was ordained as lay pastor of BNCFS.

Thus, as of September 2013, there were 4 independent Nepali Fellowships meeting in Singapore, with a total of more than 100 Nepali believers. The largest group (around 55), as might be expected, is mainly drawn from the ex-Gurkha population, most of whom now work in the Singapore Police and live near Bartley. Some others are students, domestic helpers and hotel staff. This is **Bartley Nepali Christian Fellowship, Singapore (BNCFS)** and their leader, Solomon Adhikari, is himself a migrant, having come to Singapore from Kalimpong. Unlike most of the other Nepalis, he is married to a Singaporean and was granted Singapore citizenship in June 2006.

Of the other two groups, one is the **Crown of Glory Nepali Church** (leader Kris Sharma from Darjeeling) with 30-40 members, which meets in Tai Seng / Potang Pasir and now has an extra afternoon fellowship.

The other meets at **Calvary Baptist Church** (leader Shachan Pradhan from Nepal).

The fourth meets in the **City Hall** at Marina Bay and is led by Sister Lilu Lepcha, who has been seconded to this work by Bartley. She is now in her 60s but a very faithful worker, bringing many ladies into the fellowship.

BURMA – MYANMAR

STATISTICS	
Total Nepali Population	~3 *lakh*
No. of Nepali Fellowships	~7 centres
No. of Nepali Christians	1,000

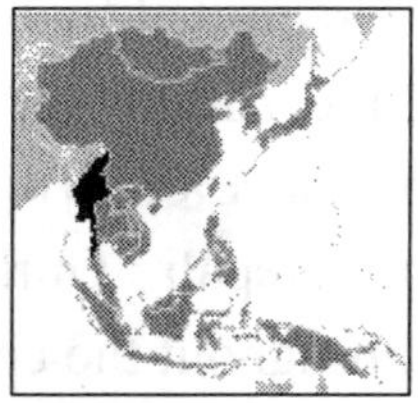

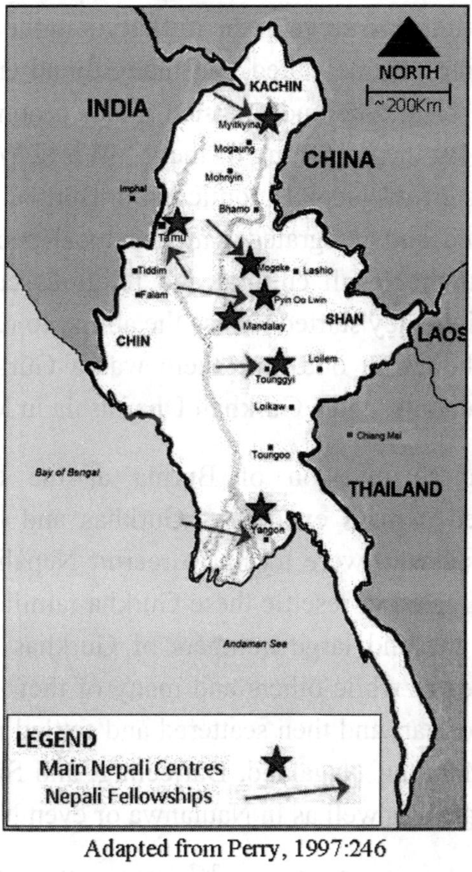

Adapted from Perry, 1997:246

Today there are ~266,000 Nepalis still resident in Burma, living mostly in the hill areas among the tribal groups.

The history of Nepali settlement in Burma dates back to the early 19th century, when Gurkhas, having recently proved their prowess in the Anglo-Nepali war of 1814-16, began to be recruited by the British, for whom they then fought in the three Anglo-Burmese wars. Thus, when Burma became a province of British India in 1887, there were huge numbers of Nepali Gurkhas and their families already settled throughout the country, the majority from the Kirant tribes of E. Nepal. The first Gurkha villages were set up in 1890.[266] Some continued to serve in the military—in the Burma Rifles as they later became called, but many found employment in the silver, lead, zinc and tungsten mines around Lashio and Karenni. By the beginning of the 2nd World War there were probably c 2 *lakh* Nepalis domiciled in Burma, but many had intermarried and integrated with the local peoples and lost some of their Nepali cultural and religious customs. This may be when they started to lose the ability to read the Nepali script, although at one time there was a Gurkha press and Sanskrit schools, and a Gurkhali Dharmsala in Mandalay.

The Japanese invasion of Burma at the end of 1941 precipitated a mass exodus of Gurkhas and their families. The British, who were trying to recruit Nepalis for the war effort, struggled to resettle these Gurkha families at the same time. In the end large numbers of Gurkhas fought in the Pacific theatre while others and many of their families were sent to Motihari and then scattered and settled in NE India—Assam, Manipur, Nagaland, Darjeeling, and Sikkim – many on tea estates, as well as in Nautanwa or even Nepal.

After the war, the final wave[267] of Nepali settlers arrived in Burma as many who had served in the Gurkha Rifles stayed in parts of NE India, Malaya and Burma. Thus, the Nepali

Diaspora in the whole of this region is inter-related. Lamichhane revealed an interesting fact that he discovered while visiting Burma in 2013. 50 years ago, when there was ethnic tension in Burma, many Nepali Burmese fled to Nepal and King Mahendra allowed them to settle in Nawal Parasi and Butwal.[268] Of those who stayed in Burma, the majority worked in agriculture, although a few made their fortunes finding and cutting precious stones.

More recently, Nepalis, like other ethnic minorities, have again fled from an oppressive regime in Burma and sought refuge, this time mostly in Thailand. "Tragically, Gurkhas from Myanmar are increasingly found in the Thai brothels of Chaing Mai [sic] and Bangkok."[269] At one time, the situation in Burma was so bad that one illegal immigrant declared that he would rather serve time in a Thai prison than return to Burma.[xcii] Nevertheless there are still large numbers of Nepalis in Myanmar. Neither return to Nepal nor taking up the benefits of NRNs in relation to Nepal is proving easy as the latest generation of Burmese Nepalis cannot provide proof that their grandparents had Nepali citizenship.[270]

Although things are slowly beginning to change, there are still many problems and challenges for doing ministry in Myanmar – both for locals and visitors. Foreigners can only stay in hotels – not private homes. Even Burmese cannot easily move around their own country without obtaining permission from a local political leader, and even relatives cannot visit without prior permission. Foreign visitors can – with difficulty – buy a SIM card for about 20 USD but it is

---

xcii Either he was treated better than other migrants who had been incarcerated or else he had never been in prison! (See p.347)

only valid for 1 month. Locals must pay 250 for the same SIM card.

Nepali Fellowships

The first outreach to Nepalis in Burma occurred at the end of the 19th century, but there was little fruit until the 1970s. Outreach was based around 4 main centres. BP Rai led the Gurkha Baptist Mission which was based in Insein (on the outskirts of Rangoon/Yangon). Kumar Limbu led the group in Myitkyina, in the north, which was part of the Kachin Baptists. The other two groups were just north of Mandalay. Harry Bahadur (of AoG) led the group in Mogoke. The fourth group was in Moe Gyaw Byit, near Maymyo (now Pyin Oo Lwin) which was the home of the 10th Gurkha Rifles.[271] By the early 1990s there were around 500 Nepali Christians although recent estimates suggest that 1% of the Nepali population are Christians. In Myitkyina there are 2 churches, 30 scattered fellowships and a small Missional Training Centre. There is a church in Pyin Oo Lwin and 2 nearby preaching centres (Naung cho & Kumbak), 2 Fellowships in Tounggyi, 1 in Moe Kyote (near Mandalay), a Church in Mogoke, and a Church and 1 Fellowship in Tamu. In Thailand, there are Nepali believers from >23 Burmese towns/villages and Daya Pradhan says that "Very soon we will see over 20 churches planted in Myanmar started in the soil of Thailand." In 1996, as a direct result of the visit of two of the original Nepali missionaries to Nepal from Kalimpong, the Myanmar Gurkhali Christian fellowship was established to link congregations in 7 locations for mutual encouragement, strategic planning, joint training and outreach.[272] One challenge in reaching out to the Gorkhalis of Burma, is that many cannot read in the Devanagri script.

THAILAND

STATISTICS	
Total Nepali Population	~ 20,000
No. of Nepali Fellowships	? 5
No. of Nepali Christians	>100

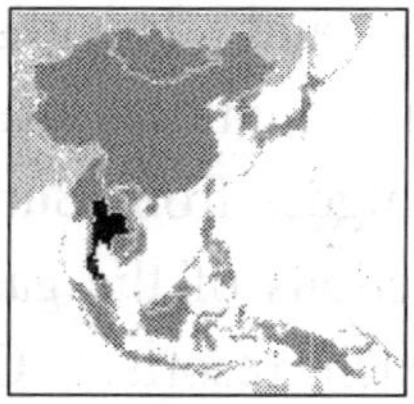

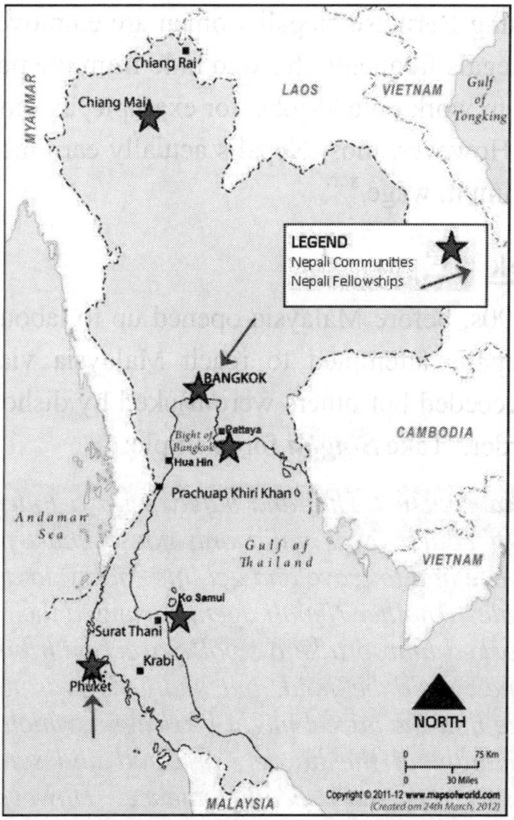

There are said to be around 20,000 Nepalis in Thailand[xciii],

---

[xciii] But see below for other figures relating to those in S Thailand.

mostly living in Bangkok and the tourist areas of Phuket, Pattaya, and Ko Samui. However, according to the Nepal Embassy in Bangkok, only 4,000 to 5,000 Nepalis work in Thailand. This discrepancy may well be due to the fact that huge numbers are illegal. More than 90% are Gorkhali refugees from Burma. Many work in tailor shops and other sections of the garment industry or selling souvenirs at the beach resorts. Others work in the hotel and restaurant industry and a few even run small restaurants themselves. Many young Burmese Nepali women are employed as house helps. Illegals frequently have to hide from the police, hence they tend to work on odd-jobs, for example, as shop-boys and waiters. However, most Nepalis actually earn more than the legal minimum wage.[xciv]

Bangkok

In the 1990s, before Malaysia opened up to labour migrants, many Nepalis attempted to reach Malaysia via Thailand. Some succeeded but others were tricked by dishonest agents at the border. Take ***Singha*** for example:

> ***Singha*** *reached Thailand safely with a tourist visa but this, of course, was valid only for a short period. He therefore had to leave and get into Malaysia as quickly as possible. Another Nepali agent arranged the crossing but also asked him to take a small parcel with him. He was told he would be paid, but sadly he was too naïve to realize that the parcel might be drugs – which it was. He was caught at the border, arrested and sent to prison where he received a death sentence. However, this was later commuted to life and then shortened even further.*

[xciv] Around 2007, this was set at 133 baht/day (approx. Rs. 385)

In all, he spent 13 years and 8 months in jail in Thailand, but during that time he accepted Christ.[273]

Wikipedia says that, "More than three dozen Nepali drug traffickers are serving long term jail sentences in Thai prisons including life imprisonment." Some are possibly innocents like Singha.

In 2004, the *Nepali Times* published the story of a Nepali who had been working in Thailand since 1993, developing a garment export business. Two years later, while on tour with a friend, they met some acquaintances of this friend. The man was drinking tea with this group when suddenly they were all arrested. He had no idea that the 6 men had been involved in a robbery. The police forced him to sign a document in Thai that he did not understand and he was then taken to the infamous Bangkwang prison in Bangkok[xcv]. He was incarcerated there for 18 months before his case was heard. When it was, it was a sham. His lawyer made little effort to help and although all his friends testified to his innocence he was sentenced to more than 17 years imprisonment. Eventually, after 9 years, he was pardoned by the king. Whether he also found Christ I do not know, but his testimony on return to Nepal was,

I have learned my lesson. I will never go after money again. I will be satisfied with what I have. The best lesson I learnt in prison is to live my new life to the fullest, to savour every moment with my family and be thankful for this gift from the Almighty. I will now find

---

[xcv] To understand what a Thai prison is like, you are referred to *Send them to Hell* by Sebastian Williams, the story of a British national who was locked up in Bangwang for many years on charges of drug smuggling, a crime of which he claimed to be innocent.

> *fulfilment by helping those less fortunate than me. I will turn into a social worker and **I'll never leave Nepal again**.* (emphasis mine)[274]

Nowadays Nepalis no longer need to enter Malaysia through Thailand; so migrant numbers have dropped although since 2009 they seem to have been increasing again.

There is an extensive sex trade in Thailand, especially in Bangkok, and many Nepali ladies have become entangled in this. I heard one story of a 20-year old Nepali girl.

> *She had been deceived by her 'lover' and was pregnant. She did not want to abort the pregnancy but also did not want to keep the child. However, unscrupulous people were trying to take advantage of her helplessness and poverty by suggesting they take and sell the child. This would then cover the costs of her confinement. Fortunately, a Nepali Christian lady somehow met this girl and rescued her. She was taken to a mission-run maternity centre and arrangements were made for the upbringing of the child.*

Not all stories have a happy ending. Some of these abused women try to find their own solution but in the wrong way. Some of the many who become HIV positive vent their anger by trying to spread the disease. Some take to alcohol or drugs. Others bury themselves deeper in the flesh trade by trafficking their own relatives from the villages.

Nepali Fellowships

There are 4 Nepali groups in Bangkok. All have grown out of one original group which met first in Calvary Baptist Church. The divisions were partly due to geography and partly to leadership issues. However, most of the believers, of whom there are around 100, still get together on special occasions.

In **Calvary Baptist Church**, A small group of 10-15 Nepalis meet together. Until 2014 they had a Myanmari pastor, but as most have come originally from Burma, language is no problem. Since 2014 they have a Nepali Pastor, Shyam Khatri. There is another group of Nepalis who meet at the **Myanmar Christian Assembly (MCA)** under the leadership of Daniel & Moemoe Subayre. At 40, they are currently the largest group, and again, most are originally from Burma. The third group is now an independent Nepali church called the **Nepali Gorkha Christian Church of Thailand (NGCCT).** Usually 15-20 Nepalis (sometimes up to 30 depending on duties) meet under the leadership of Anil & Gift Rai. The final group is the **Emmanuel Nepali Fellowship.** About 20-30 Nepalis meet under the leadership of Kailash Kharel.

Kailash told me his amazing testimony:

> *Born into a Brahmin Nepali family in Burma, from an early age he began to search for the truth but did not find it in the local Hindu and Buddhist religions. At some point he acquired a Bible, and after an interval when he attended the Jehovah's Witnesses (without understanding that they were a sect), he met a Christian pastor who led him to Christ. His conversion brought opposition from his family and he was forced to flee. That was when he first came to Thailand for a short period. Later he spent 6 months in Nepal and then returned to work in a cloth shop in Phukhet.*
>
> *And that is where he was – with his wife and 2 year old second son – at the time of the Tsunami in late 2004. They were praying when they suddenly heard a commotion on the street. Looking towards the sea he was*

shocked to see a huge black wall rapidly approaching. He rushed into the house, grabbed essentials and then tried to escape on his motorbike with his wife and son. However, the tsunami wave caught them and he was rolled over and over but eventually managed to catch hold of a tree and hold on until the water receded. Then, despite being sure that his family must have perished, he kept calling out their names. After half an hour he found them – safe in the top of a house with some foreigners.

Meanwhile, God had been working another miracle for his wife. She and the son had been washed up against a palm tree and amazingly she had managed to cling onto it and still hold little Viram safely. Carrying the child, she then started to wade towards a wooden house when another wave washed them through a window into a second storey room. She thought she was safe but then the water level began to rise and Viram was tugged away from her grasp until 4 minutes later when there was a sudden explosion in the water and he was tossed up and she was able to catch him – still alive. And that was how Kailas found them.

They had lost everything in Phuket, so after a few days they went to Bangkok, where God again provided work.

At that time many other Nepalis relocated from the south to Bangkok. Across Thailand, there are scattered Christian believers but most meet in Thai or Burmese fellowships.

South Thailand

In and around the **Phuket area**, especially on the beaches of Karon, James Bond, Katta, Rawai, Phi Phi Islands, Pathong, and Khaulak there are 40-50,000 Nepalis who have come from Burma. There is a small fellowship in the area led by a Nepali lady. Others have settled on the east of the Gulf of Thailand in and around **Pattaya**. They work in the tourist industry and in most of the shops in all these Islands one will meet at least one Nepali worker. A few even have their own shops. They are legal migrants who have been granted a *Bhat,*[xcvi] and some have even obtained permanent citizenship rights. Their work conditions are generally much better than those for Nepalis elsewhere in Thailand. In contrast, illegal immigrants have often been treated very badly by government agencies, factory owners and companies. Many were sent – without due reason – back to Burma where all too often they were punished and tortured. Daya Pradhan says there is a small fellowship in Phukhet and small preaching centres have been started in Krabi, Ong Nao and Khaulak.

North Thailand – Chiang Mai

As far as I can ascertain, there are far fewer Nepalis in the north than the south of Thailand. In **Chiang Mai** there is no formal Nepali fellowship, but there are several Christian Nepalis. One of them was Daniel, who had a tailor's shop, where he hosted a multilingual fellowship Many Nepalis in the area used to gravitate to Daniel's shop—both Christians and others; those who came from Nepal and the majority who came from Burma. ***Daniel*** also has an amazing testimony:

> *He was one of the few Nepalis in Thailand who came originally from Nepal. His early connections were with Pokhara, until the family moved to the east – Jhapa and Morang, and finally to Bhojpur. He had a traumatic childhood as his father left his mother with 4 children to bring up on her own. Eventually Daniel arrived in Kathmandu and found work, which seems to have been helping an agent to recruit overseas migrant workers. After some time he was persuaded to go overseas himself*

[xcvi] Thai work permit.

as he could earn more that way. This was many years ago – before official channels were opened for Malaysia and so he travelled with a legal tourist visa to Singapore. From there he got into Malaysia on a tourist visa and a bribe but rapidly became illegal as his visa ran out.

Before long he was arrested and on paying a 'fine' was taken to the Thai border and left there. That was the way things worked in those days. Together with six others, he crossed into Thailand. The others immediately left for Bangkok, but because he had no agent to help him, he had to stay near the border and cut trees to earn money to get there, but in due course he made it and found work. Those early years were not easy as he was illegal, but eventually he became a valued salesman, and his boss agreed to help him obtain legal status.

Confessing his illegal status, he went to immigration and paid a fine. He was kept in the detention centre for one day and then sent back to Nepal, but was soon able to return legally as this time he had a letter from his boss ensuring a job.

Around this time, he met some Christians and became a believer himself and started to attend the fellowship at Calvary Baptist church. Not long after this he was called to go and work in Hua Hin and while there he managed to set up his own business. Also, he met a local Thai Christian girl and after some time they married.

Sometime later, Daniel and his family came to Chiang Mai where they have been until recently, when he emigrated to New Zealand.

Ministry among Nepalis in Thailand is very different from that in most other parts of the Diaspora. Compared, for example, with Malaysia, there is far less support from any local churches, and little funding available. As many migrants are technically illegal, no one can have a high profile. They have to be constantly alert for any police raids, which makes fellowship meetings difficult to arrange. In view of the long working hours, migrants have little time for fellowship or teaching sessions. Factory workers usually get a day off, but maids have particular problems. If they are with western families they usually get a Sunday off and can go regularly to fellowship, even if not to a weekday house-group, but maids with Indian families are lucky to get one day off a month. Most Nepali migrants (at least in Bangkok) have been in Thailand far longer than any have been in Malaysia, but even so, they are not fully integrated. Some can speak some Thai but most converse in Nepali and/or Burmese. Those who are literate are able to read in Burmese but usually not well (if at all) in Nepali, and there is little motivation or time for them to learn to read Nepali, hence the use of Nepali medium resources is not possible. Because of the language issue, there is minimal opportunity for teaching ministry by Nepalese Nepalis or Nepali-speaking expatriates in Thailand. Maybe the way to help is to assist some committed Burmese-Nepali migrants to get further education, especially Bible training, so that they can minister in a language that is understood and acceptable.

It is theoretically possible to get a religious affairs visa – to be the pastor of a Nepali church, but in order to do that one needs support from an established Christian group in Thailand. There are more women than men, because jobs for women are easier to obtain, and this also affects the leadership. There may perhaps be a small role for Nepali-speaking visitors to interact with Nepalis who are employed in S Thailand in the tourist areas. Nepali CDs are well received and spoken Nepali is understood even if not totally. Another much needed ministry is prison visiting. Of all the groups of non-Thai prisoners in Thai jails, the Nepalis are the ones least visited, probably because most prison visitors do not speak Nepali and the Nepalis in jail know little English. From early 2014, some visits have been made to the group of more than 20 Nepalis in Bangkwang Prison in Nonthatburi, and it is known that about 9 other Nepalis are in jail in Chiang Rai.

ANDAMAN & NICOBAR ISLANDS

There are said to be around 10,000 Nepalis living on these islands, situated in the Bay of Bengal, between India and Burma. Some have lived there for several generations, having first come from places like Darjeeling and Sikkim in search of jobs. They now work mostly as night security guards, hotel cooks or waiters; and drivers, although there are also a few in the army or police force. Most of the younger generation have forsaken their Nepali language for Hindi.

Nepali Fellowships

A Christian evangelistic team from NE India, visiting the islands in 2008 said that they did not meet a single Nepali Christian but found the people very open and friendly.

OTHER ASIAN COUNTRIES

(SE Asia & East Asia)

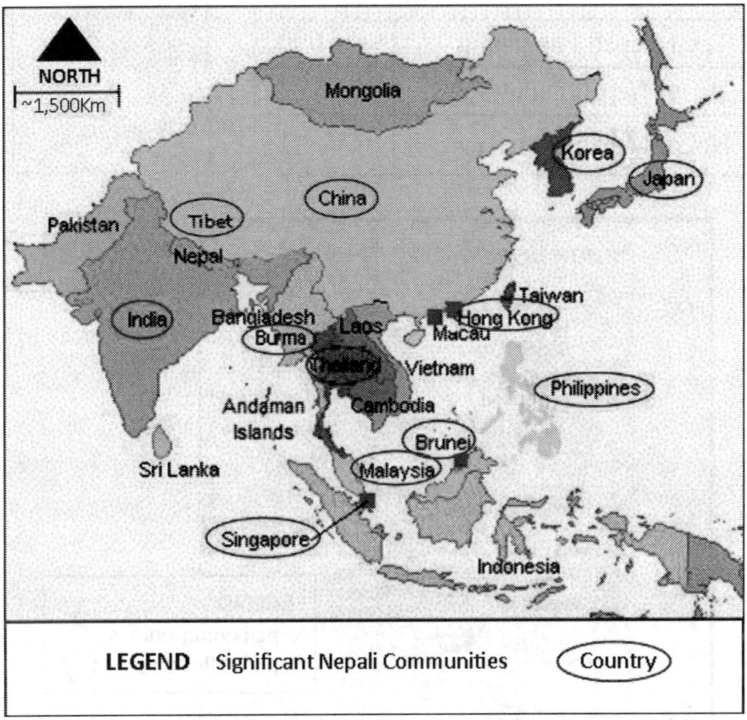

Nepalis have travelled to all the countries marked on the map, but only in 5 (apart from those already described) are there significant numbers.

SOUTH KOREA

STATISTICS	
Total Nepali Population	~ 25,000
No. of Nepali Fellowships	30-35
No. of Nepali Christians	~450

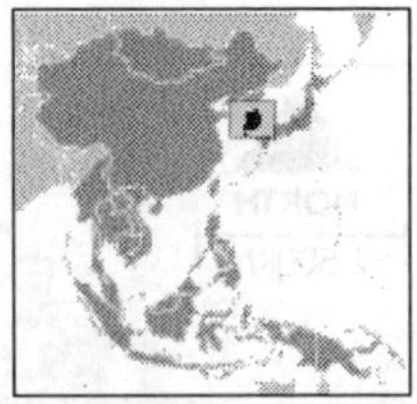

Nepalis first started to travel to S Korea only in the late 1980s as up until 1987 S Korea was itself a labour-exporting country. Thus, up to 1992, only about 4-6,000 Nepalis had gone to S Korea, but as at that time there was no work permit system, migrants had to enter on tourist visas and were therefore technically illegal and had to hide from the authorities. After 1990 more Nepalis started to travel to S Korea, but then the government stopped issuing tourist visas for Nepalis. They also made changes in the labour laws. Even in 2009, Wikipedia estimated that there were only around 8,200 Nepalis in S Korea, and the Korea Immigration Service cited 12,603 in 2011. By 2013, there were probably around 25,000, some of whom were undocumented. About 13% are women. Most live in centres like Seoul, Uijeongbu, Ansan, Gimhae, Incheon, Suwon and Gwangju. S Korea, Japan and the Philippines are slightly different from most of the other SE Asian countries in terms of the Nepali Diaspora. While the majority of Nepalis in S. Korea are labour migrants (of whom at least 2,500 were illegal in 2010), there are also businessmen and many international students [xcvii]. Some of the attraction for students is in the cost of courses being cheaper than in the west, but this is partly offset by the need for them to learn Korean – and to a standard significantly higher than that expected of labour migrants. If they do not pass the language examinations then they cannot continue their courses. There are also apparently many Nepali women married to Korean men whom they met through international matchmaking agencies. Children of mixed marriages are automatically granted Korean citizenship.

In the earlier days labour migrants had to work long hours (sometimes 12-16 hours) and the jobs were '3D'. Many did not receive their salary on time and others were beaten by their bosses or Korean co-workers. There were many industrial accidents.[xcviii]. Illegal workers were arrested and imprisoned by the Immigration Police. Despair led to many suicides. Because of this, Korean churches started to help

[xcvii] SONSIK, the Society of Nepalese Students in Korea was established in 2004

[xcviii] Up to 2003, more than 55 migrant workers had died in S Korea.

and show love to the migrant workers. They also created awareness of the migrant situation among the Korean people and appealed to their government to stop the wrong treatment and punishment of migrant workers, which had been going on since 1994. Slowly changes came and by 2003 the government had brought in more humane policies, thus making S Korea the first labour importing country in Asia to try and protect the rights of migrants through legislation making them equal with nationals.[275] Migrant workers got some facilities and it became easier for them to live and work in S Korea, but many find the work pressure a real challenge as this is not something most have been accustomed to in Nepal. Nevertheless "South Korea has [now] become the most lucrative destination for Nepali workers."[276]

> *23 year old **Biru Ghising** left his studies and went to Korea in 1992, at the time when many Nepalis were going. He spent 10 years there and confesses that especially in the beginning it was quite hard. He did not understand the language and he felt that the Korean people were not friendly and kindly towards foreign workers. However, unlike many he did not face so many difficulties and sees this as the grace of God in his life.*[277]

Nowadays the Government of Nepal is keen to promote S Korea as a suitable destination for Nepali workers. However, Nepalis who wish to work there must pass a Korean language test (TOPIK). There have been three TOPIK examinations (in 2008, 2010 & 2011) but the number of Nepalis who pass the test far exceeds the number of those who have to date been offered employment.[xcix] More than 50% of the 2011

[xcix] 13,000 have gone to work in Korea compared with 124,000 who passed the test.

aspirants were still waiting to be hired when another TOPIK examination was held in 2013.

Migrants must also register with the Employment Permit System (EPS) office. This system was established in S Korea in 2004 and an MoU was signed with Nepal in 2007. The aim was to help both Korean industry and Nepali migrants. EPS "allows the Korean companies to hire foreign migrant workers legally in five business sectors – manufacturing, construction, agriculture and livestock farming, offshore and coastal fishing, and services (restaurant, business support, social welfare, cleaning, nursing, house work, etc.)."[278] Failure to register with EPS renders migrants ineligible to receive a job offer. In this way it is aimed at eliminating illegal entry but still 33 Nepali migrants were deported in 2013 because they were using forged passports and EPS documentation.[279] In 2010 the local NRN Association opened a shelter in Dongdaemun-gu for Nepalis in trouble.

A further advantage of the EPS system is that it guarantees migrants legal 5-year work permits at a cost of only 800 USD (approx.. 72,000 Rs.), gives them equal labour rights with local employees and higher wages (1,000 USD per month or around Rs. 90,000) than unskilled workers get in Malaysia or 'Arab'.[280] Nevertheless the working conditions, especially for illegals, are still often appalling and Korean society in general remains unwelcoming. Even in the last few years there have been several deaths of Nepalis recorded in the press. The latest report was in December 2013, which indicated that 57 Nepalis had died in S Korea since 2007; 19 of them in 2013.[281] All the men were legal migrants, recruited through EPS. There were 3 cases of suicide, one of which purported to be the result of depression due to unfair dismissal and one case of serious illness for which the employer refused to take any responsibility.[282]

Nepali Fellowships

In contrast, local Korean churches have been very welcoming and tried to reach out to migrants through practical love and help. Many Nepali migrants have been attracted to Christ by this care, especially those who have been suffering from workplace problems or illness. There are around 35 main fellowships, but the list may not be comprehensive:[283]

No	Location	Name of Fellowship
1994	Seoul – Seobing-go	Onnuri Nepali Fellowship (Khadga B Rai)
	Seoul - Daerim	Nepali Worker Fellowship
	Seoul – Dongdaemun	Chowan Nepali Fellowship
2003		Nepal Mission Home (Dharma Raj Singh)
		El-Shaddai Nepali Fellowship
2006		AMI Nepali Fellowship (Prakash Kaphle)
2006	Seoul – Eujiro Samga	Youngnak Presbyterian Nepali Fellowship
1995/ 98	Seoul – Gasan Digital Media City	Jubilee Mission Nepali Fellowship (Ju Sun Mi & Phalgun Sunuwar)
	Seoul – Macheon	Ammy Fellowship
	Seoul – Sindorim (Uijeongbu)	International Calvary Church (Vicky Chaudhary)
1995	Uijeongbu	Garar Prayer Hall (Silash Rai)
1995	Incheon – Pupyeong	Juan Presbyterian Nepali Fellowship (Rana B Rana & Kim)
2005	Incheon – Seokbawi	Jesus Foreign Mission (Karna Gurung)
	Majang (nr Incheon)	Honggik Nepali Fellowship
	Yangju	Yangju Nepali Fellowship
	Goyang-si – Ilsan	Holy Nations Nepali Fellowship
	Gunpo	Gunpo Nepali Fellowship (Kaji Gurung)

	Ansan	Onnuri Emmanuel Nepali Fellowship (Bharat Rasai)
2005		Ansan Jaeil Nepali Fellowship (Amos Gurung)
2009		Ansan Nepali Community (Karna B Tamang)
		House Fellowship (Nima Lama)
2011		New Life Fellowship (Timothy Pun)
	Ansan – Gojan	Ansan Mission Nepali Fellowship
c1993	Suwon	Suwon Nepali Fellowship
	Pyeongtaek	Pyeongtaek Nepali Fellowship
	Songtan	Songtan Youngnak Nepali Fellowship
	Namseoul	Namseoul Dail Nepali Fellowship
2002	Cheonan	Heaven Central Church, Cheonan Nepali Fellowship (Ladies & Bhojraj Bhatta → Ramesh Bidari)
2005	G/Kimae	Gimae Migrant Mission Church (Yagraj Subedi)
2007	P/Busan – Haeyundae	Sooungroo Nepali Fellowship (Chu Si Yeon & Shyam Rana Magar)

According to Chandra Shrestha, who has researched the matter, the very first Nepali fellowship was in Suwon, although the exact date is unknown. From 1995 several groups started, all in the NW area around Seoul, and by 2000 there were at least 4 separate fellowships (Juan, Onnuri, Gunpo and Jubilee Mission) which joined to form a United Fellowship under the presidency of David Thapa.[c] In 2007, Nepali seminary students established NCTSA[ci] under the presidency of Ps. Shekhar Gurung.

The number of Nepali Christians is very difficult to state because some attend English or Korean fellowships and some

[c] Subsequent Presidents have been Janardan Tripathi, Jacob Chamling, Rana Bahadur Rana and Kaji Gurung.

[ci] Nepali Christian Theological Students Association

none at all – either because they work too far away from a fellowship or because they are only nominal Christians. Migrants in Korea share many of the problems found elsewhere but there are two or three other specific problems for Christians. There are now so many false sects in S Korea that knowing which group is doctrinally sound, despite their friendship, can prove difficult for theologically uneducated migrants. Because of the culture of materialism, even some, who arrived as Christians, become so busy earning money that they neglect Christian fellowship. There are also many active Nepali cultural organisations which can draw migrants away from seeking Christian fellowship.[284]

PHILIPPINES

STATISTICS	
Total Nepali Population	~ 1,000
No. of Nepali Fellowships	?1
No. of Nepali Christians	>40

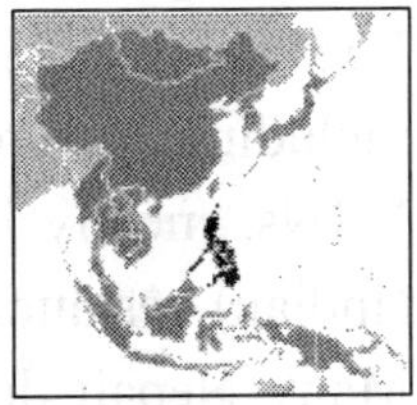

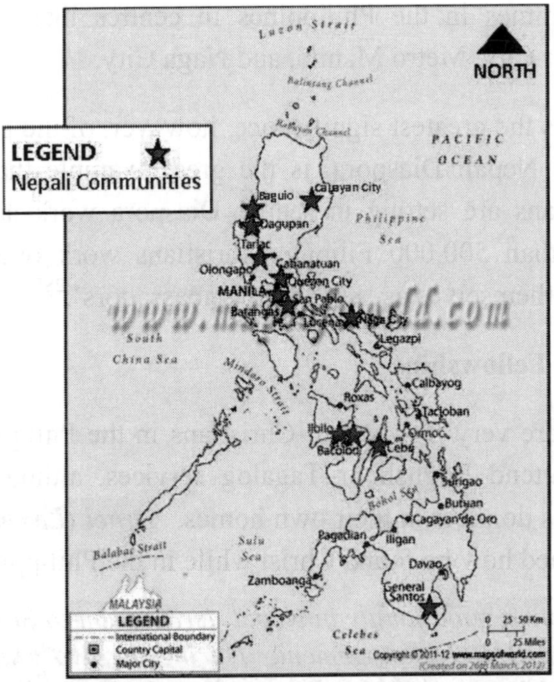

In the country census of 2000, it was estimated that there were almost 2,750 Nepalis in the Philippines, although one source suggested far fewer. They are thus a relatively small community, made up mostly of international students especially those in medical faculties. Nepali students are found in small numbers in all the main university cities of which there are about a dozen. BP Khanal reckoned that between 2005 and 2008 there were around 270 in Manila and Baguio Cities and >100 in Davao and Cebu cities. Most were singles although at the International Graduate School of Leadership (IGSL) at one time there were 17 Nepali families, including 3 from Darjeeling. There is a small group of 60-70 NRNs, mostly in mixed marriages and those who work in (Indian) restaurants, largely serving the student population. Many Nepali doctors choose to do their hospital residency programmes in the Philippines in centres like Cebu City, Quezon City, Metro Manila, and Naga City.

Perhaps the greatest significance, however, of the Philippines for the Nepali Diaspora, is the great example that Filipino Christians are setting in seeing Diaspora work as mission. More than 500,000 Filipino Christians work overseas and regard themselves as 'Kingdom ambassadors'.[285]

Nepali Fellowships

There are very few Nepali Christians in the Philippines, and most attend English or Tagalog services, although Nepali families do meet in their own homes. ***Israel (Laxmi Prasad)*** explained how he found Christ while in the Philippines:

> *From a good family in Nepal, Israel went to Singapore to study Hotel Management. During the two years he was studying, and later when working in Singapore and even for some years after he landed a good job as a Hostel Manager in the Philippines, he described his lifestyle as that of a drinker (virtually an alcoholic) and looking for a good time. Then one day he met a pastor who witnessed to him and gave him a tract. Initially Israel dismissed the matter but later the Lord started to work in his heart. One day he went to buy some beer but ended up with iced*

tea! Although he prayed for a change in his life and the longing for drink disappeared, he was still not sure that Christ was for Nepalis as well as westerners! But the peace of the Christians challenged him and eventually he accepted Christ and a year later decided to return to Nepal to share the Good News with his family and friends. By 2013, he had become a part-time pastor of a small church and was running two momo shops where he employs and trains men who are out of work.[286]

There is one small Nepali Fellowship in Quezon City, established in 2004, with a current membership of around 40. Its leadership has changed frequently as most have been students.[cii] Outreach strategy included events organized exclusively for Nepali students in Manila and Baguio, when the Christians were able to share the gospel. This led to practical help and several who came to Christ are now serving him back in Nepal. According to Dinesh Shrestha, some IGSL students meet for fellowship on Saturdays on the college compound. There may also be other small fellowships, and in Cebu city – famous for its Civil Aviation training – brothers Him Lal and Kul Bahadur Pradhan, from NE India, both married to Filipinos, reach out to Nepali students alongside their ministry in the Chinese church.

[cii] Leaders since 2006 include: Vijay Karmacharya, Bishnu Regmi, Kesang T Lama, BP Khanal, David Regami, Sher Bahadur AC, Dinesh Shrestha, Prakash Shrestha, Niraj Thapa, & Santosh Guide.

JAPAN

STATISTICS	
Total Nepali Population	20,000
No. of Nepali Fellowships	? >1
No. of Nepali Christians	??

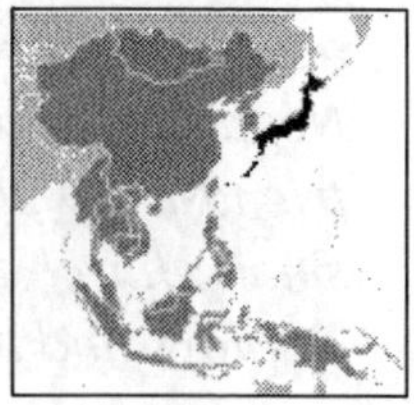

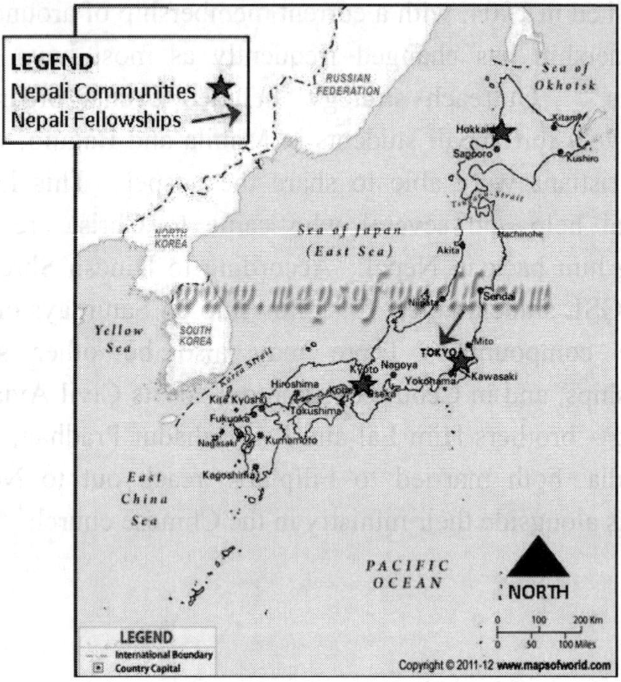

The first groups of Nepali students went to study in Japan 100 years ago under the Rana Regime, but especially since the 1950s a steady small stream have continued. In 2013, it was estimated that there were approximately 20,000 Nepalis working in Japan, most of them based in Tokyo and

Sapporo.[ciii] Most are temporary residents but a few have integrated, intermarried and settled with their families. Many Nepalis – even some Christians – going to Japan for study are influenced by the materialistic opportunity to better their lifestyle, including the temptation to work all day on a Sunday and earn more money.

When compared with other centres in SE Asia (and the Middle East), Japan is popular because even migrants in low-skilled manual jobs have been able to earn perhaps 10 times the average wage in Nepal. Nowadays IT engineers and other Nepali professionals are being recruited, while other (probably less highly skilled) migrants have joined Japan's garments industry and agriculture sector. There is also said to be a criminal network which imports large numbers of women as sex slaves, [287] but Nepalis are not mentioned in this connection: the women are mostly Thais and Filipinos.

One positive feature in labour relations between Nepal and Japan occurred in mid-2012, when the government made an offer for Nepali industrial trainees to work under the Japan International Training Co-operation Organisation (JITCO).[288] This scheme was to give around 1,000 Nepalis the opportunity to receive 2 years on-the-job work experience in industry, including hotels, agro industry and cooperatives. However, the conditions were that selected candidates should learn Japanese, and gain understanding of Japanese culture and its legal system as well as paying a fee of Rs. 65,000.[civ]

[ciii] One source gives a much higher figure (1 *lakh*)

[civ] Rs. 50,000 of this would go to the recruiting agency.

Despite this sort of provision, and the fact that "violent crime is relatively rare in Japan and the country's small immigrant population is not routinely targeted in racist attacks," not all Nepal-Japan relationships have been good recently. In 2012, a Nepali immigrant was beaten up and killed by two Japanese nationals in an unprovoked street attack in Osaka. In early 2013, there was a flood of articles in the Nepali press about a Nepali national who had spent 15 years languishing in a Japanese jail for a murder he did not commit. Amnesty International said "Mainali was denied access to lawyers after his arrest and was beaten, kicked and pinned against a wall by police officers." He also spent 3 years in prison before his trial was settled. Apparently "almost all murder cases in Japan result in guilty verdicts because so many are based on confessions." The happy ending was that "Mainali was released from jail in June [2013] when his conviction was overturned. He was sent back to Nepal by immigration authorities because he had – during his time in prison – overstayed his visa"![cv]

Nepali Fellowships

According to Andy Purja, who was converted when serving as a Gurkha in HK, an El Shaddai group meets at Tokyo Baptist Church on Sundays and for Cottage meetings on Saturdays. Richen Karmacharya, who studied in Japan, reckons that there are few – if any – other Nepali fellowships, but some students, like him, attended Japanese or international fellowships.

[cv] Most of the quotations are taken from the HK Standard, Mar 2013

BRUNEI & DARUSSALAM

STATISTICS	
Total Nepali Population	1,500
No. of Nepali Fellowships	? 1
No. of Nepali Christians	? <20

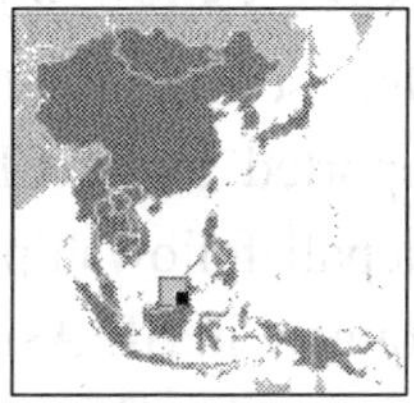

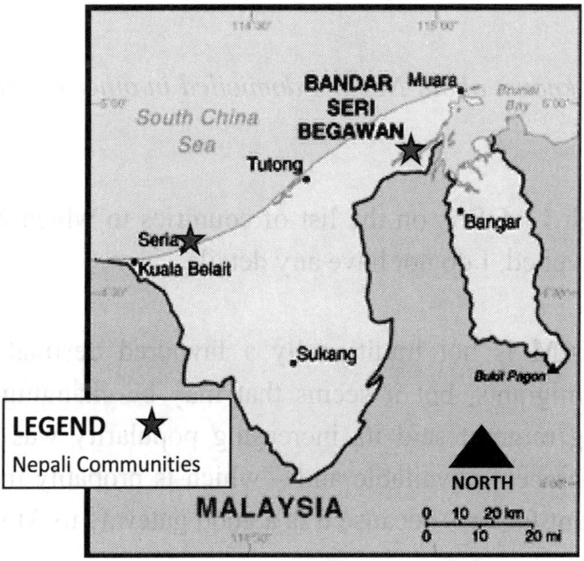

Brunei is one of the many destinations where the Gurkhas have carved out a name for themselves. There are approximately 1,500 Nepalis in Brunei and they are almost exclusively Gurkhas or ex-Gurkhas. Two thirds – the older men – are serving as security guards, especially for the royal family and in the capital city of Bandar Seri Begawan. The remainder – the younger men – are still serving British Gurkhas, and are based in the oil-rich Seria district at the request of the Sultan. They live in camps rather than integrated into the local community.

Nepali Fellowships

One source stated that 1% of the Nepali population are reported to be Christians, and I believe there is one small Nepali fellowship. However, Brunei is the strictest Muslim country in SE Asia, so it is not easy for the Nepali Christians to meet for fellowship. Some of the Brunei Gurkhas are now based in the UK and fellowshipping there in Kent.

Little is known about Nepalis domiciled in other countries in SE Asia.

Although **LAOS** is on the list of countries to which Nepalis have travelled, I do not have any details.

VIETNAM is not traditionally a favoured destination for Nepali migrants, but it seems that may be changing. One outgoing migrant said its increasing popularity was due to good jobs being available and – which is probably the most significant factor – because it is a good gateway to America.

I have not discovered any information regarding Nepalis domiciled in **CAMBODIA.**

As in 2012, the Ministry of Foreign Affairs proposed opening a diplomatic office in **INDONESIA**,[289] there may be significant numbers of Nepalis working there, but I have discovered no details.

CHINA

STATISTICS	
Total Nepali Population	>3,500
No. of Nepali Fellowships	Nil
No. of Nepali Christians	???

One source says that in mainland China (excluding HK and Macau) there are around 3,500 Nepalis. Some are Chinese citizens i.e. the descendants of mixed marriages. China is now host to international students from 175 countries, thus many of the Nepalis in China are students – studying culture or language but also technical subjects like engineering and medicine. Many Nepali students have been choosing China, despite the language problem, as the costs for medical courses in Nepal (and in India) are so high – 4 million rupees compared with 2.5 million in China. Regardless of how bright they are, most students fail to get government scholarships in Nepal as these are limited and often reserved for 'the elite'![290] The majority of Nepalis live in one of the major cities like Guangzhou, Kunming, and Dali City, as well as in HK and in cities of the Tibetan Autonomous Region'.

Guangdong / Guangzhou

The number of Nepalis – mostly traders and international students – who now live in Guangzhou, has increased so much in recent years and the city has become a significant centre for Nepali imports that the Government of Nepal has recently (in 2013) opened a Consulate General's Office there.[cvi] One reason for the increase is the internal migration of Nepalis from other parts of China, like HK and Kunming.

Yunnan

Since 2005, a steady stream of Nepali medical students has been enrolling in Dali University in Dali City, Yunnan. The latest estimate is of 175 students. However, in January 2013, a crisis occurred particularly for the medical students, when Chinese authorities gave students a month's deadline to pay their fees or else be deported. In fact, what had happened was that although the families of students had already lodged the fees with a consultancy, some of these consultancies had embezzled 45 million rupees. (from more than 70 students).

[cvi] Nepal has an Embassy in Beijing and two other Consulates General – in HK and Lhasa.

TIBET (Tibet Autonomous Region)

Tibet has a long relationship with China, dating back even beyond the Middle Ages. In the 7th century it was a unified empire but later came under Chinese sovereignty. In 1913 it again declared its own independence but this lasted only until 1951 when China invaded and the Dalai Lama was forced to flee to India. The link between Nepal and Tibet, and therefore of Nepali migration to Tibet, is one of the longest in the history of Nepali migration.

> The first expatriate Nepali community was established in Tibet… through cultural exchange and trade with Tibet… as early as the 7th century… Until the 19th century there were more Nepalis in Tibet than anywhere else outside Nepal… Sir Charles Bell, British Resident in Lhasa, reported as late as the 1920s that there were colonies of Nepalis in Tse-tang, Shigatse, Gyantse, Lhatse and the province of Kongpoi.[291]

The first Nepalis to travel to Tibet were Newar merchants and during the Malla period (1100-1480 AD) several trade routes across the Himalayas were in regular use. They travelled to the major cities of Lhasa, Shigatse and Gyantse where many settled and integrated into Tibetan culture and life and even married Tibetan women. The most famous Nepali migrant to Tibet was Arniko. In the 2nd half of the 13th century he went to Lhasa to build a golden Buddhist stupa. He also met the Mongol Emperor, Kublai Khan, in Yuan China. This was the period too, when the Jesuits and later, the Capuchin Fathers were coming and going to Lhasa via Kathmandu. The very first Nepali Christians were possibly the few converts of the last Jesuit Father Desideri, in 1721.[292]

However, in the late 18th century, Prithvi Narayan's *nakabandhi*[cvii] of the Kathmandu Valley and his subsequent conquest of the Malla kingdoms, put a stop to this trade. In the 19th century, the British opened up a shorter trade route via Kalimpong, which effectively excluded Kathmandu from the Tibet-India trade, although some traders remained and in 1943, those based in Lhasa formed the Nepalese Chamber of Commerce in order to promote and protect their own business interests.

Some Nepalis have lived in Tibet for over 300 years. They are mostly *kazara*[cviii] and multilingual but some still prefer to identify as Nepali and send their children to the Gorkha Primary School of Lhasa, established 65 years ago, which has two Nepali teachers and is paid for by the government of Nepal. As a result of these historical developments, there are nowadays two distinct groups of Nepalis in Tibet. The first group consists of those (now) Tibetan families who are descendants of earlier Nepalese traders. The second group are the hotel and restaurant workers from Nepal who come on short-term work visas. Although only about 100 in number, they are skilled in the preparation of non-Asian cuisine.

Nepali Fellowships

As far as I have been able to discover, there are no specific Nepali Fellowships today in the Tibet region or elsewhere in mainland China. Nepali students are widely scattered in the country but where a few in a college are Christians, they try to meet together for fellowship. They also seek fellowship with students from other language groups.

---

cvii Historic blockage of the (Kathmandu) Valley.

cviii Mixed race Tibetan.

HONG KONG

STATISTICS	
Total Nepali Population	~60,000
No. of Nepali Fellowships	>18
No. of Nepali Christians	>1,300

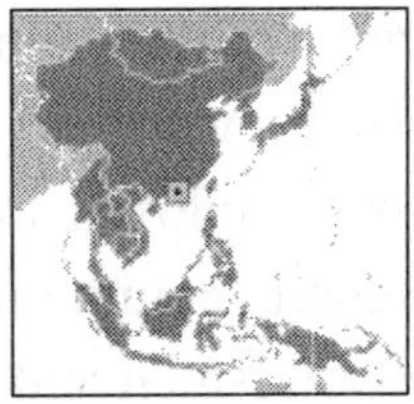

The South Asian population of HK is very largely a legacy of British rule. In the case of Nepalis, who constitute around 0.2% of the total population, a large proportion are the children of soldiers, born in HK while their fathers were serving with the Brigade of Gurkhas between 1970 and 1997 (when the British withdrew from HK and handed it back to the Chinese). These children have right of residence and can also sponsor their parents to stay on in HK on retirement from the army. Most of them still live in Shek Kong (near the old Whitfield Barracks) and in Yuen Long District.[293]

According to the Joshua Project, there are more than 14,000 Nepalis in HK, of whom 1% are professing Christians. The official 2011 Census stated a figure of 16,518 Nepalis living in HK: other sources cite figures of 19,000 and even 40,000. However, most Nepalis, like Ang Kusang Sherpa, believe that this number only represents the permanent residents and not the total Nepali population. They believe the true figure is more likely to be approximately 60,000 Nepalis who live and work in Hong Kong, including some from West Bengal in India. There may be several reasons for this discrepancy. One is that almost all the Gurkha families have British passports and spend time in the UK although many prefer the climate in HK! Also, by law they must return to HK every 36 months to maintain their right of residence.

Many of the younger Nepalis are traders; the older generation usually work as guards in the security industry but some are also employed in menial work. Most of the leaders in the Nepali community (NGOs, social workers, interpreters, businessmen and even pastors) are ex-army or their children. The conditions for work in HK are highly superior to those experienced by labour migrants in many nearby countries, but some of the same pressures remain – witness the story told by Nepal News in early 2013 – of a Nepali jeweller who committed suicide in HK "due to financial reasons".

Two other issues that have been a significant problem for the Nepali community in HK are unemployment and drug addiction. The latter is probably similar to the pattern of drug abuse seen among the youth of rich families in Nepal, but has the added complications that they are on their own overseas and there is a need also for reconciliation with their families back at home in Nepal.

One interesting and more positive feature of migrant life in HK has been mentioned by Hsai, i.e. "migrant workers from the Philippines, Indonesia, Thailand, Nepal, and Sri Lanka have worked together across nation-state, racial, and gender boundaries," in the Asian Migrants Coordinating Body.[294]

Nepali Fellowships

According to Perry, the Nepali Fellowship in HK, established after the Brigade of Gurkhas headquarters was transferred there in 1970, was the first Nepali language fellowship outside of S. Asia, and this despite opposition from the army hierarchy.[295] Even before that, some Christian Gurkhas had met off camp for Bible study and prayer in the 1960s.[296]

Swiba Lepcha speaks about the early days in the 1970s:

> *"In 1973 with a handful of Nepalese believers we started the Hong Kong Nepalese Christian Fellowship which grew in number to almost hundreds. There was indirect persecution to fellow Gurkha Christian service personnel. All these brothers were tested by many trials but they stood their ground."*[297]

He remembers colleagues like Philip Tikaram, Jarna Rai (now a pastor in Kathmandu) Bom Prasad Rai and especially Nar Bahadur Sahi, who is still serving in HK but who earlier gave up his Commission to be an officer so as not to give up his faith in Christ. Swiba also mentioned Ron and Mary Byatt, who were instrumental in setting up the Nepali Christian Fellowship; Roy and Alma Hagen and Ian Bull (British Army Chaplain), who gave much needed encouragement and support.

By 2013, there were at least 18 Nepali Fellowships including 2 mission organizations that provide Nepali fellowship – the Inner City Ministry (ICM) and Yang Memorial Methodist Social Service (YMMSC) Yuen Long and Yau Ma Tei branch, which especially focuses on drug abusing Nepalis. Four churches come under the International English Church and 3 under the local Chinese Church. The other 11 have grown by division. The total number of believers is probably around 1,300 and numbers are steadily growing in the Nepali community. The biggest church has around 350 members; others seem to have between 30 and 70 although higher figures are claimed, as some of their members may be in the

UK or on holiday. Most, but not all, are linked with the Nepali Christian Council in HK. There is also a large El Shaddai congregation and a few Roman Catholics. Jehovah's Witnesses and Church of Christ are two sects that are a problem in HK. Since 2008, the Manna Book Center has been the source of supply for Nepali Christian literature not only to HK but also to Singapore and S Korea.[298]

Although most Nepalis in HK have Gurkha connections, not all do and one has shared his testimony:

> ***Sharan*** *was born into a poor farming family in Bhojpur, one of 7 brothers and sisters, but has now been in HK for 9 years. It came about like this. His father died when he was only 6 and so he had to work hard to fund his own education. After graduation he married a lady who was working in HK, but unfortunately he was unable to get an ID to stay there and so they were separated for 3 years. During that time, his eldest brother witnessed to him but he admits that he turned a deaf ear and tried to solve his own problems through good morals, hard work and his own wisdom without involving God. When his first son was born, Sharan was able to go to HK and they were so happy. But life was still difficult. His wife had to work extremely hard. And then the HK Immigration was about to send him back to Nepal because he did not have a good job or money to rent a nice apartment. At that time when there was no way he could help himself, a missionary shared God's message with them, and this time, in their weakness, the gospel touched their hearts and they accepted Christ. After some months they were baptised and then 3 days later the miracle happened and Sharan got his ID. This confirmed God's faithfulness to them. Sharan says, "We give him all the praise... Everything is possible in God... I know the Bible is true, he took our burden & healed us spiritually." 3 years*

later they moved from the English church to the Nepali church UNCC for their spiritual growth. Today they are very happy following Jesus and say, "Life is not about the problems we face; it is about our relationship with Jesus. God is bigger than our problems."[299]

As far as I can discover, **MACAU** (which, unlike HK, was a Portuguese possession) has never had the same attraction for Nepalis. Considering Macau's reputation as a 'city of sin,' we should be grateful for this!

The island of **TAIWAN** (formally known as Formosa) has had a chequered history. Today it is a separate sovereign state although still claimed by mainland China as its 23rd province. Around 200 Nepalis live in Taiwan: many married to Taiwanese ladies, some international students and a few household helpers. Most are nominal in their own religion. Ronald Adhikari knows of only 3 Nepali Christians and no Nepali language fellowships and there appears to be virtually no specific outreach to Nepalis.

MONGOLIA was originally part of the Chinese Mongol Empire but today is a separate sovereign state. I have found no specific information on Nepali migrants.

Chapter 9

THE 'WEST'

"... you shall spread abroad to the WEST and to the east and to the north and to the south, and in you and your offspring shall all the families of the earth be blessed."
~ Genesis 28:14 ESV ~

The 'West' is not one single geographical area, but includes most of what today are regarded as 'developed' countries, of which there are three main blocs: the UK and Continental Europe, North America, and Australia-New Zealand. Japan, the Philippines and S. Korea are included with SE Asia as they also host many Nepali labour migrants as well as students, most of whom eventually return to Nepal. S Africa is listed with other African states but hosts few Nepalis.

Since the 2nd World War migrants and refugees have flooded into many western countries, and in the more recent past, the majority of them have come from Asia, many fleeing from unstable political regimes. The peak years for Nepalis to seek refuge in the west coincided with the Maoist insurgency (approximately 1996 to 2006). Although there have been – and still are – Nepali asylum seekers and some relatively unskilled workers in this region, the majority of Nepali migrants to the west are probably students and professionals, as they regard western university degrees of more value than those awarded in Asia, regardless of the actual standards and relevance of the courses. The 'West' therefore remains their first choice of destination. Europe (especially the UK), the USA and now Australia are favourites for those able to afford the cost of study in the west. This is partly because the medium of study in these countries is English, which is already known – at least to some extent – by the would-be students.

However, travel to and study in the west is extremely expensive, and it is becoming increasingly difficult for Nepali students to obtain visas – largely because of the tightened rules imposed by western governments on educational institutions. Until recently many colleges promoted courses that were only low level, but gave an easy route for poor students to change over to being workers.

Regarding professional migrants to the west and medical personnel in particular, Ahmad has highlighted the serious long-term consequences for both the sending nations and the host countries. The former lose valuable educated citizens from their work force and the latter have to rely increasingly on imported labour. The financial benefit from any remittances is vastly outweighed by the loss of intellectual and skill capital and the resulting lack of development of local health services,[300] something seen already in Nepal.

This permanent 'brain drain' is the indirect result of the difference between the status of Nepali migrants in Asia and those who travel to the 'west.' Although permanent settlement and citizenship are not easily procured (and regulations are getting more stringent each year), in almost all these countries it is theoretically possible, given time, for Nepali migrants to obtain a green card or its equivalent.

Some who achieve this, retain links to their homeland through NRN Associations and personal or family contacts, while others want to put their migrant status behind them, feeling that it is a derogatory term. Manu Brajaki gave the interesting example that a Nepali writer would prefer to be known as 'a Nepali who writes in English' rather than an 'immigrant/diaspora Nepali writer.[301] Another controversial, but pertinent, comment has been made by Ramesh Badal, Legal Advisor to GFONT: "we are also sending skilled people abroad, who rich countries have not invested in. It's time to raise the issue of a human resource development fund that rich countries contribute to in exchange for supplying them with skilled manpower."[302]

There are two special groups of Nepali migrants, who have settled in the 'West'. During the height of the Maoist insurgency, there was a steady stream of asylum seekers ending up in a wide variety of likely and unlikely destinations, but this is no longer an important issue. The **'Lhotshampas' – the (Nepali) Bhutanese refugees** are, however, a special case, and after many years of political wrangling, they are, at last being resettled in several western countries. The **British Gurkhas**, now allowed to settle in the UK, are also special, but the initial promise, won for them by Joanna Lumley in 2009, is not living up to its expectations.

Churches & Nepali Fellowships

As the majority of western countries are those with Christian cultural roots, this is a great challenge to the churches in these lands. It is a great opportunity for outreach and 'mission on the doorstep'. Conversely vibrant Nepali Christians often put lethargic local believers to shame. Some of the most rapidly growing churches in most western countries are migrant churches. However…

> The greatest challenge is finding a way to integrate first-generation immigrants with [their] second- and third-generation younger people. The integrity of the original culture and the appeal of mainstream… culture often conflict, even in church life.[303]

The older generation of Nepali immigrants usually do not know English when they arrive and find it hard to pick up. As a result, they prefer to worship in their mother tongue. In contrast, their children and grandchildren already know English or pick it up very quickly. They want to identify with their local peer group. If this very important difference is not taken into consideration when arranging Christian fellowship for the Nepali community, the younger generation may be lost to the church. One positive way around this is for Nepali fellowships to be closely linked with local English-speaking congregations.

In most western countries with significant populations of Nepali immigrants, there are Nepali fellowships. With the possible exception of the Bhutanese refugees in America, they are not growing as spectacularly as the groups in the Asian labour diaspora, and there are several reasons for this. They often have their families with them. They live scattered in the local community, not all together in hostels. New arrivals especially are under a lot of pressure with their study or work, and the influence of western secularism and materialism is strong.

EUROPE

UK is the most important country to consider in Western Europe, largely because of its Gurkha heritage. Other European countries are considered in their geographically related groups. However, it is not easy to divide Europe, as the groups of countries tend to overlap. I have therefore chosen to break them down into smaller units that seem to have similar Nepali migrant data. Only countries where I have been able to discover even a minimum of information about Nepali migrants are mentioned. This minimum may even be as little as a name on the Nepal Government list of allowed countries or a brief mention in a news article stating that Nepalis have gone there.

UNITED KINGDOM

STATISTICS	
Total Nepali Population	~80,000
No. of Nepali Fellowships	~27
No. of Nepali Christians	~2,500

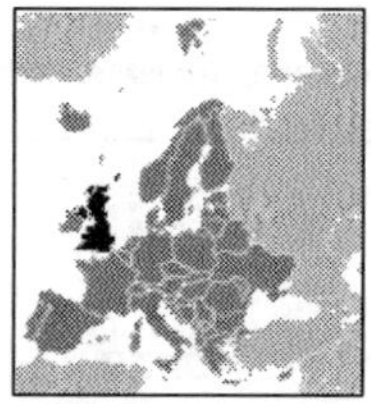

Compared with the Afro-Caribbeans, Indians and Pakistanis, Nepalis are relatively recent immigrants to the UK. When the Rana Prime Minister, Jung Bahadur, visited in 1850, he was said to be the first, although there is a story that he was met by a Nepali already living in London.[304] However, from then, for the next century, there was no tradition of Nepalis coming to Britain. The 2001 UK Census reported that there were 5,943 Nepal-born Nepalis living in the UK, but the corresponding figure from the Nepal Census was 7,221. In both cases, the overwhelming majority were males.[305] In 2005, John Bradley (an ex-Nepal missionary) researched Nepalis in Britain and came up with a figure of 30,000[cix] of whom "there could be 1,000 in Reading [alone]" At about the same time, a BBC[cx] 'Born Abroad' survey highlighted several groups close to British Army bases and in particular 844 in the Folkestone area. "By early 2006, it was clear that the Nepali population in the UK was rising rapidly, but there was no systematic source to identify their number and characteristics."[306]

[cix] Other informants were more conservative, giving figures of 15-20,000.
[cx] British Broadcasting Corporation.

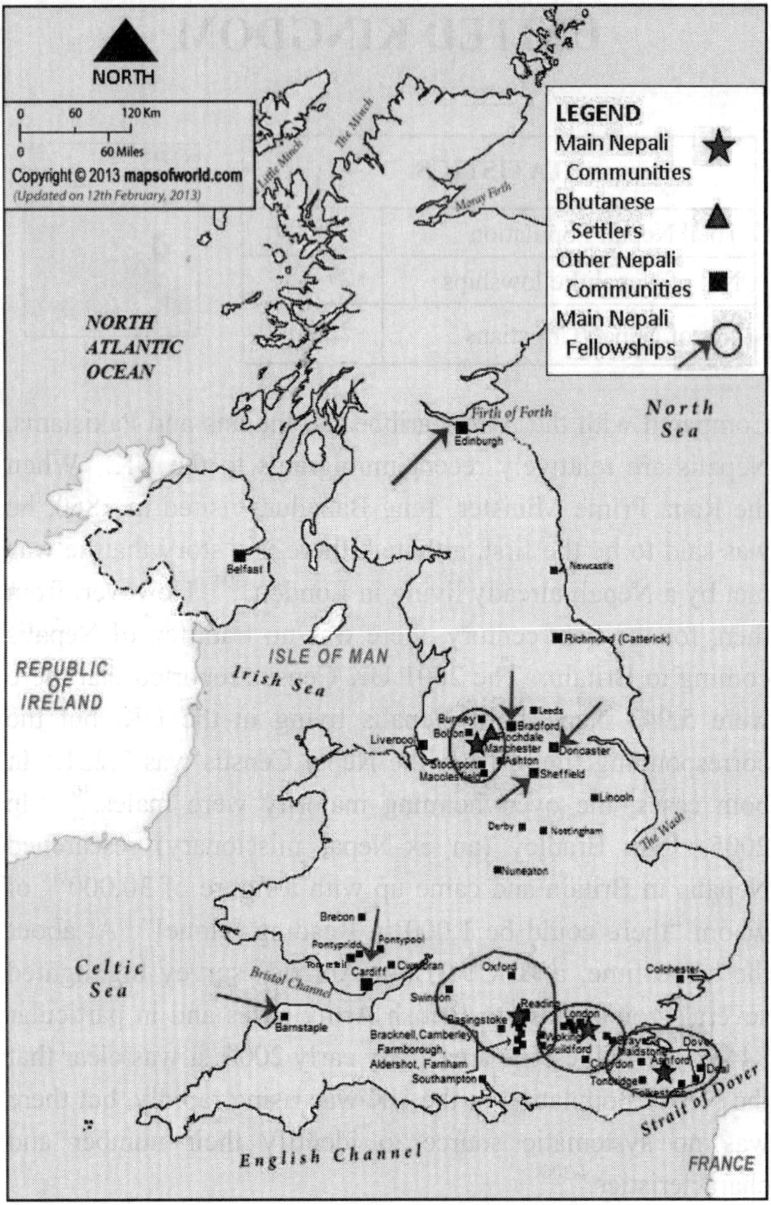

Nepali Settlement in the UK

The earlier centres of increase seem to have been London, Cardiff, Aldershot and Reading.[307] Then, in 2011, the "Office for National Statistics [ONS] estimated that 35,000 Nepali-born people were currently resident in the UK."[308] In 2012/3, Wikipedia, mentioned the 2010 ONS estimate of around 40,000 and also a possible 50,000 (Himalayan Yeti Nepalese Association estimate). However, these figures do not take into consideration the 2011 UK Census. Research by the Centre for Nepal Studies, UK (CNSUK) shows that the anomalous figures of 35-36,000 in 2011 and 41-43,000 for each of the years 2009-2010,[309] must have been under-estimates. This must be so especially in view of the big increase after the change in law in 2009 allowing large numbers of (ex)Gurkhas to settle in the UK. The number of Nepalis who had obtained British citizenship (and so had automatically lost their Nepali citizenship)[cxi] had increased from 12 in 1990 to almost 12,000 in 2011, but this should not have skewed the data as adjustments are made for the final figure to account for the differences in size between estimates of Nepalis by country of birth and Nepali citizens.[310]

Today, the figure for Nepalis domiciled in the UK, according to the UK Home Office is 41,000,[cxii] however Thomas Hieber, by making slight adjustments to the 2011 UK Census figures, suggests that the numbers are 59,902 (England), 300 (Wales) 1,200 (Scotland) and 400 (N Ireland) with clearly the majority settled in England.[311] According to CNSUK these figures are also under-estimates, "because the Census showed

---

[cxi] NRNs in the UK and ex-Gurkhas have been petitioning the GoN to make special provision for them to have a kind of dual citizenship and which would protect any UK earnings they send back to Nepal. (*Nepal News*, 29 Dec 2011)

[cxii] This presumably does not include any undocumented migrants.

over 1,000 in Wales alone. We know for fact that the figure for Scotland is many times more than this."[312]

The CNSUK survey therefore gave a much higher number even for 2008 – 72,173, including 61,835 scattered residents, 8,254 serving Gurkhas and their families, and 2,084 otherwise unaccounted for – maybe illegal immigrants. However, this was a sample estimate and not a census figure.[313] Because of the changes in immigration rules, further big increases are probably unlikely to occur although some Gurkha families will continue to come.

Dr Krishna Adhikari of CNSUK provided further clarification on the number of Nepalis domiciled in the UK but confusion and uncertainty remain.[314] In the 2011 ONS UK Census, the figure of 60,202 was given for England and Wales alone – a rise of 969% since the 2001 Census (5,630)! The 2008 CNSUK estimate was 72,173, but in 2006/7 various guesstimates of 50,000 to 130,000 were made. By 2012, Dr. Adhikari suggested the most likely figure was about 80,000,[cxiii] reached by making adjustments for temporary workers, students and elderly Gurkhas who did not participate in the census, despite this being a legal requirement. Some landlords omitted their Nepali families and some soldiers serving overseas were also missed out. As there was no specific ethnic category of Nepali to 'tick', Nepalis had to 'tick' 'Other Asian' and then write 'Nepali,' it is likely that many did not do this or perhaps recorded a sub-category of ethnicity that was not recognised as Nepali.[315]

Gurkhas and ex-Gurkhas tend to congregate in several

[cxiii] Ps. Dambar Adhikari suggested perhaps 90,000 with 20,000 students.

specific areas near to the Army camps where they used to work or family members still work: these include London, Reading, Thurrock, Catterick, Shorncliffe, Folkestone, Farnborough, Aldershot, Doncaster, Sandhurst, Camberley, Maidstone, Croydon, Basingstoke, Plumstead, Ashford, and Guildford. Other Nepalis have scattered much more widely. One group runs a village pub on the borders of Herefordshire and Gloucestershire, and there are many Nepali restaurants e.g. in Cornwall, Derby, Lichfield. Other places mentioned include Birmingham, Liverpool, Manchester, Leeds, Sheffield, Bradford, Newcastle, Derby and Nottingham besides Harrow, Willesden, Wembley, etc in Greater London, plus Cardiff (S Wales) and Edinburgh and Glasgow (Scotland). The top 20 'towns' identified by CNSUK[316] are:

<table>
<tr><td>1</td><td>Rushmoor – Aldershot – Hampshire*</td><td>6.5%</td></tr>
<tr><td>2</td><td>Shepway – Folkestone – Kent</td><td>2.2%</td></tr>
<tr><td>3</td><td>Greenwich – London</td><td>2.1%</td></tr>
<tr><td rowspan="2">4</td><td>Reading – Berkshire</td><td rowspan="2">1.8%</td></tr>
<tr><td>Richmondshire (Catterick) – N Yorks</td></tr>
<tr><td>5</td><td>Ashford – Kent</td><td>1.4%</td></tr>
<tr><td rowspan="2">6</td><td>Hounslow – London</td><td rowspan="2">1%</td></tr>
<tr><td>Surrey Heath – Surrey</td></tr>
<tr><td rowspan="3">7</td><td>Maidstone – Kent</td><td rowspan="3">0.9%</td></tr>
<tr><td>Bracknell Forest – Berkshire</td></tr>
<tr><td>Brent – London</td></tr>
<tr><td>8</td><td>Ealing – London</td><td>0.8%</td></tr>
<tr><td rowspan="5">9</td><td>Hillingdon – London</td><td rowspan="5">0.6%</td></tr>
<tr><td>Harrow – London</td></tr>
<tr><td>Dover – Kent</td></tr>
<tr><td>Swindon – Wiltshire</td></tr>
<tr><td>Basingstoke & Deane – Hampshire</td></tr>
<tr><td rowspan="2">10</td><td>Newham – London</td><td rowspan="2">0.3%</td></tr>
<tr><td>Barnet – London</td></tr>
<tr><td>11</td><td>Wiltshire</td><td>0.2%</td></tr>
</table>

* Increased to 12-15% by 2013

In all, the CNSUK study identified 327 towns where a significant number of Nepalis lived, although in most there were fewer than 100.[317] The greatest concentration is in the South East and Greater London.[318] The top 10 counties are Greater London, Hampshire, Surrey, Kent, Berkshire, Wiltshire, Essex, Lancashire, Warwickshire and Oxfordshire.

There are large numbers of international students. Many others work in restaurants, real estate and renting, wholesale and retail and health and social care. Especially during the years of the Maoist insurgency, there were many asylum seekers. Undoubtedly there are also still unquantified numbers of illegal immigrants – those who have found their way to the UK through Europe or other intermediate destinations or those who have overstayed their visa or moved outside originally legitimate student visas.

The single most important group of Nepali migrants in the UK are surely the Gurkhas. There are still 3,570 Gurkhas serving in the British armed forces, and all but one battalion are based in the UK.[319] They were given permission to settle as a result of the intervention of Joanna Lumley. Initially they saw her, and she saw herself, as their champion, but it is now becoming clear that she has actually done many of them a bad turn. Huge numbers of Gurkhas / ex-Gurkha families have availed themselves of this offer and one of the main reasons is almost certainly so that their children may get a better education. Some have even sold up in Nepal and so burned their bridges behind them. They have left behind very nice houses (I know because I lived in one) and a great deal of respect. In the UK, and out of uniform, they no longer have any special perks. They have discovered the high cost of living. Younger ex-army men find it hard to get good civilian jobs. Rental costs are huge and so sometimes families share one house. Many therefore complain of financial difficulties but to be fair, this is sometimes because they remit money back to Nepal and also visit each year. The older generation, or the parents who have emigrated with their Gurkha sons, have found themselves socially isolated and lonely – in a strange country and culture where they do not understand the language. In addition, most of their pension money and their expertise, that was going back into Nepal, is now mostly staying in the UK. Even the Government of Nepal is concerned. There was apparently a "parliamentary report [which] said the recruitment of Gurkhas should be ended, adding that since Britain has granted retired Gurkha troops the right to remain in the United Kingdom, the amount of income Nepal earns from the arrangement has declined."[320] However, AP Thapar noted that this is unlikely to happen until GoN is able to provide alternative jobs in country for young men!

I have seen some of these problems first-hand. I have seen houses where families share accommodation. My own landlord is in the UK, doing better than many, with his own house and so he invited his mother to join him. When I visited, she looked so old and sad and lonely – usually on her own in the house all day and apparently without friends. Once back in Nepal, she was again her cheerful self, shopping and socialising in the local bazaar. I was therefore encouraged to read of the pioneer crafts and conversation project started in Winchester.[321] Many church groups are also involved in this sort of outreach to Nepali migrants (see below). Even officialdom is helping in some places. "As from the beginning of… [2013], former Gurkhas and their families in

Reading have been receiving help [mediated by the Borough Council] in accessing health and social care…[and] in September… [2012] a specialist help centre for Gurkha veterans and their families opened in Reading."[322]

A significant number of older retired Gurkhas are in the UK without the younger members of their families, to whom they are expected to send part of their UK pension. Many are lonely and there is no help and no going back and they wish now they had never come to the UK. "Ombahadur Damai, 70, 11 years' service, arrived three months ago. Asked where he lived, he just said: 'Room No 8.' His polite smile never slipped but he stared into the distance. 'England too difficult.' He wanted to go home."[323] This is not an isolated case. Peter Bisset (an ex-Nepal missionary) writes that there are approximately 160 Nepali couples in Swindon, some in their seventies and eighties, and a few even older! Not many of them can speak, read or write English. While he estimates that some of them are financially better off than they were in Nepal, money does not meet all their needs. Many would actually like to be able to live back in Nepal, but only if they had better pension/support from the British Government.[cxiv]

Tula Singh Rai also confessed in 2010 that he had seen relational difficulties in some Gurkha families. The generation gap is exacerbated as the children and youth easily learn English and integrate but the "older generation often don't speak any English and feel very isolated and detached from their children and grandchildren. They [also] feel that they have lost their independence and have become socially

---

[cxiv] The generous pension support they receive while living in the UK tails off within 3 months if they return to Nepal and their UK residence visa lapses if they stay out of the UK for 2 years.

isolated. They are suffering loss of self-esteem and dignity and often feel depressed…."

The second main group of Nepalis living in the UK are the students (and professionals). In the late 1990s, many graduates, sent by research institutions in Nepal, came (with their families) to do *bona fide* Masters courses at UK Universities, usually in agriculture and development studies. A few, despite the high fees, managed to fund themselves for a further 5 years to do a PhD. However, from around 2000, a lot of small colleges opened, offering migrants low grade courses such as diplomas in computing. These colleges enabled those who had finished their university courses to continue on a part-time study-and-work basis. Their income or their spouse's paid for the college fees, visas, rent & food. In addition, an increasing stream of young adults arrived straight from Nepal to study at these colleges, although most had had to borrow money to get to the UK. Then, in 2010, the UK government began to take action against many of these institutions and placed severe restrictions on visas for those studying below degree level. Many small colleges suddenly closed. My informant gave one example:

> A *new student arrived in S. England having paid £7,000 up front for fees and visa only to find her college was now closed (bankrupt). There was no way she could get a refund and her visa had automatically become invalid. Only by raising a further similar amount from a relative (helped by UK friends) was she able to get a seat on another college course and renew her visa.*

For others it was even harder. I heard of one student whose college closed when he was 2 years through his course:

He felt he could not return to Nepal, because it would mean 'loss of face' as his family had put up the money for his studies. He also knew he would find no work back in Nepal and so he became very depressed. Then, like many others in the same situation he went to Europe (Spain and Belgium) where the employment laws are more lax.[324]

Some, who have succeeded in being perpetual students for 10 years, have been able to apply for Leave to Remain in the UK and can henceforth stay without visa renewal or study provided they are not away from the UK for more than 2 years. At the moment this route is still open. Other ex-students transferred to a 'skilled migrant' status though the jobs they found often would not normally be termed skilled. The income threshold was hiked in around 2007 but some found skilful lawyers to get round the rules.

As a result of all this, a generation of children has grown up in student towns. Although not British citizens, they speak English as their main language and go through the higher education system in Britain. Some are culturally more English than Nepali but still observe the festivals. However, some of the mothers, usually those from higher castes, faced with the drudgery of so-called low-caste work like cleaning offices, have 'had enough' and persuaded their husbands to return to their Kathmandu homes and former (higher rank) jobs in Nepal, where the family is relatively better off and the wife does not need to work. However, the teenagers retain a head start in their career because of excellent English.

Yet others in the ex-student / skilled migrant categories have obtained mortgages and bought their own homes in the UK. Many of them would return to Nepal if there were any 'real' jobs in the country, but instead they have resigned themselves to staying in the West, and sending back surplus income to their relatives in Nepal to build and maintain houses – usually in Kathmandu. They also support members of their relatives' households, many of whom are dependant young adults, students or unemployed, who are also seeking some means of escape to the West or the Gulf.

I personally know of many who have benefitted from a chance to further their education in the West and then returned to Nepal with vision and enthusiasm. In contrast, there are also many who have succumbed to the ease of living in the west and managed to stay on. ***Tshering Lama's*** story is encouraging. He had been inspired by volunteer teachers in his remote village and helped by families in the UK. After graduating PhD for his studies in telemedicine, he was on his way home to help his own people.[325] How different from the story of a Nepal government post-holder!

> An Under Secretary from the MoE who went to England 5 years ago under the Highly Skilled Migrant Programme is now working happily as a Security Guard... and has British citizenship. All his family do. Because he was a post-holder government servant he goes to Nepal from time to time, looks after his work and then again returns to the UK... Although living in the UK, this man is in line for promotion to Joint Secretary. (translation mine).[326]

The contrast of this story with one about 4 Christian Nepali students mentioned by Ps. Abraham is also striking:

> *Krishna, John, and Daniel each had a vision to return to Nepal and serve God there after getting a good education in the UK. Their studying didn't work out as planned, but Abraham encouraged them in their vision to go back to Nepal and plant churches through music ministry. Later,*

through a Bible Study group, they met another student, Sangita, who had a similar vision. Abraham and Ps. Timothy Sherpa taught them all how to do outreach and church planting and now their UK church is committed to supporting them financially and in prayer.[327]

Difficulties experienced by students and professionals are perhaps predictable. They arrive with such high hopes for their future, but then find adapting to the British culture really hard. Abraham Shrestha has discovered that in many cases either the wife comes with a student husband or else comes in advance of her husband as the visa holder and so she becomes the main family earner. This has two possible negative effects. The wife may not be able to earn sufficient to support the family well. The husband may start to feel inferior and that he is letting his family down. Add to this the fact that both are working long hours, with shift work or study and assignments, the amount of time they can spend together is minimal, and this has the potential to break up their marriage. With the increased strictness in immigration law in the UK since 2010, it is likely that fewer students will come and fewer manage to settle after their studies.

The third category largely overlaps the second. The work-related migrants are mostly professionals, many of whom originally came for their studies – and stayed on. However, a small proportion of this group are work-permit holders and domestic workers. None are temporary. Coming from a British Army background, "security has been the main field of employment for men, whereas nursing, care and 'other professions' have employed the majority of Nepali women."[328] Many also work in the catering industry and, as in Asia, in some of the unskilled dangerous, dirty and difficult jobs that local citizens refuse to tackle.[329] A few have managed to start their own businesses.

Asylum seekers made up the fourth category of immigrants. This group was at its maximum from the late 1990s until 2004, but once the conflict in Nepal was largely resolved in 2006, numbers dropped dramatically. At least 2,000 Nepalis sought refuge during the years of the Maoist insurgency, but it seems that less than 100 were granted asylum.

In 2005, Buddhimaya, visiting from Nepal, expressed shock and concern for the pastoral care of the Nepalis, many of whom were living in poor conditions – cramped accommodation, and at standards less than they would in Nepal. Some of the wives were working antisocial hours in supermarkets just so that they could send home up to £1,000 per month, sometimes used to pay off loans raised to get to the UK. On an earlier visit she had also noted that many faced cultural difficulties in adapting to British society and that their children were not being sufficiently disciplined. Some orientation classes were suggested.

John Bradley met (ex)Gurkhas, professionals, students, workers (some of whom were illegal) and asylum seekers, and noted a very interesting feature that confirms a 'Nepali network' in the UK. All you have to do is find a Nepali restaurant and enjoy a traditional *daal-bhat* meal and you are immediately in touch with the local Nepali community.

There are at least 300 Nepali community or social organisations,[330] including several 'tribal' linked societies for the Kirats (Rai/Limbu), Thakuris, Gurungs, Magars, Tamangs and Newars. One of the advantages of living in the

UK is freedom of religion and members of these sub-ethnic groups and others feel free to identify as Buddhists rather than Hindus. Other groups link together those from a common district homeland in Nepal or the location where they live in the UK. Various Nepali Samaj UK functions are arranged and they have a dedicated website. Over the years various professional societies have come into being – not just for (ex-)servicemen but also for doctors, nurses, accountants, lawyers, engineers and caterers. The Gurkha Welfare Trust, established in 1969, provides assistance to those needy ex-Gurkhas and their families who did not serve long enough to qualify for an army pension. It has an office in Salisbury and several distribution centres in Nepal. There are two academic associations: the Britain Nepal Academic Council (BNAC) and the Centre for Nepal Studies, UK (CNSUK), which conduct research and arrange seminars and conferences. CNSUK has also published an informative book on Nepalis in the UK.[331] Some groups are essentially for the benefit of Nepalis in Britain but others are also working to help their homeland. Help Nepal Network, for example, has completed 75 local educational, medical and other assistance projects since 2000 and has 5 on-going for which it is continually fundraising. The Britain-Nepal Society, established in the early 1960s, aims to foster cross-country relationships and organises various social and service events. The first-ever Walk for Nepal was held at the end of July 2013 in London. The event was planned to bring together leading UK-based Nepali social cause organisations and about half a dozen came together to pool their energy for the betterment of Nepal and Nepalese back home.[332]

Migration is one of the biggest media and political issues in Britain today, and with added economic uncertainty the tensions surrounding the issue are likely to become even greater.[333] While many ethnic minorities face racial discrimination, this is less (although not totally absent) for the Nepalis due to the legacy of the brave Gurkhas. Anti-migrant feelings are sometimes due to racial discrimination but at other times they are fuelled by the fact that a local community finds itself overwhelmed by a large minority of 'others'. This has happened in Rushmoor, Aldershot, one of the areas where Gurkhas have settled in large numbers and >6.5% of the population are now Nepalis.[334] One British MP tactlessly suggested the Gurkhas should be dispersed around the country like asylum seekers, but others see no problem. A local greengrocer in Aldershot, said, "We love the Nepalese… They have great banter, they're really patriotic and they buy a lot of tomatoes. They're proper hagglers, and they don't always understand the concept of queuing. But still, we have a great laugh." Perhaps in part linked to some of the souring of feelings towards the Gurkhas, since early 2013 there has been a flurry of articles in the press concerning the arrest of an ex-Nepal Army Colonel on charges of torture while he was working in Nepal during the Maoist insurgency. The incident created a minor diplomatic rift between London and Kathmandu.

Nepali Fellowships

In almost all the western countries to which Nepalis travel, "the church is growing among many ethnic minorities."[335] This includes the Nepalis, although the growth is perhaps less dramatic than among the labour migrants in Malaysia and the Middle East. According to the CNSUK study, 2% of the

Nepali migrants in the UK claim to be Christians.[336] However, some time ago I read an interesting report in the *Baptist Times*. A member of Anderson Baptist Church in Reading, where there is an associated Nepali fellowship, said how amazed she was to find 8 Nepalis being baptized on one day. In all her years as a member of the church, such a large number had never been baptized together! The other side of the picture is that in 2005 the Reading (Hindu) Nepali community voiced complaint about Christian evangelism.

Perhaps the first Nepali Christians in the UK were the 24 Gurkha soldiers who were baptised in the period 1960-63. In more recent years, other Nepali Christians came to the UK, but even up to 2007 little was known about them and they themselves had little contact with each other. During Buddhimaya's visit in 2005, she found a number of Nepalis who had been Christians for several years but who were weak in Biblical understanding and in Christian family practices. For some, this was due to their previous lack of fellowship, a result of Army life, and she was able to encourage them to become stronger in the faith and equip themselves through study so that if and when they return to Nepal they can perhaps be 'Christian missionaries' back into their own country. Shortly after this, small groups were discovered in Farnborough, Willesden and Harrow. Those in Harrow continue to meet on Saturday evenings but most are members of local UK churches. Another group was found in connection with Earley Christian Fellowship in Reading, a city where there are considerable numbers of Nepali students. One of them has a thrilling testimony:

> ***Prem*** *originally worked in various development projects in Nepal and had also developed his own NGO which had*

grown to a staff of 100. Then, in 1998, Prem and his wife, Indira, came to the UK so that he could do further study. After gaining a Masters degree in Rural Social Development he went on to earn a PhD. However, by 2002, Prem was experiencing many problems, including financial, social and family breakdown. He became depressed and began drinking heavily, for which he received various forms of treatment. They had Christian friends, but initially were not interested in the gospel for themselves. Later, a friend prayed for him and he was healed and as a result both Prem and Indira accepted Christ. The very next day after encountering God, Prem went to his GP and said he didn't need his anti-depressants any longer – and he hasn't used them since. He also stopped drinking and God healed their family relationships. Over the next two years God did more amazing things in their lives: in 2005 they started a home group in their house with some friends, and then in 2008 God led them to All Nations Christian College. After a year of mission studies, God called them back to Nepal – as missionaries. In 2013, Prem became the 2nd Nepali Director of INF/Nepal.

The involvement of INF/UK with Nepali ministry in the UK (as opposed to supporting missionaries going to work in Nepal) has a long history, dating back even before 2004. Right from the beginning, the aim was to support the development of the Nepali church in the UK while still allowing it to be independent. During 2005, John Bradley conducted personal informal research and established contacts with individuals, including one Nepali pastor (Bhab Ghale) who was then studying at Bible College in the UK.

In 2005, the only Nepali fellowship that Bradley discovered was the El Shaddai (Bakht Singh) Fellowship in Reading, where the pastor was Daniel Khatri. This group has tended to be rather strict and exclusive, but is now becoming a little more open towards other Christian groups.

Already, at that time, John Bradley and John Reynolds (CEO of INF/UK) began to think how the mission could have input into Nepali ministry in the UK. Some suggestions included Bible teaching (from visiting Nepali leaders and expatriates fluent in Nepali); pastoral help and counselling; provision of Scripture and other resources (hard copies and soft or via a website); possibly some translation, and publication of a newsletter. They proposed cooperating with other relevant missions, organisations and ministries in the UK and Europe and one long-term aim was to challenge UK Nepali Christians to return home as missionaries.

Another idea was perhaps to recruit a Nepali pastor to work long-term among Nepalis in the UK. However, they were hesitant about this following the advice of a visiting Nepali church leader. Part of the rationale was that a posting in the west could prove a real (financial) temptation. Therefore, during 2006, INF/UK looked into the possibility of a former expatriate missionary with good cultural understanding and language ability, but in the midst of this John Reynolds met with a Nepali visiting the UK and was so impressed with all the travelling he did and the ease with which he was invited into Nepali communities, that it seemed the Lord was in fact guiding to a Nepali pastor, who would genuinely be called to the UK. The very next day news came from Nepal that Abraham and Kate Shrestha[cxv] were already planning to settle in the UK from August-2007 and had actually been thinking

[cxv] In many ways an ideal 'compromise' on the original hesitation as Kate is British and Abraham, Nepali.

for some weeks about approaching INF concerning ministry to Nepalis in the UK. Abraham was a Mathematics teacher also serving in Nepali Isai Mandali in Lalitpur while Kate was a missionary from N Ireland. There was also the possibility that their Nepal church would be willing to stand behind them in this calling. At about the same time, INF/UK heard of another couple: Tula Singh and Chandra Rai. Again, there were many positives as he himself was an ex-Gurkha and Baptist pastor. In fact, in 2010, Tula looked back to what might be regarded as his call to this work, "Seventeen years ago I had a vision that I would serve British Gurkhas after I retired from the British Army and share the good news of Jesus Christ with them. Now I am giving most of my time doing exactly that."

In 1995, after retiring from the army, Tula founded Lalitpur Baptist Church and developed it from a small fellowship of 13 members to a church of 400 with 5 daughter churches. Later, between 2003 & 2006, as President of the Nepal Baptist Church Council, he was responsible for coordinating and mobilising 110 churches and 360 fellowships across Nepal. In 2005, at the Baptist World Alliance Centenary Congress in Birmingham, UK, to which Rev. Rai and other Baptist pastors were invited, his call was confirmed. "Many of the speakers emphasised the decline of churches in western countries and an increasing number in Asia. One of the speakers was urging Asian leaders to send missionaries to the West. I knew God was saying that it was my time to go and witness in the West," he said. In July 2007 he arrived with his wife and two of their three daughters to become the first Nepali missionary to the UK.

Thus, after various negotiations, both families came to the

UK with the blessing of their respective churches and some small financial support. Officially, to comply with UK tax and employment laws, they were employed by INF/UK, but not all their support has come through INF nor have they been formally answerable to INF/UK in their ministry. They have had considerable freedom to develop the Nepali ministry as God has individually led them.

Rev. Tula and his family settled in Reading, in the middle of a large Nepali community, of whom a significant number were (ex)Gurkhas. His "vision was to locate Nepali Christians, bring them together and establish Nepali Fellowships and bring the good news of Jesus to Nepalese and others." As he began this new ministry, he said, "I will help to address their social, cultural and spiritual needs. For Nepali people that are already Christians, I will be giving pastoral care and encouraging fellowship, outreach and evangelism. It will be a huge challenge, but very exciting."[337] Tula developed a close link with Anderson Baptist Church, and by 2012, the Nepali congregation was at least 50. His ministry has thus been fairly localised but a tremendous blessing to the Gurkha families who have appreciated all the help he has been able to give them as they settle in a new country. Tula translates the regular Sunday sermons for those who do not understand English and on Saturdays he leads a Nepali medium worship service. For the ladies there is a fellowship on Fridays. The Nepali cultural activities, English classes and advice about living in the UK have "proved to be a good way to build friendships, to bring relief to those in frustrating circumstances and help people gain confidence and independence. [They are] also a good place to share our faith," says Rev. Tula.

"There are about 3,500 Gurkha soldiers currently serving in the British Army and around 800-1,000 Gurkhas serving in Afghanistan," says Tula. "Some have been killed or wounded. Lots of those serving have families here in the UK who worry about them and struggle while they are away…' Thus, one particularly poignant area of help given to Gurkha families is prayer for them when members are serving in dangerous places like Iraq and Afghanistan. In 2010, Tula himself shared, "I want to thank people for praying for my son-in-law, Deepak. He has been serving in the British Army in Afghanistan and has recently returned safely to the UK." Not all soldiers return safely: sometimes Tula has opportunity to comfort their relatives. Because of his army contacts, Tula has also had opportunity to meet with new recruits training in Catterick (N. Yorkshire).

Abraham's ministry has developed quite differently, as he spends a considerable amount of time travelling to visit Nepali groups scattered across the British Isles. When he began his ministry, there were just 4 local groups: at the end of 2010, there were 18, and by 2013, there were at least 27 Nepali fellowships/churches with around 2,500 Nepali believers in the UK. Most fellowships serve Nepali communities grouped in 3 or 4 distinct areas but others are more scattered around the country:

1. **The Greater London area** covers Harrow, Hillingdon, Wembley, Harlington, Hounslow West, Brent, Feltham, Shepherd's Bush in the west; Plumstead, Greenwich & Woolwich in the east; Barnet in the north; Wimbledon and Morden as well as Croydon in Surrey in the south.
2. **The Reading area** covers Reading town in **Berkshire;** Aldershot, Rushmoor, Bracknell, Sandhurst,

Farnborough, Farnham, Southampton, & Basingstoke in **Hampshire;** Swindon in **Wiltshire;** Camberley, Surrey Heath, Blackwater, & Woking in Surrey; and also Oxford in **Oxfordshire.**

3. **The SE area** covers Ashford, Folkestone, Dover, Deal & Tonbridge in **Kent**; as well as Colchester & Grays (Thurrock) in **Essex**.
4. **The Northern area** covers Rochdale, Manchester Bolton, Ashton, and Macclesfield in Greater Manchester, plus Liverpool, Burnley, and Catterick (Richmondshire), Sheffield, Doncaster and Bradford & Leeds) in N, S & W Yorkshire respectively.

Other Scattered groups or individuals are found in the Midlands, Scotland, Devon, S Wales and N Ireland.

There are also seven Churches linked with the El Shaddai group in Reading, Woolwich, Hounslow, Camberley, Aldershot, Swindon, and Dover.

In 2007 there was one Nepali fellowship in Harrow: by 2010 there were 6 fellowships in the **GREATER LONDON** area, with a combined membership of 60-70; today there are more.

The **Plumstead** fellowship started in 2008 with three families meeting together in the flat of a Burmese family, but, after 18 months, numbers had grown so much that they moved to East Plumstead Baptist church. They are now a church and known as the Nepali Christian Fellowship, Plumstead, having a regular membership of 60-70. In 2013 they appointed their own elders and deacons. Abraham says that "This group is slightly different from most other Nepali Christian groups [in the UK] in that there are Nepali-speaking Burmese, Nepali speakers from North India, as well as Nepalis from Hong

Kong and Nepal." Local churches in the area are getting involved and some Nepalis have begun attending those churches.

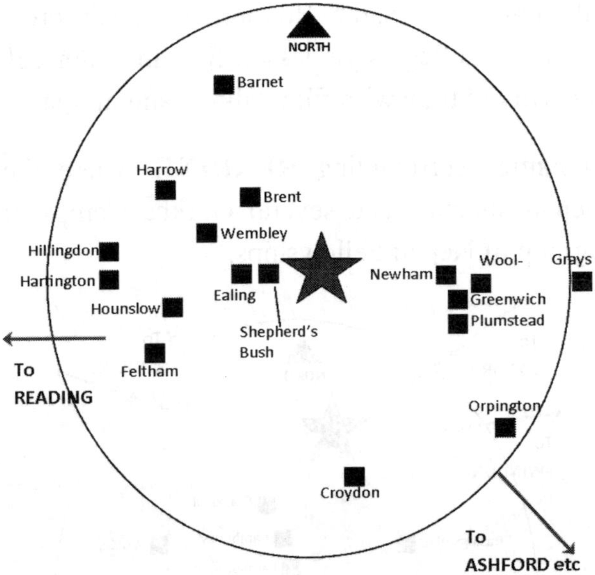

Nepali Communities in Greater LONDON – within the M25
(Approximate locations – Diagram not to scale)

The United Nepali Fellowship, **Harrow** (membership 25-30) is active in outreach into its community and has organised events like a prayer walk and gospel tract distribution. A meal and a trip to Bournemouth beach attracted outsiders who saw their faith in action. Two groups meet in **Hounslow**: the Nepali Christian Community Church (membership 40-45) and the Melchizedek Nepali Mandali (membership 30-35). The Shepherd's Bush group merged with NCCC and Feltham people also go to Hounslow for fellowship. Other Nepali groups include the United Nepali Revival Church, (at Sudbury Methodist Church), **Wembley** (membership 40-50), which began in 2009; and Elohim Nepali Church, **Harlington** (membership 50-55)

There is an English class in **Orpington** (Kent) facilitated by ex-Nepal missionary, Sarah Bottomley. Their programme has two parts: a college style lesson first and after coffee, an interactive Bible Study with film, talking and drama.

In the counties surrounding **READING** where there are many Nepali students and several Gurkha Camps, there is another group of Nepali Fellowships.

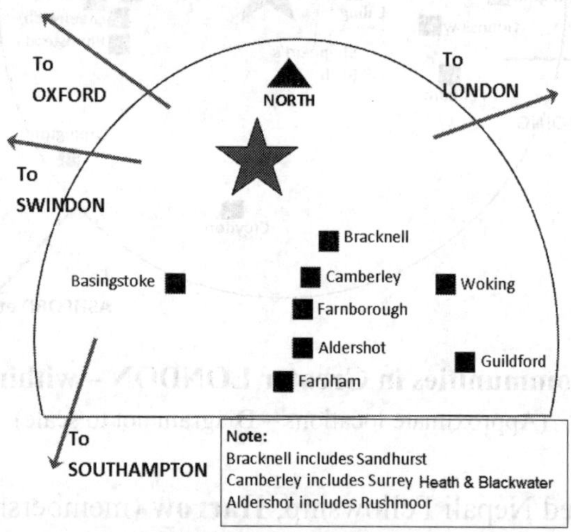

Nepali Communities in the READING area
(Approximate locations – Diagram not to scale)

In **Reading** itself there are 3 groups: the Nepali Fellowship at Anderson Baptist Church (membership 50-60) 13), Earley Nepali Christian Fellowship (membership 10-15) and Jyoti Mandali, (just 3-4 families). The biggest church in the area is the Nepali Christian Church, **Aldershot** (membership >120: maybe 180-200). It is growing and uses the buildings of Holy Trinity Church for its Sunday services. Despite some of the problems in the town (see p.399) caused by the large numbers of ex-Gurkhas settled there[cxvi], Ursula Johnston (an ex-Nepal missionary) is encouraged with developments but admits that one of the major problems is that many of the new arrivals are elderly retired Gurkhas who need considerable support. The British Government even gave the Borough Council an extra £200,000 to try and help the situation, but despite this, the local MP said that they still cannot cope with the extra burden on doctors, facilities and social services. The women are invariably over 60 and their husbands significantly older. When the men die, the women are extremely lonely. The older couples usually opt to settle in the UK for reliable utilities, cleanliness and the NHS benefits but their children, being well over 18 do not qualify and so a widow will often end up living on her own – not the Nepali cultural norm. Sadly, the children expect the parents to do this so that money can be sent back to help educate the grandchildren. As a result the old folks live frugally and many deny themselves adequate heating in the winter.[338]

Ursula and friends experimented with a social group for Nepali ladies, offering cooking and knitting plus English classes and conversation. Many ladies, including younger wives, feel very isolated if they do not speak English and so the training was to help boost their self-confidence and empower them. This trial programme lasted for 3 months and now they just run the English classes but with plenty of fun social time mixed in with outings and parties. About 60 ladies were already attending in 2011, bringing Nepali snacks to share with their *chiya*,[cxvii] but by 2013 it had grown to

---

[cxvi] 14% of the total population in 2011.
[cxvii] Nepali tea – usually sweet and milky.

about 85. At festival times, like Easter, they have a chance to share the true meaning, and at the time of the 2011 census, they also invited the menfolk and offered help with completing the forms.

They also saw the need for a regular men's group and one was formed in 2012, but has not had the same take-up as the ladies' one. This might be partly because of the local betting shops, which give free food and hot drinks as incentives to stay and maybe because the men do not feel the same need to improve their English (although many in fact do need to). In 2010, Jos Johnston began training with the local Citizens' Advice Bureau as so many Nepalis are in need of this kind of help. Ursula has also seen some of the problems for Nepali schoolchildren, who find it culturally difficult to question or challenge their teachers. This is gradually being overcome since a young Nepali Christian joined the permanent full time staff of Aldershot comprehensive school. Her main role is to provide assistance and teaching to Nepali students, and she is the link person between the school and Nepali parents. In **Farnborough** there are 15,000 Nepalis, and a local church is running English classes and has a real heart to reach out to the group. There is a small Nepali Christian group – the British Nepalese Christian Community Church (membership 12-15). There are fewer Nepalis in **Southampton** but 80 of them live near Lizzie Cox (an ex-Nepal missionary). Initially, only two were Christians, and Lizzie, Liz Taylor (another ex-Nepal missionary) and Anne from Southampton Community Church began to reach out to the group, inviting them to social and community activities and even starting a low-key Alpha course. They also arranged English classes and even received a grant of £6,000 from the Ministry of

Defence (MoD) to develop community links with Nepalis. By 2011 a group of 5 families were meeting monthly, but most have now moved from the area.

Nearby, in Surrey, there is the **Camberley** Nepali Fellowship (membership 35-40) and the **Woking** Nepali Fellowship (membership 12-15), whose members are mostly from the Darjeeling/Kalimpong area).

In **Swindon**, there are 3 Nepali groups: the Prabhu Yeshu Christ Gorkha Mandali (membership 30-40), Swindon Nepali Christian Church (just 3 families) and the Gateway Nepali Fellowship (membership 15-20) in which Peter Bisset and Bedlap (previously in Kent) are involved. In 2012 this group was only 17-strong but because Gateway Church is host to many different language groups as well as the Nepalis, they planned to set up simultaneous translation into Nepali during the Sunday Service, but also to continue with a Nepali language fellowship to fulfil a need for those who speak no English. The **Oxford** Nepali Christian Fellowship, (membership 15-20) meets with Gateway once a month.

The SOUTH EAST is another area where there are many Gurkha families settled. **Ashford** Nepali Christian Fellowship (membership 40-45) is the oldest group but Emmanuel Nepali Mandali (Church), **Folkestone** (membership 110-140) is now the biggest. This group began among the local Nepali community from a small fellowship meeting in Laxmi Limbu's house in 2000, serving unattached soldiers. In the middle of that year, the army moved the Gurkha regiments from Church Crookham to Folkestone and with this move came the opportunity for soldiers' families to come to England for up to 3 years, while their husbands were based in England. This therefore created a Nepali community with children and elderly parents needing support in the Folkestone area. In the beginning many parents did not understand the British school system and Helen (see below), a trained teacher working in the area, was able to obtain a Nepali translation of school information letters for them. I remember helping her do this and the amusement it caused when the Nepali working with me translated 'trainers' not as sports shoes but rather more literally!

Originally, Christian soldiers met twice a week for prayer and fellowship. At the beginning there were just 3 families and a number of single men, but the group soon began to grow and by 2005 there were 20-30 people involved. That same year, Subash (an ex-Gurkha) and Helen (daughter of ex-Nepal missionaries) moved to a bigger house, which they were able to open for the fellowship to meet on a Sunday. This was really the beginning of the actual church, and a very encouraging time for the growing fellowship, as many of the soldiers were leaving the army and staying in the Folkestone area. In 2007, the rules for serving Gurkhas and retired soldiers changed, they were given the same entitlement as the British soldiers and allowed to have their families permanently with them. As accommodation problems followed, the Gurkha families were spread out to nearby towns like Canterbury, Dover, Hawkinge and Ashford.

By September 2007 the group had outgrown Subash and Helen's house but fortunately they were offered the use of a local primary school in Cheriton, where Helen was a teacher. At this time they became known formally as Emmanuel Nepali Church: it was the first official Nepali Church in the UK. The Nepali fellowship continued to meet in this school on Sunday mornings until they were offered the use of Cheriton Baptist Church in 2010. From then on they began to meet in the church but on Sunday afternoons. This move was advantageous in many ways, one being that the venue was easier for members to invite friends to attend. It also meant a closer relationship with the local English-speaking church, especially helpful for the Nepali youth; and it opened the possibility for some joint meetings. The pastor was also able to give support to the leaders. Although some of the members were transferred with their regiments to Brunei in 2009 and others moved away from Folkestone when they were demobbed from the army, the membership is now over 100 with more than 60 attending Sunday services plus weekly house groups, a monthly ladies' fellowship and regular youth and Sunday School classes.

In Essex in **Grays** (Thurrock), SE of London, there is the Anugraha Mandali (membership 20-30), and in **Colchester**, the Colchester Nepali Fellowship (just 4 families). Although the members are involved in local churches, they are keen to reach out to other Nepalis in their respective areas.

Ps. Barnabas, from Gorkha, who lives in **Lincoln,** is involved in helping Nepali groups in Sheffield and Doncaster in the north and Barnstaple in the SW.

The groups in **the NORTH** are more spread out although there are links between them. There are currently just 4 Christian groups meeting regularly – in Rochdale, Sheffield, Doncaster and Bradford.

Ina Herd (an ex-Nepal missionary) writes about the group in **Doncaster.** Because many families in this area are younger and have come to the UK largely for the sake of their children's education, this can put a lot of pressure on the children. Their parents have often sacrificed a lot to help them but some Nepali children find it very hard to adapt to the style of teaching in British schools, even though they were doing really well back in Nepal. The result is tension between the generations.[cxviii] To try and bridge this, some of the local church members have given informal help and also ran a day seminar called 'Me and my Teenagers' to help the parents to see things from their children's perspective. Help with homework and career counselling has also been organized. A youth club called *Mitra Mit* (Friends) has helped new arrivals in particular, but its weakness is that it does not encourage integration into the local community. As elsewhere, English classes are much appreciated by the ladies who have often had little formal education back home. They have also proved to be a forum for discussing health issues. Finding ways to help the older people is perhaps the most challenging. Through this outreach the Doncaster Nepali Church (membership 20-30) has come into being.

Under the UNHCR Resettlement Programme, a total of 750 **Bhutanese refugees** are due to be settled in UK by 2014/15. Most of them are being sent to Rochdale, but others are located in Manchester, Sheffield, Burnley, Bradford, Stockport, Bolton, Ashton and Macclesfield. It is reckoned that about a third of them are (new) believers.

In around 2012, more than 100 **Bhutanese refugees** came to the UK. In the Greater **Manchester** area 12 Christian

---

[cxviii] This is part of the problem of Hybrid identity – see Jonathan Ingleby, "Globalisation, Glocalisation and Mission, *Encounter Mission EZine*, Aug 2004

families meet weekly as the Himalayan Nepali Church, Rochdale (membership 30-35). Their leader is Ps. Samuel Lepcha. Ps. Abraham has an interesting story of Rochdale:

> *A Newari couple from Patan emigrated to the UK about 40 years ago and first lived in London, where Elizabeth Franklin (an ex-Nepal missionary) used to take them to church in Wembley. Later they moved north to Rochdale and at some point accepted Christ and were baptized in around 2000. However, even in 2012, the wife still only spoke Newari and Abraham found himself preaching for them in that language.*[339]

A group of about 60 Bhutanese Nepali refugees have also settled in **Sheffield** and among them there were about 17 Christians, although most of them were very new believers. Ina Herd visited in 2012, "We had an impromptu meeting together where it was possible to teach them some Nepali songs and introduce them to the Bible. It was a great experience seeing their smiling faces and their enthusiasm to learn more about Jesus." Again, Ina enthusiastically records, "One week about 17 of them came [by bus] from Sheffield to our Saturday Nepali fellowship meeting [in Doncaster]." As it is clearly not practical for them to do this regularly, she noted that they were trying to link them up with English churches in Sheffield, but felt that as their English was weak, it would be good to them to have a Nepali worship service as well. In fact they have become the Himalayan Nepali Church, Sheffield (membership 40-45).

There are also a few Bhutanese Nepalis in **Bradford** as well as some Gurkha families, and Ps. Samuel is trying to reach out to them from his own base in Rochdale. Just 3 families make up the Himalayan Nepali Fellowship, Bradford. Before this and for many years, Barbara Gill (an ex-Nepal missionary) had been exercising a generous ministry of hospitality to Nepali families in the town.

In **Richmondshire**, (N Yorks, **near Catterick Camp**) John and Angela Dickenson (ex-Nepal missionaries and John himself also an ex-Gurkha officer) are running an ESOL[cxix] group. They organised a 16-week literacy course for the older relatives now living at the garrison. There have been two groups of 12 students each and their average age is well over 50, but so far this has not led to a fellowship meeting.

OTHER SCATTERED GROUPS have developed similarly across the UK, with more or less help and encouragement – and later teaching – from Abraham or Tula. Some are still quite small but growing.

In the West Midlands / Warwickshire area there were Nepali Christians at the barracks in **Nuneaton**, but all have now been transferred elsewhere. In Brampton there are still a couple, who have opted to join the local El Shaddai fellowship. Joyce and Richard Odell, who live in **Derbyshire**, are developing contacts among the local Nepali community of more than 200: no Christians as yet.

In **Scotland**, the only group of which I am aware is the small (12-15 member) **Edinburgh** Nepali Fellowship, but again some have recently left.

There is a North Devon Nepali Fellowship (membership 8-10) which meets quarterly in **Barnstaple.**

There is a Gurkha camp in Brecon and in the past I heard that

---

[cxix] English for Speakers of Other Languages.

2-3 families were Christians, but understand there are none now (2013). Other Christian Nepalis live in the Cardiff area. Dorothy Evans (an ex-Nepal missionary) mentioned two nurses, Jyoti Gautam and Jyoti Shrestha, who have tried to reach out to Nepalis over many years. In late 2013 the first meeting of the **South Wales** Nepali Christian Fellowship was organised by Gautam Neupani from Pyuthan, who had accepted Christ through the witness of a flatmate while he was living in Wales. It was held in Cardiff and about 10-12 attended, but Nepalis live in Pontypool, Pontypridd and Tonyrefail. (in the Rhondda) as well as Cardiff. Prabhat Shah and his wife, Vicky, who formerly worked for the Nepal Leprosy Trust in Lalgadh, also have contacts among the 300 Nepali Gurkha migrants in Cwmbran.

There are 3-5 Nepali Christians in Belfast (**N Ireland**) but to date no fellowship.

Abraham tries to visit each group regularly and give Bible training and leadership seminars. He also plans counselling and other practical trainings, all of which will help Christian Nepalis to reach out to their fellow nationals. Some of the problems encountered in Nepali fellowships in the UK are rather different from those in other countries because the large numbers of Gurkhas has tended to skew the usual or 'normal' leadership, ethnic or caste tensions. For those with an army background, rank is extremely important and their process of decision-making is often different from that of non-army church groups. Tula (himself an ex-Gurkha) explained that Gurkhas will not be ruled by anyone, and this therefore makes church leadership quite a challenge. The fact that many UK Nepalis have not lived in Nepal and experienced Nepali Church life also raises different issues.

In 2009 Ina and Abraham together with INF/UK office staff arranged a Nepal Day in Doncaster. The afternoon part of the programme was an open session with a short evangelistic message. Since then there have been several other Nepali days in different parts of the country – Reading and Sheffield. In 2011 Joyce and Richard Odell relocated from Nepal. They have been able to give much help to developing a UK Nepali fellowship network and have also been involved in training for local Christians to be more involved in Nepali ministry. Apart from the two major inputs that most groups request – supply of Nepali Christian literature and English classes, they and Peter Bisset have found that the following are all ways or potential ways of ministering to the Nepali migrants:

- Discipling for Nepali young people (especially in relation to drug abuse).
- Supporting Bible studies, prayer meetings, etc.
- Production of a tract for use especially in the UK.
- Placing good Nepali books in local libraries.
- Building effective leadership.
- Accompanying and translating for those needing to visit doctors, hospitals and various offices, etc.
- Reading/translating/explaining official letters and helping migrants respond to these by phone calls, visits or giving help with form-filling.
- Assisting with the production of relevant CVs to help migrants get better jobs.
- Being a 'furniture agent' (matching unwanted furniture with needs).
- Acting as the guardian for some children or young people in relation to their school or college when parents cannot understand English.
- Educating and helping churches with a vision to reach out to the Nepali community.

When we compare this list with the services envisaged on p. 402, it is clear that practical help as well as spiritual is very important in outreach. Significantly, this list reflects the needs expressed by the Nepalis themselves for help in the areas of education, security, health, English language, employment and transportation.[340] With the arrival of elderly Gurkha families, illiteracy in Nepali (and not just English) has also become a problem. Together, ex-missionaries and the two Nepali pastors have worked untiringly and now they have established a link with Triangle Christian bookshop in Farnborough to ensure a sustainable supply of Nepali Christian literature – Bibles, commentaries, hymnbooks, tracts, DVDs so important for discipling.

In late 2011 a new **'Nepali Christian Council UK' (NCCUK)** was formed. It came about as from time to time, Nepali groups in close proximity to each other began to arrange joint meetings approximately every 2 months. In October 2006 the 1st historic meeting of **Nepali Christian Fellowships & Churches (NFC)** took place at Sudbury Methodist Church in London, initiated by Ps. Bhab Ghale. It was attended by around 150 (Nepalis and others) with the aim of encouraging partnership amongst all the Nepali Christian groups in the UK. The 2nd joint gathering was held in December of that same year, when the Nepali believers in Cheriton, Kent hosted a Christmas celebration at Subash Limbu's home. 89 people came from groups all over the SE of England. At this time they decided to meet quarterly. The 3rd meeting was in February 2007. After that further combined gatherings were organised by the various groups in rotation and held bi-monthly to unite the different fellowships and help them grow together in Christ. Initially, this was done mainly to support the many Gurkha fellowships in the south of England, but as more and more Nepali Fellowships began in different parts of the UK, there was a need to establish a wider network to include groups in the Midlands and the North. It also became clear that a more formal mechanism for correcting any Biblical errors and giving regular advice to the fellowships was needed. As a result Rev. Rai suggested to the NFC leaders that they should reshape their organisational structure and develop a clear mission and vision – and these issues were discussed prayerfully and in depth at the next three meetings in June 2008 (in Farnborough), July 2010 (in Sudbury) and October 2011 (in Aldershot). Finally, at the 7th formal gathering, on 26th November 2011 at Holy Trinity Church in Aldershot, Elder Capt. Laxmi Limbu led the meeting to select the first executive committee.[cxx] Ps. Abraham said that the committee was created in order to build up and maintain deeper relationships among UK Nepali fellowship groups and Churches. Then, the 8th gathering – which was of the executive committee – was held on 14th January 2012 in Wellington Hounslow Community Church, hosted by Hounslow Nepali Community Church, the Organisation was given its official name – the **Nepali Christian Council United Kingdom (NCCUK**, and its Aim and Objectives were specified. Tula says that in 2013 there were officially 8 churches and 16 fellowships, together known as Nepali Fellowships and Churches (NFCs). Of these, 14 had already signed up to membership of the NCCUK. (see also below)

[cxx] Chair: Capt. Laxmi Prasad Limbu, Vice Chair: Rev. Samuel Lepcha, Secretary: Rev. Tulasi Rai, Treasurer: Elder Bed Labh Rai, Members: Som Kumar Sunuwar, Rudra Rai, Kumar BK and Man Sunuwar.

He also says that, "the main aims of NCCUK are to: preach the gospel of Christ and be witnesses to the Nepali community; to bring Nepali believers together in fellowship; to train NFC leaders and develop new Nepali Christian leaders." The vision is to:

The aim of NCCUK is to support church leaders, to communicate the Gospel among Nepalis and to build the kingdom of God.

1. Locate (all) Nepali Christians and families living in the UK.
2. Encourage all Nepali Christians to be part of NFCs.
3. Maintain close relationships among (all) NFCs.
4. Identify & train potential future leaders in the NFCs.
5. Mobilise leaders for pastoral care and awareness of their autonomy.
6. Encourage integration (especially for the youth) into local English Churches.
7. Encourage the establishment of new Nepali fellowships in Nepali communities.
8. Provide training and seminars for local leaders.
9. Share difficulties related to sickness, death, and biblical error between NFCs.
10. Maintain close contact with all ex-Nepal missionaries.

There are 4 churches that have not joined the NCCUK but meet monthly as the **Pawitra Aatma Fellowship**: Hounslow Melchizedek Nepali Mandali, Swindon Prabhu Yesu Christ Gurkha Mandali, Grays Anugraha Mandali and Camberley Nepali Fellowship.

At the same time links have been developing between individuals and English-speaking churches called to help Nepali migrants in their midst. Shortly after the establishment of the NCCUK, a new **UK Nepali Network** was also formed. Because of the increasing number of

Nepali people coming to live in the UK, and the many challenges and exciting opportunities to show God's love and share faith, the aim was to bring together like-minded people with a heart to help Nepalis and so enable people to share experience and resources regarding different ministries. The UK Nepali Network membership is currently 157, of whom 7 are outside the UK. Its purpose is to foster unity, helping Nepali believers to integrate into the English church, whilst still retaining their Nepali identity.[cxxi] The network is facilitated by Joyce and Richard Odell, and in early 2012 they brought together a number of people working with Nepalis in the UK[cxxii] or who have an interest in doing this. One was a GP, who did her elective in Nepal in the 70's and had felt a call to Nepalis but for various reasons was unable to serve in Nepal. Her practice has a list of 10,000 patients of which 900 are Nepali. She said, ***"I couldn't go to Nepal, so the Lord brought Nepal to me".***

[cxxi] This is integration with contextualisation but not assimilation – see Darrell Jackson, "Europe and the Migrant Experience: Transforming Integration," *Transformation: An International Journal of Holistic Mission Studies,* 2011 28:14

[cxxii] 40 attended but others indicated interest.

S. IRELAND/EIRE

There is little information about Nepalis in S Ireland, but anecdotal evidence suggests that there are more settled in the south than the north and that the numbers are growing as more come for study, business and employment. The first Nepali apparently arrived in 1984. The latest figure given in Wikipedia, with which Hieber generally agrees, is 400-500 of whom 150 are settled around Dublin and some others in Limerick. Despite the low numbers, in 2000 they formed a Nepal-Ireland Society and since then have arranged community activities and been involved in social support, developed a website and were planning a Newsletter.

I have not discovered any information about Nepali Christians or Nepali Fellowships, but Ps. Abraham is planning an exploratory visit for 2014.

THE REST OF EUROPE

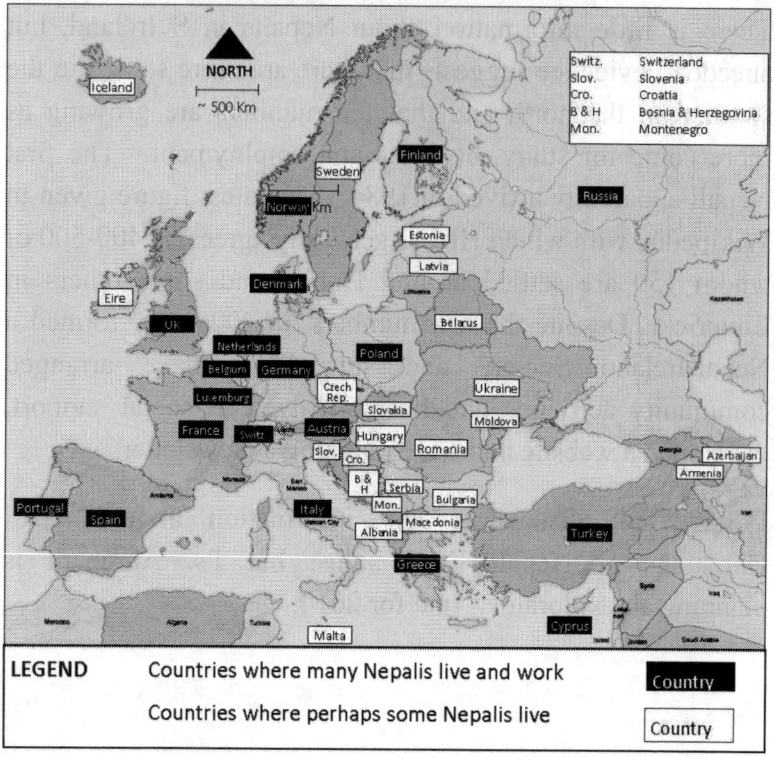

Nepali migrants are known to have travelled to all the countries marked on the map, but few details or numbers of any Nepali Christians or fellowships are available for many of these countries, especially in Eastern Europe.

Most of the outreach to Nepalis in WESTERN EUROPE – specifically Germany and the countries surrounding it, has been done by Ps. Dambar Adhikari since 1990. He was the first Nepali missionary in this area. Together with a group of others he was involved in developing a spiritually active multicultural church. He also has an evangelistic travelling ministry spread across several European countries. In addition, a number of individuals who earlier worked in Nepal (with INF or UMN) are involved in Nepali ministry in some way.

GERMANY

STATISTICS	
Total Nepali Population	~4,500
No. of Nepali Fellowships	Nil
No. of Nepali Christians	~70-80

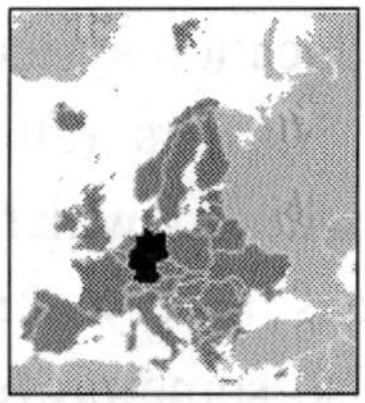

Hieber estimates that there are around 4,540 Nepalis living in Germany. Other figures range from 4,000 to 8,000. Dambar

Adhikari reckons that the numbers of Nepalis domiciled in Germany has dropped from around 13,000 a few years ago to 6,000 because of the strict immigration laws that have been introduced and enforced in Germany.

Many work in the catering business, and in 2008, Adhikari opined that 90% of Nepalis working in restaurants were there illegally. There are also large numbers of international students and this has increased recently due to changes in the education system in Germany. Nowadays it is possible to do a Masters (although not a Bachelors) Degree in English medium, which makes Germany with its minimal college fees, a very attractive option for Nepali students. There are also some professionals, entrepreneurs and businessmen and an increasing number of maids. During the Maoist insurgency, hundreds of others arrived, seeking political asylum. The biggest number of Nepalis (around 200, although this possibly excludes students) appears to be in Munich, where there is a Nepali restaurant, school and pagoda temple. Others are found especially in Berlin, Hamburg (600) and Göttingen.

The situation in continental Europe differs significantly from that in the UK and also from country to country. A lot of students deliberately overstay their visas, hoping to find work and settle. Many arrive, deliberately intending to settle and work, even if they enter Europe on a student visa. Others get themselves an invitation letter to a business or other conference, in Germany, for example, and therefore enter the country legally on their own passports. However, they never go to the conference, but find work or travel to another European country for work. Some get married and achieve residence that way. Many change their names and hide or destroy their passports so that they can claim to be refugees. While many Bhutanese refugees were flooding into Europe, it was a favourite ploy to claim to be Bhutanese. Once they have become illegal, it is almost impossible to change that status, although if they have been exceptionally good workers, their employers may help them. This involves admitting their original deceit to the immigration authorities, obtaining an exit pass, returning to Nepal and coming back legally under their proper name. It also involves legal fees and the cost of a return airfare. If they voluntarily present themselves to immigration as above, they can later return legally. However, if they are discovered by the police, who sometimes do spot checks on restaurants, then they are deported and are not allowed to return.

Nepali Fellowships

The Nepali community in Germany is largely scattered and unevangelized. There are many students but few Christians among them. Ps. Dambar pointed out that working with illegal immigrants has required a lot of sensitivity. Many of those who change their names, do not like to attend church – perhaps because they are ashamed of 'living a lie'? Even some who have come from churches in Nepal have not been encouraged to find fellowship in European countries. It seems that their pastors in Nepal have instructed them to send their tithe back to Nepal and perhaps this has been (mis)interpreted as also not joining a church overseas. This could be because some churches in Nepal teach that all one's tithe should be given to one's own church. This has saddened Dambar who believes that home-church pastors need to keep in touch with their migrant members.

However, as in many other European nations, there is an exciting increase in immigrant or diaspora churches, which have the potential and opportunity to reach out to groups like the Nepalis.[341] Again Dambar said that, "the challenge lies in encouraging churches in Germany to 'receive' and nurture new Nepali believers." He himself is one of the pastors in Stadtmission Wanne-Eickel in Ruhrgebiet, Central Germany. His vision is for Nepalis to enrich local churches rather than for specifically Nepali churches. There are two main reasons for this. There are few older Nepalis who need Nepali language services, and many Nepalis are in mixed marriages. Dambar believed that the 70-80 Nepali believers, who are scattered across the country, should attend local or multicultural churches. Some who arrived as Christians, have struggled with this, finding the German worship style very different from that in Nepal.

Dambar*'s* own testimony is interesting, but far from unique:

> *Born in 1962, he initially practised as a Hindu priest and for many years rejected the Gospel. Then, when he was 21, a great miracle changed his entire life, and he accepted Christ. This led to persecution in which he lost everything and had to flee from Nepal. He spent 2 years in Bahrain and one in Egypt before he arrived in Germany, with the intention of going on to America to attend Bible College. However, the spiritual needs of Europe touched his heart and so he settled in Germany. In 1991 he was ordained to work with the Baptist Mission for the American army as an assistant pastor, and three years later he began his evangelistic work which now takes him all over Europe.*

Nepalis have settled – albeit in relatively small numbers in all 3 of the 'LOW / BENELUX COUNTRIES (Netherlands, Belgium, Luxemburg).' Ps. Dambar has been instrumental in much of the outreach here.

NETHERLANDS/HOLLAND

STATISTICS	
Total Nepali Population	~2,000
No. of Nepali Fellowships	2
No. of Nepali Christians	>200

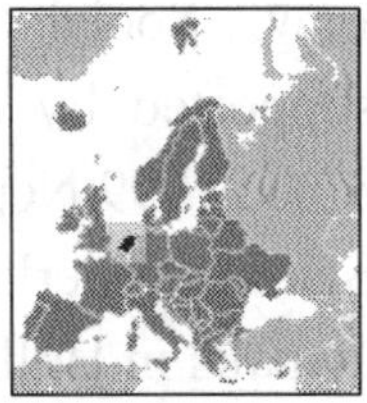

In 2010, the Central Bureau of Statistics gave a figure of 1,505 for Nepalis residing in Holland. Hieber has estimated that in 2013, the figure had risen to 1,617, and, according to Ps. Dambar it may now even be as many as 2,000. The main centres are Amsterdam, Utrecht and The Hague.

Nepali students have been studying in the Netherlands since the early 1970s and to date about 2,000 have graduated from different institutions all over the country in Engineering, Law, Social Sciences and Management. Many were supported by the Netherlands Fellowship Program (NFP). Since 1999 Nepalis have organised themselves into the Nepal Samaj Nederland, an apolitical and social association of Nepalis in Holland and Dutch people interested in Nepal.

Since 2009, the Netherlands has also been accepting around 100 **Bhutanese Nepali refugees** each year. By November 2011, around 350 refugees had been resettled. About 98% of the Nepali ethnics in Holland are Bhutanese.

Nepali Fellowships

Not just Nepalis, but other migrant ethnic minorities are increasing in numbers and diversity. By 2050, it is predicted that one-third of the whole country will be immigrants.[342] Immigrant churches are a ray of hope but integration into the national church life is also important.

Around 2008, when groups of Bhutanese refugees began to arrive in Holland, a Dutch couple, Kees and Karin Everaars, from the Rafaël Fellowship in Amersfoort and who had a heart to help refugees, began to get involved with these Bhutanese Nepalis. Wim and Margreet Korstanje (ex-Nepal missionaries) were also involved at the beginning when

Margreet translated at the baptism of 2 Bhutanese girls. As they were friends of Tjerk and Corrie Nap (fellow ex-Nepal missionaries) they invited them also to get involved. Kees and Karin then asked Tjerk to help them with their work among Nepali refugees (mainly from Bhutanese origin) in Amersfoort because they needed a translator. They also wanted a Nepali speaking Christian to help them nurture the Nepali believers some of whom had already been Christians back in the refugee camps while others had believed and been baptized since arriving in Holland. One of the Nepalis (from Nepal), Ram Subbha and his wife Shanti, had a keen interest in seeing a Nepali Christian church being established and so Tjerk invited Ps. Dambar from Germany to get involved, knowing that he was called to evangelism and church work amongst Nepalis in Europe. Dambar and Tjerk had first met in Nepal when Tjerk was working in Okhaldunga in the late 1980s. According to Dambar the link-up happened like this: Dambar and Tjerk had been trying to start a Nepali Fellowship. One day they went to pray in the house of two Bhutanese girls to cleanse it from the evil one and there they met Kees and Karin, who were like parents to all the Bhutanese in Holland. This led to them working together.

As a result, Tjerk, Dambar and Ram Subba visited several Nepali families who had left the refugee camp in Amersfoort already and had been resettled by the government in various towns like The Hague, Amsterdam, Lienden, Ingen and Maurik. Since that time Ps. Dambar has returned to Holland many times to work together with Kees and Karin and the growing group of Nepali people. He has given Bible studies, counselling and been involved in other pastoral activities. However, in a later group of refugees there were a few who had themselves been pastors already in the refugee camps. In the Nepali community, the work also has grown: there have been at least two Nepali baptismal services and even one wedding in 2011, which was conducted jointly by the Rafaël church pastor and Ps. Dambar.

In May 2011 Ram asked Tjerk to join a group of Nepali Christians on their visit to a Notary in Terheijden to discuss the possibilities of establishing a Nepali Christian Church in Holland. By November the **Nepali Christian Church of the Netherlands** had come into being and in mid-2012, twenty seven Nepalis were baptized in a river in Maurik. The main leadership is from a Rai family. Sadly, not long after this, the leadership broke up, part of the reason being a difference in aim between integrating into Dutch churches and developing Nepali ones. A second church was officially established in October 2012 under the name of **Immanuel Nepali Church of the Netherlands**. It has about 12 families with a total of 55 to 65 people. A great Christmas celebration was held in Zaandam in 2012. Their pastor is Dawa Tshering Tamang, who is based in Terheijden. Ram is a board member and Tjerk an advisor.

There are therefore now 2 registered Nepali Churches, ministering to a total of more than 200 Nepali believers, and served by 5 pastors. Both are national churches; neither has its own church building or a clear location for its activities. Rather they are both trying to bring some coherence to a community that lives scattered throughout the Netherlands in places like Venlo, Terheijden, Maurik, Tiel, Zaandam, Leiden, Raalte, Breda, Someren, Baarlo and Harderwÿk. The overall aim is to get the Bhutanese particularly to fully integrate in local fellowships as they are permanent settlers.

Thus most Nepali Christians attend a local Dutch (denominational) church in their neighbourhood on Sunday mornings, but they also go to house groups and monthly Nepali language fellowships.

The Nepali language activities of the Immanuel Church are additional: once or twice monthly small regional gatherings and 4 times a year nationally (e.g. Christmas). They cooperate with local Dutch churches although there is no official affiliation, thus for the Nepali fellowships, they hire rooms in local churches in places where groups of Nepalis are living. The aim is to help those Nepalis who do not really understand the Dutch language. Each regional group is led by a pastor/elder, who receives training from time to time. Also there are discipleship trainings and small group inductive Bible studies for the members. Services are conducted in Nepali for the older members and also in English and Dutch for the younger generation.

BELGIUM

STATISTICS	
Total Nepali Population	~6-9,000
No. of Nepali Fellowships	2
No. of Nepali Christians	~30

Estimates of Nepali residents in Belgium vary greatly. Hieber suggested 2,101 and Martine Muczerniuk (an ex-Nepal missionary) 6,000, but Ps Dambar reckons there may be as many as 3,000 legal migrants and twice that number of illegals. They are found mostly in the Flemish area of Belgium in Antwerp and Ghent in the west as well as Leuven (near Brussels). Most Nepalis in Belgium are refugees who are trying to reach the UK. Many stay in crowded accommodation and share beds. Some have paid ~10 *lakh* Nepali Rupees to get to Belgium, where they then work in a restaurant. Many do not really learn the local language and integrate, but one family in Leuven (known to colleagues from when they were in Burtibang, run a Belgian restaurant.

Nepali Fellowships

The first outreach to Nepalis in Belgium was made by Ps. Dambar in around 2001. In 2012 there were possibly only 15 Nepali Christians in Belgium, but by 2013 this number had increased to about 30-35, most of whom, including Min's group (see below) get fellowship from Ps. Dambar monthly.

Martine Muczerniuk has described how ***Ananda*** came to Christ. It was largely through the love and care of a local retired pastor who befriended him and his Pakistani companion. They had thought that having a child would help them to get papers to get married and stay in the country but it proved not that easy. However, now they are married and have (unofficial) work, are studying the language and attending a church in Antwerp.

A few Nepalis worship in Flemish churches. Many foreign evangelical Christians in Belgium choose to worship in international churches so that they can reach out to locals.[343]

Min Gurung's story illustrates this.

> ***Min****, from a hill village in Gorkha, found Christ while studying in Kathmandu and determined to go to Bible*

College. He chose Belgium, partly because he was not aware of any academic colleges in Nepal and partly "because some of [his] family members gave [him] information about the school." He completed his BA and continued to his Masters and at the same time was involved in running a small Nepali fellowship and Bible Study attached to ICEL (International Church of Evangelical Christians) in Leuven.[344]

LUXEMBOURG

STATISTICS	
Total Nepali Population	~100-300
No. of Nepali Fellowships	Nil
No. of Nepali Christians	~25-30

Hieber has estimated that there are 100 Nepalis in Luxemburg but others suggest a figure as high as 300. Most Nepalis in Luxemburg are professionals.

Nepali Fellowships

Ps. Dambar has been visiting Luxemburg and reaching out to Nepalis since around 2005. There are no known specifically Nepali Fellowships, but around 20-25 scattered believers. Some of these are Nepali-speaking Darjeeling businessmen who attend international fellowships.

Of the countries comprising GREATER SCANDINAVIA (Denmark, Norway, Sweden, Finland & Iceland), Ps. Dambar has only visited Denmark and has some knowledge of that. However, at least two of the Scandinavian countries (Denmark & Norway) have accepted Bhutanese refugees. Other than these, numbers of Nepalis from Nepal are relatively small.

DENMARK

STATISTICS	
Total Nepali Population	~4-5,000
No. of Nepali Fellowships	2
No. of Nepali Christians	~170

Like so many European countries, there are many Asian settlers in Denmark, Nepalis among them. Hieber and Adhikari agree that there are around 1,849 Nepalis in Denmark, but others suggest a figure as high as 3,000 or even 4-5,000, including around 800 **Bhutanese refugees**. In Denmark, migrants are required by law to become integrated into the society[345], but, especially the Bhutanese, after years of living in refugee camps, have found difficulty in settling into European life. The policy of scattering them across the country has perhaps strangely not facilitated this. There are also some international students, but they tend to live together in adjacent flats so that they can support each other socially.[346] Denmark was a popular student destination until 2005, when it started charging heavy fees. Some students had to give up their studies because of this: others found their studies suffering because they had to work to earn money for their fees. Legally students in Denmark are only supposed to work for 60 hours a week maximum, but the amount they can earn in this time is insufficient to support them. The NRN Association, Denmark commented that "it seems Denmark is either supplying labour through students from third world or maintaining state revenue in the form of tuition fee."[347]

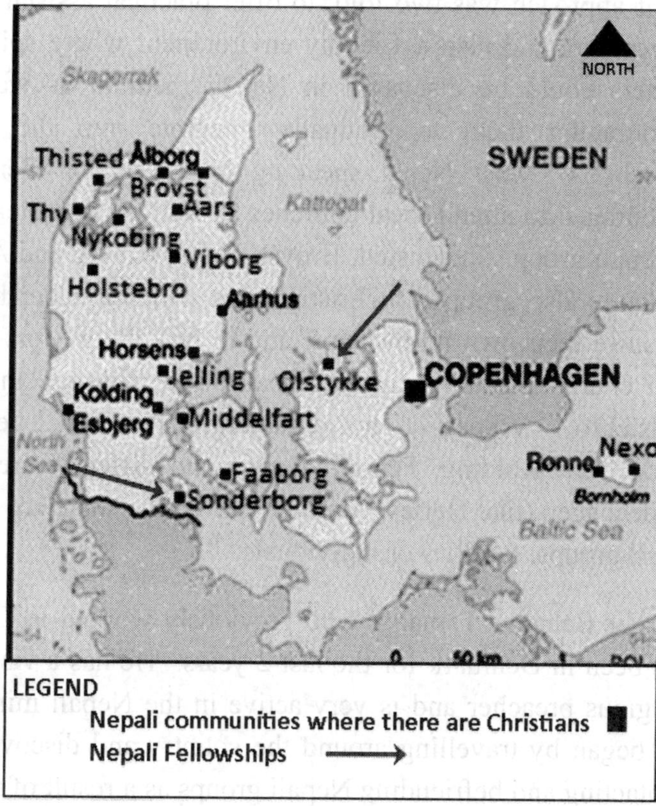

Nepali Fellowships

Migrant churches are the growing edge of Christianity in the country. Ps. Dambar has been visiting Denmark since around 2008, and according to him there are now more than 100 and maybe 170 Nepali believers. There are 2 Nepali Fellowships – in Sønderborg and Ølstykke, both of which are attached to local churches; an arrangement common in many Western countries and which seems to provide stable and secure development for long-term migrants. This point is emphasised by Ole Kirchheiner (an ex-Nepal missionary), who with his wife has been involved in establishing a Nepali fellowship alongside the other activities of their own church. Their approach was two-fold: to offer practical assistance to newcomers and also a friendly environment where spiritual matters could be discussed in Nepali medium as well as encouraging them to gradually integrate into the local church.[348] Most Nepali-speaking believers are therefore encouraged to attend local churches as well as, or instead of, a Nepali group. In Thisted, Brovst, Nexø, Ålborg and Århus there are also groups of Christians but without leadership to organise their own fellowships; and in Nykøbing Mors there is a church reaching out to Nepalis. In addition, in Års, Holstebro, Viborg, Thy, Esbjerg, Horsens, Jelling, Middelfart, Kolding, Fåborg, Rønne and different areas of Copenhagen (like Herlev, Amager and Valby) there are many small groups, families or individuals.[349]

Ps. Bir Bahadur Tamang, who previously worked in Dubai, has been in Denmark for the last 2 years. He has a visa as a religious preacher and is very active in the Nepali ministry. He began by travelling around the country and discovering, contacting and befriending Nepali groups as a result of which 20 people accepted Christ in the first year.[350] He has had opportunity to witness at funerals and new fellowships are beginning to spring up. He also runs a fruitful local and international skype ministry.

NORWAY

STATISTICS	
Total Nepali Population	>2,000
No. of Nepali Fellowships	2
No. of Nepali Christians	??

Adhikari agrees with Hieber's estimate of around 1,030 Nepalis in Norway, although others give figures ranging from 200 to 2,000. Some Nepali students are in Trondheim.

In addition, Norway accepted about 200 **Bhutanese refugees** and resettled them in Trondheim (54), Vadsø (40) & Alta (>30) in the far north, and Kopervik in Rogaland (60) in the south. They seem to have settled well and started to arrange Nepali cultural programmes. Larger family units and relatives have been able to settle in the same community.[351]

Nepali Fellowships

There are said to be 2 Nepali fellowships in the country.

SWEDEN

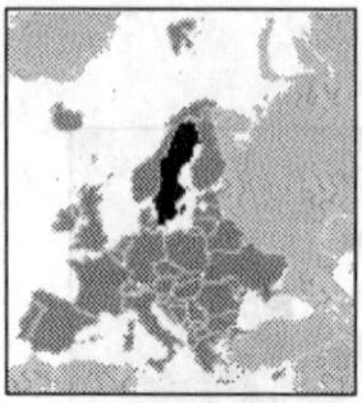

Nepali migrants are just one small group among 35 Asian nationalities who have found their way to Sweden. Hieber suggests that there may be as many as 823.

FINLAND

STATISTICS	
Total Nepali Population	~3,000
No. of Nepali Fellowships	1 or 2
No. of Nepali Christians	15-30

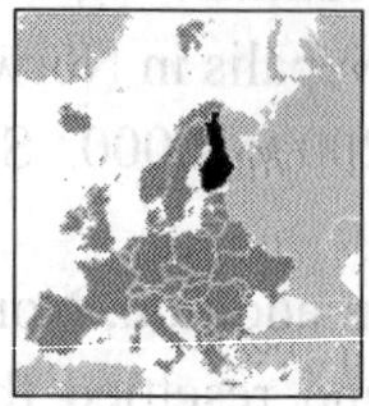

There are fewer foreign migrants in Finland than in many European countries. Hieber suggests 1,389 Nepalis living in Finland. Official records say approximately 1,850. Nepalis themselves say 3,000. 63% live in the area around Helsinki. Only 25% are women. Most of the earlier migrants came to work in restaurants, but in recent years there has been an increasing number of students.

Nepali Fellowships

Very few churches apart from the Pentecostal and Free Church are active in reaching out to foreigners, including Nepalis. However, there are said to be 2 Nepali fellowships but only a handful of believers (maybe 15-30). One problem is that they are so scattered. Another is pressure of time and work. The Nepali Christians themselves are committed to spreading the Word of God to other Nepalis. Accordingly, the Nepali Finnish Christian Fellowship runs annual Nepali outreach camps in Helsinki. Since the first camp, some of the Christian families have started a Nepali Fellowship group and some have even moved house to enable them to live closer together.[352] As elsewhere many ex-Nepal missionaries have become involved with this – befriending Nepalis, giving them Christian literature and helping with the summer camps. One told me this lovely story:

> *In 2007, Matti, a Finnish man very active in reaching out to foreigners, befriended a young Nepali student called Shyam, who was interested in Christianity and started to go to an English church service with Matti. After some time the church got a Nepali New Testament for him. When given it, he looked at it and asked, "Didi, I see that there are many chapters in this book and the first one seems to be written by a person called Matti, but it doesn't give his last name. Is it written by this Matti that we know?" Mari-Sisko says she will always remember that question – a reminder to always cover the basics for enquirers with no Christian background.*[353]

ICELAND

The estimate given by Hieber for Nepalis domiciled in Iceland is only 94. I have not discovered any information about any Nepali Christians or Nepali Fellowships.

Nepalis have settled in all the other main WESTERN EUROPEAN countries, but far less is known of these: they are not countries that Ps. Dambar has been visiting. The majority are – somewhat surprisingly – based in Spain, Portugal and Italy, almost certainly because it is relatively easy to obtain residence permission, especially in Portugal.

SWITZERLAND

STATISTICS	
Total Nepali Population	~1,000
No. of Nepali Fellowships	?1
No. of Nepali Christians	5-12

There may be around 1,000 Nepalis in Switzerland. Hieber estimates 955. Many are illegal. I heard one amusing story about a missionary from Switzerland. An illegal Nepali in the country asked him to marry his (the Nepali's) wife in Nepal and so bring her to Switzerland for him!

Nepali Fellowships

"Switzerland has the highest proportion of foreign residents of any major state in Europe.... A number of agencies and churches are committed to ministry among them..."[354]

There are at least 5 Nepali Christians. One source also indicated that there is one Nepali church with 12 believers.

FRANCE

STATISTICS	
Total Nepali Population	~2-5,000
No. of Nepali Fellowships	Nil
No. of Nepali Christians	7

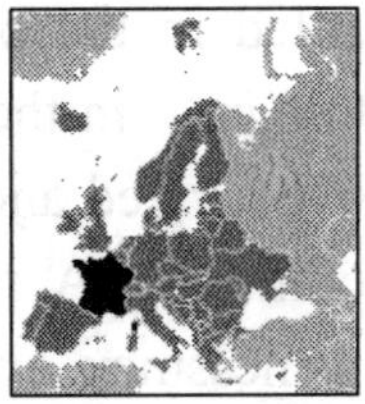

Hieber estimates that there are 2,000 Nepalis in France, but others have suggested a figure as high as 5,000. Probably a large number of them are international students. There is a Nepali community in Paris.

Nepali Fellowships

There are no known Nepali Fellowships but I have heard that there are 7 individual believers.

ITALY & the HOLY SEE

STATISTICS	
Total Nepali Population	~9,000
No. of Nepali Fellowships	Nil
No. of Nepali Christians	?

The figure given to me for Nepalis in Italy was 10,000, but I found this surprising, although perhaps it is correct as in 2012, the Ministry of Foreign Affairs proposed opening a diplomatic office in Italy.[355] Other sources, including Hieber, have estimated a much lower figure (2,000-2,500), but Adhikari veers towards the higher number and suggests 9,000. Most are settled in the big cities of Milan, Rome, Venice, Pisa and Bologna. In the last few years, a greater variety of migrants have arrived and some have transferred from other European countries. A few Nepalis are professionals, academics or businessmen, but most migrants work in factories and restaurants in the private sector. As in many European countries, "illegal immigration is a major challenge… Italy functions as a gateway into the EU."[356]

Nepali Fellowships

There are no known Nepali Fellowships, although there may be some scattered believers.

AUSTRIA

STATISTICS	
Total Nepali Population	~800-1,000
No. of Nepali Fellowships	Nil
No. of Nepali Christians	1-2

Wikipedia sources state that there are around 1,250 Nepalis in Austria, but Adhikari and Hieber give more conservative figures of 800-1000 and 570 respectively. Most are based in Vienna. They are a mixture of temporary and permanent residents and refugees. As in many western countries, there are many international students – at least 125 at graduate or post-graduate levels. Because of free movement within the

European Union, it is hard to state a specific number, but some suggest it may even be as high as 1,000! In contrast, only about 100 Nepalis have settled permanently in Austria: they are professionals and those working in UN posts.

Some **Bhutanese refugees** have also been settled in Austria.

After 1998 (2 years into the Maoist conflict) and especially after the 'peace accord' of 2006, the numbers of asylum seekers in Austria increased drastically, the official number being 450. Some Nepalis from Nepal have obtained asylum in Austria by pretending to be refugees from Bhutan. However Somnath Ghimire believes that there are only about 200 Nepali refugees in Austria. Pathak and Niraula tell the fascinating story of how Somnath reached Austria:

> *In 2001,* ***Somnath*** *left Kathmandu and travelled via Mahendranagar to New Delhi, where, after 2 days he flew to Moscow. From there, a broker sent him, along with a group of other Nepalis and Indians, hidden in a container, to Ukraine. However, they were discovered, arrested and imprisoned under harsh conditions for a month but then freed on the condition that they leave the country within 24 hours. Instead, they walked through jungle and later hid in the snow for 6 months before eventually reaching Kiev. After hiding near the border for a couple of months, they were taken across in a convoy-truck but again immediately arrested on the Slovak side. They escaped but were later re-arrested for a month. Then, with the help of other brokers they reached Bratislava, near the western border of Slovakia, but they were still in hiding and in terrible conditions. In the end they gave themselves up to the police. After 11 months' further incarceration – and almost exactly 18 months after leaving Nepal – Somnath finally reached Austria and applied for refugee status. This was granted*

for he is now Vice President of the Institute for Nepali Social Culture in Vienna![357]

There is quite a different story of three other Nepalis. "On the evening of October 13 [2002], they reached Kathmandu's international airport, received boarding passes from a broker, and rushed onto the Austrian Airlines flight. Instead of checking them, the security personnel told them to hurry-up. The next day they reached Vienna and applied for refugee status." They had paid over 12,000 USD to a broker to make these arrangements, and probably some of that money had been passed to the security personnel in TIA. This group and others like them were not as lucky as Somnath: however, once in the EU they have been able to move on to other places like Portugal. One ironic – even laughable – story was also told by Pathak and Niraula. In 2006 a group of Nepalis arrived in Vienna via Tel Aviv, intending to ask for asylum:

> *They remained at the airport for 24 hours waiting for the police to arrest them. [Nothing happened.] Then they called the police [but] the police officer on duty told them to call later since he did not understand English. They went to immigration at the airport and said that they were refugees from Nepal...*[358]

This then led to their arrest and detainment but ultimately to their receiving temporary residence permits, although they were not yet truly free for the 'white card' only entitled them to restricted residence and did not permit them to work. Less than 20% of Nepalis receive a UN Passport, entitling them to travel to anywhere except their home country.

Nepali Fellowships

There is only 1 Nepali Christian in Austria and no fellowship.

There are considerable numbers of Nepalis working in both of the countries of the IBERIAN PENINSULA.

PORTUGAL

STATISTICS	
Total Nepali Population	~10,000
No. of Nepali Fellowships	1
No. of Nepali Christians	?

The figure given for Nepalis in Portugal is 10,000, which I found surprising, although perhaps it is correct as in 2012, the Ministry of Foreign Affairs proposed opening a diplomatic office in Portugal.[359] Hieber suggests that the figure should be only 1,000, but Dambar Adhikari thinks 10,000 is about right, because in Portugal it is relatively easy for 'refugees' to obtain official permanent residence. If they pay 3 years' tax (even without working for 3 years) they are eligible! Most live and work in Lisbon. Many work in the fields.

Nepali Fellowships

There is just one small Nepali Fellowship (8 people) in Lisbon, and probably other scattered believers elsewhere. A friend in Malaysia was suddenly asked one day in 2008 whether she knew of any Nepali fellowships in Portugal. One of the labour migrants, who had accepted Christ while working in Malaysia, was concerned because his company was thinking of transferring him. Sadly we had no contacts to give him, so, after much prayer and fasting, this young believer decided not to take up this opportunity because it would be hard for him to find fellowship there. Instead, he returned to Nepal to witness to his family. Not all (Christian) migrants are this wise: many keep crossing borders always hoping for a better deal.

SPAIN

STATISTICS	
Total Nepali Population	~10,000
No. of Nepali Fellowships	Nil
No. of Nepali Christians	?5

Similarly, the figure given to me for Nepalis in Spain was 10,000, and again I found this surprising. Adhikari suggests around 9,000 while Hieber is far more conservative, giving an estimate of 1,344. Perhaps the higher number is correct as in 2012, the Ministry of Foreign Affairs proposed opening a diplomatic office in Spain, even though it was later decided that this was unnecessary.[360] It is suggested that the popularity of Spain and Portugal is due to the ease of obtaining residence permits. They can be a step on the way to the UK or a haven to escape when a UK visa has expired!

Nepali Fellowships

There are no known Nepali churches, but perhaps around 5 scattered believers. In 2007, Heike heard from a German lady running a Bible Study group in Madrid. A Nepali man, deported from Germany had ended up in Spain and was now attending this group (presumably in Spanish medium). The lady asked for a Nepali Bible for him: it duly arrived safely.

There are far fewer Nepalis known to have settled in the SE part of Europe, including the BALKANS than in Western Europe.

GREECE

Although there is an active NRN association, total numbers of Nepalis are unknown. "Many thousands of immigrants and asylum seekers pour into Greece every year from Iraq, Afghanistan, Pakistan, Iran and other places [including some from Nepal]."[361] However, it is likely, especially since the economic collapse in Greece, that most of them are using Greece as a stepping stone into more affluent EU countries.

There is no known Nepali church as yet in Greece. I am also not aware of any individual Nepali Christians.

There are not so many Nepalis known to have settled in EASTERN EUROPE; rather it seems that many who travel there are actually hoping to make these countries a jumping off place to reach Western Europe.

Wikipedia says that the first Nepali settled in **POLAND** in 1965. In 2007, according to the NRN-NCC in Poland, there were about 100 Nepalis living in the country, most of them having arrived since the 1990s. By 2008/9 the DoFE in Nepal noted that 121 Nepalis were employed in Poland, but by 2013, Hieber estimated 315. Many international 'students' find their way to Poland, but some actually go with the hope of getting entry to western European countries where work is better paid. Early Nepali migrants came to work in restaurants and in Indian textile companies. Today, Nepalis often work in industry, building, services and the finance sector. The majority of Nepali migrants are today found in 3 specific regions: in the central plain region of Mazovia, around Warsaw, in the SE region of Lesser Poland, around Krakow, and in the northern coastal region of Pomerania, around Gdansk. I am not aware of any Nepali Fellowships or of any individual Nepali Christians in Poland.

Hieber estimates there may be 115 Nepalis living in the **SLOVAK REPUBLIC**. I have no information on any Nepali Fellowships or Nepali Christians.

In 2010 there were maybe 1,000 Nepalis resident in **RUSSIA**, although Hieber estimates the number in 2013 as 1,000 (*including* those in **UKRAINE**). During the heyday of the Soviet Union, Russia was a popular destination for international students. Wikipedia claims that over 6,000 Nepalis have graduated from Russian and former Soviet universities as lawyers, journalists, doctors and engineers. Some stayed on, married and settled. Since the fall of the USSR, some have been able to invest in private hydropower projects and other ventures in their home country. Russia is a huge country but most Nepalis live in and around Moscow or in the far east of the country. I am unaware of Nepali Fellowships and have not even heard if there are any individual Nepali Christians.

In the MEDITERRANEAN countries, there are some Nepalis, but not huge numbers.

As with Eastern Europe, some Nepalis have managed to reach **TURKEY** and then gone on from there to the west. In 2013, the Ministry of Foreign Affairs was considering opening a diplomatic mission in the country.[362]

I do know there are Nepalis working in **CYPRUS** and Hieber estimates there may be as many as 472. However, I have not discovered any information about them or whether there are any Nepali Fellowships.

There is a lot of immigration in **MALTA**, but I have no information on Nepali migrants there.

NORTH AMERICA

UNITED STATES of AMERICA

STATISTICS	
Total Nepali Population	? >1.5 *lakh*
No. of Nepali Fellowships*	c 100
No. of Nepali Christians*	10,300

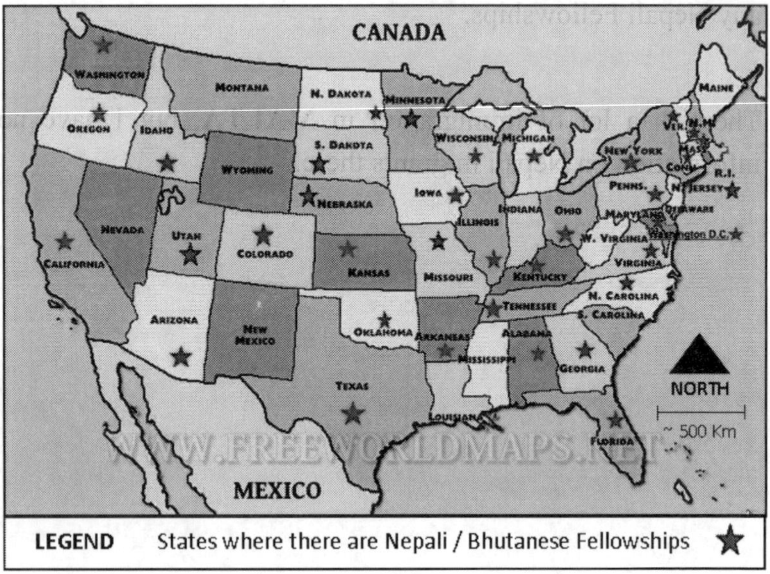

* In the USA (at least) Nepali-speaking Bhutanese often identify as Bhutanese rather than Nepali. 10,000 of the Christians are Bhutanese.

Because early records are not wholly reliable, it is not clear exactly when Nepalis started to travel to the States. Wikipedia says that "the first Nepalese to enter the United

States were classified as 'other Asian'." According to Ps. Dan BK, the first Nepali in the USA was in the 1940s but he was not an immigrant. Probably the first to emigrate to America did so after 1950 but it was only in 1974 that Nepalis were classified as a separate ethnic group. Up to 1992, less than 100 Nepalis entered the USA each year. This changed significantly in the following decade. By the turn of the century, there were around 6,000 Nepalis arriving each year and by 2008 this figure had risen to almost 16,000.

In the 2000 census, there were almost 12,000 Nepalis in America but as of 2010, it was said that there were almost 60,000,[cxxiii] although local Nepalis reckoned that this was a gross under-estimate.[363] The 2011 census suggested 86,256 (apparently excluding undocumented migrants and students). Cynthia Hale suggests that the number may be around 1 *lakh*. Ps. Dan BK thinks the figure is 5 *lakh* for those of Nepali origin and 70,000 for **Bhutanese refugees.** 5 *lakh* is probably an over-estimate,[cxxiv] although taking into consideration the fact that not only illegals, but also students, new immigrants like DV winners and some professionals without Green Cards will not have been included in the census, the true figure is still likely to be at least 1.5 *lakh*. Also, it is important to remember that there are 3 groups of Nepali-speaking peoples in the USA: Nepalis, 'Bhutanese' and Indians,[364] which may also have confused the statistics.

[cxxiii] The sources do not make it clear whether this figure is including or in addition to the resettled Bhutanese. Either way, with 60,000 Bhutanese alone, this figure must now be a lot higher. Joshua Project gives a figure of 55,000 of whom 3% were thought to be Christians.

[cxxiv] However, Dan BK asserts that there are 50,000 Nepalis in New York City and 30,000 in Washington DC alone, plus at least 15,000 in most of the other major cities.

As in most other western nations, the majority of Nepalis are professionals or students. Even in 2007/8 the total number of Nepalese students enrolled in colleges and universities in the USA was 8,936,[365] and many have stayed on to work and subsequently obtained citizenship. Others come via the US Diversity Visa (DV) lottery system[cxxv] which has increased the possibility of Nepalese migration to the United States, hence more of the recent migrants are less educated.[366]

Although spread throughout the country, the most populous states are said to be New York, Georgia, Texas, California, Virginia, Maryland, Massachusetts and Colorado and also Washington DC. Another list of cities includes New York City, Dallas, Houston, Atlanta, San-Francisco, Los-Angeles, Boston, Chicago, Denver, Gainesville (Florida), Portland (Oregon), and Saint Paul (Minnesota).

One of the reasons that Nepalis with professional qualifications are willing to take relatively menial jobs in America is because they have bought into the 'American Dream' for the sake of their children. Similarly, they appreciate the freedom and respect they can get in America regardless of gender or caste.[367] Thomas recounts the following story from Perry's book:

> In the late 1980s a former PC [Peace Corps] worker invited two Nepali students to Bellvue University [in Nebraska], and they gradually made way for their friends. Within ten years (by the late 1990s) there were nearly 600

[cxxv] According to Dan BK, this DV program is "congregationally-mandated and allows up to 55,000 persons from nations that are historically under-represented in terms of migration to the United States to qualify each year for immigrant visas." (www.dvlottery.com)

> Nepali students at Bellvue! Today about 400 remain, many with green cards and work visas and they've started their own Nepali organisation and web-site.[368]

America is one of the favourite destinations for Nepali students and some will do almost anything to prolong their stay. However, one of the requirements is that students have to prove that they have sufficient funds to maintain themselves (and their families, if they are also living in the States) in order to obtain or renew their visas. In 2008, a group of post-graduate students at Kansas State University committed visa fraud. "The students temporarily obtained funds from fellow Nepalese students and deposited the funds in their bank accounts. After getting the notarized bank letter, they returned the funds…" In 2013 an indictment was brought against them and if convicted they will face 10 years in prison and a heavy fine.[369] However, not all Nepali students are like that. Khadaroo tells the story of Surya Karki who came from a remote hill village but by winning scholarships, was eventually able to study in America. Even before he had completed his studies he had begun several schools back home, inspiring fellow students and businessmen in the west to support his venture.[370] Another heart-warming story of a Nepali migrant giving back to his own country is that of Ang Chhongba Sherpa, who is an evening manager in a branch of Dunkin' Donuts, but also works with an NGO, Moving Mountains Trust, to help the people back in his home village in Solukhumbu:

> *The Nepal group has built two primary schools and plans to expand each to include 12th grade, refurbished two monasteries… built a hydro-electric power plant, developed eco-friendly stoves, that create hot water, and*

placed them in 67 homes, built a water distribution system and run medical camps. Ang called this "the most satisfying work" he has ever done.[371]

One issue which is common in all the western destinations where Nepali professionals settle long term concerns the generations in some way. The parent's generation is at home in Nepali and misses their Nepali culture. The younger generation prefers to use English is are rapidly being integrated into American society. This is a problem for both Hindus, some of whom have now acquired their own temples[372] and also those who are/become Christians.

The USA was one of the countries that agreed to accept a large number of **Bhutanese refugees**, and since 2008, around 68,000 Bhutanese have been resettled.

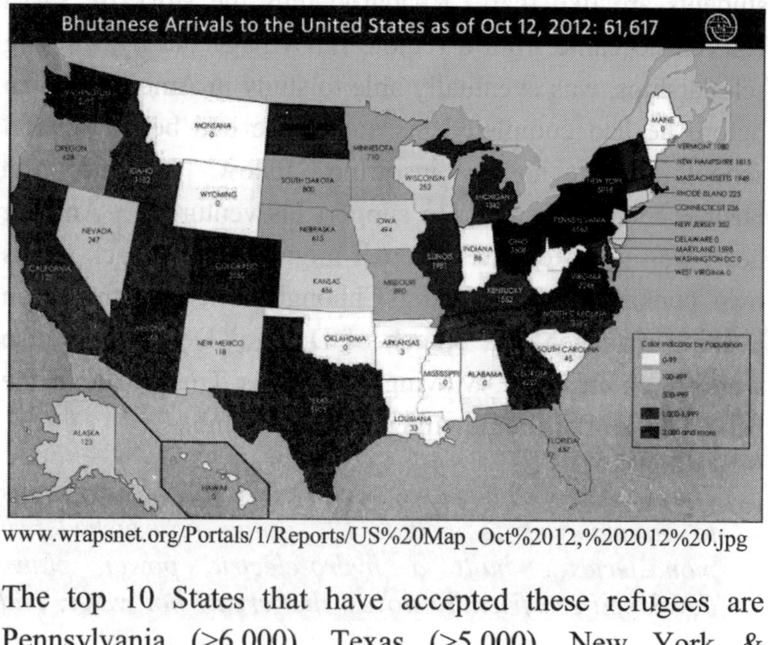

www.wrapsnet.org/Portals/1/Reports/US%20Map_Oct%2012,%202012%20.jpg

The top 10 States that have accepted these refugees are Pennsylvania (>6,000), Texas (>5,000), New York &

Georgia (>4,000 each), Ohio (>3,000), Arizona, Colorado, Washington, Virginia & North Carolina (> 2,000 each). Another 12 states have accepted more than 1,000 refugees each.[cxxvi] There are also 17 cities that individually each host more than 1,000 Bhutanese.[cxxvii][373] All these numbers refer to the primary settlement figures as published by the Office of Refugee Resettlement: they therefore give no indication of subsequent movements within the country.

Despite the resettlement, some Bhutanese refugees are still under stress and their suicide rate remains much the same as it was in the Jhapa Camps, or three times higher than the national average in the USA.[374] The main reason seems to be depression related to unemployment, lack of money, communication difficulties, worry about families back home and not being able to maintain their own religious and cultural traditions. However, many others are beginning to settle in their new homes and some have even demonstrated about the issues of human rights abuses in Bhutan.

While some refugees talk of trying to 're-emigrate' to Nepal, the majority are settling and after 5 years, the first groups are becoming eligible to take the examination to obtain American citizenship. This is relatively easy for the youth who have good English and can memorise all the facts about the USA. Many of those over 40, however, are illiterate even in Nepali

---

[cxxvi] 11. Illinois, 12. Massachusetts, 13. New Hampshire, 14. Maryland, 15. Kentucky, 16. Michigan, 17. California, 18. Idaho, 19. N Dakota, 20. Tennessee, 21. Utah & 22. Vermont.

[cxxvii] 1. Erie PA, 2. Denver CO, 3. Houston TX, 4. Rochester NY, 5. Syracuse NY, 6. Tucson AZ, 7. Dallas TX, 8. Phoenix AZ, 9. Pittsburgh PA, 10. Buffalo NY, 11. Decatur GA, 12. Fort Worth TX, 13. Baltimore MD, 14. Clarkston GA, 15. Lancaster PA, 16. Louisville KY, and 17. Salt Lake City UT.

and find the test almost impossible. One problem is that if they take the test and fail, they stand to lose their residency status and benefits like medical care, although if they keep resitting the test the benefits may not be removed. Another serious problem concerns numbers of independent youth who have joined gangs and got into trouble with drinking.

Nepali Fellowships

There are more, and more varied immigrants in the USA than anywhere else in the world, many coming from restricted access countries, and this is a great challenge to the American churches.[375] In fact, the same source notes that "Ethnic minority churches are the growing edge of US evangelicalism today." Only since 1990 have significant numbers of Nepali Christians migrated to the USA.[376] A critical mass has therefore probably not yet been reached for the Nepali community, but undoubtedly God is moving amazingly among the Nepali-speaking people of Bhutanese extraction.

The first Nepali Christians to arrive in the USA attended local American churches, but in some cases were disillusioned by the worldly behaviour they saw and so began to meet in their own homes for praise and worship.[377] In contrast, some local churches have welcomed Nepali congregations to use their facilities, mostly free, or else contacted Nepali pastors for help when new groups of Nepali-speaking migrants arrived on their doorstep.[378] The earliest Nepali Fellowships (circa 2006-8) were in Dallas, Atlanta, Denver, and San Francisco: later in Boston, New York City[379] and Baltimore[380], but the Church Planting movement was really 'ignited' by the arrival of the Nepali-speaking Bhutanese.[381] Ps. Dan and others have mentioned many pastors who have been deeply committed to this growth.[cxxviii] In many towns there are now several Nepali churches, though sadly often the result of splits.

Whereas in 2008, there were just 20 Nepali language fellowships in the States, by 2011 this number had increased to 100, although the majority are Bhutanese Nepali-speaking fellowships. "Ps. John Magar, of International Restoration, Austin, TX,[cxxix] claims that 'Bhutanese Churches are one of the fastest growing ethnic churches in America.'"[382] Part of the explanation is due to the fact that those arriving almost destitute, after years of life in refugee camps, have responded positively to the Christian love extended to them. In addition, there have been significant numbers of experienced Bhutanese pastors who have come to the States among the refugees. Nevertheless, as seen elsewhere among all Nepali-speaking groups, the response is greater among the tribals and 'lower' castes. Although the same growth phenomenon is not seen among the professional immigrants to America, as there are a number of IT professionals among the Nepali Christians, they have arranged their own link up over the Internet and a members-only Facebook page. There are many exciting testimonies of Nepalis now in America:

[cxxviii] These Pastors include: Dan BK (Dallas & Boston), Paul Rai (Bethel Nepali Church, New York City), Samuel Cho (Nepal Baptist Church, Baltimore), Silas Thapa (Emmanuel International Church, Atlanta), Michael Magar (Atlanta Nepali Christian Church), John Thapa (Restoration International Church, Austin), Samuel Khawas, (United Jyoti Church, Rochester NY), Shankar Rai (Pennsylvania), Basu Prasai (Seattle), Kris Kafle (Dallas), Nima Ghising (New Hampshire), Bijay Lama, and Prakash Gurung (Washington DC) to name just a few.

[cxxix] See also p. 465 where his name is written as Monger.

Jyoti, from Amp Pipal, tells how – after various setbacks and time in Norway – she ended up living in Baltimore in the USA where she is a worship leader in the Nepal Baptist Church.

> *While studying in Kathmandu, she met her future husband, Rabin, but he then went to the USA. Jyoti, who was keen to go to Bible College, applied to one in Canada with the help of Canadian friends but the visa was denied. Instead she went to Norway and worked as a nanny. During her time there she resumed contact with Rabin who invited her to visit him in the States, which she did. They decided they wanted to marry but "because of the seriousness of the issue, we decided to defer this decision for another year. I went back to Norway to continue my job. We prayed and fasted and finally God answered our prayer." They married in 2008 and Jyoti received a Diversity Visa to go to America. "Since then life has never been the same." They were even able to invite Jyoti's parents to visit at the time of the birth of their second child in 2013.*[383]

By rights, ***Asha*** should neither be living in Nepal nor in the Diaspora:

> *As a small child she suffered a near-fatal illness from which she recovered through the prayers and medical skill of the mission team in Amp Pipal Hospital. Then, after completing her schooling in Kathmandu, Asha had the opportunity to study medicine in India and later got a chance to do residency training in the States. She is now settled in America, married to a classmate, a devout Christian, and working for an under-served community in Connecticut.*[384]

One of the striking things about stories I have heard from the Diaspora is the involvement of Nepal or ex-Nepal missionaries. In most cases this is friendship when Nepali migrants reach the home countries of the missionaries:

> *For **Rajan** it began in childhood as his father worked with INF in Pokhara, and continued later as he himself joined a band set up by the son of UMN missionaries. He himself had also started a band – possibly the first in Nepal, as he longed to witness through singing. For several years Rajan visited India and toured around Nepal but when his father died he returned home and worked with the local church for 4 years until, with the support of family and a missionary friend, he started the first Christian recording studio. Unfortunately this did not do well and so he began a coffee house ministry which was initially very fruitful. However, when they moved the business to Kathmandu it was affected by the Maoist uprising and his partner had to leave, but in 2002 Rajan was invited to visit him in the States. On return to Nepal Rajan started a smaller coffee shop but with the same vision. Then God called his family to emigrate to the USA. They sold the shop and it has been thriving ever since! At first, Rajan and his family struggled to settle in America and wondered if they had mistaken God's guidance. Finally in 2007 they were introduced to Immanuel Baptist Church, which was looking for someone to reach out to the Nepalis in NYC. The ministry has not been easy but slowly the Nepali numbers have grown to around 30 and Rajan, as well as being involved in worship and interpretation in the English services, has been commissioned as Youth Pastor for the Nepali group. He has also helped Taraman to establish a daughter fellowship in Syracuse.*[385]

Dr Joe Lemaster (an ex-Nepal missionary) tells how he got involved with the Bhutanese. Having lost his Nepal visa in 2000, he and his family returned to the States where he did further study. About 10 years later he heard from Dr Cynthia

Hale (another ex-Nepal missionary) of the Nepali-speaking community in Kansas City and subsequently he moved there and now runs a refugee clinic. There are around 1,000 refugees and maybe a total of 3,000 Nepali speakers in the city but no other Nepali-speaking doctors. Sadly there is little mixing between the Nepalis from Nepal, who are more educated, and those from Bhutan. The former helped the refugees initially to get settled and then stepped back. In 2010 also the first Bhutanese Christians arrived and from that time on a fellowship began to grow, especially as one Rai family became Christians 'overnight'. It happened like this:

> *A young Rai man had heard of Christ while in the refugee camp. Then he and his family went to America. Suddenly he decided – without any contact with Christians – that he wanted to be a Christian and be baptised. At that time, his father was dying of cancer, but when prayed for by some local American Christians he improved. Father and son were subsequently baptised together in a Presbyterian church for Asian Indians. Then the father died and at the wake the question was asked, 'What does a Christian son have to do to get his father into heaven?' When the answer was given, "If the father is a Christian – nothing, as he will go straight to heaven," the whole family decided there and then to become Christians. They did not want a family division about this with some doing Hindu rites and others not! Shortly after this those who really understood were baptised and so began the Rai house fellowship.*
>
> *This family did not join with the Bhutanese group as at that time many of its members were 'messed up' with loose morals, inconsistency and hypocrisy. There was also an issue over legalism. Slowly, however, things are beginning to change.*

In recounting the beginnings of the Bhutanese fellowship in

Albany, Cynthia Hale highlights some of the problems associated with this sort of ministry. In 2008, hearing that Bhutanese refugees would soon arrive in the States, Drs Tom and Cynthia Hale volunteered to help if any were sent to their home town, and their church (Loudonville Community Church) supported them in this. In due course refugees began to arrive, the Hales started an International Friendship Team and began to recruit fellow Christians to welcome the refugees, guide them around town, help them with doctor's visits, shopping, welfare provisions, English classes, driving instruction, etc. All this generated a great deal of goodwill within the community. Right from the beginning, their motivation was based purely on the Biblical injunction to love the 'alien' (see p.11). They therefore made it clear that they would help anyone, regardless of whether they were interested in becoming Christians, although invitation and transportation to church were given.

For the first eighteen months, almost all the arrivals were high caste Hindus, but many showed interest in attending church and even becoming Christians. However, when older family members arrived, they dissuaded them. Then from the end of 2009, low caste families also began to arrive. Slowly, some of these accepted Christ as did one high-caste couple, and a Saturday house fellowship was started. House visits and discipleship classes were also begun, although sadly, many seemed more interested in the physical help they received than the spiritual. They were also not enthusiastic about reaching out to Hindus in their community. However, 4 years on this group had evolved via a Sunday morning Nepali-language Bible Study, led by Cynthia, into a typical church, attendance 60-70, with an emphasis on praise and worship and led by a young man called Santosh.

Then, in early 2013 attendance dropped to 10-12 for which there were probably multiple reasons. One big factor was the loss of the use of a school bus that had been used to bring the Bhutanese to church – needed because there was no local transport. Another factor has been internal migration, as refugees moved elsewhere to find work. There was some disagreement among the members regarding the appointment of a young pastor. Hindu visitors may have experienced some discomfort regarding the worship style and also felt that Christianity was only for low-castes. The Saturday house fellowship also ceased as the refugees settled and were working then or used their day off for shopping or visiting. Overall it seemed that lifestyle transformation had not really occurred. However, after a couple of discouraging months, numbers again began to rise. Now Hindus are attending, some of the discord has been addressed and reconciliation has begun. A few high school students have professed faith, and there is an increasing desire to reach out to Hindus. The Bhutanese community in Albany is very small, only about 300, and unlike other areas, no mature pastors who had previously served in the refugee camps were resettled in Albany. In time, however, God will surely bless this small group so that it matures into a church with its own leaders.[386]

Since the resettlement programme, an amazing spiritual work has occurred among the Bhutanese refugees. Cohn mentioned World Relief, how some ethnic churches have started and partnerships been established with local churches, whose congregations have been able to help meet some of the needs of the refugee community – helping them settle culturally and providing language lessons[387] – an experience similar to that of those who have been involved in helping the Gurkhas settle in the UK. Monger's story, as recorded by Cohn, underlines this:[cxxx]

> ***Monger*** *was converted when he was 17 in a church in the jungle in Bhutan, he became an outspoken witness, but when arrested by the police he had to flee for his life to avoid renouncing his Saviour. In Nepal he began evangelizing in the refugee camps and was again arrested and this time spent 15 months in jail. After that he went to Nagaland and studied at Kohima Bible College, where he also met his wife and then returned to Nepal and founded Restoration Ministries. Four years later they arrived in Austin, Texas. Now Monger [aka John] is "probably serving a couple of hundred refugees in his community."*

Some of the practical ways that he has been able to help his fellow Bhutanese as they tried to adjust to America include driving them to a shop that will accept their food stamps, interpreting, helping them obtain medical care, etc. while the local church members have donated second-hand computers, clothes, furniture, a van and Nepali Bibles and also help with transport to fellowship meetings and practise English conversation with the refugees. Other groups have donated mobile phones or TVs, rice cookers, etc. to new arrivals.[388]

Cody Lorance also has stories of two Bhutanese Nepali speakers now in America:

> ***Krishna*** *was born into a prosperous farming family in Galephug in Bhutan, but in the 1990s his family were forced out of the country and into one of the refugee camps in SE Nepal. Because he had completed high*

[cxxx] See p. 459 where his name is written as (John) Magar.

school he worked there as a teacher, until in 2008, he, his wife and 3 grown-up children were able to go to America. Once in Chicago, they were befriended by a Christian Karen family and started attending a Bible Study, where they heard the Gospel in a mixture of Karen, English and Sanskrit! Then, largely through the healing of their daughter, the whole family turned to Christ. Krishna became one of the first deacons of the Nepali-speaking church.

***Ganesh** also came originally from Bhutan and had met Krishna in the refugee camp. He and his family arrived in the USA a year after Krishna. In due course Krishna shared the Gospel with Ganesh who subsequently committed his life to Christ, and like Krishna, also became a deacon in the church.*

Mark Kiser, an American citizen, who formerly served as a missionary in Nepal and who now lives in Omaha, Nebraska, has also been very involved in helping the Bhutanese refugees who started being resettled in the USA in 2008. At that time there were approximately 10 Nepali Fellowships in the USA but since the Bhutanese started coming that number has grown to 100 or so. Not only have the number of fellowships grown, but so also has the number of new believers in the fellowships. For example, in Omaha in 2009 there were 6 Bhutanese Nepali speakers meeting in an apartment in Omaha, but now there are approximately 150 adults and 50 children meeting weekly in a church with two thirds of them having become baptized believers since arriving in the States. This group has both a Bhutanese leader and a Nepali leader. Phurba Tamang was born in Bhutan and had become a Christian in the refugee camp in Nepal. He had received Bible training in North India and was serving as an associate pastor before being resettled in the USA. Min Thapa was previously a church leader in Pokhara. He has been instrumental in setting up Nepali language Theological Education by Extension (TEE) and training has been started in a few centres to provide basic discipleship courses. An inexpensive source of Nepali language Bibles has also been located in the States. Mark has been in touch with other Americans and Canadians involved in this ministry, sometimes by teleconference. They have their own Facebook group and are involved in a North American Refugees' Round Table.

RC Bhandari (Silvanus) has also been involved in ministry to Bhutanese refugees in America. He spoke excitedly about his involvement with the Bhutanese Nepali-speaking Fellowship, in Manchester, NH. There was a time in 2012 when he said it felt like they were in a revival. The group in Boston run their own radio programme.

According to Ps. Silas Thapa most fellowships are situated in the big cities. A composite list taken from several sources confirms that there are about 100 Nepali-speaking fellowships, although some identify as Bhutanese. Baptized membership varies from 15 to 300:

State	Cities
Arizona	Phoenix, Tucson
California	Los Angeles, Sacramento, San Francisco
Colorado	Denver
Florida	Jacksonville
Georgia	Atlanta, Clarkston (2), Decatur, Lilburn, Stone Mountain, Tucker (2), Warner Robins
Idaho	Boise
Illinois	Chicago, Glen Ellyn
Kansas	Kansas City

Kentucky	Louisville
Maryland	Baltimore (3), Gaithersburg, Worcester
Massachusetts	Boston, Cambridge, Lynn, West Springfield
Michigan	Lansing
Minnesota	Minneapolis, Saint Paul
Missouri	Saint Louis
Nebraska	Omaha
New Hampshire	Concord (2), Manchester
New Jersey	Freehold, Princeton
New York	Albany, Buffalo, Loudonville, NY City, Rochester, Syracuse, Utica, Woodside
North Carolina	Charlotte, High Point, Matthews, Winston Salem
North Dakota	Fargo, Grand Forks
Ohio	Cincinnati, Columbus (2)
Oregon	Beaverton (2), Portland
Pennsylvania	Erie, Harrisburg, Lancaster, Pittsburgh
South Dakota	(no major cities named)
Tennessee	Memphis, Nashville (3)
Texas	Abilene, Austin, Dallas, Fort worth, Houston (2), Irving
Utah	East Salt Lake City
Vermont	Essex Junction
Virginia	Charlottesville, Fredericksburg, Herndon, Richmond, Roanoke, Woodbridge
Washington	Burien (nr Seattle), Kent, Spokane, Tuwkila
Wisconsin	Madison

Dan BK, Church Planter and Catalyst, first came to the States to study Theology in 2001, but in 2006 God called him to plant a church in Dallas and that same year a Korean missionary planted another church in Baltimore. Nowadays Dan is based in Boston but continues to plant churches, mainly on the eastern seaboard, and recruit and mentor their leaders. He has been involved in this phenomenal growth of Nepali-speaking churches in the USA and has documented it in a paper entitled "The Spread of Christianity among the Nepali-Speaking Population in the United States," based on interviews conducted with 10 Nepali speaking pastors (5

Bhutanese and 5 Nepali) and one Korean-American. Since 2006, he has worked with Southern Baptist church plants in 16 cities in 7 states mostly in the north east. Other Nepali (or Bhutanese) fellowships have affiliation with Presbyterian, Four Square, Free Will Baptist, and Methodist Churches, etc. Yet others have no denominational affiliation – being independent Pentecostal or Charismatic groups.

Although the greatest spiritual fruit has so far been seen amongst the Bhutanese, Bijay Lama shared with me how God worked among two IT professionals, neither of whom had ever been to church before they left Nepal. Both are now serving in Nepali churches and also involved in the 'Nepali Speaking Christian Students and Professionals Fellowship,' a group who reach out to Nepali speaking students in High Schools, Colleges and Universities across the USA.

*While **Parmeshwor** was studying at graduate school in Missouri, he heard the Gospel through some American friends and went with them to church. However, it was only after he moved to Texas and met Nepali Christians, that he found the answers to his questions and personally accepted Christ.*

***Deep** has a similar testimony. After completing his graduate studies in California he also moved to Texas where he found himself living in the same apartment as Parmeshwor. As a result he got to know many Nepali Christians and when he moved to Massachusetts, Deep attended an American church. In 2012, he returned to Dallas and he and his wife formally accepted Christ.*

One interesting development, despite the huge size of the USA, is that since 2009, there have been annual Nepali Christian gatherings, increasingly involving representatives from all across the States.[389] Ps. Dan has organized Christian Leaders' Conferences (as below), Ps. Silas & John Magar Bhutanese Nepali Conferences and Ps. Bijay, with Samuel, and Maya, Students' and Professionals' Conferences.

2009	Boston	40	Pastors from Dallas, Houston, California, New York, Ohio, Illinois, Maryland, Boston, and Scotland, UK
2010	Rochester	300	
	Atlanta	200	
2012	Phoenix	4-500	
	Lancaster		
2013	W Springfield	c1,200	Celebration for pastors, lay leaders, and members
	Washington DC/Virginia	c124	for pastors & lay leaders only

In addition, there are local seminars being organised each month in different states. Nepali leaders are also proving adept at networking with other Nepali and American leaders, as well as within their local communities – to develop relationships and promote funding for their ministries.

Dan mentions some of the problems faced by the Nepali Fellowships. One is the generation gap: should they start English-speaking congregations or Nepali language schools? Another is denominationalism, and its relationship to theological training, which has never really been an issue in Nepal. A third is that of the influence of cults. Despite all these, perhaps the biggest single factor behind the phenomenal growth is, however, the tradition, common in Nepal, of setting aside one day a week for prayer and fasting.[390]

CANADA

STATISTICS	
Total Nepali Population	? c 5,000
No. of Nepali Fellowships	>6
No. of Nepali Christians	?

Nepalis have only recently started to emigrate to Canada. Only a handful arrived in the 1960s and early 1970s. Even in 1991, there were only 125. In the 2006 census, the number of Nepalis domiciled in Canada was recorded as 3,780. Just over half live in Ontario and smaller populations are found in Alberta (Edmonton & Calgary), British Columbia (Vancouver), Quebec and Manitoba. Once a family has been welcomed in a local town, other Nepali families join them to make a small community.[391] Although the majority travel directly from Nepal, small numbers have come via India, Burma, Bhutan, Fiji, Hong Kong, the UK and the USA.

Most Nepalis in Canada are well-educated professionals, students or businessmen. ***Indu,*** who had worked for 7 years in various NGOs in Nepal, including the two main missions, described how she experienced God's guiding her to Canada:

> *Originally,* ***Indu*** *was determined to stay back in Nepal even though so many of her friends had left for foreign lands 'chasing their dreams'. She admitted to uncertainty and lack of confidence in herself and she also had a fear of being lonely if she crossed the 'seven oceans'. Then one day, a simple thought came to her – Canada. After that everything worked so well and she received her visa within a record time of 7.5 months. Everyone was surprised, including Indu and it made her realise that this really was God's plan for her. That was confirmed each step of the way. In around 2011 she flew to Canada with nothing but loads of prayers from her family and with a bible verse: "Look in the scroll of the Lord and read: None of these will be missing, not one will lack her mate. For it is his mouth that has given the order and his spirit will gather them together. He allots their portions; his hand distributes them by measure, they will possess it forever and dwell there from generation to generation.(Isaiah 34:16-17).*
>
> *From her very first day in Canada, God opened new doors for her. She had a Nepali family already waiting for her, who out of the blue, came in contact with her*

even before she left Nepal. They were able to help and guide her start this new life for which she had a dream that she would one day have a home there. Since then, she has completed her International Development studies and is now volunteering with a Christian Children's organisation. However, she writes, "The greatest thing that Canada has given me is my life partner, for which I had struggled and suffered a lot back home. It was and is God's plan for me; I realize this every moment and find hundreds of reasons to praise him. I am happy and content with my life now and believe that I am here for a reason."[392]

Some Nepalis work in restaurants or factories as Nepalis can be hired for employment in Canada through personal contacts in various sectors. A few arrived as asylum seekers. Wikipedia gives us an interesting addition by saying that "a small group of Nepalis came through the Gurkha Welfare Appeal (Canada), which was established by Canadian military veterans after World War II."

Nepali Fellowships

Canada, like Australia, is a nation of immigrants and it has deliberately embraced multi-cultural pluralism, but this makes outreach and evangelization difficult.[393] Nevertheless, these immigrants, including the Nepalis, are almost all living on the doorstep of urban churches. Where Nepalis are scattered, rather than in discrete communities, new immigrants much appreciate it if there is someone to welcome them. This is how it happened for ***Jyoti and Narayan***:

Because Jyoti was related to our NeMUN Chairperson, she asked me if I knew any Nepali contacts in Canada. The only person I could think of was Betty Neumann, an ex-Nepal missionary, but she was living in a very different city. However, she managed to find a contact for us and it turned out they lived in exactly the same road as where the family would be settling.

According to Ps. Dan BK, who is based in the USA as a Church Planter Catalyst with the Southern Baptists, he was instrumental in starting 6 Nepali fellowships in 3 provinces in 2012:– in Calgary (Alberta), Toronto & Ottawa (Ontario) and Quebec City, Montreal & Sherbrook (Quebec). There are other fellowships in Joliette and Saint Jerome in Quebec.

Many Nepalis move around the Diaspora. Swiba Lepcha, an ex-British Gurkha, arrived in Canada with his family in 1990, and he is now a part of the Nepali fellowship in Mississauga, Ontario. Earlier, he was a member of the fellowship in HK in the 1970s. His testimony of that time is on p.377.

C. AMERICA & CARIBBEAN

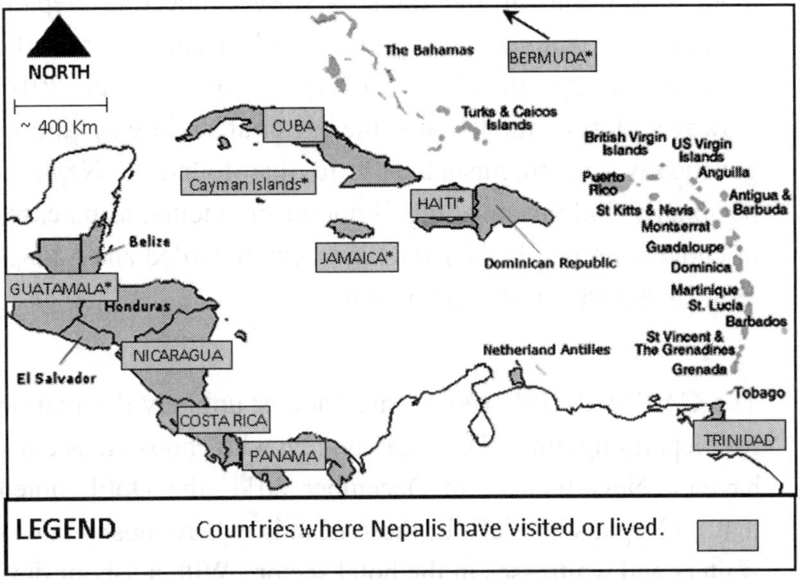

Nepali migrants are known to have travelled to all the countries marked on the map but few details or numbers of any Nepali Christians or fellowships are available.

In the colonial era some went to **TRINIDAD** as indentured labour.[394]

HAITI* is not on the Nepal Government list of allowed destinations for Nepali migrants. Hardly surprising then that one story I have discovered about Nepalis in Haiti is about trafficking. Rather like the story already quoted of a circuitous route to Austria, 2 Nepali men paid agents (aka smugglers) to get them to the USA but ended up being prisoners held to ransom in Haiti, after travelling for 11 months through Singapore, China, Brazil, and Panama. The other – well-known and tragic – story connecting Nepalis with Haiti is that concerning the spread of cholera from the camp of the Nepali UN peacekeeping force in late 2010. However, despite the fact that the bacterial strain was 'almost genetically indistinguishable'[395] to that found in Nepal, I personally find this puzzling, if not unconvincing, as no cases of cholera among the Nepalis have been recorded and a long-term carrier state is extremely rare.

The **CAYMAN ISLANDS*** are another unlikely destination for Nepali migrants. There can be few who choose it as a tax haven! Nevertheless, in December 2011, the DoFE noted that 20 Nepalis had left for these islands, where most work as waiters and waitresses in the hotel sector. With a 9-hour day, good facilities and the possibility of earning up to 10-15 USD an hour, life in the Caymans is a far cry from the situation of most Nepali labour migrants. Although Manpower agents cannot recruit for such jobs in the Cayman Islands because they are not on the GoN allowed list, private arrangements are not illegal, but professional work experience in international standard hotels is a prerequisite. Another possible hurdle is the need to obtain a US transit visa.

SOUTH AMERICA

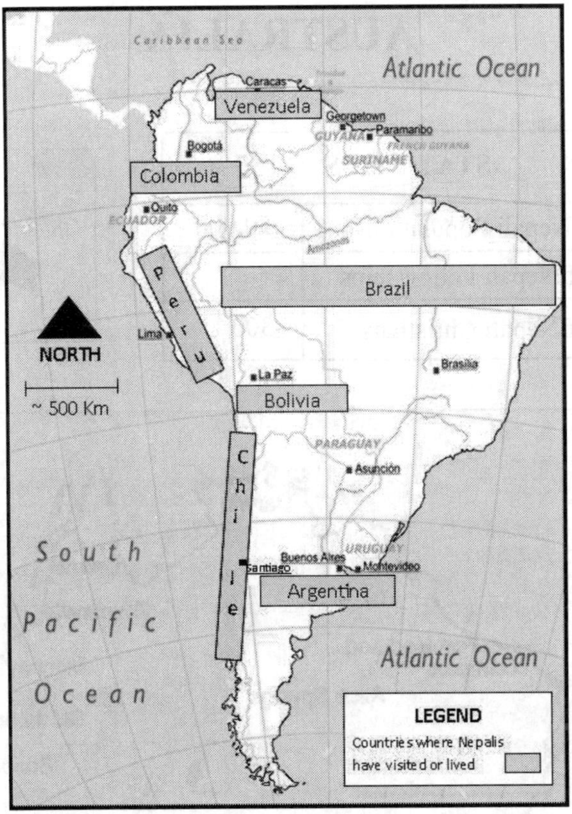

Nepali migrants are known to have travelled to all the countries marked on the map but few details of numbers or of any Nepali Christians or fellowships are available.

During the Colonial era Nepalis were shipped as indentured labourers and Perry mentions **BRITISH GUIANA** (now **GUYANA**) as one destination.

AUSTRALASIA and OCEANIA

AUSTRALIA

STATISTICS	
Total Nepali Population	>50,000
No. of Nepali Fellowships	4+
No. of Nepali Christians	~300

Nepalis first travelled to Australia in the 1960s. In 2009, it was estimated that there were approximately 17,000 Nepalis domiciled in Australia, of whom almost half were international students. This figure may well have now increased due to the current popularity of the country as a student destination. Wikipedia noted that graduations increased 500% in 2007 alone, such that Nepal is now Australia's 11th biggest source country for international students. In fact, a recent personal communication suggests that there are around 47,000 Nepalis in Sydney of whom the vast majority (30-35,000) are students. Like most estimates of Nepali populations in other countries, this conflicts with both the census figure of 27,600 in 2011 (up from 7,000 in 2006) and an NRNA estimate of 70,000.[396] Uttam GC suggests a figure of around 50,000. Most Nepalis live in Sydney and Melbourne and there are also some in Brisbane, Adelaide and Darwin.

Australia also agreed to accept around 5,000 **Bhutanese Refugees.** Recent information suggests that there may actually be 6-7,000 Bhutanese refugees resettled in Australia now, mostly in Adelaide (S Australia), Albury (NSW), Launceston (Tasmania) and Melbourne (Victoria).

Sustained immigration in Australia has created a multicultural country, which has readily accepted Nepali (and Bhutanese) settlers.[397] "Yuba Sansar, weekly Nepali language radio programme run by young Bhutanese in Adelaide… was awarded the 'Multicultural Youth Program of the Year 2012'" and "a Nepalese-run radio programme from Melbourne was one of the finalists for Women's Program of the Year."[398]

Nepali Fellowships

As in Malaysia, Uttam GC was one of the pioneers. Some four years after returning from Malaysia in 2003, he discovered that many Nepalis were going to Australia to study. Sensing a new challenge, he prayed about it and applied for a professional visa and then a small miracle occurred! When the email of acceptance arrived, long before he anticipated a response, he threw it in the junk box, not realising what it was, but happily he later checked and found it was actually his visa. In Australia he found a similar situation to that in Malaysia and used a similar tent-making strategy to motivate other Nepalis. Some Nepali migrants were attending local English-medium churches, but a lot were just 'rice Christians'. They had arrived on visitors visas and become asylum seekers and were then hoping that Australian Christians would help them. Uttam, after talking with Lokman, started a Nepali fellowship: it was hard-going at the beginning but then blessing came. He was instrumental in founding the Sydney Nepali Christian Church, whose leader is Lokman; and also of the United Nepali Christian Community (UNCC), both of which are continuing to grow. Others then copied the pattern, like Andy Limbu and the Korean churches in Sydney.

Then the Bhutanese refugees started to arrive and God opened a door for them too. A group of them turned up at a small Australian church, in Albury, a town 6 hours south of Sydney on the border of NSW and Victoria. The church had no idea what to do, but contacted the INF/Australia office, who put them in touch with Uttam who began to help them. At first he visited at weekends and also preached via skype, but nowadays he lives in Albury. At first he and his family were reluctant to leave good jobs and the opportunities in the city of Sydney, but God made it clear that they should go. By 2013 (after 18 months), between 60 and 80 Bhutanese Nepalis were attending, about half of whom were baptised believers and the others serious enquirers.

In the whole country there may be at least 6 Nepali churches and around 1,000 Nepali Christians. In Sydney alone there are now 4 registered Nepali churches and several small unregistered fellowships, serving more than 300 Nepali Christians. The **Australian Nepali Christian Community (ANCC) Church**, Liverpool, Sydney, was the first registered Nepali church organisation in Australia in around 2008. It now has around 15 members and the pastor is Lokman Limbu. The **Sydney Nepalese Fellowship (SNF) Church** was established around 2009 and is closely associated with a Korean Church. It has around 40 members (25 meeting regularly on a Saturday) and is pastored by Anurag (Andy) Limbu. They also run mid-week Bible studies, and are currently using ITEEN material. The **United Nepali Christian Community (UNCC)** is one congregation of St Luke's Anglican Church in the Liverpool area, which meets in one of their halls every Sunday morning. They also run mid-week Bible studies. It was formed out of ANCC in 2010, has a regular congregation of about 30, and its original leader was Uttam GC before he moved to Albury. The current leaders now are Rudra Paudel and Anil Shrestha. **Rockdale Uniting Church** is a small group of around 5-10 who meet on Sunday evenings and are coordinated by Sarah Cox, while **Campsie Baptist Church** is another small group established around 2010, and which now has around 10 members meeting each Saturday. One of their leaders is

Gagan Gharti Magar. In addition to these there is also a multi-national church (Jesus family church) with a large Nepali membership (at least 30) in the Cabramatta area. Simon Limbu is a member of their leadership team.

Most of the work to date has been in the area around Sydney but now the outreach is extending to Nepalis in Melbourne, Adelaide and Tasmania. There are large Nepali (Bhutanese) congregations worshipping in Nepali/English in at least 4 places: Thurgoona Baptist Church, **Albury**, has 40 members and is led by Uttam GC. The Reformed Church and Gateway Baptist Church, both in **Launceston**, have congregations of about 15 each, while **Hobart** Nepali church has around 20 members. Maybe as many as 100 individual Nepali Christians also go to other churches in Melbourne, Brisbane and Adelaide.

INF/Aus (like INF/UK) seeks to encourage and network with Nepali people, helping individuals to find fellowships, and fellowships to build relationships with churches and groups. In particular, the annual conference in Sydney has been a good opportunity for leaders of nearby fellowships to come together, share what is happening and their prayer needs. The INF office has helped people to access Nepali Christian resource materials, including lists of materials available free of charge on the Internet, tracts printed by the Nepal Bible Society, 'Jesus Film' DVDs (as produced by Campus Crusade), plus Bibles and New Testaments.

Many Australian Christians come into contact with Nepali people in hospitals and care homes, going to visit a sick relative, getting into conversation with a Nepali person and then wanting a tract or Bible to give them. One church in

Melbourne has been active in outreach to Nepalis in the city, especially to a community of 18 families who live in an area of low-cost housing. Most of the families – who are high caste Brahmins from Chitwan – are inter-related. They arrived about 6 years ago when migration was easier, and have been sponsored by one man who migrated many years previously and started several restaurants in the city. They mostly work as chefs or have other jobs in hotels but some are personal care assistants. Others are students who work part-time in similar jobs. Since 2012, 8 Australians from the church who had visited Nepal or worked there short-term developed a love for Nepalis and so started this ministry, with the aim of seeing a Nepali Christian fellowship established among this community. They have been involved in various types of friendship evangelism, visitation, children's club activities and Bible story telling. To date, there has been little response except from the children.

Most Nepali Christians are young students, who have come to faith through contact with other Nepali Christians while in Australia, although some have accepted Christ through the witness of Australians. Many are now actively sharing their faith back in Nepal and some have built relationships with Nepali churches and have financially supported outreach programs / church plants in their home areas. One student reported first coming into contact with Christians through an INF programme being based in his district in Nepal, while others have been challenged by the commitment of INF workers and come to faith through their testimony.[399]

Australian Nepali Fellowships face some specific problems. Most members are first generation believers and so need good strong Biblical teaching: SNF has been able to teach the

ITEEN course 'Abundant Life,' which has helped many new Christians to study the Bible effectively. They also need to discover how to connect their culture with their new faith. While the younger generation find it easier to communicate in English, the church tries to get them to retain their Nepali language and the good things from Nepali culture. Many church members have heavy schedules which leave them little time for church attendance and any extra fellowships, nevertheless Andy says:

> *I am blessed to walk with these young saints of God [young international students]. Their life and commitment encourages my faith. Most of them study and work. They need to pay their bills and school fee. Many of them sleep around 5 hours a day but they still come for prayers and fellowship. They give time for worship training and teaching.*[400]

The majority of Nepali migrants are young and separated from their families and thus from any parental control. Many therefore, in the Australian culture, start to drink, take drugs or party excessively and so need special help and ministry when they come to Christ. Some young couples have also been living together. Again Andy says, "Our church has become a family where we care and pray for each other. It is great to see God's word and His Holy Spirit changing the hearts and lives of people." As a result many have believed and then decided to get married. "We have been blessed by 7 weddings till now."[401] Not all students remain overseas: some return and some even return as new Christians. I remember trying to help a doctor settle back into Nepal:

> *Coming from a Hindu family and converted in Australia,* ***Smriti*** *had no church contacts in Nepal. An ex-Nepal*

missionary in Australia put her in touch with two of us working in Nepal and we met her and took her to church.

One exciting thing is to see Nepalis who come to Christ in western countries being challenged to return to serve him back in Nepal. Like Prem (from the UK), ***Asha Lal*** has recently arrived as a missionary from Australia to work as the Programmes Director for the INF. He tells his own story:

My family & I lived in Australia from 2008 to 2012 while I was studying PhD in Sociology and Anthropology at the University of Newcastle. I met a friend through the University and he invited us to his church, although we were not Christians... In April 2009, while in Nepal for my PhD fieldwork, I was suffering terrible pain in my spine and legs. When no medical treatment or traditional ways of pleasing gods was working, I received a 'holy call' from God: "Accept Jesus Christ, you will be healed." I was completely healed from that moment. I learnt that my friend and congregation in Australia had prayed for me while I was sick, so I started reading the Bible, praying, talked with Christians about their experiences and tried to learn more about the Lord. I took a foundation course on Christian faith and living and in 2010, I was baptised. [My children], Rhoswen and Rhythm were baptised in 2011 and Dimpal [my wife] in 2012. After becoming a follower of the Lord, I explored more about Christianity. One night, I heard a voice in my dream saying, "I am the truth, I am the life ..." I woke and searched the bible. Was the Lord speaking to me? I was so happy that in John 14:6 Jesus answered, "I am the way, the truth, and the life. The only way to the Father is through me." My faith became stronger because He is the one I belong to.

NEW ZEALAND

STATISTICS	
Total Nepali Population	1,500+
No. of Nepali Fellowships	?4
No. of Nepali Christians	?

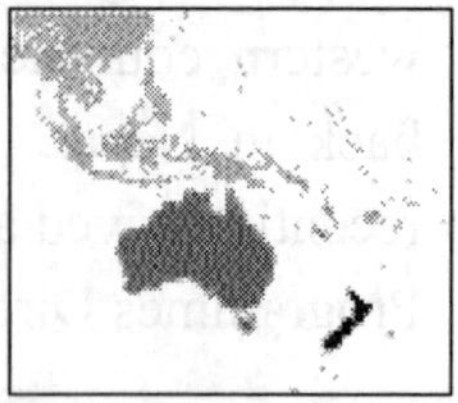

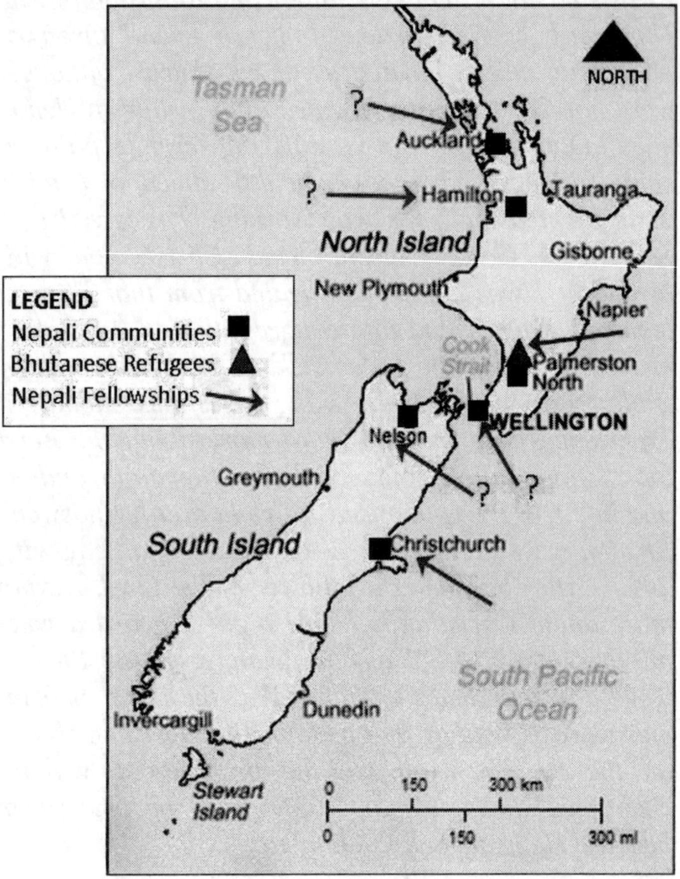

Despite the strong links through Edmund Hilary, there are

relatively few Nepali residents in New Zealand. One estimate is approximately 1,500.[cxxxi] Most are found in Auckland and Hamilton, the former being mainly a receiving point into the country. Some, who were later resettled in Christchurch are now again drifting back there after the earthquake. There are also Nepali communities in Palmerston North, Wellington, and Nelson. Some are students: others are settlers. Many work in the dairy industry. As in Australia, Nepalis in New Zealand are keen to keep Nepali culture alive: they host an annual 'Nepal Festival' in Auckland.

In 2008, New Zealand agreed to resettle 600 **Bhutanese refugees** over 5 years. By 2013 at least 450 had already settled around Palmerston North. As in most of the other countries in which they have been settled, there is a distinction between them and other Nepalis (from Nepal) – partly because the latter feel that the Bhutanese have received preferential treatment from the government.

Nepali Fellowships

There are Nepali fellowships in most of the main centres where Nepalis have settled, and in many there is a link with former Nepal missionaries. In **Palmerston North** a small group (10 adults, 5-6 teenagers and a few children) is supported by Rosemary Teulon and Kevin and Anne Bellringer. In **Christchurch**, there are several Nepali fellowships and support is given by Rodger and Shirley Vickers. There are Christian contacts and scattered believers in Wellington and other towns.

[cxxxi] It is not clear whether this includes the Bhutanese refugees or not.

A few Nepalis have found their way to some of the Pacific Islands.

After the 2nd World War, some Gurkha soldiers settled in **PAPUA NEW GUINEA*** and **SAMOA***. In addition, some Nepalis have apparently also gone to **PALAU***.

FIJI

STATISTICS	
Total Nepali Population	>10,000
No. of Nepali Fellowships	?
No. of Nepali Christians	?

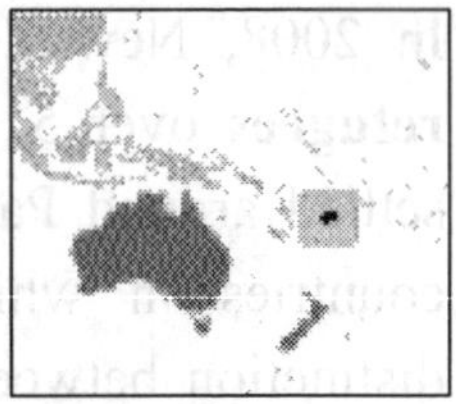

The biggest group of Nepalis in this area of Oceania is in Fiji, where they have an interesting history. Most are descendants of *Girmityas* (indentured labourers)[cxxxii] [402]brought to Fiji by the British colonial rulers together with Indian labourers from 1870 onwards. Shivadatta Neupane explains:

> During the time of the British rule, before the 2nd World War, for the first time in January 1879, the British brought 31 Indian workers to Fiji. They were put in Tabeorni. Then between the two wars the British brought many other workers from S. Asia. In the same way the British East India Company brought workers from India – Gonda (UP), Maharanjganj, Valmiki Nagar (Bihar) and Hariyana and Jharkhand. With these workers also came some Nepalis on the ships. In addition in 1896/7, 30 Nepalis came from the Tea Estates of W. Bengal/Darjeeling. (rough translation mine)[403]

One Indian researcher from the Fijian Indian community has also noted that Brahmin pandits came from Kathmandu and with the Gorkha regiment. Nepalis have therefore been in Fiji for more than 100 years. Originally only men were sent to Fiji and apart from the Brahmins, brought to cater for the religious needs of the earlier workers, there was no real second wave of Nepali migrants, although more Indians came. This led to much intermarriage with Indian women. Their families kept much of their Nepali / Hindu culture and largely remained distinct from the native Fijians.

The earliest settlers went to Suva, then Navua and then Kavanagasau, Sigatoka, probably because that area, with its

---

[cxxxii] *Girmityas* basically sold themselves to alleviate the financial problems of their families, and were then transported overseas as indentured labourers. They were virtually slaves and treated even worse – especially on the journey out – than today's labour migrants.

misty hills and valleys reminded them of Nepal. Today, there is a small community of Nepalis – maybe as many as 10-11,000 – scattered over the two main islands, but especially around Suva (the capital) and between there and the airport. Only in Sigatoka is there a significant number of Nepalis (c 6,000). They are also found around Lautoka, on Viti Levu and Labasa on Vanua Levu. Officially Nepalis are counted among the 'Other Hindus,' but because of their Mongolian features, they are often confused with the Chinese population and so numbers may not be wholly reliable.

Most Nepalis were and still are peasant farmers, involved in the sugarcane and paddy industries, although some have taken to goat rearing as this is more lucrative. Others are fishermen. However, nowadays a few who have been better educated are teachers or work in various types of business enterprise, including running their own sugar mills. There has also been a small but significant emigration to Australia or New Zealand. Others have travelled to Nepal for study as it is cheaper for them than colleges in the Pacific area.

Nepali Fellowships

I have no details of any Nepali Christians or fellowships.

REFERENCES FROM SECTION 3

[1] Mallika Aryal, *Nepali Times*, Issue 421, 17-23 Oct. 2008
[2] Thomas / Perry, *LOT Quarterly*, July 2003
[3] Perry, 1997:18 & compare Perry, 2001:36
[4] David Seddon, Jagannath Adhikari & Ganesh Gurung, *The New Lahures: Foreign Employment and Remittance Economy of Nepal*; Kathmandu: Nepal Institute of Development Studies, 2001:xx
[5] *Nepal Migration Year Book 2011*, NIDS & NCCR, 2012:16
[6] David Seddon, "Nepal's Dependence on Exporting Labor – Country Profile," Migration Information Source, Jan 2005
[7] *Nepal Migration Year Book 2011*, NIDS & NCCR, 2012:17
[8] BC Upreti, *The Marginal Migrants (A Study of Nepali emigrants in India)*, 2002:47
[9] *The Kathmandu Post*, 3 Aug, 2001, quoting Seddon et al 2001:xi-xii
[10] Nandita Baruah & Srijana Chettri, "Demand for Migrant Labor Grows, Opportunities for Women Emerge, But Risks Prevail," *Asia Foundation*, 7 Mar 2012
[11] *Nepal Migration Year Book 2011*, NIDS & NCCR, 2012:18
[12] *Nepal Migration Year Book 2011*, NIDS & NCCR, 2012:18
[13] *Passage to India*, 2008:3
[14] Mahendra Bista, "More than 20 lakh Nepalis in Malaysia & the Gulf alone, *Gorkha Patra*, 13 Oct 2011 (26 Asoj 2068)
[15] Elvira Graner in Philippe Ramirez (Ed), "Special Double Issue: Nepalese migrations:, European Bulletin of Himalayan Research, 35-36, Autumn-Spring 2009-10:35
[16] Roshan Sedhai, "Air ticket shortage in Gulf route leaves thousands of Nepalese workers stranded," *The Kathmandu Post*, 23 May 2013
[17] "The Challenge for Nepal's migrant workers," *The Diplomat*, 26 Dec 2012
[18] *Himal Media's* roundtable discussion on the challenges and issues of migrant labour, *Nepali Times* #532, 17-23 Dec 2010
[19] Madan K Dahal(Ed), *Impact of Globalization in Nepal*; Kathmandu: Nepal Foundation for Advanced Studies, 2005:92
[20] "Nepali aspirants for overseas job increases by 40 pc," *Nepal News*, 26 Oct 2011
[21] Ramesh Shrestha, "Nepali migrant workers struck by wanderlust," *The Kathmandu Post*, 13 Dec 2011
[22] Shrestha, *The Kathmandu Post*, 13 Dec 2011
[23] Shrestha, 13 Dec 2011
[24] Upreti BC, 2002:47
[25] Perry, 2001:36

[26] Upreti BC, 2002:47

[27] Raju Bhattrai, "International migration, multi-local livelihoods and human security: Perspectives from Europe, Asia and Africa, *Institute of Social Studies*, The Netherlands, Aug 2007:3

[28] Andrew Hall, *Himalayan Exodus: Nepalese Migrant Groups* 1995:133

[29] Seddon et al 2001:xiii-xiv

[30] *Operation World*, 2010:406

[31] Michael Lokshin, Mikhail Bontch-Osmolovski & Elena Glinskaya, *Work-Related Migration and Poverty Reduction in Nepal,* 2007:7

[32] Ganesh Gurung, "Lahure workforce," *Himal Magazine*, Dec 2012

[33] Bishwa Rai, Paluwa HIV/AIDS Section – INF Technical Proposal, 16 Aug 2009, quoting the UNGASS Report of 2005

[34] Seddon et al, 2001:75; HB Jha (ed.) 1995, Nepal-India Border Relations Centre for Economic and Technical Studies (CETS), 1995:48

[35] *Operation World*, 2010:412-413

[36] Mahesh Acharya, "Agents in Mumbai swindle millions from Nepalis," *The Kathmandu Post*, 22 Oct 2012

[37] *Passage to India*, 2008:10

[38] Upreti, BC 2002:3

[39] Jit Bahadur; Jiwan Gurung, Jiwan Giri, Reinhold Betz, Reinhold & Bertjan Bouman, *Findings Beyond the Border* INF Mugu Programme: In-House Document (unpublished), 2002:5

[40] *Passage to India*, 2008:8

[41] Ibid 17

[42] Ibid

[43] Tara Bhattarai, "Nepalese Migrants Working in India", *Nepal National*, 2 Jan 2013

[44] *Passage to India*, 2008:8

[45] Government of Nepal Report.

[46] Bahadur et al, 2002:14

[47] Gurung, *Himal*, Dec 2010

[48] Janak BC, *A Tragedy at Diaspora,* unpublished, 2010

[49] Seddon et al 2001:55

[50] Personal communication from Janak BC

[51] Niyama Rai, "Trafficker Behind Bars: A Counter-Trafficking Success Story," *Asia Foundation*, 13 Jul 2011

[52] Mary Crawford, & Michelle R Kaufmann, "Sex trafficking in Nepal: Survivor Characteristics and Long-Term Outcomes", *Violence Against Women*, Aug 2008, Vol. 14, Issue 8, p905-916

[53] Kamala Gautam, "Survivors Continue to Fight Sex Trafficking, Raise Awareness in Nepal," *Nepal National*, 4 Oct 2011

Katie Orlinsky, "Women bought and Sold in Nepal," *New York Times*, 31 Aug 2013

[54] Rachel Williams, "Nepal struggles to contain human trafficking problem, *The Guardian*, 8 May 2013

[55] Narayan Namboodiri, "Rickshaw puller kills another for calling him 'Nepali'," *Times of India*, 24 Jul 2012

[56] J Pandey, "Card provision hits Nepalis, *Kathmandu Post*, 5 Dec 2008

[57] Bhattrai, Aug 2007:2

[58] "The musician from Nepal who wants to strike it big in India," *Meri News*, 22 Jul 2013

[59] Peter Heslem (Ed), *Globalization and the Good*; London: SPCK, 2004:106

[60] J Pandey, "Nepalis being killed and robbed", *Kantipur,* 12 Oct. 2011

[61] "Campaigning to raise awareness of increasing border theft," *Gorkha Patra*, 13 Oct 2011

[62] Seddon et al 2001:64,65, 111-112

[63] Hall, 1995:133

[64] Lopita Nath, "Migration, Insecurity and Identity: The Nepali Dairymen in India's Northeast", *Asian Ethnicity*, Volume 7, Number 2, June 2006:133

[65] Seddon et al, 2001:115-116 (who also refers to Jha, 1995:35)

[66] Janak BC, personal communication

[67] Hall, 1995:133

[68] Perry, *Dharma Deepika*, Jul-Dec 2001:41

[69] Philip Lepcha, personal communication

[70] Perry, 1997:190

[71] Leo Rose, http://news.meronepalma.com/readnews/7112-via-meronepalma.com

[72] Perry, 1997:191

[73] Ibid 204

[74] Ibid 170

[75] Cindy Perry, "The Nepali Diaspora and the Gospel," Dharma Deepika, Jul-Dec 2001:40

[76] Perry, 1997:204 & 219

[77] Ibid 205 & 219

[78] Joseph Gadal, personal communication

[79] Perry, 1997:205

[80] Perry, *Dharma Deepika*, Jul-Dec 2001:40

[81] Perry, 1997:222 & Perry, *Dharma Deepika*, Jul-Dec 2001:40

[82] Perry, 1997:231

[83] Perry, *Dharma Deepika*, Jul-Dec 2001:40

[84] Perry, 1997:233

[85] Ibid 211 & Ps. Joseph Gadal, personal communication

[86] Perry, 1997:217
[87] Ibid 213-4
[88] Perry, *Dharma Deepika*, Jul-Dec 2001:40
[89] Perry, 1997:218
[90] Hall, 1995:133
[91] Ibid 133
[92] Perry, 2001:38
[93] *Operation World*, 2010:439-440
[94] Perry, 1997:88ff
[95] Robin Chhetri citing the United Christian Welfare Society of Sikkim survey
[96] Bahadur et al, 2002:11
[97] Ibid 31
[98] Cindy Perry, *Dharma Deepika*, Jul-Dec 2001:41
[99] Janak BC, personal communication
[100] Ibid
[101] Perry, *Dharma Deepika*, Jul-Dec 2001:41
[102] Bishop Narayan Sharma, personal communication.
[103] http://kufit.wordpress.com/2012/07/20/181/ [22 May 2013]
[104] Renate Riek, personal communication – from whom much of this section is taken.
[105] Perry, 1997:261
[106] Ibid
[107] Perry, *Dharma Deepika*, Jul-Dec 2001:41
[108] Janak BC, personal communication
[109] *Operation World*, 2010:423
[110] Perry, 1997:310
[111] *Operation World*, 2010:423
[112] Upreti, BC 2002:4
[113] Seddon et al, 2001:65 (who refers to Dixit et al, 1997:11)
[114] Augustine Kanjamala SVD. *Migration and Mission in India*. 2007: 20-21
[115] Perry, 1997:312
[116] Hall, 1995:133
[117] *Operation World,* 2010:151
[118] Geocities, 2006
[119] Himali Dixit, “Repatriation or Resettlement: Resolving the Lhotshampa Dilemma,” *Himal South Asia*, Vol. 20, No. 6, June 2007:39
[120] Ibid
[121] Kamatchy Sappani, “Refugee problem haunts Bhutan,” *The Star*, ? Dec 2011
[122] Dixit H, *Himal*, June 2007:39

[123] Ibid 42
[124] Ibid 40
[125] Ibid 41
[126] "Beldangi," *The Kathmandu Post*, 12 Aug 2013
[127] "Nepali engineer serving time in Bhutanese jail on 'false charges' *Nepal News*, 1 May 2013
[128] "Nepal to add diplomatic missions in China, Gulf countries," *China Daily*, 22 Feb 2013
[129] Perry, 1997:135ff
[130] Ibid 137-8
[131] Ibid 155, 158
[132] Ajit Sherpa, personal communication.
[133] "Nepal to add diplomatic missions in China, Gulf countries," *China Daily*, 22 Feb 2013
[134] "Nepali migrant workers duped under false promises," *Himalayan Times*, 13 Dec 2011
[135] Remigio in Luis Jr., Pantoja, Sadiri Joy B Tira & Enoch Wan (Eds), *Scattered: The Filipino Global Presence*, 2004:10
[136] "Nepal: Nepali women victims of prostitution and slavery in Arab countries," *Spiro News,* 9 June 2011
[137] "Nepali migrant women victims of abuse and exploitation, *Weekly Nepal*, 2 Aug 2011
[138] *Operation World*, 2010:622
[139] "Handful of takers for low-paying jobs in Gulf," *Ekantipur*, 17 Mar 2012
[140] Brigitte Suter, *Labour Migration in the United Arab Emirates: Field study on Regular and Irregular Migration in Dubai*, 2005:36
[141] Rubeena Mahato, "Woman Power," *Nepali Times*, No. 597, 23-29 Mar 2012
[142] Mahato, *Nepali Times*, No. 597, 23-29 Mar 2012
[143] Sedhai, *Kathmandu Post*, 23 May 2013
[144] Anil Giri, *The National AE*, 16 Dec 2010
[145] Baruah & Chettri, *Asia Foundation*, 7 Mar 2012
[146] "Five Nepalese dying in gulf countries weekly," *Nepal News*, 18 Dec 2005
[147] Wikipedia
[148] Suter, 2005:30
[149] "Hundreds of Nepali workers 'trapped' in three Gulf countries," *Ekantipur*, 6 July 2012
[150] "Nepal to add diplomatic missions in China, Gulf countries," *China Daily*, Feb 2013
[151] "Nepali workers suffer in Qatar due to fake visa," *Ekantipur*, 20 Nov 2009

[152] "5 Young Women get their Money back in Qatar," K*antipur*, 4 Jul 2011

[153] "No jobs no hope Nepal's workers head to the Gulf and Malaysia," *The Star,* c 28 Oct 2013

[154] Tristan Buslé in Philippe Ramirez (Ed), "Special Double Issue: Nepalese migrations," *European Bulletin of Himalayan Research*, 35-36, Autumn-Spring 2009-10:157-8

[155] "Mobile Money service to Nepal launched," *Gulf Times*, July 2012

[156] Francesca Astorri, "Qatar's Nepali workers want higher min wage", *Arabian Business*, 16 Jan 2013

[157] Wikipedia information

[158] Buslé in Ramirez, *EHBR* 2009-10:168

[159] "Qatar asks Nepal to send skilled workers," *Nepal News*, 4 July 2013

[160] Astorri, *Arabian Business*, 16 Jan 2013

[161] "No jobs no hope Nepal's workers head to the Gulf and Malaysia," *The Star,* c 28 Oct 2013

[162] Pete Pattisson, "Revealed: Qatar's World Cup 'slaves'," *The Guardian*, 25 Sep 2013

[163] Ibid

[164] Ibid

[165] *The Dark side of Migration*, AI Report, 2013, p 5

[166] Ibid, p 8

[167] Ibid, pp 8,15

[168] Sedhai, "At what cost? Migrants' deaths shroud economic benefits," *Ekantipur*, 19 Dec 2013

[169] "Qatar court sentences Nepali to 3 years in jail," *Ekantipur*, 11 Jul 2012

[170] Alois von Flüe, Personal communication

[171] "Nepali wins 1 million dollars in Qatar Duty Free lottery," *Nepal National*, 27 Apr 2013

[172] "Accused of insulting Islam Nepali teacher fired, detained in Qatar," *Nepal News*, 9 May 2013

[173] Pantoja et al, 2004:341ff

[174] Wikipedia

[175] Suter, 2005:61

[176] Courtney Trenwith, "UAE, Nepal ink deal to expand air travel services," *Arabian Business*, 17 Apr 2013

[177] Suter, 2005:41ff

[178] Ibid 65

[179] Ibid 44 & 76-80

[180] Ibid 58

[181] Preeti Kanaan, "Nepal may impose guarantees for hiring nannies," *The National*, Apr 2011

[182] Anwar Ahmad, "Nepalese workers flood in after ban lifted," *The National*, 26 Jul 2012

[183] Suter, 2005:34, 69

[184] Ibid 30

[185] Ibid 70

[186] Ibid 32

[187] Ibid 30

[188] *Operation World*, 2010:849

[189] Ibid

[190] "Duped workers cry for help," *Ekantipur*, 25 Dec 2011

[191] Anjali Subedi, "Migrant workers long for work at home," *Republica*, 20 Dec 2012

[192] Anwar Ahmad, "'I was sold for Dh 7,000', says Abu Dhabi maid," *The National*, 29 Jan 2013

[193] Anwar Ahmad, "Nepalese maids at UAE shelter tell of abuse," *The National*, 14 Apr 2013

[194] Ahmad A, *The National*, 14 Apr 2013

[195] Personal communication.

[196] Ahmad A, *The National*, 29 Jan 2013

[197] Ahmad A, *The National AE*, 14 Apr 2013

[198] Roshan Sedhai, "Illegal Nepali workers in Saudi Arabia return in droves," *The Kathmandu Post*, 18 Jul 2012

[199] "114 agents responsible for 90 pc illegal departure of Nepali woman to Saudi Arabia", *Nepal News,* 15 May 2013

[200] "130,000 Nepalese to benefit from Saudi amnesty scheme", *Asia News Net, Kathmandu Post*, 16 May 2013

[201] Lochana Sharma, "Women in Nepal warn of foreign employment exploitation," *Global Press Institute*, *Nepal National*, 6 Aug 2011

[202] "3,000 Nepalis die in Saudi in 12 years", *Ekantipur*, 2 Jul 2012

[203] *Operation World*, 2010:730

[204] "Nepal established first embassy in Bahrain," *Republica*, 23 Oct 2013

[205] *Operation World*, 2010:131

[206] Arpana Adhikari, "Gulf countries not safe for Nepali migrant workers: study," *Gorkha Patra*, 19 Dec 2011

[207] "60 Nepali run-away housemaids sent home from Kuwait," *Nepal News*, 1 Jul 2011

[208] Gokarna KC, "A bitter truth of Ramkumari," *Maiti Nepal Magazine*, Jan 2007

[209] "Kuwait- Bangladeshi men 'rape' Nepali housemaid after kidnapping her," *Arab Times*, 24 Feb 2013

[210] "Live sex show by a Kuwaiti & Nepali attracts children, passersby", *MENAFN - Arab Times,* 22 Oct 2012

[211] "60 Nepali run-away housemaids sent home from Kuwait,, *Nepal News*, 1 Jul 2011

[212] "Over 50 Nepali migrant workers deserted in Kuwaiti desert", *Nepal Human Rights News*, 19 Mar 2011

[213] Andrew Thompson, *The Christian Church in Kuwait. Religious freedom in the Gulf*, Kuwait: Saeed & Sameer, 2010:4-5

[214] *Operation World*, 2010:515

[215] "Women going to banned Oman from TIA," *Karobar Daily*, 9 Jan 2013

[216] Sangam Singh & Prem Subedi, personal communication.

[217] "Nepali women suffering in Jordan," *The Kathmandu Post*, 15 Feb 2013

[218] "Nepali workers rescued over working conditions in Jordan," *Albawaba*, 11 Mar 2013

[219] Roopa Abraham, Personal Communication

[220] "Report sheds light on plight of Nepali women in Qatar, Lebanon", *Nepal News*, 6 Feb 2013

[221] Adhikari A, *Gorkha Patra*, 19 Dec 2011

[222] Ram Pokharel, email communication, 31 May 2013

[223] Ibid

[224] "Nepal Army soldier killed in action in Lebanon, *Nepal News,* 19 May 2013

[225] "Nepal to send peacekeepers to Syria," *Nepal National (IANS)*, 11 Jul 2013

[226] "Govt ignoring Nepali migrant labourers", Himalayan News Service, 17 Dec ?2008

[227] "Nepalese woman who accused Israel PM's wife fired," *Ekantipur*, 1 Sep 2011

[228] "200 students from Small Farmers families leaving for Israel for advanced agricultural training," Nepal News, 19 Jul 2013

[229] Bijay & Bindu Rai, personal communication

[230] "Preparation to bring back 125 Nepali from Libya," *Ekantipur*, 8 Mar 2011

[231] "Gov't ponders reopening Iraq, Afghanistan, Libya for Nepali workers," *Xinhua*, 28 Aug 2012, quoting PC Bhattarai

[232] "Nepali killed in French military strike in Central African Republican, *Nepal News*, 29 Mar 2013

[233] "Stranded in Madagascar: Missions asked to rescue Nepalis," *Ekantipur*, 20 Jul 2012

[234] *KR* Sigdel, "Human Traffickers dumping Nepalis to Afghan jails," *Look & Gaze*, 27 Apr 2013

[235] Ibid

[236] "Nepal to add diplomatic missions in China, Gulf countries," *China Daily*, 22 Feb 2013

[237] "Freed from Afghanistan, Nepali Workers Return Home," *Ekantipur*, 9 Jul 2012

[238] Masoud Popalzai, "7 die in attack on companies' Kabul compound…," *Cable News Network*, 1 Jul 2013

[239] Aryal A, *Nepali Times*, Issue #421, 17 Oct-23 Oct 2008

[240] Seddon, Jan 2005

[241] Heike Priebe, personal communication.

[242] Ramchandra Giri, "2766 Nepali migrants get amnesty in Malaysia," *Kathmandu Post*, 18 Dec 2011

[243] Kalpit Parajuli quoting Dr Rishi Adhikari, former Ambassador to Malaysia, "Crackdown in Kuala Lumpur: 65 thousand Nepalese migrants risk expulsion, *Asia News Net*, 31 Aug 2013

[244] Ibid

[245] Nicholas Cheng, "M'sia begins crackdown on illegal immigrants," *Asia News Net*, 1 Sept 2013

[246] Bloomberg, "Malaysia's cheap labour crackdown," *South China Morning Post*, 3 Sep 2013

[247] Cheng, *Asia News Net*, 1 Sept 2013

[248] Disappointed by Hope, 2010:10

[249] "13 Nepalis stranded in Malaysia after they refuse to do work other than stated in their contract," *Nepal News*, 17 Apr 2013

[250] "One Nepali dies in Malaysia," *Nepal News*, 18 Jul 2013

[251] Modh Farhaan Shah, "Johor police deny Nepali worker deaths after brawl," *The Star*, 29 Mar 2013

[252] Elizabeth Zachariah & Nadirah H Rodzi, "Nepali workers cause chaos at hostel", *New Straits Times*, 8 Feb 2013

[253] Rani Rasish, "Stop exploitation: Implement minimum wage now!" *Aliran*, 13 Apr 2013

[254] "PUTRAJAYA: The Cabinet has agreed to reinstate a 1992 ruling putting the burden of levy on foreign workers instead of their employers," Mar 2013

[255] Ram Chandra Giri, "Nepal govt hopes to sign labour agreement with M'sia," *Kathmandu Post*, 19 Jun 2013

[256] "Ray of Hope – Nepali migrant workers," *Republica*, 25 Jul 2012

[257] "1,850 Nepali workers dead in Malaysia since 2003," *Ekantipur*, 12 Jul 2012

[258] "One Nepali killed, two injured in Malaysia quarry blast, " *Nepal News*, 21 Jul 2013

[259] "Cheated migrant workers return home empty-handed," *The Himalayan Times*, 25 Jul 2011

[260] Perry, 1997:328ff

[261] Kosh Raj Dahal, KRAMS Ministry Report, March 2013
[262] Kosh Raj Dahal, KRAMS Ministry Report, June 2013
[263] Heike Priebe, personal communication.
[264] Ibid.
[265] Perry, 1997:330
[266] Thomas Sodemba, *How the Church's Evangelism and Mission might have an Impact on Its Community – Reflection on a case study of Ghill Basti Gurkha Mission in Myanmar (1993-2010),* University of Wales MA Thesis, np, 2010
[267] Perry, 1997:247
[268] Jiva Lamichhane, "I went to Burma – with work," *Koseli*, 1 June 2013
[269] Thomas/Perry, *LOT Quarterly*, July 2003
[270] Lamichhane, *Koseli*, 1 June 2013
[271] Perry, *Dharma Deepika*, Jul-Dec 2001:40
[272] Perry, 2001:40
[273] Singha, personal communication.
[274] "I will never leave Nepal again", *Nepali Times*, 26 Nov-2 Dec 2004
[275] Chandra Prakash Shrestha, *A Study on an Effective Evangelization Strategy for the Nepali Migrant Workers in South Korea*, M.Div. thesis, Chongshin University and Theological Seminary, Yangji, S Korea, 2010
[276] "South Korea to hire 8,200 Nepalis next year," *Himalayan Times*, 26 Jul 2013
[277] Biru Ghising, personal communication
[278] KC, *Nepal News*, 24 Jul 2013
[279] "33 Nepali workers under EPS deported from Korea for using fake passports," *Nepal News*, 28 Feb 2013
[280] KC, *Nepal News*, 24 Jul 2013
[281] 57 Nepalis died in South Korea since 2007, *Kathmandu Post*, 13 Dec 2013
[282] Kang and Yoon-seung, "Nepali worker in S. Korea found dead after losing job," Seoul/The Korea Herald, 14 Jun 2011
[283] Debendra Niraula, personal communication.
[284] Chandra Shrestha, thesis page 53
[285] *Operation World*, 2010:684
[286] Laxmi Prasad, personal communication
[287] *Operation World*, 2010:493
[288] "Govt issues guideline to send trainee workers in Japan," Nepal Biz News, 9 Jul, 2012
[289] "Nepal to add diplomatic missions in China, Gulf countries," *China Daily*, 22 Feb 2013
[290] Manish Gautam, "High fees forcing Nepali medical students to study abroad," *The Kathmandu Post*, 23 Jul 2013

[291] Thomas/Perry, *LOT Quarterly*, July 2003
[292] Perry, *Dharma Deepika*, Jul-Dec 2001:35
[293] Wikipedia, Dec 2011
[294] Hsaio-Chuan Hsai, "The Making of a Transnational Grassroots Migrant Movement," *Critical Asian Studies*, Mar 2009, Vol. 41, Issue 1, p113ff
[295] Cindy Perry, "The Nepali Diaspora and the Gospel," *Dharma Deepika*, Jul-Dec 2001:42
[296] Perry, 1997:332
[297] Swiba Lepcha, personal communication
[298] Ang Kusang Sherpa, personal communication
[299] Sharan Tamang, Personal communication via Olak Sunuwar.
[300] Omar B Ahmad, *British Medical Journal,* 2 July 2005:43
[301] Manu Brajaki, "Jews say Diaspora is a discarded rotten sack," *Koseli*, 8 June 2013
[302] Himal Media's roundtable discussion on the challenges and issues of migrant labour, *Nepali Times #532*, 17-23 Dec 2010
[303] *Operation World*, 2010:867
[304] Krishna P Adhikari (Ed), Nepalis in the United Kingdom: An Overview, 2012:3
[305] Ibid 26
[306] Ibid 9
[307] Ibid 9
[308] Wikipedia, Dec 2011
[309] Adhikari KP, 2012:27
[310] Dr Krishna P Adhikari, personal communication & "Census Results: Demographic Confusions and Surprises," *Europe's NepaliPatra Epaper*, Nos. 343, 29 Jan–4 Feb 2013
[311] Thomas Hieber, personal communication
[312] Dr Krishna P Adhikari, personal communication & Census Results, *Europe's Nepali Patra ePapers* No. 343:16, 22-28 Jan 2013; 344:16, 29 Jan-4 Feb 2013
[313] Adhikari, KP, 2012:28
[314] Dr Krishna Adhikari, "Census Results: Demographic Confusions and Surprises" and "Census Results: Adjusting Estimated Nepali Population in the UK," *Europe's NepaliPatra Epaper*, Nos. 343 & 344, 22 Jan & 29 Jan 2013
[315] Adhikari KP, "Census Results: Adjusting Estimated Nepali Population in the UK," *Europe's NepaliPatra Epaper*, No. 344, 29 Jan–4 Feb Jan 2013
[316] Krishna P Adhikari, KP, "Nepalis in the United Kingdom-Exaggerated Population and Politics," *Our Service- Souvenir of the Gulmi District Society UK,* August 2013:16-18 [Nepali]

[317] Adhikari KP,2012:28

[318] Ibid 33

[319] *Nepal Migration Year Book 2011*, NIDS & NCCR, 2012:29

[320] "Gurkha service in Britain armed forces set to end under new Nepal law," *Nepal National*, 20 March 2012

[321] "Ex-Ghurkhas in pioneering project to reduce social isolation". *This is Hampshire*, 17 Dec 2012

[322] *Jai Masih*, May 2013

[323] Martin Evans, "Disperse Gurkhas like asylum seekers, urges minister," *The Telegraph*, 20 Sep 2011

[324] Jos & Ursula Johnston, personal communication

[325] Tony Henderson, "From Nepal to Newcastle: A life-changing journey for Nepalese student," *North-East News*, 13 Dec 2012

[326] Nabin Pokhrel, "High level postholders as security guards," *Ekantipur*, 6 Apr 2013

[327] Abraham Shrestha, *Jai Masih*, Sep 2012

[328] Adhikari KP, 2012:76

[329] Ibid 78

[330] Ibid 128

[331] *Nepalis in the United Kingdom: An Overview,* 2012

[332] "First 'Walk for Nepal' to be held in London," *Nepal News,* 28 May 2013

[333] R David Muir, Don't be a Stranger, Evangelical Alliance Report, 2008:3

[334] Dr Krishna P Adhikari, personal communication, who suggests that the 1 in 10 previously quoted figure was a political incited inflation, ttp://www.cnsuk.org.uk/?option=articles&id=13

[335] *Operation World*, 2010:852

[336] Adhikari KP, 2012:45. Ps. Abraham reckons it may be higher now in 2013.

[337] Rev. Tula Singh Rai, personal communication

[338] Jos & Ursula Johnston, person communication

[339] Abraham Shrestha, personal communication

[340] Adhikari KP, 2012:142

[341] *Operation World*, 2010:363

[342] Ibid 627

[343] Ibid 142

[344] Min Gurung, personal communication.

[345] Ole Kirchheiner, *Mission and Migrated People – Case Denmark*, 2013:8

[346] Ibid 8

[347] http://www.nrndk.com/nepali-students-in-denmark.php

[348] Kirchheiner, 2013:10

[349] Ole Kirchheiner, personal communication
[350] Kirchheiner, 2013:9
[351] Asbjørn Voreland, personal communication
[352] Abraham Shrestha, personal communication, 2010
[353] Mari-Sisko Khadgi, personal communication
[354] *Operation World*, 2010:801
[355] "Nepal to add diplomatic missions in China, Gulf countries," *China Daily*, 22 Feb 2013
[356] *Operation World*, 2010:485
[357] Bishnu Pathak & Chitra Niraula, "A Different Diaspora: Story of Nepali Refugees in Austria:, 28 Jun 2007
[358] Ibid
[359] "Nepal to add diplomatic missions in China, Gulf countries," *China Daily*, 22 Feb 2013
[360] Ibid
[361] *Operation World*, 2010:373
[362] "Nepal to add diplomatic missions in China, Gulf countries," *China Daily*, 22 Feb 2013
[363] Adhikari, Dr Krishna "Census Results: Demographic Confusions and Surprises" *Europe's NepaliPatra Epaper*, No. 343, 22 Jan 2013
[364] Dan BK, "The Spread of Christianity among the Nepali-Speaking Population in the United States," TH 847 Rise of Global Christianity Class Paper, Boston University, unpublished, May 2013
[365] BK, 2013, citing Sijapati 2009-2010:140.
[366] Dan BK, 2013
[367] June Ghimire, :Postcards from America: Lessons for Nepal," Asia Foundation, 17 Dec 2008
[368] Thomas/Perry, *LOT Quarterly*, July 2003
[369] "Nine Nepali students in US charged with Visa fraud, may face 10 yrs in prison if convicted," *Nepal News*, 4 Jul 2013
[370] Khadaroo, Stacy Teicher, Maya Universe Academy, 28 June 2013
[371] Barbara Rybolt, "Photos: Nepal native is helping move mountains at home, while working at Dunkin' Donuts in Chatham Township," *NJ.com*, 22 Jul 2013
[372] Dan BK, 2013
[373] Mark Kiser, personal communication
[374] "The Bhutanese agony," *The Kathmandu Post*, 17 Apr 2013
[375] *Operation World*, 2010:868
[376] Dan BK, 2013
[377] Ibid
[378] Ibid
[379] Dan BK, 2013 citing Ps Paul Rai
[380] Dan BK, 2013 citing Ps Samuel Cho

[381] Dan BK, 2013
[382] Dan BK, 2013, citing Ps John Magar
[383] Jyoti Rimal, personal communication
[384] Asha, & Cynthia Hale, personal communications
[385] Rajan Shahi, personal communication
[386] Cynthia Hale, personal communication
[387] Alicia Cohn, "Migrating Ministry," *Christianity Today*, 11 May 2011
[388] Dan BK, 2013, citing Ps John Magar
[389] Dan BK, 2013
[390] Ibid
[391] Andrea Sands, "Edmonton school sees upsurge in Nepalese students," *Edmonton Journal*, 5 Sep 2013
[392] Indu Shah, personal communication
[393] *Operation World*, 2010:197
[394] Perry, 1997:18 & 2001:36
[395] "Nepalese troops brought cholera to Haiti with earthquake relief", *The Los Angeles Times*, 6 Jul 2013
[396] Adhikari, Dr Krishna "Census Results: Demographic Confusions and Surprises" *Europe's NepaliPatra Epaper*, No. 343, 22 Jan 2013
[397] *Operation World*, 2010:119
[398] Indra Adhikari, "Bhutanese in Australia host multicultural festival," *Nepal News*, 7 Nov 2012
[399] Phil Morris, personal communication
[400] Anurag (Andy) Limbu, personal communication
[401] Ibid
[402] Amitav Ghosh, *Sea of Poppies,* London: Penguin, 2009
[403] Neupane, Nepalis in Fiji (2013)

SECTION 4

MIGRANTS, MINISTRY & MISSION

"As you sent me into the world,
so I have sent them into the world."
~ John 17:18 ESV ~

People are on the move. God is on the move. "God in His sovereignty is moving people so that they may seek Him and know Him… [and] the Church of Jesus Christ is also on the move!" God is using "se*emingly ordinary* people on the move carrying the extraordinary Good News to the furthermost corners of the globe.[1]

In *Scattered to Gather – Embracing the Global Trend of Diaspora*, the Lausanne Committee for World Evangelization (LCWE) appealed "to church and mission leaders to recognize and respond to opportunities in world evangelization presented by the realities of the global diaspora." (p.13) The LCWE (pp.27-29) also distinguished between mission *to* the Diasporas, mission *through* the Diasporas and mission *beyond* the Diasporas. This means simply that there are three major dimensions of Diaspora Mission. The first is simply the reaching of Diaspora peoples as they are scattered around the world and not just found only in their own – often gospel-restricted – countries. This is especially a challenge to all host nations. The second dimension is that of these Diaspora peoples reaching out to their own people group, while they are outside their homeland. The third dimension is that of these Diaspora peoples reaching out cross-culturally to those among whom they have settled in the diaspora. These peoples may be other migrant groups or the local residents.

As a result, "'Diaspora missions' is the practice including ministering to (in evangelism and service), ministering through (motivate and mobilize) the diasporic groups and ministering beyond them (to other groups in the fulfilment of the Great Commission."[2] This concept encompasses the whole spectrum of Christian outreach from evangelism to cross-cultural mission. However, it is also dependent on the Diaspora peoples themselves receiving appropriate ministry – care, discipleship and teaching – to enable them to mature and move on into mission. We may find this easier to understand if, in the Nepali context, we break it down into 3 slightly different component parts or steps.

- The (evangelistic) outreach to migrants both by their fellow-countrymen and by locals in the host countries. This is outreach or mission *to* (and also *through*) migrants. We will look at this in Chapter 10.

- The care and discipling of migrants, both those who go out as Christians and those who are converted while working overseas. This is ministry or mission *for* migrants. We will look at this in Chapter 11.
- The cross-cultural mission that migrants can themselves embrace and propagate in the diaspora, both to fellow migrants from other countries and also to the locals in their host country. This is mission *through* (and *beyond*) migrants. We will look at this in Chapter 12.

Already, in the Nepali Diaspora, we have seen something of Step 1: God's amazing work among groups of Diaspora Nepalis especially in Malaysia and the Middle East. Huge numbers of Nepalis have found Christ as their Saviour and Lord while working overseas. We have also seen a little of Step 2: how Nepalis and others are gaining knowledge of diaspora issues and ministering to those overseas. What we have still to see, except in a few isolated examples, is Step 3: the Nepali church embracing the broader opportunities (and difficulties) of Diaspora, not only to witness to other Nepalis, but to be lights for Jesus in many dark places of the world. With the restrictions on proclamation of the Gospel that existed inside Nepal until 1990, it is not surprising that the Nepali church – once a degree of freedom was given – has concentrated largely on its own people group at home and later, overseas. The concept of mission overseas through the diaspora is still in its infancy.

I believe that to truly serve the migrant community, and promote diaspora mission a strong global network is needed, linking together local Nepali churches in Nepal, who almost all have migrant members, and Nepali fellowships scattered throughout the Diaspora. The network needs a hub to facilitate all these strategic partnerships and it should also embrace mission groups working in Nepal and churches and organisations in host countries who have concern for the migrants in their midst.

To my knowledge there is as yet only one organisation that is beginning to network globally. The **Nepali Pravasi Ekata Sanjaal** (Nepalese Migrant Unity Network or NeMUN) together with **Mitra Niwas** (Friends' Home), has been pioneering a role as a hub in Kathmandu for growing a strong Diaspora Network. The ministry came about like this:

When Franklin and Sapana moved from Malaysia to Nepal in 2008, they wanted to keep in contact with many Nepali converts and friends and so they began a small monthly prayer gathering in their home. At first all their contacts were returnees from Malaysia but later others from Qatar and Emirates began to attend. The fellowship grew and in 2010 it was formally registered as a local NGO.

Overlapping and even pre-dating this, during the time of the Maoist insurgency, Malaysians linked with MMK supported the establishment of a small flat in Kathmandu as a returnees drop-in centre (RDC) where migrants coming home or on holiday could stay if it was unsafe for them to go to their villages. However, it was only when a host and hostess were appointed in 2008 and the place renamed Mitra Niwas that this ministry of hospitality began to be really effective.

Gradually these two groups came closer together with their common vision and in 2013, NeMUN and Mitra Niwas signed a more formal Memorandum of Understanding. Today they share the same premises and the work overlaps.

As well as NeMUN there are a few other groups of ex-migrants who have built up small networks with their contacts from specific countries. Returnees from Qatar have opened the Peace Zone Guesthouse. Those from Emirates have set up the Nepali Overseas Christian Fellowship, linked back to the original organisation in UAE.

At Lausanne III, in 2010, Patrick Fung declared that many Christians study the Word but not so many study the world and understand it. I trust that what I have written especially in the previous three chapters of this book and what I am about to summarise in these last three chapters will help us to remedy that in terms of the Nepali world.

Chapter 10

OUTREACH TO MIGRANTS

"And he said to them, 'Go into all the world and proclaim the gospel to the whole creation.'"
~ Mark 16:15 ESV ~

Church growth in Nepal has rocketed from zero in 1950 to an estimated 1 million Christians or more in 2013. According to research conducted by The Center for the Study of Global Christianity, based at Gordon Conwell Seminary, and published in June 2013, Nepal vies with China for the world's highest Christian Annual Average Growth Rate – of nearly 11% per annum. Some of the first outreach to Nepalis actually occurred in the Diaspora as Christians in Raxaul, Gorakhpur, Nautanwa and Shillong contacted the Gurkhas in their camps,[3] and other Nepalis travelling between Nepal and India. Nepalis are natural sharers of the Gospel, and they have now extended their witness to most of the places to which they have been scattered, such that Nepali fellowships, especially among the labour migrants in SE Asia and the Middle East are also growing very rapidly.

The Nepali Church – the fastest growing in the world.

Gospel Receptiveness

The fact that 'immigrants travel with their religion'[4] has both positive and negative effects for evangelism in the diaspora. It is a known fact that when people are removed from their own society and family and set down in a new socio-cultural environment, they are more open to any kind of new ideas – including the Gospel. They become more curious, question their old beliefs and explore new alternatives.[5] Even those who might never have considered the claims of Christ in their home villages, have an opportunity to do so in Malaysia and 'Arab' and are turning to Christ in large numbers. This is clearly a new global opportunity that God has given to the church. However, Wan implies that this receptiveness is maximum when migrants are in transition and adjusting to their new situations,[6] which suggests that outreach is likely to be most effective among newcomers. Despite this, Chandran says that although many are "open to discussing God, religion and prayer… a syncretistic mindset [so often a characteristic of Hinduism] often prevents them… accepting the gospel…"[7] Not only are diaspora people usually "more open to the gospel than their compatriots back at home,"[8] but also Christian "migrants from poor countries [like Nepal] who travel in search of economic survival [may] carry the Christian message… with them."[9]

Diaspora people – more open to the Gospel.

Gospel Outreach

There are two avenues for outreach to Nepali migrants: One

is from Nepali migrants themselves (and a few visiting Nepalis or Nepali-speaking people) to other Nepali migrants; and the other is through the witness of local people (including other expatriates of various nationalities) to Nepali migrants. In some (western) destinations and among some (of the more educated) groups of Nepali migrants, the primary witness is through host nation Christians who are able to share directly with the migrants. However, language is a barrier, resulting in the outreach to most Nepali (labour) migrants being primarily through the witness of fellow Nepalis. Ps. Bhakta Yonghang has found one innovative way of building links with migrants – creating a church football team which participates in matches with other teams a couple of times a year. This attracts young men who have few other pastimes in the midst of their hard work schedules. He also plans to print shirts advertising some Christian ministry.[10]

Ps. ***John Aite***, also working in Malaysia, has shared some of his excitement about the unique opportunities in his ministry:

> *I am serving the Lord now among the Nepali people in Malaysia. It take [sic] many days to visit some villages in Nepal due to the lack of road and resources but I can easily meet people from all over Nepal in the hostels here. Malaysia has given me the golden opportunity to reach out to my people from all kinds of people groups. Therefore I need your serious Prayers and Passionate hearts for Jesus so that God will use me to win all my Nepali people and disciple them while they are here so that they may be able to win their families, neighbors, friends and communities when they go back home in future!*

Anil Lama, who worked for several years in Penang, tells how God called him to Malaysia:

During the 2 months' village outreach part of his Discipleship Training School Anil was sent to the Far West. He says, "During that time I had many opportunities for sharing the gospel and I went to many villages but could not meet any young people there. I tried to find out where they were and asked, 'Where is your son, your uncle, your husband?' Then some of them told me, he has gone to Malaysia and others said he has gone to Saudi Arabia... So it was at that time that the Lord spoke to my heart and I realized that I had to go to these same places and share the gospel with them." Later he shared this vision and burden with his leaders and they advised him first to take further training with the International School of Frontier Missions. One of the teachers on this course was Kai Lee didi from Penang in Malaysia and through her Anil learnt much about the country. Eventually she helped him get a visa to work as a tentmaker in Malaysia.[11]

In contrast, despite the enormous challenges for evangelism in the diaspora, "in general the churches' response... in host nations has been poor."[12] Reflecting on this comment, I see different reasons and different responses related to the different regions of the Nepali Diaspora. In India, the whole cultural milieu is so similar, the challenge to the migrants is necessarily far less. In the West, political implications of migration and the prevailing secularism and materialism have permeated many churches. In the Middle East, there are no local Christian congregations to take up the challenge, although some international churches or expatriates give valuable assistance to groups like the Nepalis. In Malaysia we see a significantly different picture. There are many large and active churches but all are precluded from local evangelism among the native Muslim population by law. Instead, many have turned their missionary zeal towards the migrants (including Nepalis), generously giving assistance to help them start and build up fellowships linked with local churches. Most Indian Malaysians are Tamil speakers and so only a handful of Indian or Chinese Malaysians have learnt enough Nepali to communicate effectively at a deeper level. However, the practical help (accommodation for fellowship meetings, transportation, food, medical clinics, etc), they give when involved in migrant ministry combined with the zeal and witness of Nepali leaders has been an important factor in showing God's love and bringing many to accept Christ.

One of the most effective methods of outreach is through this showing of Christian love when migrants are in trouble or need. In late 2013, I was told that there were 77 Nepalis in Pekan Nanas jail (in southern Malaysia) alone – because they had no documentation. Local pastors are working to get these men released and repatriated and if a ticket is bought for them, they can usually be released. However, the church cannot buy tickets for everyone and contact with their families is not so easy to establish from overseas. This is where a network can help by getting in touch with the families back home and when trust has been established, transferring their funds to purchase the tickets.

Many non-Christians think that if they go to church God will help them stop drinking or gambling.

> *Kali is an Indian Tamil Malaysian who sells meat and rakshi*[i] *to migrants on credit. However, if they appear drunk, he sends them to the church. He even calls the church leaders when he sees a man drinking too much and tells them to take him.*[13]

---

[i] Nepali-style alcoholic beverage.

Even the Nepal Embassy in Kuala Lumpur has sent many needy Nepalis to MMK for shelter in the mission house while they are waiting for their exit pass from immigration. This provides added opportunities to share the good news.

Outreach to Ladies

Outreach to ladies is complicated by three important factors. The total numbers, although increasing, are still small compared with those of men. Any Christians are scattered and there is no critical mass for a group to form as in the men's hostels. Secondly, the male leaders are not allowed to visit the ladies in their hostels. A third serious problem is entanglement in immorality: many girls, away from home and family, succumb to the attraction of freedom and sexual relationships.

Ladies' ministry is not easy.

Tentmaking & Pre-Evangelism

In most countries where Nepali migrant labourers are found, there are no full-time pastors: outreach must be done by tentmakers, and ***Anil Lama*** speaks about some of the difficulties of working like this:

> *When I went to serve in Malaysia, I went on a workers' visa, and it was not easy to work as well as to be involved in ministry. I used to work for 8 hours and then I still had to go for the sangati in the evening; I was never able to rest. For six days a week I used to work in construction – digging foundations, carrying cement bags, mixing*

cement, etc. and all day Sunday, from morning till evening was spent in the Nepali fellowships and that was also very hard for me. Therefore, I prayed and wept before the Lord, but he reminded me that he had died for me on the cross. Then I realized how much the Lord had done for me in comparison to what I was doing for him. I realized that my physical discomfort was not so great and this gave me inner strength and I was able to continue. Later, however, the Lord gave me the opportunity to spend all my time in Nepali ministry.[14]

The situation is similar and yet rather different in the Middle East, but, with the exception of Saudi Arabia, where no churches are permitted, large international churches host up to 20 different language congregations. In Qatar, the Nepali fellowship was originally encouraged by the Filipino fellowship. Where there are Christian professional expatriates, who themselves may employ migrant maids or drivers, they can be a tremendous witness in their relationships and also advocates for migrant rights.

Tentmakers are usually welcomed.

In India, the context is different yet again, and in many ways, all too similar to that in the Nepali homeland. However, there are strong social networks and, perhaps surprisingly, lack of caste difference among the migrants, both of which are factors that facilitate outreach. However, contact is sometimes difficult as labourers have little recreational time.

The situation and needs of migrants in the West are very different. Local outreach usually begins with pre-evangelism, including the provision of English classes, translation, assistance with dealing with government and other authorities, and accompaniment on visits to the doctor, hospital, etc. Several churches have pioneered these activities, especially among the Gurkhas in the UK and Bhutanese refugees in the USA. Ps. Abraham tells the amusing story of a lady in Plumstead (London) who knew no English on arrival in the UK. She had not even been able to understand which meal the stewardess on the plane had been offering her. After attending a language class she declared, "Now I will be able to choose my own meal!" Some training to help British people teach basic English to Nepalis was planned in 2013.

English classes are popular.

Friendship Evangelism

Migrants in both India and the West tend to live scattered among and more integrated into local communities, although many do live near to each other. Many have their families with them and they also have more personal freedom to spend their time off in any way they choose. In India, they can visit a temple – as at home. In the West, they can visit a supermarket or freely go to a church.

In contrast, labour migrants are usually herded into single-sex hostels or labour camps and their lives are very largely regimented. Many are lonely and seek friendship. Some choose the wrong friends and squander their wages on drink, etc. Others find more wholesome friends and save their money to send home. Working and living together in close-knit groups can lead to close friendships, which in turn can lead to their joining the Christian fellowships. In this context, Pohl's question, "How is the gospel 'good news' to these [dispersed, displaced] people?" is pertinent and the answer she gives is all about mutual friendship and hospitality.[15] Most outreach to labour migrants is therefore 'friendship evangelism' – with Christian migrants who are work colleagues and who live in the same hostels – offering help and friendship, advice and a Saviour to their friends.

Special Programmes

At festival times or on national holidays the Nepali fellowship group may arrange a special programme and invite all their workmates, give them a meal and share the Gospel in some way. This leads many to Christ but is easier in Malaysia where it is possible for churches to celebrate Christmas and Easter as well as other local holidays like Chinese New Year and Hariraya (the end of Ramadan). It is far harder in 'Arab' with only Muslim festivals and restrictions on other religious celebrations.

Holiday 'Camps' are great opportunities.

At another level, positive contact with Christian employers, locals or visitors, especially those who can speak Nepali, may be one link in the chain of God's working in their lives. A friend told me of one man she shared with in 2007. He came from Dang, where my friend had also worked for a while:-

> *He looked so tired I felt strongly that I needed to share the gospel with him. I did not say much but managed to give him a tract and a Christian newspaper a few days later. The next day he was transferred to a very faraway*

place. As I had given him my mobile number at our first meeting, he has been in touch twice since he moved. Last weekend he phoned me with the good news that he has managed to get himself transferred to Klang...[16]

There is a large Nepali group in Klang and my friend visited that specific area regularly. Another divine appointment!?

Outreach to migrants' families

Outreach goes far beyond just those living in the diaspora. As soon as they accept Christ, they are concerned for their families back home. Many phone home to share with their wives; a few are afraid to do this. They all pray hard.

One returnee had asked specifically for prayer for his family before he left in May. Krishna called at the end of July to testify that most of his immediate family members have come to Christ.[17]

An organisation like NeMUN (see p.83 & other references), based in Kathmandu, also has a place in diaspora outreach – by praying; and by helping to connect outgoing and returning migrants and their families, so that the actual on-the-spot outreach becomes far more effective. The hospitality through Mitra Niwas (Friends' Home), as in the mission houses in Malaysia, is a Biblical demonstration of respect for migrants as people and of Christ's love towards them.[18] Devendra, host of Mitra Niwas, tells a story of one of their guests:

One day we had a surprise phone call from ***Hiramoti*** *in Dang. She greeted us with 'Jai Masih' and so we thought she was a Christian believer. When she arrived at Mitra Niwas late one evening we discovered that although she was not a Christian, her husband had told her to come to us. The next day* ***Mahendra*** *arrived home from Qatar* *and what a happy reunion they had! It was even more exciting when Mahendra shared his testimony – how he had been ill but through that had met Jesus and accepted him as Lord. This so touched Hiramoti's heart that she also immediately gave her life to Christ.*

It is this kind of story that makes diaspora outreach so exciting and worthwhile.

Chapter 11

MINISTRY FOR MIGRANTS

"Go therefore and make disciples of all nations, baptizing them in the name of the Father and of the Son and of the Holy Spirit, teaching them to observe all that I have commanded you. And behold, I am with you always, to the end of the age."
~ Matthew 28:19-20 ESV ~

Our mission is only fulfilled when new believers have themselves become mature disciples, leading others to the Lord. Sometimes it is not appreciated that Matthew actually used one main verb in his Great Commission verse: 'make disciples' and all the others (go, baptize, teach…) were participles, meaning that they are simply the ways and means to make disciples. Like many English Bibles, the Nepali Bible (NRV) does not make this fact clear. Also, within Nepali churches, evangelism is prioritised to such an extent that sometimes discipleship and teaching have not received the emphasis they should have had. As a former Obstetrician, I think of human babies. At the delivery I have only started the process that the parents then need to continue for many years! Of course, the boundaries between pre-evangelism and evangelism; and between explaining the faith before baptism and further on-going teaching can – and should – overlap significantly.

It is easy to over-emphasise the needs of Nepalis overseas which are often very significant and urgent, and yet forget that our ministry to migrants should start before they leave Nepal and continue after they have finally returned home. It should also encompass their families. Ministry for migrants can be envisaged in two ways: Geographically there is ministry in Nepal and ministry in the diaspora. Chronologically ministry relates to outgoing migrants, overseas workers and returnees – the same people but at different times in their lives.

Links between Nepal & Diaspora are vitally important.

Ideally these two ways of looking at migrant ministry should be linked together. This is exactly what NeMUN is seeking to do. Based in Kathmandu, through which most labour migrants going to destinations in Asia other than India have to travel, NeMUN is gradually building a network of contacts in Nepal and the diaspora. One important aim is to link outgoing Christian migrants with diaspora fellowships and returning new Christian migrants with churches in their home villages. Another is for NeMUN staff to give advice to outgoing migrants and provide practical help for migrants who have returned with problems, especially legal or medical. The office building also has rooms where migrants and their families can stay.

Ministry as Networking

All NeMUN staff have overseas experience which gives them real understanding and empathy with migrants in trouble.

Ramesh Baidewar, who was born into a staunch Hindu family in Palpa, tells how he accepted Christ while working in Malaysia and later came to work in NeMUN.

> *My grandfather was a dhami and a priest, who started to teach me. Because he loved me I followed his instructions – for temple worship, pilgrimage and washing in the river, etc. but I did not understand why I was doing them.*
> *In 2002 I went to Malaysia in search of work, but found myself in a very hopeless situation working hard for very little pay. At that time, a fellow Nepali, Uttam GC, shared the good news of Jesus Christ with me. He gave me a Bible and as I read Mathew 11:28*[ii] *my heart was touched and I accepted Jesus Christ as my Saviour. I was baptized on Christmas Day 2002 and began to attend the Nepali fellowship regularly; so I could grow in my faith.*
> *When I returned to Nepal in 2005 l faced opposition from my family, my wife and my society. Especially, my wife was very angry with me but I kept praying and sharing the good news and the Lord answered my prayer, so that today my whole family has accepted the Lord. My wife and I are now leaders in the church and I am also working as a pastoral networker in NeMUN.*

Ramesh is strengthening NeMUN's social ministry, as he concerned about migrants who return as Christians but then backslide due to opposition or lack of fellowship.

Sajit Shrestha's story is a little different.

> *When he went to Malaysia to work and earn money, Sajit was already a Christian, but not yet a mature one. He says, "It was so hard for me in the initial days to stay and work because I lost my bag in which I had put my Bible." But he prayed and God answered him. "I got a Bible as*

[ii] "Come to me, all who labor and are heavy laden, and I will give you rest."

well as the opportunity to meet Christian friends. I went to church with them and with their help, I started growing spiritually."

During his holidays Sajit had many opportunities to work alongside church leaders, sharing the gospel with Nepali migrant workers. It was at that time that he became aware of the many problems that are faced by migrants. He realised that many had no one to help them in time of need. They, like him, had not received any proper guidance or counselling about working abroad. He realised then that it was only by God's grace that he had come into contact with helpful Christian friends. He saw the outworking of the vision of the Nepali leaders to win Hindu Nepalis for Christ in Muslim Malaysia and equip them to return home to spread the good news.

On return to Nepal, Sajit enrolled in Bible College and also became involved in church ministry. Some time later, he came to know about the Nepali Christian Returnees' Fellowship run by NeMUN and saw that their ministry of pre-counselling and networking was a small fulfilment of the needs he had sensed while in Malaysia. As a result, Sajit joined the staff of NeMUN and now has particular responsibility for office administration.

Ministry as Hospitality

Ministry for migrants has a very strong Biblical basis and motivation with the example of "offering hospitality to migrants and the identity of the people of God as resident aliens."[19] In line with this, Devendra and Ram Maya Joshi, with the help of Anil Lama, are today running Mitra Niwas (Friends' Home), the hospitality programme of NeMUN. Their aim is to help those who return to Nepal or are in the process of going overseas as well as some who need to visit Kathmandu to obtain compensation or medical treatment by offering them a place to stay. To help migrants obtain their rights, they are also involved in giving assistance and counselling to those with legal or other problems. God gave Devendra and Ram Maya the vision to start this work while they were on a short-term visit to Malaysia in 2008:

> ***Ram Maya*** *remembers that while in Penang they met a group of 6 undocumented Nepalis. They were able to give them accommodation for a week and organize travel documents and persuade the work boss to pay their due salaries. However, they did not know anyone in Nepal who would meet them off the plane, give them hospitality and help them get back into life at home.*
> ***Devendra*** *adds that during their time in Malaysia they also met many Nepalis who had accepted Christ there but who needed to be linked into a fellowship when they returned home to Nepal so that they could grow in the Lord.*

Others – usually ex-migrants themselves – are involved with similar ministries. 'Peace Zone' is a hostel for students and returnees especially from Qatar, while many individuals informally offer hospitality to returning migrants. Others have established businesses which then employ returnees.

Ministry and the Local Church

Local churches in Nepal also have an important role to play in ministry for outgoing and returning migrants. However, I have discovered that churches do not always understand that all the time a church member is working

> ***Local churches need to understand migrants' problems.***

overseas he/she remains, at least in part, the spiritual responsibility of his/her home church. Migrant workers are not just a source of somewhat larger tithe monies to be sent home like the remittances to their families, but they are themselves in need of care and prayerful support from their home churches. So too are their families. Another of NeMUN's aims is therefore to inform and help churches and church leaders to better support their absent migrant members and their families.

While migrants are overseas, they become temporarily members of local Nepali Fellowships overseas, hence the importance of linking outgoing migrants with a fellowship in the place to which they are going.

OUTGOING MIGRANTS AND THEIR FAMILIES

"The Spirit of the Lord is upon me, because
he has anointed me to proclaim good news to the poor..."
~ Luke 4:18-19 ESV ~

In earlier chapters, we have already discovered the challenges and problems that face many outgoing migrants. Difficulties are less acute for those leaving for India but when people are planning to go as labour migrants to Asia or as students to the west, they need help and support in several specific areas.

Ministry through the Local Church

The first need is for wise and informed practical advice, including health awareness: 'Don't send your wives/daughters to the Middle East however attractive the offer is made to sound.' 'Be very wary of trusting local agents.' 'Make sure you know all the necessary details before you leave.' 'Do attend the government training and orientation programme.' 'Don't go as an undocumented migrant.' 'Know the risks of contracting HIV.' 'Remember to take your Bible with you!' Ideally local Nepali churches should support these men and women as they prepare to leave for a term of at least 3 years away from home, but sadly few church leaders know enough about migration and the diaspora to give such advice. And non-church-going migrants also need similar advice and help.

The second need is a promise of support to the families who will be left behind. Wives will be left to cope, often for months without funds until the first remittances arrive. Children will suffer from having no father in the home. Elderly parents will worry about their offspring overseas. The migrant will be concerned for the family he leaves behind, but it is not right to assume that keen Christians will simply manage these changed circumstances. Again, many Nepali churches do not fully realise what pressures outgoing migrants and their families are about to face. Too often they, like the migrants themselves, think of the Diaspora as Utopia.

The third need is to link their outgoing members with a Nepali fellowship in the diaspora. Sadly, most (smaller and remote village) churches have no idea about overseas Nepali fellowships and so cannot do this.

And a fourth need is for prayer! This sounds obvious and the Nepali church is very good at praying, but sometimes 'out of sight is out of mind'. The responsibility lies both with the church leaders – to initiate prayer, and with the migrant him/herself – to keep in touch and send back news.

Ministry by Ex-Migrants

These areas are exactly those where an organisation like NeMUN can help, but regional or sub-regional groups of churches can also mutually stimulate and encourage each other in this practical and prayer ministry for migrants.

MIGRANTS IN THE DIASPORA AND THEIR FAMILIES BACK HOME

"For I was hungry and you gave me food, I was thirsty and you gave me drink, I was a stranger and you welcomed me,"
~ Matthew 25:35 ESV ~

Nepali ministry often starts as Nepali Christians overseas meet newcomers to their company or as Christians in the host country make contact in the places where Nepalis congregate on their days off: Nepali *Chowk* in Doha, Central Market in Kuala Lumpur, a park near La Chapelle subway station in Paris, West Hounslow Station in London and Dongdaemun station in Seoul, for example.[20] In the UK (and probably in other countries too) you only have to drop into a Nepali restaurant for a meal and you are immediately in touch with the local Nepali network.

The Home Church

Although the main needs during this time in a migrant's life are probably those that must be met in the host country, I believe it is vitally important that for Christians, their home church continues to support them and their families. And – even if family members are not yet believers – this does not absolve the church of its responsibility. While overseas, a Christian migrant will be concerned about his family: is his wife coping, are his children doing well in school, are his parents keeping well…? And the family back home will continue to be concerned about their overseas member: is he well, is the job working out as he hoped, is the news he sends home the truth or a cover-up for their sakes, does he have friends, is he going to church…? If the pastor can keep in touch with both the migrant and his/her family or at least ensure that husbands and wives or children and parents are communicating regularly, this will be a great blessing.

All too often the concerns on both sides become reality. Christian migrants – unless they are linked into a network – may not find a Nepali language Christian fellowship for some time, and in countries like Saudi there is none to find. If they are strong in their faith, they will persevere and maintain their personal spiritual life through prayer and Bible reading. If they are not strong in their faith, they may yield to one of the many temptations – alcohol, drugs, women or just simply give up on Christianity. At home, especially if the wife is not with the extended family, she may succumb to the greatest temptation in loneliness and find a male companion. This is part of what Charito Basa means by "the overriding social costs of international migration that were breaking up families in Third World countries,"[21] although she was also concerned about the female migrants who were suffering long separation from their families and sexual exploitation.

Many children also suffer trauma when one or more of their parents disappears for years at a stretch. For Christian families, it is so important that the home church realises these dangers and becomes positively involved in family support.

The Diaspora Fellowship

In the diaspora, the onus falls onto Nepali Christian colleagues to provide help, especially when bad news comes from home. This might be serious illness or accident to one of their family or information that their wife has run off with another man. All these factors can upset migrants and even lead them to suicide. Nepali churches therefore often have to function as substitute family, providing social activities and spiritual nourishment.[22]

Diaspora Fellowships – a 'home from home'.

One example from India is the India Migrant Initiative (IMI), which works through partnerships with churches to facilitate integral mission in India. Ps. Keshab Mijar, one of the core group members of the IMI team in Delhi, says:

> *I think IMI has tried to empower the local Nepali churches in order to serve the Nepali migrants holistically. One of the things that we have learnt through IMI is to work holistically. This opened a platform to reach the community, therefore IMI has bridged the gap between the community and the Nepalese churches through their initiative works. Children programmes have been special to the migrants as most of the parents do not have privileges for the better education. Hence, IMI looks to support such groups of Nepali migrants.*

However, churches or fellowships in Nepal and the Diaspora need information in order to give the support that is needed, and this can best be transmitted through an international network. Then they can contact new arrivals as soon as possible or help in contacting the church or family when something goes wrong. Especially for the labour migrants in other parts of Asia, the network can be a spiritual lifeline.

Ministry as (Social) Service

Nepali diaspora fellowships, together with local Christians (where feasible) are able to offer friendship, fellowship, and help in general. When special needs arise, the Christian community may also be able to provide – or at least put a migrant in touch with someone who can provide – special legal or medical help. Experienced migrants can give useful advice on do's and don'ts and also help newer migrants access the services at the Nepal embassy. They can put those in trouble in touch with the network so that if and when the migrants arrive back in Nepal there is help at hand before they have to face their families. Three examples of different situations in which NeMUN has helped are…

> ***Bhupendra*** *(from Dharan) landed in jail in Malaysia because he had become 'illegal'. Back home in Nepal, his sister, Nita, tried three times to send him a return ticket, but to no avail. Then one day in Dharan, she was chatting with her friend, Gita, who usually lives and works in Penang with her family. Gita told Nita about NeMUN. Immediately Nita got in touch with NeMUN in Kathmandu and found out the name of a reliable person to whom to send the ticket. When the travel agent sent it, it did not work out, but later the NeMUN office managed to forward the ticket to Ps. Rohn in Johor Bahru. He*

delivered it safely to Bhupendra, who was at last able to return to Nepal.

***Sudan** obtained a 3-year work permit for Malaysia and for the first year all went well. Then — for no apparent reason — his company did not renew his visa for a second year. The company also, despite requests, refused to send him back to Nepal. Two months later, while he was out shopping, he was arrested by the police and put into jail. When his family heard about this, a neighbour and himself an ex-migrant, Gyan Bahadur Magar got in touch with NeMUN, and the NeMUN staff managed to phone the Labour Attaché in the Nepal Embassy in Malaysia to enlist his help. Then Janak, one of the NeMUN board members, who has a travel agency, sent an air ticket which enabled Sudan to return home to Nepal. On arrival in Kathmandu, Sudan stayed in Mitra Niwas and NeMUN staff helped him visit the FEPB and Ministry of Labour and so submit his case against the Manpower Agency who had sent him to Malaysia. At the time of writing he was awaiting the outcome.*

***Prem** (from Chitwan) went to Malaysia, but was not given the job he had been promised: he had to work for a lower salary and was made to do work he was not used to. As a result, he became ill and had to return to Nepal after 2.5 months and without his salary. He reported all this to the Manpower Agency, but they did nothing. Prem therefore went home and got medical treatment. When he was better, he heard about NeMUN from their representative in Chitwan. He therefore returned to Kathmandu, stayed in Mitra Niwas, and Devendra helped him visit offices and get compensation.*

Ministry as Fellowship

The nurturing of migrants who arrive in the diaspora as

Christians is vitally important, but neither the leaders nor the fellowship members have much spare time to do this. In Asia long working hours and a shift system make regular meetings and teaching sessions almost impossible although the close fellowship in hostel groups partly offsets this. In the west, a different kind of busyness, as students or their wives work to support themselves, stops many being able to freely join in fellowships. Finding ways to disciple new believers is equally problematic. Even in Malaysia, where there are some full-time pastors, all their pastoral work and teaching has to be done in the evenings or between shifts – with flexibility as working hours frequently change. Considering all the hindrances, it is amazing how much is achieved and how full of zeal are returning migrants who have been converted overseas. However, one area that is not yet covered so well is concerning preparation for their return and how to fit into (or back into) the Nepali church in Nepal.

Discipling migrant believers is a big challenge.

Ministry as Training

Visitors to Diaspora fellowships are welcomed especially those who can teach and preach in Nepali. They can run training seminars for the leaders and teaching sessions for the members. One-off seminars are easier to arrange but fitting longer seminars, like Bible Yatra seminars and ITEEN training, into the minimum time available is a challenge for both teachers and participants!

Ministry as Pastoring

In most of the Asian Diaspora there is no possibility for full-time Nepali pastors to be appointed. The only alternative is lay leadership, and so Nepalis are gradually incorporating the concept of 'tent-making' which the Filipino diaspora has been using profitably for some time. This is not easy especially for those employed in factories. They have long working hours, strenuous work and little time off for preparing sermons, discipling new believers or to do any pastoral visits as Anil discovered. (see p.512-13) Most have no Bible School training to equip them for these leadership roles. It is a real challenge but "young Asian diaspora Christians [including Nepalis] are waking up to God's call to the Great Commission"[23] in this way.

Nepali pastors/leaders in the Diaspora have to deal with some special problems in their ministry which they may not meet (or meet in the same way) back in Nepal. One is immorality:

> ***Kanchhi*** *(not her real name) was already married with 2 small children when she arrived in the Diaspora. She was a gifted dancer and her first contact with the Christian group was at a Gospel Camp when she danced a (secular) love song. After that she started to come to church on and off. A few months later she accepted Christ, but continued to have relationships with many boys and even had an abortion. This entanglement lasted for 2 years, and she felt guilty. Finally, she decided to leave the boy, was baptised and changed completely.*[24]

Another difficult issue for Diaspora pastors is dealing with members who suffer bereavement. Some can travel home to be with their family at this time; others cannot.

> ***Sudip*** *was a new believer; he had accepted Christ in*

Malaysia. Not so long after that his mother, back home in Ilam, died suddenly aged only 50. Ps. Bhakta counselled him to go home and even purchased a ticket for him. However, after prayer he decided not to go. He said, "If I go, my brother will insist I do 'kiriya'[iii] and if, as a Christian, I refuse it will cause a quarrel in the family. It is better not to do that." Instead Ps. Bhakta arranged a short memorial service – Christian style – and also stayed with him for 3 days of mourning. Sudip later refunded the money for the service saying that the church should not pay as "it was for ***my*** *mother."*[25]

Ministry as Networking

All of this is important but unless there is a network in place to maintain contact between overseas migrants and their home churches and promote an effective partnership to meet the needs of the migrants and their families, it will be less than effective. ***Maya's*** story illustrates the value of having such world-wide contacts:

> ***Maya*** *is from Nepalgunj in Mid-Western Nepal. Her husband worked for INF but she went to Kuwait to augment the family income, and then, like so many others, she faced problems. In the end she ran away from a bad employer and so became illegal, not working according to her contract and not having her passport. Knowing that she would soon be arrested, she managed to phone home for help. Her husband had no idea what to do but contacted his former boss, who was by then working in Kathmandu for another mission. Mark also could offer no practical advice but turned to his wife for suggestions, and through her I heard about the situation. Email to my one Nepali contact in Kuwait did not work, but then I had a brainwave. An old school friend knew*

[iii] Hindu funeral rites.

someone (Andy) serving with the Anglican church in Kuwait. That contact worked and then Andy, urged on by a Nepali friend of Maya's, was able to help. Having discovered that Maya was in the lockup, Andy visited, but was told Maya was not there. In fact she was there as she responded immediately when he called out her name! This put the policeman in a difficult position and Andy pressed home his advantage by threatening to report him on two counts – refusing to acknowledge Maya was in the lock-up and then saying that she had been arrested for prostitution when the real reason was 'absconding'. Andy eventually got Maya out of detention and his church helped her return safely to Nepal.

Before NeMUN had come into existence, the forerunner of Mitra Niwas, a Returnees Drop-in Centre, had already been established in Kathmandu, and some of us were involved in the story of ***Narayan and Bimala:***

For the three years he had been working in Muar, ***Narayan*** *had not sent any money back to his family, nor had he repaid the loan he had taken to get to Malaysia. This left his family in severe need, always thinking that soon remittances would start to arrive. Then, as the result of an accident Narayan lapsed into coma and died two weeks later. Just before that it seems he was befriended by Christians and had committed his life to Christ. After his death, his Christian friends in the church in Muar decided to send some financial help to* ***Bimala****, his widow, and this was duly delivered by a Nepali church leader. To get there it took 12 hours by bus, 3 hours by jeep and half an hour's trek through the hills. Bimala's house was very small and poor, and she had hardly any means of support for herself and the 3 children, unless the lawyer, who agreed to fight her case pro bono, won some compensation. There was not even a local church whose members could befriend her.*

Such stories are common, but already NeMUN and Mitra Niwas are beginning to make a difference for a few families. However, there is huge scope to expand the networking and for other groups to take up the same challenge.

Christian Ministry and Other Organisations

In several countries, the NRN Associations play an important role as they can "form a basis for acts of solidarity and… give migrants a sense of belonging."[26] Although this belonging is often associated with the Hindu culture, I see potential for relationships between the NRNs and local Christians involved in Nepali ministry in host countries. Perhaps the NRNA's greatest strength lies in their links between destination and homeland and their official status in the eyes of GoN. An encouraging 15-point Kathmandu declaration at their conference in 2007 expressed "commitments to explore new employment destinations for Nepali youth in developed countries, utilize skills obtained by returnee migrants in trade schools, establish workers' welfare funds for people on short-term employment, and establish a $100 million Nepal Investment Fund within a year,"[27] although I am not sure how much has been achieved.

In SE Asia – in Malaysia in particular – several organisations or groups work towards migrants' rights and/or give specific practical assistance in time of need. The Love Penang Network (LPN) in Malaysia is part of an NGO network called JUMP.[iv] They organise workshops on handling cases of migrant issues and run free medical clinics. They have also produced an information booklet which tells migrants

[iv] Jaliran Utara Migrasi dan Pelarian

their rights and duties and provides a list of useful contact addresses and phone numbers.[28] Migrant Ministry Klang (MMK) is active in spiritual ministry but also maintains mission houses for the use of migrants. Because of this, the Nepal Embassy in KL has often asked them to shelter needy people who are waiting for their exit pass from the Malaysian immigration. This therefore becomes an opportunity for these migrants to hear the gospel as they experience Christian love and many have responded to the gospel. Similarly, the MMK medical clinics reach out to migrants in a non-threatening way, making it easy for them to come to the church service after the clinic.[29]

In India, there are two other very important needs in the Nepali migrant community. Janak BC reckons that the problem of illiteracy in the Indian metros is far worse than in Nepal's villages. The other problem is the lack of health awareness especially in relation to the risk of HIV infection. One of many Christian groups trying to meet these needs is the INF India Migrant Initiative working through local churches.

In the west, the problems faced by migrants are different because most of the migrants are different. Ministry needs are being met through missions and student Christian organisations. English classes and Bible teaching, provision of literature and pastoral care as well as establishing links with local churches are perhaps the most important. These can be met by local Christians with a heart for migrant ministry, or better still, by retired or home leave missionaries who have served in Nepal and are fluent in the Nepali language. This is already a noticeable feature of the ministry. Even missionary recruits could serve as interns in Nepali fellowships in their homelands.[30]

RETURNEES AND THEIR FAMILIES

"Then the LORD said, 'I have surely seen the affliction of my people... I know their sufferings, and I have come down to deliver them... and to bring them up out of that land to a good and broad land... I will be with you...'"
~ Exodus 3:7-12 ESV ~

Returnees are a very special group of migrants. Those who went out as Christians, who have maintained their spiritual life and growth and been able to visit their families every 1-2 years, may have minimal problems settling back into life in Nepal. But even some strong Christians have remained separated from their families for many years and for them settling back can be difficult. Local Nepali churches need to be involved, understanding, show patience and perhaps give counselling.

Resettlement is not easy.

Returnees and Fellowship

Returnees who accepted Christ while overseas face special problems. Many do not appreciate the big difference between Nepali churches and the congregations they attended overseas. Those were almost exclusively young male fellowships but they are now part of a family church, where members have work and family responsibilities and are not free after work in the evenings to arrange fellowships any time they like. Such returnees may feel rejected or neglected by the church because they miss that close fellowship.

Unlike in Malaysia, no food is provided at the church and no transport to and from the services! Add to this, negative family pressure, and some inevitably backslide. How many is unknown but the issue needs addressing. Local churches often have no real understanding and even sometimes are rejecting. This may be because the leaders doubt the sincerity of the new believers (perhaps because they were anti-Christian before they went overseas) or because the leaders themselves feel threatened by new people coming in who may want to change things.

Returnees and Work

A problem in which all returnees share – whether or not they are Christians – is that of what they will do back home. It is a sad fact that huge numbers return overseas within a couple of months because there is no work for them and they have no savings. This situation is stressful and contributes further to family breakdowns. Many return keen to go to Bible School and become pastors. For some this may be right but surely not for most. Vocational training and help in setting up small business enterprises is one of the most needed ministries, alongside good advice about Bible training. I do not advise Bible College if the migrants' families are not yet believers, but short basic Bible training could help new believers mature and settle into the Nepali church.

Part of NeMUN's vision is to see that returnees receive not only immediate practical help, like accessing medical care or obtaining compensation, but also good advice on 'what next'. The long-term aim is to link returnees into appropriate training courses that will enable them to find work in Nepal and remain home with their families.

Chapter 12

MISSION THROUGH MIGRANTS

"And how is it that we hear, each of us in his own native language? Parthians and Medes and Elamites and residents of Mesopotamia, Judea and Cappadocia, Pontus and Asia, Phrygia and Pamphylia, Egypt and the parts of Libya belonging to Cyrene, and visitors from Rome, both Jews and proselytes, Cretans and Arabians—we hear them telling in our own tongues the mighty works of God."
~ Acts 2:8-11 ESV ~

Historically the link between migrants and mission is well established. "Christianity is a migratory religion, and migration movements have been a functional element in its expansion."[31] Even "traditional Western missionaries were essentially transmigrants."[32] Today, as in Bible times, God continues to use dispersion or diaspora as one context for kingdom expansion.[33] Jackson is probably right to make the "migration of Jesus to our world" the basis for this. He came to us so that we could 'migrate' back to God and then help others to do the same.[34]

Mission Agencies and Manpower Agencies!

One Mission Agency CEO has said that, "Mission societies

are not the key spearhead of mission despite what they may think of themselves. It is actually big global emigrational movements." This has been so since New Testament times, and yet is also a new missionary force today; which can penetrate places that traditional 'western' missionaries cannot reach.[35] "Christian believers in diaspora… are one of the most strategic 'missionary' forces in the history of missions."[36] As Christian migrants witness transculturally for Christ, diaspora work will be the cutting edge of our mission activities in the coming years.

Global emigrational movements are the key spearhead of mission today.

Many countries today are 'closed' to the Gospel, meaning that traditional forms of mission activity are disallowed. Many of these countries are in the 10/40 window, which is exactly the area where most of Nepal's labour migrants are found. (see p.134) In fact some say, "there are no closed countries for the Gospel but only places where we are not prepared to speak up for the Lord."[37] Nepali believers already have much experience of speaking up in difficult and sometimes dangerous situations and have proved that they have both zeal and courage.

From Witness to Mission

To date, most Nepali (labour) migrants have been witnesses (to their own people) rather than 'missionaries', i.e. there has so far been relatively little cross-cultural outreach from the Nepali Diaspora. They may be in a new culture, but their outreach is primarily to their own people group in that context. Some reach out to other migrant groups, but for those in SE Asia and the Middle East, witnessing to local Muslims is not just difficult, it is forbidden by law. In addition, most migrants have relatively little contact with local people, even the management cadre of their own company. A further factor is that most Nepalis are used to witnessing to Hindus and know little about Muslims. They need special training to help them speak effectively, without causing offence and without getting themselves into trouble.

Interestingly, the Average Annual Christian Conversion Rate in Nepal is reportedly 10.93 (or 8.74 when corrected for population growth) i.e. no. 2 in the world. Even more surprising is that UAE, Saudi, Qatar, Oman & Kuwait also are in the top 20, however…

> Much of this growth has come as a result of immigration, partially by those displaced from other countries in the region, but primarily through the influx of migrant workers to the service industries of the region's wealthy nations. Many of these workers are Christians, coming from countries such as the Philippines and working in Western Asia for two or three years at a time.[38]

Although the primary growth factor in this region is currently immigration not conversion, it gives hope and challenge for mission through these migrants in the days ahead.

Nepal and Mission

Modern Nepali mission actually began in the diaspora (mainly India), first with the flow of prayer from the Nepal Border Fellowship, and then, from 1952, a steady flow of missionaries into the country. Now, the flows are reversing, with Nepali Christian churches and organisations beginning to target the diaspora in prayer and as mission destinations. A new generation of missionaries – both Nepalis and others – have before them a whole range of new opportunities as tentmakers in 'closed' countries. Domestic workers, construction labourers, diplomats, businessmen, academics, doctors, etc. all have roles where they can live for Jesus.[39]

Witness in 10/40 window countries is a challenge.

After being on the receiving end of the gospel for 60+ years, Nepalis are now beginning to move out in (cross-cultural) mission. The Nepal Gospel Outreach Centre extended its correspondence courses and church-planting activities to Nepali communities in other countries. The Nepal Missions Training Centre and others conduct training courses, preparing pastor/evangelists for outreach extending beyond Nepal's borders. Several (big) churches have formed overseas links. Other churches, parachurch organisations and individuals are slowly reaching out to and networking with the diaspora. At a Missions Conference (Oct 2005) in Shillong young people committed themselves to cross-cultural mission in NE India. At the Nepali summit, HIMGlo 2011 in Hong Kong, the participants were challenged to plan towards cross-cultural mission in Malaysia and Thailand, although at that time, the practical issues of training Hindu Background Nepali Christians in understanding Muslim or (non-Tibetan) Buddhist outreach and what resources they could use for Nepali ethnics who do not read in the Devanagri script (as in Burma and Thailand) were not addressed. Nor was there any discussion with local people. However, by HIMGlo 2013 in Malaysia, ideas were beginning to crystallise. Emerging leaders began to plan more strategically and an outreach to Burma in partnership with the Burmese Nepalis was fixed. Since then regional groups have carried forward the movement.

The Filipino International Network (FIN) is a good role model for the Nepali diaspora in mission as it has been amazingly successful in its aims of motivating and mobilising Filipinos for worldwide mission.[40] In Qatar, Filipinos have reached out to help other migrants, Nepalis in particular,[41] and Nepalis have in turn begun to reach out to other groups of fellow migrants in Malaysia and 'Arab'.

"Migration movement was—and remains—a prime factor in the global spread of world religions, notably… Christianity."[42] Nevertheless, Diaspora Missiology is a relatively new concept in mission and one which has come about in response to Globalisation and the recent vast flows of people back and forth across the world. I have identified at least 9 overlapping migratory flows in the Nepali context.[v] Cho envisioned these people flows as "a new highway for missions…"[43] and already some mission agencies are trying to set up connections that will allow them to serve within the framework of this migration movement.[44]

One example of mission involvement is that of the International Nepal Fellowship (INF), which has worked with the poor and marginalised in Nepal for the last 60 plus years. Now it continues to work with communities in remote areas of the Mid and Far West but is also involved in Safe Migration measures at two points on the Indian border, and,

---

[v] These are Urban Drift, IDPs, Street Children, Brawn Drain, Brain Drain, Gurkhas, Refugees & Asylum Seekers, Flesh Trade and Expatriates.

under the aegis of the India Migrant Initiative, works in an integral mission partnership with local churches in Delhi and 3 centres in the hills of NW India. INF is also a partner of NeMUN, helping to facilitate their ministry to labour migrants in SE Asia and 'Arab'.

Nepalis and 'Reverse Mission'

In the UK, Australia, New Zealand and the USA, the traditional home ends of many missionaries to Nepal, staff and ex-missionaries are working to motivate and mobilize local churches and believers to seize the opportunities to reach diasporas in their neighbourhood by practising "missions at our doorstep."[45] In an exciting development of what might be called 'reverse mission' migrant churches, which in so many (western) countries are the vitally alive and growing ones, could be the channel for a revival of local Christianity.[46] This is just part of the new mission 'from the rest to the west'[47] and one in which Nepalis can now be involved.

The exciting potential of 'Reverse Mission'.

CONCLUSION

"So then you are no longer strangers and aliens [migrants], but you are fellow citizens with the saints and members of the household of God,"
~ Eph. 2:19 ~

If you have ever moved house, you will know that it is an unsettling, disruptive and expensive exercise but also a wonderful chance to have a clear-out and a new start. This epitomises migration. It can be both negative and positive. It can be a source of many problems or a challenge. "To live as a migrant may well evoke the pain of loss and of not being firmly rooted in a secure place; but it is also to live in a world of immense possibility…"[48]

Living as a migrant is to live in a world of immense possibility.

As the labour force of Nepal is estimated to double in 30 years[49] and as there is no obvious increase in employment opportunities inside Nepal on the horizon, the issues of migration and diaspora are not likely to go away in the near future – if at all. We, therefore, need to understand and participate in God's redemptive mission among people living outside their place of origin.[50] This "diaspora missiology may well be the most important undigested reality in missions thinking today,"[51] but to facilitate mission through a diaspora paradigm, new strategies need to be adopted both by missionaries and Nepali churches:

New mission strategies are needed for the new Diaspora mission paradigm.

Bible and Missionary Training Colleges [in host countries and in Nepal] will need to include diaspora issues within their curricula.[52] Churches and missions should continue their activities of "establishing, supporting, and networking with migrant congregations; promoting social and cultural integration; and providing welfare and advocacy services for… migrants" but a new theology of migrant mission will also need to be developed as the basis for these.[53] If diaspora really is "a missional means decreed and blessed by God," then Diaspora Missiology must be firmly established as a new branch of Missiology,[54] and include subjects like globalisation, multi-culturalism, ethnicity, inter-racial relationships and Christian hospitality.[55]

"Global partnerships of churches will be indispensable…"[56] Networking and partnership will be key activities.[57] The partnerships should be genuinely mutual – hosts reaching out to migrants and migrants reaching out to their hosts.[58] The networking should be inclusive but in a way that avoids competition and duplication. Organisations like NeMUN can facilitate this networking by themselves functioning as a hub. Diaspora is an amazing opportunity to demonstrate Christian unity in the context of diversity.[59]

Churches in the home (or origin) countries need to be deeply involved and fully embrace the concept of Diaspora Mission. They can help prepare migrants for their overseas roles[60] as well as support them later. They must be part of the network. Churches in the host countries, wherever feasible, must also be part of the network, partnering with missions and migrants to reach out to those living in diaspora. "Never before have there been so many opportunities to reach people with the message of Jesus Christ. This is why congregations must be motivated and mobilized to participate in this new missions' strategy."[61] However, motivation needs to be linked with information on the issues of mission and migration. "If the church is responsible to reach this world on its doorstep [and it is], it must be informed."[62] However…

> The church must not be satisfied with merely binding up the wounds resulting from migration or providing a placebo for the underlying problems; rather it must strike at the roots of this social malaise. In order to bring about justice and to help improve the lot of the poor and underprivileged immigrant the Church in both emigrant and immigrant countries must speak with one voice on the related social issues. Above all, it must act in unison to protect and promote the dignity of man and human rights.[63]

Christians in Nepal – and in host countries – need to become advocates for migrants' rights, including recruitment practices, orientation briefing and training, employment policies and practices, trade union activities, debriefing and resettlement training and assistance. "If the Government of Nepal gives priority to safe migration then that would benefit thousands of workers and their families every year, and would also benefit the economy if it takes initiative to protect its citizens abroad."[64] One important way of achieving this is to lobby for fair provisions for Nepali migrant workers in the top labour destination countries. Another is to solve the problem of undocumented migrants leaving the country through informal or illegal channels. A third is to establish reliable data on the status of all Nepalis working overseas. And a fourth is to make attendance at pre-departure orientation and training programmes truly compulsory.[65]

Christians with advocacy skills need to be deployed to improve the lot of migrants. A migrant who speaks some English (or one of the other local languages) starts with a tremendous advantage. A migrant with a trade skill is far more likely to get a better-paying job overseas and also find employment on return to Nepal. Professional migrants can work as tentmakers in almost all countries.

As socio-economic push and pull factors are unlikely to be eliminated in the near future, Nepali migration will continue for many years, but I would love to see two changes. I want to see migration becoming safe and voluntary for all who want to participate. And I want to see the God factor prioritised, with Christian migrants going out as tentmakers because they know that that is their mission from God.

This is the sort of book that will be out of date almost before it is published. Because of all that God is doing in and through the Nepali Diaspora these days, some of the problems I have mentioned will be solved, some of the challenges will be taken up and many of the statistics will be altered. Nevertheless, if you have learnt something and been challenged to be part of all these amazing things that God is doing then my aim will have been achieved, and one of you can write the next instalment!

I can conclude in no better words than those that Dr Perry used almost 20 years ago: "If Christianity is to continue to expand throughout the Nepali diaspora, the vision [and prayer] of the mid-20th century missionaries… for reaching the whole Nepali world needs to be revived… this challenge is chiefly to Nepali Christian churches and organisations themselves, both within and without Nepal."[66] All I would add is that this challenge is actually to all of us who love Nepal and its people wherever they are.

"…in the whole world

it [the Gospel] is bearing

fruit and growing…"

~ Colossians 1:6 ~

"Diaspora…

God's strategic tool

to achieve His Mission."

(Jung, *Connections,* 2005 Vol. 4 No. 3.)

REFERENCES FOR SECTION 4

[1] Sadiri Joy Tira in T.V. Thomas, Sadiri Joy Tira, Enoch Wan, *Ministering to the Scattered Peoples, Lausanne III Paper*, July 2010:4

[2] Enoch Wan in Thomas et al, *Lausanne III Paper*, July 2010:2

[3] Perry, 2001:37

[4] Jehu Hanciles, "Migration and Mission: Some Implications for the Twenty-first Century Church, *International Bulletin of Missionary Research*, Vol. 27, No 4, Oct 2003:146

[5] TV Thomas in Thomas et al, *Lausanne III Paper*, July 2010:2

[6] Wan in Luis Pantoja Jr., Sadiri Joy B Tira & Enoch Wan (Eds), *Scattered: The Filipino Global Presence,* 2004:117

[7] Emil P Chandran, 'South Asian Diaspora – Challenges and Opportunities' *Evangelical Missions Quarterly* 10/04 pp453-4

[8] Min-Young Jung, "Asian Diaspora: Strategic Resource for World Mission" *Connections,* Vol. 4 No. 3, Autumn 2005

[9] Samuel Escobar, *A Time for Mission: The Challenge of Global Christianity* 2003:66

[10] Bhakta Yonghang, personal communication

[11] Anil Lama, personal communication.

[12] Chandran, *EMQ*, 2004:453

[13] Bhakta Yonghang, personal communication

[14] Anil Lama, personal communication

[15] Christine Pohl, "Biblical Issues in Mission and Migration," *Missiology,* Jan 2003, Vol. XXXI No. 1, pp4-5

[16] Heike Priebe, personal communication, 2007

[17] Kai Lee Wong, personal communication, 2009

[18] Pohl, *Missiology*, Jan 2003, Vol. XXXI No. 1, pp.9-10

[19] Ibid p. 3

[20] Bruslé in Ramirez, *EBHR* 35-35, 2009-10:20

[21] Stanley Johnson, *The Politics of Population*, 1994:166

[22] Pantoja et al, 2004:117 quoting Wan 2003

[23] Jung, *Connections*, 2005 Vol. 4 No. 3.

[24] Personal communication from 'Kanchhi's' pastor.

[25] Bhakta Yanghang, personal communication

[26] Bruslé in Ramirez, *EBHR 35-36*, 2009-10:157-8

[27] Jugal Bhurtel, "Global Nepalis come home They have stopped complaining, and started getting things done," *Nepali Times*, Issue # 373, 9-15 Nov 2007

[28] Kai Lee Wong, personal communication, 2008/9

[29] Heike Priebe, ppersonal communication, 2011

[30] Bill Lottis, "How to meet the needs of Immigrants, with a bonus" *Evangelical Missions Quarterly* 7/89 pp256ff

[31] Hanciles, *IBMR*, Vol. 27, No. 4, 2003:149

[32] Ibid

[33] Santos in Pantjoja et al, 2004:51, 62

[34] Darrell Jackson, "Europe and the Migrant Experience: Transforming Integration," *Transformation: An International Journal of Holistic Mission Studies,* 2011:15 from the Commission for World Mission and Evangelism, 2010:118

[35] Escobar, 2003:15-6

[36] LCWE, *Scattered to Gather…*, p.27

[37] Michael Ramsden in a Plenary Session at Lausanne 3, 2010

[38] "The Top 20 Countries where Christianity is Growing the Fastest", Center for the Study of Global Christianity, June 2013

[39] *Operation World*, 2010:69

[40] Pantoja et al, 2004 p 161, 163

[41] Ibid, 163, 343-4

[42] Hanciles, *IBMR*, Vol. 27, No 4, Oct 2003:146-153

[43] Stan Guthrie, *Missions in the Third Millennium: 21 Key Trends for the 21st Century*, 2000:134

[44] Escobar, 2003:66, 164

[45] Wan in Thomas et al, *Lausanne III Paper*, July 2010:6

[46] Hun Kim, "Receiving Mission: Reflection on Reversed Phenomena by Migrant Workers from Glocal Churches to the Western Society," *Transformation: An International Journal of Holistic Mission Studies,* 2011 28:62

[47] Peter Vethanayagamony, "Mission from the Rest to the West," in Amos Yong, pp.60-68

[48] Robert JC Young, *Postcolonialism: A Very Short Introduction*, 2003:215

[49] Madan K Dahal (Ed), *Impact of Globalization in Nepal*, 2005:156

[50] *Scattered to Gather*, Lausanne III, 2010:12

[51] Ralph Winter

[52] Tira in Thomas et al, *Lausanne III Paper*, 2010:6

[53] Jackson, 2011:24

[54] LCWE, *Scattered to Gather…*, p.21

[55] Pantoja et al, 2004:106, 107, 110

[56] Escobar, 2003:164

[57] Pantoja et al, 2004:113

[58] Pantoja et al, 2004:115, citing Marcel Durst's thesis, *Mission Initiatives of Latin American Migrants in Switzerland*, 2002:xiii

[59] Pantoja et al, 2004:106, 107, 110

[60] Ibid, 175

[61] Tira in Thomas et al, *Lausanne III Paper*, July 2012:5
[62] David L Ripley, "Reaching the World at our doorstep," *EMQ*, Apr 1994:148
[63] GE Gorman, Migration, Immigration and the Church, Commmuno viatorum, XXI, 1978.114, quoted by Janak BC in his Literacy Report
[64] "Nepali migrant workers duped under false promises," *The Himalayan Times*, 13 Dec 2011, quoting Norma Kang Muico, Amnesty International Researcher on Asia-Pacific Migrants' Rights
[65] "Ray of Hope – Nepali migrant workers," *Republica*, 25 Jul 2012
[66] Cindy L Perry, *Nepali around the world*, 1997:376-7

BIBLIOGRAPHY

Abrahams, Pema, "New Act a Blow to Human Rights in Nepal," *Asia Foundation*, 14 Mar 2012, http://asiafoundation.org/in-asia/2012/03/14/new-act-a-blow-to-human-rights-in-nepal/ [17 Sept 2013]

Acharya, Mahesh, "Agents in Mumbai swindle millions from Nepalis", *The Kathmandu Post*, 22 Oct 2012, http://www.asianewsnet.net/home/news.php?id=37970 [29 Oct 2012]

Adhikari, Arpana, "Gulf countries not safe for Nepali migrant workers: study," *Gorkha Patra*, 19 Dec 2011, http://www.gorkhapatra.org.np/detail.php?article_id=61152&cat_id=4 [20 Dec 2011]

Adhikari, Indra, "Nepali Literature Blooming in the Diaspora", N*epal News* [16 Jul 2008]

Adhikari, Indra, "Bhutanese in Australia host multicultural festival", *Nepal News*, 7 Nov 2012, http://www.nepalnews.com/archive/2012/nov/nov07/news01.php [3 Dec 2012]

Adhikari, Krishna P (Ed), *Nepalis in the United Kingdom: An Overview*, Reading: Centre for Nepal Studies, United Kingdom, 2012

Adhikari, K.P. "Nepalis in the United Kingdom- Exaggerated Population and Politics," *Our Service- Souvenir of the Gulmi District Society UK,* August 2013, pp*16-18* [Nepali]

Adhikari, Krishna, "Census Results: Demographic Confusions and Surprises," *Europe's NepaliPatra Epaper*, No. 343:16, 22-28 Jan 2013, http://www.nepalipatra.com/epaper/Main.php [5 Sep 2013]

Adhikari, Krishna, "Census Results: Adjusting Nepali Population in the UK," *Europe's NepaliPatra Epaper*, No. 344:16, 29 Jan – 4 Feb 2013, http://www.nepalipatra.com/epaper/Main.php [5 Sep 2013]

Ahmad, Anwar, "'I was sold for Dh 7,000', says Abu Dhabi maid", *The National News AE*, 29 Jan 2013, http://www.thenational.ae/news/uae-news/i-was-sold-for-dh7-000-says-abu-dhabi-maid [31 Jan 2013]

Ahmad, Anwar, "Nepalese maids at UAE shelter tell of abuse," *The National News AE*, 14 Apr 2013, http://www.thenational.ae/news/uae-news/nepalese-maids-at-uae-shelter-tell-of-abuse [16 Apr 2013]

Ahmad, Anwar, "Nepalese workers flood in after ban lifted," *The*

National News AE, 26 Jul 2012, http://www.thenational.ae/news/uae-news/nepalese-workers-flood-in-after-ban-lifted [31 Jan 2013]

Ahmad, Anwar, "Rising number of Nepali girls lured and sold in UAE", *The National News AE*, http://www.thenational.ae/news/uae-news/rising-number-of-nepali-girls-lured-and-sold-in-uae?utm_source=rss&utm_medium=UAE%20news&utm_campaign=feed [31 Jan 2013]

Ahmad, Omar B, "Managing medical migration from poor countries", *British Medical Journal*, 2 Jul 2005: 43-45

Aryal, Mallika, "The Gurkhas and Lahore In the city where it all started, they don't even know who Lahures are, *Nepali Times*, Issue #421, 17-23 Oct 2008, http://nepalitimes.com/news.php?id=15294#.UZ3eHaz_j6M [22 May 2013]

Astorri, Francesca, "Qatar's Nepali workers want higher min wage", *Arabian Business*, 16 Jan 2013, http://www.arabianbusiness.com/qatar-s-nepali-workers-want-higher-min-wage-485940.html [17 Jan 2013]

Bahadur, Jit; Gurung, Jiwan; Giri, Jiwan; Betz, Reinhold & Bouman, Bertjan, *Findings Beyond the Border* INF Mugu Programme: In-House Document (unpublished), 2002

Banskota, Pratima, "Released from pledge but 9 Nepalis in detention in Turkey," *Kathmandu Post*, Jun 2013

Baruah, Nandita, "Nandita Baruah Examines Realities & New Approaches to Combating Human Trafficking," *Asia Foundation*, 5 Jun 2013, http://asiafoundation.org/in-asia/2013/06/05/nandita-baruah-examines-realities-new-approaches-to-combating-human-trafficking/ [17 Sept 2013]

Baruah, Nandita & Shareen Tuladhar, "Nepal's Migrants Boost Economy, But Greater Protection of Rights is Needed", *Asia Foundation,* 19 Dec 2012, http://asiafoundation.org/in-asia/2012/12/19/nepals-migrants-boost-economy-but-greater-protection-of-rights-is-needed/ [20 May 2013]

Baruah, Nandita & Srijana Chettri, "As Demand for Migrant Labor Grows, Opportunities for Women Emerge, But Risks Prevail," *Asia Foundation*, 7 Mar 2012, http://asiafoundation.org/in-asia/2012/03/07/as-demand-for-migrant-labor-grows-opportunities-for-women-emerge-but-risks-prevail/ [17 Sept 2013]

Batchelor, Simon, "Sending money outside the envelope", http://www.developments.org/articles/loose-talk-saves-lives/?searchterm [? Date]

BBC – The Forum (Sun 5 Jun 2011)

BC, Janak, *A Tragedy at Diaspora* [Pune blast], unpublished, 2010

BC, Janak, *Investigation of Illiteracy among Diaspora Nepalis with special reference to three Indian Metros (Chennai, Delhi and Mumbai)*, Pune, UBS: unpublished College Report, 2011

BC, Janak, *Diaspora on the Net* (2012) – network links

BC, Janak, "Situations of Nepalese Migrants in India" *NepaliChurch.com* [10 Jun 2013], Originally presented for NeMUN, Aug 2012

BC, Janak, "Growing Nepali-speaking Diaspora Churches in Urban India: A Review, NepaliChurch.com [24 Jun 2013]

Bhattarai, Devendra, "Son died but questions remain," 27 Jul 2011

Bhattrai, Raju, "International migration, multi-local livelihoods and human security: Perspectives from Europe, Asia and Africa, *Institute of Social Studies*, The Netherlands, Aug 2007

Bhattarai, Tara, "Trafficking, Poverty and Illiteracy Force Girls into Nepal Flourishing Sex Trade," *Nepal National*, 14 Oct 2011

Bhattarai, Tara, "Nepalese Migrants Working in India", *Nepal National*, http://www.nepalnational.com/index.php/sid/211729338/scat/7399985502eaed63/ht/Lack-of-Policy-Risks-Health-Safety-of-Nepalese-Migrants-Working-in-India [3 Jan 2013]

Bhurtel, Jugal, "Global Nepalis come home – They have stopped complaining, and started getting things done, *Nepali Times*, Issue 373, http://www.nepalitimes.com/issue/373/Nation/14168 [20 Dec 2011] from Nov 2007

Bista, Chirangivi, "What Growing Student Migration Means to Nepal?" *Nepal News*, http://www.nepalnews.com/archive/2013/others/guestcolumn/feb/guest_columns_03.php [6 Feb 2013]

Bista, Mahendra, "More than 20 lakh Nepalis in Malaysia & the Gulf alone, *Gorka Patra*, 13 Oct 2011 (26 Asoj 2068) – Nepali

BK, Dan, "The Spread of Christianity among the Nepali-Speaking Population in The United States", College Course Paper TH 847 Rise of Global Christianity, May 2013 (unpublished)

BK, Dan, "God's Work among Nepali Ethnic in North East, US & Canada – Southern Baptist Works among Nepalese," a PowerPoint Presentation, 2013

Bloomberg, "Malaysia's cheap labour crackdown," *South China Morning Post*, 3 Sep 2013, http://www.scmp.com/news/asia/article/1302144/thousands-illegal-workers-arrested-malaysias-cheap-labour-crackdown [3 Sept 2013]

Bradley, John, *Report on Work amongst Nepalis in the UK to INF/UK Council of Management International Nepal Fellowship* (unpublished in-house document), 2005

Brajaki, Manu, "Jews say Diaspora is a discarded rotten sack," *Ekantipur – Koseli,* 8 Jun 2013, http://www.ekantipur.com/kantipur/news/news-detail.php?news_id=297775 [12 Jun 2013]

Burbank, John, *Culture Studies: A Guide to Customs and Etiquette,* np, nd

Bute, Amanda, *A Voice for the Voiceless – Developing INF/W's capacity in advocacy* In-House Document (unpublished), c 2006-7

Bute, Amanda, *Combating trafficking and caring for victims of trafficking – What could INF/W's role be?* In-House Document (unpublished), 2006

Bute, Amanda, *Proposal to help transform the lives of Nepali migrants*, (unpublished in-house document), 2006

Celebrating 10 years UNCA, Souvenir 2012, Delhi

Chalke, Steve & Wilson, Hannah, "Slave Releasers" & "Lidia's Story", Modern Day Slaves, *BMS World Mission*, Mar/Apr 2007

Chandran, P Emil 'South Asian Diaspora – Challenges and Opportunities' *Evangelical Missions Quarterly* 10/04 pp450-454

Cheng, Nicholas, "M'sia begins crackdown on illegal immigrants," *Asia News Net*, 1 Sep 2013, http://www.asianewsnet.net/Msia-begins-crackdown-on-illegal-immigrants-51035.html [3 Sept 2013]

Cohen, Robin & Paul Kennedy, *Global Sociology*, London: Macmillan, 2000

Cohn, Alicia "Migrating Ministry", *Christianity Today*, May 2011, http://www.christianitytoday.com/ct/2011/may/migratingministry.html?start=2 [16 May 2011]

Cohn, Alicia "Migrating Ministry", *Christianity Today*, 9 Nov 2011, http://www.christianitytoday.com/ct/2011/may/migratingministry.html?start=2 [16 May 2011]

Crawford, Mary & Michelle R Kaufmann, "Sex trafficking in Nepal: Survivor Characteristics and Long-Term Outcomes", *Violence Against Women*, Aug 2008, Vol. 14, Issue 8, p905-916

Dahal, Madan K (Ed), *Impact of Globalization in Nepal*; Kathmandu: Nepal Foundation for Advanced Studies, 2005

Diep, Karen, "Former Nepalese Colonel Appears Before Court for Torture Charges", *Impunity Watch*, http://impunitywatch.com/former-nepalese-colonel-appears-before-court-for-torture-charges/?utm_source=feedburner&utm_medium=feed&utm_campaign=Feed%3A+ImpunityWatchHeadlines+%28Impunity+Watch+Headlines%29 [27 Jan 2013]

Dhital, Mina, "Remittance Extravagance", *Kantipur*, 20 Jul 2013

Dixit, Himali, "Gorkhalis still flock to Gorakhpur", *Nepali Times,* Feb 2005, http://nepalitimes.com/news.php?id=1188#.UZxWxqz_j6M [22 May 2013]

Dixit, Himali, "Repatriation or Resettlement: Resolving the Lhotshampa Dilemma", *Himal SouthAsia*, Vol. 20, No. 6, Jun 2007:38-44

Dixit, Kundar, "Less food, more mouths to feed," *Nepali Times*,7 Aug

2009,
http://www.nepalitimes.com.np/issue/2009/08/07/Nation/16199 [20/08/2009]

DNCF Silver Jubilee, Celebrating 25 years, 2012, Delhi

DOFE – Government of Nepal has given permission for Nepalese to work for given foreign countries, http://dofe.gov.np/recognized-destination-27-en.html [24 Jul 2011]

Dugger, Elia W, "Asia: Nepal: Migrant workers Help alleviate Poverty", *New York Times* 23 Nov 2006, p24 (abstract only)

Escobar, Samuel "Migration: Avenue and Challenge to Mission" *Missiology: An International Review*, Vol XXXI Number 1 Jan 2003 Mission and Migration pp17-28

Escobar, Samuel, *A Time for Mission: The Challenge of Global Christianity*, Leicester: IVP, 2003 (excerpts only)

Evans, Martin, "Disperse Gurkhas like asylum seekers, urges minister", *The Telegraph*, 20 Sep 2011, http://www.telegraph.co.uk/news/8775687/Disperse-Gurkhas-like-asylum-seekers-urges-minister.html [20 Sep 2011]

Farley, Melissa, "Prostitution, Trafficking and Traumatic Stress", Tables of responses, 2003

Fernandez, Irene, "Immigration Act in Malaysia," *Tenaganita*, 2011-2

Fisher, William F & Thomas Ponniah (Eds), *Another World is Possible: Popular Alternatives to Globalization at the World Social Forum*, London: Zed Books, 2003

Flüe, Alois von, *New Start Project: Naya Suruwath – Ministry among Nepalis in Delhi*, (unpublished in-house document), c 2006

Galpin, Mark, *Proposal for Work among Karnali Migrants*; INF Mugu Programme: (unpublished in-house document), 2005

Galpin, Mark, *In their footsteps: a paper submitted to INF/N & INF/W boards, proposing the initiation of work with Nepali migrants in border areas and NW India*; INF Mugu Programme: (unpublished in-house document), 2005

Gautam, Kamala, "Survivors Continue to Fight Sex Trafficking, Raise Awareness in Nepal," *Nepal National*, 4 Oct 2011

Gautam, Manish, "High fees forcing Nepali medical students to study abroad," *The Kathmandu Post*, 23 Jul 2013

Gayathri, Amrutha, "Nepal urged to revoke ban on young women migrating to Gulf", *IB Times*, 15 Aug 2012, http://www.ibtimes.com/articles/373831/20120815/nepal-urged-revoke-ban-young-women-migration.htm [24 Aug 2012]

Geocities, Bhutanese Refugees, http://www.geocities.com/bhutaneserefugees/ [13 April 2006]

Ghimire, Anita et al (eds), *Nepal Migration Year Book 2009*, Kathmandu: Nepal Institute of Development Studies (NIDS), 2010

Ghimire, Anita et al (eds), *Nepal Migration Year Book 2010*, Kathmandu: NIDS & NCCR North-South, 2011
Ghimire, June, "Postcards from America: Lessons for Nepal," *Asia Foundation*, 17 Dec 2008, http://asiafoundation.org/in-asia/2008/12/17/postcards-from-america-lessons-for-nepal/ [17 Sept 2013]
Ghosh, Amitav, *Sea of Poppies*, London: Penguin, 2009
Ghosh, Palash R, "Thousands of Nepali Girls Trafficked to India as Sex Workers every Year," *IB Times*, http://www.ibtimes.com/articles/362387/20120712/nepal-india-sex-trafficking-brothels-aids-court.htm [30 Jul 2012]
Ghosh, Shamik, "4-year-old critical in hospital; alleged rapist arrested in Bihar", NDTV, http://www.ndtv.com/article/india/4-year-old-critical-in-hospital-alleged-rapist-arrested-in-bihar-357967 [25 Apr 2013]
Giri, Anil, "Nepal must help to protect women working in the Gulf", *The National News AE*, http://www.thenational.ae/thenationalconversation/comment/nepal-must-help-to-protect-women-working-in-the-gulf [31 Jan 2013]
Giri, Jeewan & Anga Rokaya, *Seasonal Migration Research in India;* INF Mugu Programme: In-House Document (unpublished), 2004
Giri, Ramchandra, "2,766 Nepali migrants get amnesty in Malaysia", *Kathmandu Post*, 19 Dec 2011
Giri, Ram Chandra, "Nepal govt hopes to sign labour agreement with M'sia", *Kathmandu Post*, 19 Jun 2013, http://www.asianewsnet.net/Nepal-govt-hopes-to-sign-labour-agreement-with-Msi-48149.html [20 Jun 2013]
Gugler, Josef (Ed), *The Urbanization of the Third World*, Oxford: Oxford University Press, 1988
Gurung, Dorje, "How I landed in jail", *Koseli*, 18 May 2013
Gurung, Ganesh, "Lahure workforce", *Himal Magazine*, Dec 2010, http://www.himalmag.com/component/content/article/3467-.html [22 May 2013]
Gurung, Manju (Ed), *Addressing Vulnerabilities of Women Migrant Workers to HIV & AIDS*, Kathmandu: Pouraki / NIDS, 2008
Guthrie, Stan "Does Global Culture mark the end of missions history?'" *Evangelical Missions Quarterly* 7/96 pp328-334
Guthrie, Stan, *Missions in the Third Millennium: 21 Key Trends for the 21st Century*; Carlisle, Cumbria; Paternoster, 2000
Hall, Andrew, *Himalayan Exodus: Nepalese Migrant Groups,* 2001 (Originally presented in 1995)
Hamdan, Nurbaiti, "Teenager charged with robbing Nepali", *The Star*, 6 Sep 2012, http://thestar.com.my/news/story.asp?file=/2012/9/6/nation/2012090

6170608&sec=nation [11 Sept 2012]

Hanciles, Jehu, "Migration and Mission: Some Implications for the Twenty-first Century Church, *International Bulletin of Missionary Research*, Vol 27, No 4, Oct 2003:146-153

Harvey, Alan, "Diaspora: A Passage to Mission", *Transformation: An International Journal of Holistic Mission Studies,* 2011 28:42

Hausner, Sondra & David Gellner, "New home, new religion? New lives for Nepalis in the UK, np, nd

Heide, Susanne von der & Hoffmann, Thomas (Eds), *Aspects of Migration and Mobility in Nepal*; Kathmandu: Ratna Pustak Bhandar, 2001

Held, D & McGrew, A, Goldblatt, D & Perraton, J, *Global Transformations: Politics, Economics and Culture*, Cambridge: Polity, 1991

Henderson, Tony, "From Nepal to Newcastle: A life-changing journey for Nepalese student", *North-East News*, 13 Dec 2012, http://www.journallive.co.uk/north-east-news/todays-news/2012/12/13/from-nepal-to-newcastle-a-life-changing-journey-for-nepalese-student-61634-32421943/2/ [17 Dec 2012]

Heslem, Peter (Ed), *Globalization and the Good*; London: SPCK, 2004

Himal Media Round Table, "Helping Workers Abroad", *Nepali Times*, Issue 532, 17-23 Dec 2012

Hiyama, Hiroshi, Nepal man cleared after 15 years in Japan jail, *Arab News*, http://www.arabnews.com/nepal-man-cleared-after-15-years-japan-jail [8 Nov 2012]

Ho, Shaun, "Nepali nabbed for alleged rape of 15-year-old missing girl", *The Star*, 5 Feb 2013, http://thestar.com.my/news/story.asp?file=/2013/2/5/nation/20130205192830&sec=nation [6 Feb 2013]

Hollingshead, Iain, "The Gurkhas in Aldershot: Little Nepal", *The Telegraph*, http://www.telegraph.co.uk/news/uknews/defence/8339467/The-Gurkhas-in-Aldershot-Little-Nepal.html [21 Feb 2011]

Hornby, William F & Melvyn Jones, Studies in Human Geography: *An Introduction to Population Geography*; Cambridge: Cambridge University Press, 1980

Hsai, Hsaio-Chuan, "The Making of a Transnational Grassroots Migrant Movement", *Critical Asian Studies*, Mar 2009, Vol. 41, Issue 1, p113-141

"Implications of the Great Commission for the 21st Century," The Center for the Study of Global Christianity, www.globalchristianity.org/globalcontext [27 Sept 2013]

Inchley, Valerie M, How Globalisation has affected by 'local' community (Kathmandu, (Class paper produced for MA though Redcliffe

College, University of Gloucestershire), Jul 2005

Inchley, Valerie M, *Globalization, Migration and Mission in the Nepali Context*, (Globalization Assignment produced for MA though Redcliffe College, University of Gloucestershire), 2006

INF, "Diaspora Figures from the INF Website, INF, 2011

Ingleby, Jonathan, "Globalisation, Glocalisation and Mission", *Encounter Mission EZine*, Issue 1: August 2004, www.redcliffe.org/mission [c 20 December 2005]

International Labour Conference – Provisional Record – "15A Text of the Convention concerning Decent Work for Domestic Workers", Geneva: ILO, 2011

International Labour Conference – Provisional Record – "15B Text of the Recommendation concerning Decent Work for Domestic Workers", Geneva: ILO, 2011

International Seminar on Nepali Diaspora in the Globalised Context, 28-30 Nov 2011: I was privileged to read some draft papers but have not quoted from them – as requested.

IOM, *World Migration Report 2010 – The Future of Migration: Building Capacities for Change*, Geneva: International Organisation for Migration, 2010 (ONLY pdf)

Jackson, Darrell, "Europe and the Migrant Experience: Transforming Integration," *Transformation: An International Journal of Holistic Mission Studies,* 2011 28:14

Johnson, Stanley, *The Politics of Population: Cairo 1994: The International Conference on Population and Development*, London: Earthscan Publications, 1994 Part of Chapter 9 "International Migration"

Jones, Harry & Yurendra Basnett, "Foreign employment and inclusive growth in Nepal: what can be done to improve impacts for the people and the country?" *ODI*, Jun 2013, http://www.odi.org.uk/publications/7424-foreign-employment-inclusive-growth-nepal-can-be-done-improve-impacts-people-country [17 Sept 2013]

Jones, Harry et al, "Prospecting policy issues for the Nepal Centre for Inclusive Growth," *ODI*, May 2011 to April 2014, http://www.odi.org.uk/projects/2520-policy-nepal-centre-inclusive-growth-cig [17 Sept 2013]

Jung, Min-Young "Asian Diaspora: Strategic Resource for World Mission" *Connections* Vol. 4 No. 3 ?Autumn 2005

Kanaan, Preeti, "Nepal may impose guarantees for hiring nannies," UAE: *The National News. AE*, Apr 2011

Kang & Yoon-seung, Nepali worker in S. Korea found dead after losing job, *The Korea Herald / Asia news Network*, 14 Jun 2011, http://sg.news.yahoo.com/nepali-worker-korea-found-dead-losing-

job-110002966.html [16 Jun 2011]
Karki, Hom, "2 Nepali prisoners in UAE," *Ekantipur*, 27 Jun 2011
Karki, Hom & Dinesh Regmi, "Returning Women," *Ekantipur*, Jul 2011
Karki, Hom, "Nepali Passport sold for 3 lakh," *Ekantipur*, Apr 2013, http://www.ekantipur.com/kantipur/news/news-detail.php?news_id=293348 [5 Jun 2013]
Karki, Hom, "Outpass for 13,000 leaving Saudi in 4 days", *Kantipur*, 19 May 2013
Karki, Hom, "88 Workers in trouble in Doha," *Ekantipur,* 16 Jestha 2070, http://ekantipur.com/np/2070/2/16/full-story/369026.html [5 Jun 2013]
KC, Gokarna, "A bitter truth of Ramkumari," *Maiti Nepal Magazine*, Jan 2007
KC, Rebanta, "Korean EPS and Growing Joblessness," *Nepal News*, 24 Jul 2013, http://www.nepalnews.com/archive/2013/others/guestcolumn/jul/guest_columns_09.php [24 July 2013]
KC, Thir, Overseas Employment Problems and Migrant Fellowships, *Ashish Patrika*, 2011 (Nepali)
Kett, Maria "ABC of conflict and disaster - Displaced populations and long term humanitarian assistance", *BMJ* 9 Jul 2005: 98-100
Khadaroo, Stacy, "US college student Surya Karki builds schools back home in Nepal" *Maya Universe Academy*, 28 Jun 2013
Khadka, Ramkala, "Remittances – Family Troubles", *Annapurna Post*, 27 Dec 2012
Khadka, Sudip, "Doing the Lord's work in Nepal while living overseas" (Nepali), *Bachan*, Jestha 2069, p.6
Khatiwada, Yogesh & Dinesh Regmi, "Nepalis coming home on leave and returning freed of paperwork", *Gorkha Patra*, 14 Jul 2011
Kilbourn, Phyllis (Ed), *Healing the Children of War* Monrovia, CA: MARC, 1995 Foreword iii-iv & pp1-3, 7-8, 11-12, 14 ##, 19-20, 23-24, 26, 29-30
Kilbourn, Phyllis (Ed), *Street Children: A Guide to Effective Ministry*, Monrovia, CA: MARC, 1997
Kim, Hun, "Receiving Mission: Reflection on Reversed Phenomena by Migrant Workers from Glocal Churches to the Western Society," *Transformation: An International Journal of Holistic Mission Studies,* 2011 28:62
Kirchheiner, Ole, *Mission among Migrated People* – Case Denmark, 2013
Koirali, Kosh Raj, "Nepali workers on visitor visas in a fix, *Republica*, http://www.myrepublica.com/portal/index.php?action=news_details&news_id=43644 [22 May 2013]
Lamichhane, Jiva, "I went to Burma – with work", *Koseli*, 1 Jun 2013,

http://www.ekantipur.com/kantipur/news/news-detail.php?news_id=297279 [5 Jun 2013]
LCWE, *Scattered to Gather: Embracing the Global Trend of Diaspora*, 2010
Lechner, F & J Boli (Eds), *The Globalization Reader*, Oxford: Blackwell, 2000
Levitt, Peggy, "God needs no passport: Immigrants and the changing American religious landscape," *IBMR* 2009, Vol. 33 No. 2, pp 107-8 (Review of a 2007 book)
Li, Shengjie, Presentation re ILO Convention concerning Decent Work for Domestic Workers", Kathmandu: Pauraki et al, 2011
Lokshin, Michael, Mikhail Bontch-Osmolovski & Elena Glinskaya, *Work-Related Migration and Poverty Reduction in Nepal*, Washington DC: The World Bank, 2007
Lorance, Cody, *Pursuing Cruciformity in Diaspora Mission*, Carol Stream, IL: Trinity International Baptist Mission, 2010
Lorance, Cody, *Pursuing Cruciformity in Diaspora Mission*: With Emphasis on Ministry Among Refugees, Presented at Himalayan Global Summit in Hong Kong, 2011
Lottis, Bill, "How to meet the needs of Immigrants, with a bonus" *Evangelical Missions Quarterly* 7/89 pp256-260
Lundy, David "Globalization and the Support of Nationals" *Evangelical Missions Quarterly* 4/03 pp166-174
Lusher, Adam, Aldershot: the town turning away the Gurkhas, *The Telegraph*, http://www.telegraph.co.uk/news/features/8786802/Aldershot-the-town-turning-away-the-Gurkhas.html [25 Sep 2011]
Lutz, Wolfgang, *The Future Population of the World: What can we assume today?* Laxenburg, Austria: International Institute for Applied Systems Analysis, 1996 – Sections by Hania Zlotnik and Sture Öberg
Mahato, Rubeena, "Woman Power", *Nepali Times*, Issue 597, 23-29 Mar 2012
Mahato, Rubeena, "To hell and back", *Nepali Times*, Issue 598, 30 Mar – 5 Apr 2012
McClung, Grant, *Moving with God among "People on the Move,"* www.MissionsResourceGroup.org [March 2011]
McLeod, J, *Beginning Postcolonialism*, Manchester: Manchester University Press, 2000
Mishra, Surya Nath, "Diplomacy for Migrant worker," *Ekantipur,* 10 Jul 2012
Mishra, TP, "A Diaspora Begins" [re Bhutanese], *Himal SouthAsia*, Vol 23, No. 5, May 2010 pp58-9
Ministry of Health & Population, National Centre for AIDS & STD

Control, Cumulative HIV & AIDS Situation of Nepal, 17 Aug 2007
Ministry of Labour & Transport, Foreign Employment Dept, Labour Migrants departing Nepal in Baisakh 2068
Namboodiri, Narayan, "Rickshaw puller kills another for calling him 'Nepali'," *Times of India*, 24 Jul 2012, http://articles.timesofindia.indiatimes.com/2012-07-24/mumbai/32827343_1_rickshaw-drivers-rickshaw-puller-victim [30 Jul 2012]
Napit, Shree, "Nepali Second Generation in Australia," *Europe's NepaliPatra Epaper*, No. 374:16, 27 Aug 2 Sept 2013, http://www.nepalipatra.com/epaper/Main.php [5 Sep 2013]
Nath, Lopita, "Migration, Insecurity and Identity: The Nepali Dairymen in India's Northeast", *Asian Ethnicity*, Volume 7, Number 2, Jun 2006, pp129-148
Nazari, Hamzah, "Merry-making of different kind", *Malay Mail* –14 Nov 2012, http://my.news.yahoo.com/merry-making-different-kind-034800759.html [3 Dec 2012]
Nepal National Census, 2011 (excerpt)
Nepali Samaj Nederland, http://www.nepalsamaj.nl/index.php [15 Oct 2013]
North, Andrew, "Nepal's World Cup trail brings misery," *BBC News*, 19 Nov 2013, http://www.bbc.co.uk/news/world-asia-india-24964807#FBM309645 [20 Nov 2013]
Orlinsky, Katie, "Women, Bought and Sold in Nepal," *New York Times*, 31 Aug 2013, http://www.nytimes.com/2013/09/01/opinion/sunday/women-bought-and-sold-in-nepal.html?smid=fb-share&_r=0 [4 Sept 2013]
Owen, Wilfred, *Transportation and World Development*, London: Hutchinson, 1987
Pandey, J, "Card provision hits Nepalis, *Kathmandu Post*, 5 Dec 2008, http://www.ekantipur.com/the-kathmandu-post/2008/12/05/related_articles/card-provision-hits-nepalis/169136.html [22 May 2013]
Pandey, J, "Nepalis being killed and robbed", *Kantipur*, 12 Oct 2011
Pantoja, Luis Jr, Sadiri Joy B Tira & Enoch Wan (Eds), *Scattered: The Filipino Global Presence*, Manila: Lifechange Publishing, 2004
Parajuli, Kalpit, "Crackdown in Kuala Lumpur: 65 thousand Nepalese migrants risk expulsion," *Asia News Net*, 30 Aug 2013, http://www.asianews.it/news-en/Crackdown-in-Kuala-Lumpur:-65-thousand-Nepalese-migrants-risk-expulsion-28882.html [3 Sept 2013]
Parashar, Utpal, "Campaign to free Nepali jailed in Qatar for 'insulting' Islam, *Hindustan Times,* 10 May 2013, http://in.news.yahoo.com/campaign-free-nepali-jailed-qatar-

insulting-islam-183000029.html [15 May 2013]

Pathak, Bishnu & Chitra Niraula, *A Different Diaspora: Story of Nepali Refugees in Austria*, http://blog.com.np/2007/06/28/a-different-diaspora-story-of-nepali-refugees-in-austria/ [28 Dec 2012]

Pattisson, Pete, "Revealed: Qatar's World Cup 'slaves'," *The Guardian*, 25 Sep 2013, http://www.theguardian.com/world/2013/sep/25/revealed-qatars-world-cup-slaves [27 Sep 2013]

Payne, Heather, "Nation's Pulse", *Namkeen*, Feb 2010:1

Payne, JD, "Peoples on the Move: A God-ordained opportunity for reaching the unreached", *Mission Frontiers*, Nov/Dec Issue 2012

Perry, Cindy L, *Nepali Around the World*, Kathmandu: RC Timothy, 1997

Perry, Cindy, "The Nepali Diaspora and the Gospel", *Dharma Deepika,* July-December 2001:35-41

Poertner et al, "Migration in Far West Nepal Intergenerational Linkages between Internal and International Migration of Rural-to-Urban Migrants, *Critical Asian Studies*, Vol 43:1, 2011, pp 23-47

Pohl, Christine D "Biblical Issues in Mission and Migration" *Missiology: An International Review* Vol. XXXI Number 1 Jan. 2003 Mission and Migration pp 3-15

Pokhrel, Nabin, "High level postholders as security guards, *Ekantipur*, 6 Apr 2013, http://www.ekantipur.com/kantipur/news/news-detail.php?news_id=293349 [5 Jun 2013]

Popalzai, Masoud, "7 die in attack on companies' Kabul compound - Four Nepali guards, Afghan civilian and 5 attackers die, *CNN*, 1 Jul 2013, http://www.news4jax.com/news/7-die-in-attack-on-companies-Kabul-compound/-/475880/20797390/-/13ul2jsz/-/index.html [3 Jul 2013]

Pradhan, Sanjay, "Premature Gorkhaland," *Himal SouthAsia*, Vol 23, No. 7, Jul 2010, pp24-25

Rahim, Rahimy et al, "Illegals play hide-and-seek during biggest operation," *The Star, Malaysia*, 2 Sep 2013

Rai, Bishwa, Paluwa HIV/AIDS Section – INF – Technical Proposal, 16 Aug 2009

Rai, Niyama, "A Trafficker Behind Bars: A Counter-Trafficking Success Story," *Asia Foundation,* 31 Jul 2011, http://asiafoundation.org/in-asia/2011/07/13/a-trafficker-behind-bars-a-counter-trafficking-success-story/ [17 Sept 2013]

Ramirez, Philippe (Ed), "Special Double Issue: Nepalese migrations, *European Bulletin of Himalayan Research*, 35-36, Autumn-Spring 2010

Rana, Caesar & Suman Lamichane, "A remittance economy", *Boss*, May-Jun 2009

Rasiah, Rani, "Stop exploitation: Implement minimum wage now!"

Aliran, 13 Apr 2013, http://aliran.com/12995.html [14 Apr 2013]

Regional Symposium on Deployment of Workers Overseas: A Shared Responsibility, *ILO et al*, 2008

Renchen, Kesang, *National Consultation on Global Forum for Migration and Development (GFMD) in Nepal*, (Report), Kathmandu: Pouraki, 2009

Riek, Renate, Nepali Migrants in Ladakh, October 2011 (unpublished, private communication)

Ripley, David (1994) "Reaching the world at our doorstep". *Evangelical Missions Quarterly*, Vol. 30, No. 2, April 1994 pp142-150

Rose, Leo, http://news.meronepalma.com/readnews/7112-via-meronepalma.com [11th September, 2010]

Rybolt, Barbara, "Photos: Nepal native is helping move mountains at home, while working at Dunkin' Donuts in Chatham Township," *NJ*, 22 Jul 2013, http://www.nj.com/independentpress/index.ssf/2013/07/photos_nepal_native_is_helping.html [24 July 2013]

Samuels, Fiona et al, "Vulnerabilities of movement: cross border mobility between India, Nepal and Bangladesh," *Overseas Development Institute Background Note*, November 2011

Sands, Andrea, "Edmonton school sees upsurge in Nepalese students," *Edmonton Journal*, 4 Sep 2013, http://www.edmontonjournal.com/story.html?id=8875677 [17 Sept 2013]

Sappani, Kamatchy, "Refugee problem haunts Bhutan", *The Star*, http://biz.thestar.com.my/news/story.asp?file=%2F2011%2F10%2F22%2Fbusiness%2F9729877&sec=business [19 Dec 2011]

Satyal, Yajna Raj, *Tourism Scene in Nepal*; New Delhi: Adroit Publishers, 2000

Satyal, Yajna Raj, *Tourism in Nepal: A Profile*; New Delhi: Adroit Publishers, 2004

Seaman, Alistair, "A Stranger in My Own Land: how INF is helping Nepal's refugees" *Today in Nepal*, No. 202, October 2005

Seddon, David; Jagannath Adhikari & Ganesh Gurung, *The New Lahures: Foreign Employment and Remittance Economy of Nepal*; Kathmandu: Nepal Institute of Development Studies, 2001

Seddon, David, "Nepal's Dependence on Exporting Labor – Country Profile," *Migration Information Source*, Jan 2005

Sedhai, Roshan, "726 died last year, govt report says," *The Kathmandu Post*, 17 Aug 2013

Sedhai, Roshan, "A wait too long in whole of S Asia Nepali passport processing fee is also the highest in region," *Ekantipur*, 5 Jun 2013, http://www.ekantipur.com/2013/06/05/fullnews/a-wait-too-long-in-whole-of-s-asia/372758.html [5 Jun 2013]

Sedhai, Roshan, "Air ticket shortage in Gulf route leaves thousands of Nepalese workers stranded," *Kathmandu Post*, 23 May 2013, http://www.asianewsnet.net/Air-ticket-shortage-in-Gulf-route-leaves-thousands-47089.html [24 May 2013]

Sedhai, Roshan, "At what cost? Migrants' deaths shroud economic benefits," *Ekantipur*, 19 Dec 2013, http://www.ekantipur.com/2013/12/19/top-story/at-what-cost-migrants-deaths-shroud-economic-benefits/382559.html [19 Dec 2013]

Sedhai, Roshan, "Illegal Nepali workers in Saudi Arabia return in droves," *The Kathmandu Post*, 18 Jul 2012, http://www.ekantipur.com/2012/07/18/top-story/illegal-migrant-workers-in-saudi-arabia-returning-in-droves/357331.html [31 Jul 2012]

Sedhai, Roshan, "Nepali missions in labour nations 'overburdened'", *The Kathmandu Post*, http://www.asianewsnet.net/Nepali-missions-in-labour-nations-overburdened-45725.html [23 Apr 2013]

Sedhain, Roshan, "Nepal airport facing crisis of too many dead bodies flown in", *The Kathmandu Post*, 26 Jun 2013, http://www.asianewsnet.net/Nepal-airport-facing-crisis-of-too-many-dead-bodie-48462.html [28 Jun 2013]

Shah, Modh Farhaan, "Johor police deny Nepali worker deaths after brawl", *The Star*, 29 Mar 2013, http://thestar.com.my/news/story.asp?file=/2013/3/29/nation/20130329160839&sec=nation [30 Mar 2013]

Shahi, Raj Bahadur, "Mugu folk desert villages to escape cold", *Kathmandu Post* 13 Dec 2013, http://www.ekantipur.com/the-kathmandu-post/2013/12/08/top-story/mugu-folk-desert-villages-to-escape-cold/256699.html [13 Dec 2013]

Sharma, Bhadra, "Nepal teams to study Thai, Philippine, Korea diaspora voting rights," *The Kathmandu Post*, [30 Jul 2012]

Sharma, Janak Raj, "Nepali Migrants' Meeting, Kathmandu," *Turahi,* Year 1, No. 8, Asoj 2069 (2012)

Sharma, Kritika, "19-year-old Nepalese woman gangraped in Delhi", *India Today*, http://indiatoday.intoday.in/story/gangrape-in-delhi-nepalese-woman/1/266519.html [21 Apr 2013]

Sharma, Lochana, "Women in Nepal warn of foreign employment exploitation", *Global Press Institute*, *Nepal National*, 6 Aug 2011

Shrestha, Ramesh, "Half of Nepali households have member working abroad: Survey", *The Kathmandu Post*, 29 Jun 2011

Shrestha, Ramesh, "Returning Migrant Workers Freed of Paperwork", *Kathmandu Post*, 13 Jul 2011

Shrestha, Ramesh, "Nepali migrant workers struck by wanderlust", *The Kathmandu Post*, 13 Dec 2011, &

http://www.ekantipur.com/2011/12/14/national/nepali-migrant-workers-struck-by-wanderlust/345516.html [31 Jul 2012]

Shukla, Kavita & Michelle Brown, "India: Nepali migrants in need of protection", *Refugees International*, 28 Feb 2007

Sigdel, KR, "Human Traffickers dumping Nepalis to Afghan jails.doc, *LookandGaze*, 27 Apr 2013, http://lookandgaze.blogspot.com/2011/04/human-traffickers-dumping-nepalis-to.html [22 May 2013]

Sijapati, Bandita & Amrita Limbu, *Governing Labour Migration in Nepal: An Analysis of Existing Policies and Institutional Mechanisms*, Kathmandu: Himal Books for the Centre for the Study of Labour and Mobility, 2012

Singh, Sukhlal & Rita Thapa, Introduction of Rescue, Nepalgunj, Banke, 2006

Singh, Sukhlal & Rita Thapa, Progress report of Rescue, Nepalgunj, Banke, 2005-6

Sinha, AC, "Beyond Lhotshampa Resettlement", *Himal SouthAsia*, Vol. 20, No. 10/11, Oct-Nov 2007:96-98

Sinjali, Ram Bahadur, INF Mugu Programme – First Quarter Report Aug-Sep 2011, INF, unpublished

Samarika 2001-2012, New Revival Nepali Church, Abu Dhabi, 2012

Sodemba, Thomas, *How the Church's Evangelism and Mission might have an Impact on Its Community – Reflection on a case study of Ghill Basti Gurkha Mission in Myanmar (1993-2010),* University of Wales MA Thesis, np, 2010

Stackhouse, Max L with Obenchain, Diane B (Eds), *God and Globalization Volume 3: Christ and the Dominions of Civilization*; Harrisburg, PA; Trinity Press International, 2002 – incl. Sections by Scott Thomas & M Thomas Thanaraj

Steger, Manfred B, *Globalization: A Very Short Introduction*, Oxford: Oxford University Press, 2003

Subedi, Anjali, "Migrant workers long for work at home," *Republica*, 20 Dec 2012, http://www.myrepublica.com/portal/index.php?action=news_details&news_id=46786 [28 Dec 2012]

Sundelin, Gaelle, "Asian community shares prayers, memories in Mafraq, (a Jordanian Newspaper), c 20 Jul 2013

Sunderaraj, Francis "Girding up for missions in Asia in the 21st Century"' *Evangelical Missions Quarterly* 1/99 pp40-47

Suter, Brigitte, *Labour Migration in the United Arab Emirates: Field study on Regular and Irregular Migration in Dubai*, Master Thesis, IMER, Malmo University, Sweden, 2004/5

Thapa, Anu, "Gang-rape case in Nepal sparks protests," *Top News*, 28 Jun 2013, http://www.upi.com/Top_News/World-

News/2013/06/28/Gang-rape-case-in-Nepal-sparks-protests/PC-2011372456200/?spt=hs&or=tn [1 Jul 2013]

Thapa, Sangeeta & Manju Gurung, *Miles Apart....... Experience From Foreign Labour Migration*, Kathmandu: Pouraki / UNIFEM, 2009

Thieme, Susan et al, "Addressing the Needs of Nepalese Migrant Workers in Nepal and in Delhi, India "*Mountain Research and Development*, Vol. 25, No. 2, May 2005 pp109-114

Thomas, Andrea (Ed), "Book Review of Nepalis (sic) around the world", INF *LOT Quarterly* No. 18, Jul 2003

Thomas, TV, Sadiri Joy Tira, & Enoch Wan, "Ministering to the Scattered Peoples", Lausanne III Paper, Jul 2010

Thompson, Andrew, *The Christian Church in Kuwait. Religious freedom in the Gulf*, Kuwait: Saeed & Sameer, 2010

Toumi, Habib, "Nepal to open embassies in Bahrain, Oman", *Gulf News*, http://gulfnews.com/news/gulf/bahrain/nepal-to-open-embassies-in-bahrain-oman-1.1150389?utm_content=1.1150389&utm_medium=RSS&utm_source=Feeds&utm_campaign=Nepal_to_open_embassies_in_Bahrain%2C_Oman&localLinksEnabled=false&utm_term=News_RSS_feed [25 Feb 2013]

Trenwith, Courtney, "UAE, Nepal ink deal to expand air travel services," *Arabian Business*, 17 Apr 2013, http://www.arabianbusiness.com/uae-nepal-ink-deal-expand-air-travel-services-498408.html [21 Apr 2013]

Upreti, Aruna, "Put your money where your mouth is", *Nepali Times*, 15-21 Jun 2007

Upreti, BC, *The Marginal Migrants (A Study of Nepali emigrants in India)*; Delhi: Kalinga Publications, 2002

Vethanayagamony, Peter, "Mission from the Rest to the West", by Amos Yong, pp 60-68

Wan, Enoch "Mission Among the Chinese Diaspora" *Missiology: An International Review*, Vol XXXI Number 1 Jan 2003 Mission and Migration pp 35-43

Wan, Enoch, "Diaspora Mission Strategy in the Context of the United kingdom in the 21st Century", *Transformation: An International Journal of Holistic Mission Studies*, 2011 28:3

Wan, Enoch, "The Phenomenon of Diaspora: Missiological Implications for Christian Missions", *Global Missiology* English, Vol 4, No 9 (2012) http://ojs.globalmissiology.org/index.php/english/article/view/1036 [24 Aug 2012]

Wang, Yuanyuan, "Gov't ponders reopening Iraq, Afghanistan, Libya for Nepali workers", *Xinhua*, 28 Aug 2012, http://news.xinhuanet.com/english/world/2012-

08/28/c_131812525.htm [28 Dec 2012]
Ward, Victoria, Joanna Lumley targeted in online campaign against 'influx' of Gurkhas, *The Telegraph*, http://www.telegraph.co.uk/news/uknews/defence/8768670/Joanna-Lumley-targeted-in-online-campaign-against-influx-of-Gurkhas.html [17 Sept 2011]
WHO, Code of Practice on International recruitment of health personnel adopted by WHO, 2000
Williams, Rachel, "Nepal struggles to contain human trafficking problem, *The Guardian*, 8 May 2013, http://www.guardian.co.uk/global-development/poverty-matters/2013/may/08/nepal-struggles-human-trafficking-problem [9 May 2013]
Williams, Sebastian, *Send them to Hell: The Brutal Horrors of Bangkok's Nightmare Jails*, Edinburgh: Mainstream, 2012
Winter, Ralph, LCWE, nd
Xavier, Joachim, *Jiwan Kumar & Injustice in Malaysia*, Press Release – Penang: Penang Office for Human Development, 4 Dec 2008
Young, Robert JC, *Postcolonialism: A Very Short Introduction*, Oxford: Oxford University Press, 2003
Yadav, Arjun, "The musician from Nepal who wants to strike it big in India," *MeriNews*, 22 Jul 2013, http://www.merinews.com/article/the-musician-from-nepal-who-wants-to-strike-it-big-in-india/15888193.shtml [22 July 2013]
Youth Action Nepal, "Endorsing Foreign Employment Act: A Welcoming Effort", 2 Mar 2012
Zachariah, Elizabeth & Nadirah H Rodzi, "Nepali workers cause chaos at hostel", *NST.com*, http://www.nst.com.my/latest/nepali-workers-cause-chaos [8 Feb 2013]

PRESS ARTICLES / EDITORIALS (no Authors noted)

"1.83 pct working population leaves Nepal in 8 months," *Global Times*, Xinhua, http://www.globaltimes.cn/content/771354.shtml#.UVanq6z_j6M [30 Mar 2013]

"2 Nepali women die in Riyadh," *Ekantipur*, 24 Dec 2009, http://www.ekantipur.com/2009/12/24/top-story/2-nepali-women-die-in-riyadh/305031.html [5 Jun 2013)

"3 Nepali workers killed in Bahrain accident," *Ekantipur*, 26 Mar 2012, http://www.ekantipur.com/2012/03/26/national/3-nepali-workers-killed-in-bahrain-accident/351226.html [31st Jul 2012]

"5 Nepali labourers die of electrocution," *New Kerala*, http://www.newkerala.com/news/2011/worldnews-34626.html [26 Jul 2011]

"3 Nepali workers die in Doha road accident, "*Nepal News*, 20 Jun 2013, http://www.nepalnews.com/archive/2013/jun/jun20/news03.php [21 Jun 2013]

"5 Young Women get their Money back in Qatar," *Kantipur*, 4 Jul 2011

"13 Bangladeshi nationals arrested with fake Nepali passports", *Nepal News*, 22 Feb 2013, http://www.nepalnews.com/archive/2013/feb/feb22/news03.php [25 Feb 2013]

"13 Nepalis stranded in Malaysia after they refuse to do work other than stated in their contract", *Nepal News*, 17 Apr 2013, http://www.nepalnews.com/archive/2013/apr/apr17/news01.php [21 Apr 2013]

"24 Nepalis die in one month in Qatar," *NepalNews.com* [26 Jun 2009]

"25% of migrant workers in the Emirates are clinically depressed," http://www.migrant-rights.org/2011/12/15/25-of-migrant-workers-in-the-emirates-are-clinically-depressed/ [20 Dec 2011]

"33 Nepali workers under EPS deported from Korea for using fake passports," *Nepal News*, 28 Feb 2013, http://www.nepalnews.com/archive/2013/feb/feb28/news07.php [3 March 2013]

"57 Nepalis died in South Korea since 2007," *Kathmandu Post*, 13 Dec 2013, http://www.ekantipur.com/the-kathmandu-post/2013/12/12/top-story/migrant-workers/256866.html

"60 Nepali run-away housemaids sent home from Kuwait," *Nepal News,* 1 Jul 2011, *Nepalnews.com* [1 Jul 11]

"64 Officials charged with corruption," *The Kathmandu Post*, 3 Dec 2013, http://www.ekantipur.com/the-kathmandu-post/2013/12/03/top-story/64-officials-charged-with-corruption/256498.html [12 Dec 2013]

"70 Families awaiting bodies of kin abroad," *Ekantipur*, 22 Jan 2012, http://www.ekantipur.com/2012/01/22/top-story/migrant-workers-70-families-awaiting-bodies-of-kin-abroad/347609.html [31 Jul 2012]

"82 Nepali women migrant workers commit suicide in 18 months," *Nepal News*, 8 Oct 2012, http://www.nepalnews.com/archive/2012/oct/oct08/news03.php [11 Oct 2012]

"100 Nepali workers stopped from holding protest over minimum wage," *The Star MY*, http://thestar.com.my/news/story.asp?file=%2F2013%2F3%2F17%2Fnation%2F20130317213655&sec=nation [18 March 2013]

"102 Nepalis in Malaysian custody," *Ekantipur*, 4 July 2012, http://www.ekantipur.com/2012/07/04/top-story/102-nepalis-in-malaysian-custody/356558.html [31 Jul 2012]

"114 agents responsible for 90 pc illegal departure of Nepali woman to Saudi Arabia", *Nepal News,* 15 May 2013, http://www.nepalnews.com/archive/2013/may/may15/news11.php [18 May 2013]

"200 students from Small Farmers families leaving for Israel for advanced agricultural training," Nepal News, 19 Jul 2013, http://www.nepalnews.com/archive/2013/jul/jul19/news02.php [22 July 2013]

"1,357 migrant workers 'died' in 3-and-a-half years," *Ekantipur*, 12 Jan 2012, http://www.ekantipur.com/2012/01/12/business/internal-report-1357-migrant-workers-died-in-3-and-a-half-yrs/347057.html [31 Jul 2012]

"1,850 Nepali workers dead in Malaysia since 2003," *Ekantipur*, 12 Jul 2012, http://www.ekantipur.com/2012/07/12/business/1850-nepali-workers-dead-in-malaysia-since-2003/356975.html [31 Jul 2012]

"3,000 Nepalis die in Saudi in 12 years," *Ekantipur*, 2 Jul 2012, http://www.ekantipur.com/2012/07/02/editors-pick/3000-nepalis-die-in-saudi-in-12-yrs/356463.html [31 Jul 2012]

"13,000 undocumented Nepali workers apply for exit permits," *Nepal News,* 19 May 2013, http://www.nepalnews.com/archive/2013/may/may19/news10.php [20 May 2013]

"45,000 left Nepal within one month," *Kantipur*, 22 Aug 2011

"80,000 Nepali workers to get amnesty in Saudi Arabia," *Global Times*, Xinhua, http://www.globaltimes.cn/content/764260.shtml [26 Feb 2013]

"130,000 Nepalese to benefit from Saudi amnesty scheme," *Asia News Net, Kathmandu Post*, 16 May 2013, http://www.asianewsnet.net/130000-Nepalese-to-benefit-from-Saudi-amnesty-sche-46790.html [18 May 2013]

"A Shy Entrepreneur?" INF *Today in Nepal* No. 224, Jun 2013
"Accused of insulting Islam Nepali teacher fired, detained in Qatar," *Nepal News*, 9 May 2013, http://www.nepalnews.com/archive/2013/may/may09/news14.php [10 May 2013]
"AI criticizes Nepali envoy in Qatar for her attempts to deport migrant worker," *Nepal News*, 19 Jun 2013, http://www.nepalnews.com/archive/2013/jun/jun19/news02.php [20 Jun 2013]
"AI report: Migrant workers suffer at hands of dishonest recruitment agents," *Ekantipur*, 14 Dec 2011, http://www.ekantipur.com/2011/12/14/national/ai-report-migrant-workers-suffer-at-hands-of-dishonest-recruitment-agents/345503.html [31 Jul 2012]
"An owner of a manpower agency swindled youth two million rupees before fleeing", Manpower Agency Nepal, 14 Aug 2010, http://www.manpoweragencynepal.com/Manpower-news-65-1.html [9 Jan 2012]
"Another Nepali commits suicide by jumping off building in South Korea," *Nepal News*, 26 Jul 2012, http://www.nepalnews.com/archive/2012/jul/jul26/news07.php [30 July 2012]
"Bandipur Diaspora meet in NA," *Nepal.com* [early Jul 2009]
"Beldangi," *Kathmandu Post*, 12 Aug 2013
"Big fake certificate racket busted in Nepal, 15 in police net," *Kathmandu Post*, 6 Jun 2013, http://ph.news.yahoo.com/big-fake-certificate-racket-busted-nepal-15-police-060003272.html [10 Jun 2013]
"Bodies of six Nepali migrants found in Himachal's Kinnau," *IANS*, 22 Jun 2013, http://en-maktoob.news.yahoo.com/bodies-six-nepali-migrants-found-himachals-kinnaur-140523980.html [24 Jun 2013]
"Campaign for Nepali teacher's release from Doha jail starts," *Nepal News*, 10 May 2013, http://www.nepalnews.com/archive/2013/may/may10/news07.php [15 May 2013]
"Campaigning to raise awareness of increasing border theft," *Gorkha Patra*, 13 Oct 2011
"Changes at DoFE relieve foreign job seekers." *Ekantipur*, 13 May 2012, http://www.ekantipur.com/2012/05/13/entertainment/changes-at-dofe-relieve-foreign-job-seekers/353873.html [31 Jul 2012]
"Cheated migrant workers return home empty-handed," *The Himalayan Times*, 25 Jul 2011, http://www.thehimalayantimes.com/rssReference.php?headline=Cheated+migrant+workers+return+home+empty-handed&NewsID=296876 [26 Jul 2011]

"Cheers and jeers for maids' day off in Singapore," *The Himalayan Times*, http://www.thehimalayantimes.com/rssReference.php?headline=Cheers+and+jeers+for+maids\%27+day+off+in+Singapore&NewsID=323136 [7 Mar 2012]

"Consultation on Gender, Migration & Law/Human rights: India, Nepal & Bangladesh," *India Habitat Centre*, Jan 2007

"Convicted Nepalese not guilty in retrial," *(10-29 13:01),* http://www.thestandard.com.hk/breaking_news_detail.asp?id=26950 [30 Oct 2012]

"Departure of Nepalis for overseas jobs up by 20 pc," *Nepal News*, http://www.nepalnews.com/home/index.php/business-a-economy/12026-departure-of-nepalis-for-overseas-jobs-up-by-20-pc.html [20 Dec 2011] from Jul 2011

"Diplomat says Indian expatriate demand for Nepali maids the highest," *Nepal National*, http://story.nepalnational.com/index.php/ct/9/cid/7399985502eaed63/id/203983504/cs/1/ht/Diplomatsays%20Indian%20expatriate%20demand%20for%20Nepali%20maids%20the%20highest/ [5 Mar 2012]

Disappointed by Hope, YWAM Penang & Raise their Voice against Injustice, 2010

"Dozens of Nepalis' bodies rot in Arabia," *Word Press*, 9 Mar 2011, http://onwuhk.wordpress.com/2011/03/09/dozens-of-nepalis%E2%80%99-bodies-rot-in-arabia/ [20 Dec 2011] from Mar 2011 also in *Ekantipur*, http://www.ekantipur.com/2011/03/09/national/dozens-of-nepalis-bodies-rot-in-arabia/330629.html [31 Jul 2012]

"Duped workers cry for help," *Ekantipur*, 25 Dec 2011, http://www.ekantipur.com/2011/12/25/national/duped-workers-cry-for-help/346126.html [31 Jul 2012]

EDITORIAL: "The Bhutanese agony," *The Kathmandu Post*, 17 Apr 2013, http://ph.news.yahoo.com/editorial-bhutanese-agony-060003203.html [21 Apr 2013]

"Ex-Ghurkhas in pioneering project to reduce social isolation," *This is Hampshire*, http://www.thisishampshire.net/news/10106939.Ex_Ghurkhas_in_pioneering_project_to_reduce_social_isolation/?ref=rss [17 Dec 2012]

"False Promises Exploitation and Forced Labour of Nepalese Migrant Workers," *Amnesty International*, Index: asa 31/007/2011, http://www.amnesty.org/en/library/asset/ASA31/007/2011/en/b58f0185-455d-425c-bc4f-d6b7fe309524/asa310072011en.pdf [22 Nov 2013]

"First 'Walk for Nepal' to be held in London," *Nepal News,* 28 May 2013, http://www.nepalnews.com/archive/2013/may/may28/news06.php

[29 May 2013]
"Five arrested for raping Bangalore law student," *Nepal National*, 20 Oct 2012, http://www.nepalnational.com/index.php/sid/210206512/scat/7399985502eaed63/ht/Five-arrested-for-raping-Bangalore-law-student [3 Dec 2012]
"Five Nepalese dying in gulf countries weekly: report," Newspaper report, 2006
"Five Nepalis knocked down by car in Qatar," *Nepal News*, 13 Jul 2013, http://www.nepalnews.com/archive/2013/jul/jul13/news09.php [15 Jul 2013]
"Four held for sending Nepali women to Gulf on fake papers," *Calcutta News*, http://www.calcuttanews.net/index.php?sid/208713109/scat/701ee96610c884a6/ht/Four-held-for-sending-Nepali-women-to-Gulf-on-fake-papers
"Four-year-old Nepali minor allegedly raped in New Delhi," *Nepal News*, 9 May 2013, http://www.nepalnews.com/archive/2013/may/may09/news13.php [10 May 2013]
"Freed from Afghanistan, Nepali Workers Return Home," *Asia News Network/Ekantipur*, 9 Jul 2012, http://www.ekantipur.com/2012/07/09/national/freed-from-afghanistan-workers-land-in-ktm/356825.html [31 Jul 2012]
"Girls sold for sexploitation in India's residential areas," *The Kathmandu Post,* kantipuronline [3 Jan 2006]
"Goa turns into an employment hub for Nepalese," *Nepal National*, http://www.nepalnational.com/index.php/sid/214774481/scat/7399985502eaed63/pp/2 [27 May 2013]
"Govt ignoring Nepali migrant labourers," *Himalayan News Service*, Kathmandu , 17 Dec ???)
"Govt issues guideline to send trainee workers in Japan," *Nepal Biz News*, 9 Jul 2012
"Gurkha service in Britain armed forces set to end under new Nepal law," *Nepal National*, 20 March 2012
"Gurkhas Demand Release Of Nepal Army Officer," *Sky News*, http://news.sky.com/story/1034629/gurkhas-demand-release-of-nepal-army-officer [9 Jan 2013]
"Gurkhas demand retention of citizenship in the new constitution," *Nepal News*, 29 Dec 2011, http://www.nepalnews.com/archive/2011/dec/dec29/news11.php [30 Dec 2011]
"Handful of takers for low-paying jobs in Gulf," *Ekantipur*, 17 Mar 2012, http://www.ekantipur.com/2012/03/17/national/handful-of-takers-

for-low-paying-jobs-in-gulf/350698.html [31 Jul 2012]
"Happy to get money but not bodies!", Jul 20##
"House directs for support to deceased migrant workers' kin," *Himalayan Times*, 8 Jan 2012, http://www.thehimalayantimes.com/rssReference.php?headline=House+directs+for+support+to+deceased+migrant+workers\%27+kin+&NewsID=315746 [9 Jan 2012]
"HRW lauds UK Police move to arrest Nepal torture suspect," *Nepal National*, http://www.nepalnational.com/index.php/sid/211740010/scat/7399985502eaed63/ht/HRW-lauds-UK-Police-move-to-arrest-Nepal-torture-suspect [15 Jan 2013]
"Hundreds of Nepali workers 'trapped' in three Gulf countries," *Ekantipur*, 6 Jul 2012, http://www.ekantipur.com/2012/07/06/top-story/hundreds-of-nepali-workers-trapped-in-three-gulf-countries/356669.html [31 Jul 2012]
"India denies setting up immigration check posts in Nepal," Nepal *National (IANS)*, 16 Jul 2013, http://www.nepalnational.com/index.php/sid/215868980/scat/7399985502eaed63/ [18 July 2013]
"India dismisses reports of setting up check points in Nepal," *India Times*, 17 Jul 2013, http://articles.economictimes.indiatimes.com/2013-07-17/news/40635399_1_indian-embassy-lumbini-immigration-check [22 July 2013]
"India silent on Ktm airport issue, says media distorted Lumbini, Ilam check posts' issue," *Nepal News*, 6 Jul 2013, http://www.nepalnews.com/archive/2013/jul/jul16/news18.php [18 July 2013]
"Introduction of Non-Resident Nepali Association (NRNA)," http://www.nrn.org.np/nrna/intro.php#sthash.9avkTJSw.dpbs [6 Jun 2013]
"IOM Nepal – An Overview," *Nepal IOM*, http://www.nepal.iom.int/ [31 May 2013]
"IOM – Labour Migration, *Nepal IOM*, http://www.nepal.iom.int/index.php?option=com_content&view=article&id=32&Itemid=38&lang=en [31 May 2013]
"IOM – Trafficking Risk Reduction in Nepal, *Nepal IOM*, http://www.nepal.iom.int/index.php?option=com_content&view=article&id=31&Itemid=37&lang=en [31 May 2013]
"I will never leave Nepal again," *Nepali Times*, 26 Nov-2 Dec 2004
"Institutional departure of Nepali migrant workers decreases," *The Kathmandu Post*, http://www.asianewsnet.net/home/news.php?id=23177 [27 Oct 2011]

"Int'l forum issues Kathmandu Resolution on migrant workers," *The Kathmandu Post*, http://www.asianewsnet.net/home/news.php?id=39525 [30 Nov 2012]
"IOM praised for providing 'constructive support' to Nepal to facilitate migration, counter trafficking," *Nepal News*, 30 Nov 2012, http://www.nepalnews.com/archive/2012/nov/nov30/news02.php [3 Dec 2012]
"Japan man jailed for killing Nepalese," *IOL*, http://www.iol.co.za/news/world/japan-man-jailed-for-killing-nepalese-1.1484786#.UT_m_6z_j6M [13 March 2013]
"Japanese duo caged for murderous street attack on Nepalese," *The Standard HK*, http://www.thestandard.com.hk/breaking_news_detail.asp?id=33107 [13 March 2013]
"Japanese justice condemns innocent Nepali," *The Standard HK*, http://www.thestandard.com.hk/breaking_news_detail.asp?id=27470
"Japanese man convicted of murdering Nepali national," *Nepal News*, 12 Mar 2013, http://www.nepalnews.com/archive/2013/mar/mar12/news13.php [18 March 2013]
"Kuwait- Bangladeshi men 'rape' Nepali housemaid after kidnapping her," *Arab Times*, 24 Feb 2013, http://www.menafn.com/menafn/1093612207/Kuwait-Bangladeshi-men-rape-Nepali-housmaid-after-kidnapping-her?src=RSS [25 Feb 2013]
"Last lot of 125 Nepalis head to Tunisia," *Ekantipur*, 7 Mar 2011, http://www.ekantipur.com/2011/03/07/national/last-lot-of-125-nepalis-head-to-tunisia/330578.html [31 Jul 2012]
"Legalised Nepalis in Malaysia qualify for security guards," *Jhoomka*, http://jhoomka.com/news/detail/3887/149/1/Legalised-Nepalis-in-Malaysia-qualify-for-security-guard-jobs [30 Dec 2011]
"Live sex show by a Kuwaiti & Nepali attracts children, passersby," MENAFN - *Arab Times,* 22 Oct 2012, http://www.menafn.com/menafn/1093572053/Live-sex-show-a-Kuwaiti-&-Nepali-attracts-children-passersby?src=RSS [29 Oct 2012]
"Lottery officials searching for Nepali man who won US$ 1 million," *Nepal News*, 28 Apr 2013, http://www.nepalnews.com/archive/2013/apr/apr28/news01.php [28 Apr 2013]
"Lucky to be alive," *Nepali Times*, 23 Mar 2012, http://www.nepalitimes.com.np/issue/2012/03/23/ThisIsIt/19121
"Malaysia blacklisted for human trafficking," ??? [17 Jun 2009]

"Malaysia lifts ban on hiring of security guards," *Ekantipur*, 30 Jun 2012, http://www.ekantipur.com/2012/06/30/top-story/malaysia-lifts-ban-on-hiring-of-security-guards/356386.html [31 Jul 2012]

"Malaysia sets minimum wage at RM 800-900," *Ekantipur*, 2 May 2012, http://www.ekantipur.com/2012/05/02/national/masia-sets-minimum-wage-at-rm-800-900/353307.html [31 Jul 2012]

"Migrant Worker killed in Saudi road accident," *Nepal National*, http://story.nepalnational.com/index.php/ct/9/cid/7399985502eaed63/id/203984055/ [5 Mar 2012]

"Migrant workers burdened by high interest rate," *Ekantipur*, 8 Jul 2012, http://www.ekantipur.com/2012/07/08/national/migrant-workers-burdened-by-high-interest-rate/356786.html [31 Jul 2012]

"NEPAL – Migration & HIV in Nepal", *UNDP*, http://asia-pacific.undp.org/practices/hivaids/documents/HIV_and_Mobility_in_South_Asia_web_Nepal.pdf [19 Dec 2012]

"Nepal peacekeepers in Lebanon redeploying to Golan," *The Daily Star Lebanon News*, 17 Jul 2013, http://www.dailystar.com.lb/News/Local-News/2013/Jul-17/224017-nepal-peacekeepers-in-lebanon-redeploying-to-golan.ashx#axzz2Zk3kKkTd [22 July 2013]

"Migration officials rescue 2 Nepalese in Haiti after 11-month smuggling ordeal," *The Associated Press,* 23 Oct 2012, http://www.canada.com/news/world/Migration+officials+rescue+Nepalese+Haiti+after+11month+smuggling/7431632/story.html?utm_source=feedburner&utm_medium=feed&utm_campaign=Feed%3A+canwest%2FF77+%28canada.com+World+News%29 [29 Oct 2012]

"Minor girl raped by Nepali youth in AP," *PTI News*, http://www.ptinews.com/news/3244300_Minor-girl-raped-by-Nepali-youth-in-AP [27 Dec 2012]

"Mobile Money service to Nepal launched," *Gulf Times*, http://www.gulf-times.com/site/topics/article.asp?cu_no=2&item_no=520839&version=1&template_id=36&parent_id=16 [30 Jul 2012]

"More Nepali women workers leave for foreign employment," *Global Times*, http://www.globaltimes.cn/NEWS/tabid/99/ID/722706/More-Nepali-women-workers-leave-for-foreign-employment.aspx [30 Jul 2012]

"Nearly 4,00,000 Nepali youths abroad looking for better employment opportunities," *Nepal News*, 17 Jul 2012, http://www.nepalnews.com/archive/2012/jul/jul17/news02.php [30 Jul 2012]

"Nepal appoints team to manage its upcoming embassy in Muscat," *Muscat Daily*, 27 Jun 2013, http://www.menafn.com/1093673970/--Nepal-appoints-team-to-manage-its-upcoming-embassy-Muscat?src=RSS [28 Jun 2013]

"Nepal army officer on torture charge granted bail," *BBC*, http://www.bbc.co.uk/news/uk-21638945 [4 Mar 2013]
"Nepal Army soldier killed in action in Lebanon," *Nepal News,* 19 May 2013, http://www.nepalnews.com/archive/2013/may/may19/news08.php [20 May 2013)
"Nepal government lifts Iraq working ban Aug-16-2010, *Manpower News*, http://www.manpoweragencynepal.com/Manpower-agency-nepal-66-1.html [Jan 2012]
"Nepal govt mulls lifting Iraq, Afghanistan work ban," *China Daily,* http://www.nepalnational.com/index.php/sid/211744482/scat/7399985502eaed63 [15 Jan 2013]
"Nepal: HIV Awareness amongst MSM still low," *IRIN Asia English Reports*, 22 Apr 2007
"Nepal (Tier 2) – re trafficking issues," Nepal, nd
"Nepal man cleared of Japan murder after 15 years in jail", *BBC*, http://www.bbc.co.uk/news/world-asia-20234596 [8 Nov 2012]
"Nepal: Nepali women victims of prostitution and slavery in Arab countries," *Spero News Nepal National* [15 Jun 2011]
"Nepal to add diplomatic missions in China, Gulf countries", *China Daily*, 22 Feb 2013, http://www.chinadaily.com.cn/world/2013-02/22/content_16249197.htm [23 Feb 2013]
"Nepal to send peacekeepers to Syria," *Nepal National (IANS),* 11 Jul 2013, http://www.nepalnational.com/index.php/sid/215768125/scat/7399985502eaed63/ht/Nepal-to-send-peacekeepers-to-Syria [15 July 2013]
"Nepal, UAE sign air service agreement for operating upto 70 flights a week," *Nepal News*, 17 Apr 2013, http://www.nepalnews.com/archive/2013/apr/apr17/news06.php [21 Apr 2013]
"Nepal women banned from Middle East," *Sunday Observer*, 12 Aug 2012, http://www.sundayobserver.lk/2012/08/12/wld03.asp [13 Aug 2012]
"Nepal women banned from Middle East over exploitation," http://www.tert.am/en/news/2012/08/09/nepal-women-work/ [28 Dec 2012]
"Nepalese army officer denies 2 torture charges in London court," *The Associated Press*, 28 Jun 2013, http://www.canada.com/news/Nepalese+army+officer+denies+torture+charges+London+court/8593293/story.html?utm_source=feedburner&utm_medium=feed&utm_campaign=Feed%3a+canwest%2fF77+%28canada.com+World+News%29 [1 Jul 2013]
"Nepalese demands compensation after 15 years in Japan jail," http://au.news.yahoo.com/thewest/a/-/world/15736782/nepalese-

demands-compensation-after-15-years-TOKYO (AFP) [31 Dec 2012]

"Nepalese in India flee amid rumors," *China Daily*, 21 Aug 2012, http://www.chinadaily.com.cn/world/2012-08/21/content_15694498.htm [24 Aug 2012]

"Nepalese troops brought cholera to Haiti with earthquake relief," *The Los Angeles Times*, 6 Jul 2013, http://triblive.com/usworld/world/4318540-74/haiti-cholera-samples?utm_source=feedburner&utm_medium=feed&utm_campaign=Feed%3A+alltribstories+%28TribLIVE+News%29#axzz2YQ9uyRmh [8 Jul 2013]

"Nepalese woman who accused Israel PM's wife fired," *Ekantipur*, 1 Sep 2011, http://www.ekantipur.com/2011/09/01/national/nepalese-woman-who-accused-israel-pms-wife-fired/340062.html [31 Jul 2012]

"Nepali aspirants for overseas job increases by 40 pc," *Nepal News*, http://www.nepalnews.com/home/index.php/business-a-economy/14126-nepali-aspirants-for-overseas-job-increases-by-40-pc.html [20 Dec 2011] from 26 Oct 2011

"Nepali businessman murdered in India, protests in native town," *The Times of India*, 3 Feb 2013, http://articles.timesofindia.indiatimes.com/2013-02-03/india/36720578_1_nepali-nepalese-chambers-protests [5 Feb 2013]

"Nepali couple found dead in Delhi," *Nepal National (IANS)*, http://www.nepalnational.com/index.php/sid/212863846/scat/7399985502eaed63/ht/Nepali-couple-found-dead-in-Delhi [3 March 2013]

"Nepali domestic help held for Delhi realtor's murder," *IANS Indo Asian News Service,* http://en-maktoob.news.yahoo.com/nepali-domestic-help-held-delhi-realtors-murder-150018106.html [26 Feb 2013]

"Nepali embassies in Bahrain, Oman on cards," *Nepal News*, 21 Feb 2013, http://www.nepalnews.com/archive/2013/feb/feb21/news11.php [23 Feb 2013]

"Nepali engineer serving time in Bhutanese jail on 'false charges'," *Nepal News*, 1 May 2013, http://www.nepalnews.com/archive/2013/may/may01/news03.php [2 May 2013]

"Nepali gets 21 years jail term in Malaysia," *Nepal News*, 11 Jul 2013, http://www.nepalnews.com/archive/2013/jul/jul11/news24.php [15 Jul 2013]

"Nepali girl dies in car crash in Australia," *Nepal News*, 4 Apr 2013, http://www.nepalnews.com/archive/2013/apr/apr04/news05.php [6 Apr 2013]

"Nepali girl repeatedly raped and kept in illegal confinement for two months in Delhi," *Nepal News*, 6 Dec 2012, http://www.nepalnews.com/archive/2012/dec/dec06/news02.php [10 Dec 2012]
"Nepali Gov't to explore potential job sectors," *SINA*, 7 Jul 2012
"Nepali held after truck he was driving kills two Iranian pilgrims in Saudi," *Nepal News*, 6 Apr 2013, http://www.nepalnews.com/archive/2013/apr/apr06/news04.php [8 Apr 2013
"Nepali Immigrants to USA," (details unknown)
"Nepali in Afghanistan (updated)," Press Release – MOFA, http://www.mofa.gov.np/news/metadata.php?ID=354&bread=Press%20Release [28 Dec 2012]
"Nepali jeweler found dead in HK," *Nepal News*, 31 Jan 2013, http://www.nepalnews.com/archive/2013/jan/jan31/news14.php [31 Jan 2013]
"Nepali killed in French military strike in Central African Republican [sic]," *Nepal News*, 29 Mar 2013, http://www.nepalnews.com/archive/2013/mar/mar29/news05.php [3 Apr 2013]
"Nepali kills self in Malaysia," *Ekantipur*, 26 Apr 2012, http://www.ekantipur.com/2012/04/26/top-story/nepali-kills-self-in-malaysia/353018.html [31 Jul 2012]
"Nepali maid commits suicide in Kuwait", *Nepal News*, 27 Dec 2012, http://www.nepalnews.com/archive/2012/dec/dec27/news08.php [28 Dec 2012]
"Nepali man arrested in UK over torture allegations," http://hosted.ap.org/dynamic/stories/E/EU_BRITAIN_NEPAL_TORTURE?SITE=FLTAM&SECTION=HOME&TEMPLATE=DEFAULT&CTIME=2013-01-03-06-41-54 [3 Jan 2013]
"Nepali man convicted of rape, sentenced to four years in prison in HK," *Nepal News*, 23 Jan 2013, http://www.nepalnews.com/archive/2013/jan/jan23/news02.php [23 Jan 2013]
"Nepali man found dead in Bollywood actor Khurana's home in Mumbai," *Nepal News*, 6 Mar 2013, http://www.nepalnews.com/archive/2013/mar/mar06/news14.php [8 Mar 2013
"Nepali migrant women victims of abuse and exploitation," *Weekly Nepal*, 2 Aug 2011, http://www.weeklynepal.com/index.php/2011-08-02-03-02-51/232-world/1944-nepali-migrant-women-victims-of-abuse-and-exploitation [20 Dec 2011] from Aug 2011
"Nepali migrant worker died," *Ekantipur*, 12 Jan 2012, http://www.ekantipur.com/2012/01/12/business/nepali-migrant-

worker-died/347112.html [31 Jul 2012]
"Nepali migrant worker sentenced in Malaysia," *Ekantipur*, 17 Feb 2012, http://www.ekantipur.com/2012/02/17/business/nepali-migrant-worker-sentenced-in-malayasia/349111.html [31 Jul 2012]
"Nepali migrant workers duped under false promises," *The Himalayan Times*, 13 Dec 2011, http://www.thehimalayantimes.com/fullNews.php?headline=Nepali+migrant+workers+duped+under+false+promises+&NewsID=312588 [20 Dec 2011]
"Nepali missions understaffed: 2.5m workers at receiving end," *Ekantipur*, 26 Jun 2012, http://www.ekantipur.com/2012/06/26/top-story/nepali-missions-understaffed-2.5m-workers-at-receiving-end/356164.html [31 Jul 2012]
"Nepali national among 11 killed in north Pakistan shootout," *Nepal News*, 23 Jun 2013, http://www.nepalnews.com/archive/2013/jun/jun23/news12.php [25 Jun 2013]
"Nepali national held with illegal foreign currency at TIA," *Nepal News*, 26 Oct 2012, http://www.nepalnews.com/archive/2012/oct/oct26/news05.php [29 Oct 2012]
"Nepali slits his throat near Delhi Metro station," *Nepal National (IANS)*, 5 Jul 2013, http://www.nepalnational.com/index.php/sid/215646383/scat/7399985502eaed63/ht/Nepali-slits-his-throat-near-Delhi-Metro-station [8 Jul 2013]
"Nepali student gang-raped in Bangalore," *Nepal News*, 15 Oct 2012, http://www.nepalnews.com/archive/2012/oct/oct15/news10.php [17 Oct 2012]
"Nepali students in China fear deportation," *China Daily*, Xinhua, 1 Jan 2013, http://www.chinadaily.com.cn/world/2013-01/01/content_16074425.htm [2 Jan 2013]
"Nepali wins 1 million dollars in Qatar Duty Free lottery," *Nepal National*, http://www.nepalnational.com/index.php/sid/214105006/scat/7399985502eaed63 [27 Apr 2013]
"Nepali woman alleges she was raped by three men in 24 hrs," *IN News*, http://in.news.yahoo.com/nepali-woman-alleges-she-raped-three-men-24-183000001.html [24 Dec 2012]
"Nepali woman found murdered in UK," *Nepal News*, 5 Jun 2013, http://www.nepalnews.com/archive/2013/jun/jun05/news13.php [6 Jun 2013]
"Nepali woman commits 'suicide' inside Kuwait jail," *Nepal News*, 7 May 2013,

http://www.nepalnews.com/archive/2013/may/may07/news02.php [15 May 2013]
"Nepali woman gang-raped in Delhi," *Nepal National*, http://www.nepalnational.com/index.php/sid/213919315/scat/7399985502eaed63/ht/Nepali-woman-gang-raped-in-Delhi [21 Apr 2013]
"Nepali woman raped multiple times in India, two held," *Nepal News*, 23 Dec 2012, http://www.nepalnews.com/archive/2012/dec/dec23/news19.php [24 Dec 2012]
"Nepali woman raped and murdered in England," *Ekantipur*, 5 Jun 2013, http://www.ekantipur.com/2013/06/05/top-story/nepali-woman-raped-and-murdered-in-england/372784.html [5 Jun 2013]
"Nepali woman 'raped thrice on her 1st day' in Mumbai," *Asia News*,
"Nepali women suffering in Jordan," *The Kathmandu Post*, 15 Feb 2013, http://www.asianewsnet.net/Nepali-women-suffering-in-Jordan-42781.html [18 Feb 2013]
"Nepali women victims of prostitution and slavery in Arab countries," *Nepal National*, 9 Jun 2011
"Nepali worker commits suicide in Korea," *Ekantipur*, 25 Jul 2012, http://www.ekantipur.com/2012/07/25/business/nepali-worker-commits-suicide-in-korea/357716.html [31 Jul 2912]
"Nepali worker stabs fellow Nepali to death in UAE," *Nepal News*, 19 Jan 2013, http://www.nepalnews.com/archive/2013/jan/jan19/news12.php [22 Jan 2013]
"Nepali workers fearful of being mistaken as northeast people in India, leave Mumbai, Pune fearing targeted attacks," *Nepal News*, 21 Aug 2012, http://www.nepalnews.com/archive/2012/aug/aug21/news07.php [23 Aug 2012]
"Nepali workers in Qatar: Embassy unveils new rules," *Ekantipur*, 2 May 2011, http://www.ekantipur.com/2011/05/02/business/nepali-workers-in-qatar-embassy-unveils-new-rules/333384.html [31 Jul 2012]
"Nepali workers rescued over working conditions in Jordan," *Albawaba*, 11 Mar 2013, http://www.albawaba.com/business/jordan-nepal-workers-476409 [13 Mar 2013]
"Nepali workers suffer in Qatar due to fake visa," *Ekantipur*, 20 Nov 2009, http://www.ekantipur.com/2009/11/20/top-story/nepali-workers-suffer-in-qatar-due-to-fake-visa/303214.html [5 Jun 2013]
"Nepali youth held for rape of minor girl," *PTI News*, http://www.ptinews.com/news/3245748_Nepali-youth-held-for-rape-of-minor-girl [27 Dec 2012]
"Nepalis in Malaysia," details unknown

"Nepalis to overseas job up by 14 pc," *Nepal News*, 20 Feb 2013, http://www.nepalnews.com/archive/2013/feb/feb20/news04.php [23 Feb 2013]

"Nepal: Protect Nepalese migrants from 'false promises' of work abroad," http://www.amnestynepal.org/campaigns/ai-nepal-activities/nepal:-protect-nepalese-migrants-from-%E2%80%98false-promises%E2%80%99-of-work-abroad.html [20 Dec 2011]

"Nepal's Colonel Kumar Lama charged in UK with torture," *Nepal National*, http://www.nepalnational.com/index.php/sid/211752382/scat/7399985502eaed63 [9 Jan 2013]

"Nine Nepali students in US charged with Visa fraud, may face 10 yrs in prison if convicted," *Nepal News*, 4 Jul 2013, http://www.nepalnews.com/archive/2013/jul/jul04/news02.php [5 Jul 2013]

"No Data on trafficked nationals," The Kathmandu Post, 5 Sep 2013, http://www.asianewsnet.net/No-data-on-trafficked-nationals-says-Nepalese-govt-51251.html [17 Sept 2013]

"No jobs no hope Nepal's workers head to the Gulf and Malaysia," *The Star*, c 28 Oct 2013, http://www.thestar.com.my/Business/Business-News/2013/10/05/No-jobs-no-hope-Nepals-workers-head-to-the-Gulf-and-Malaysia.aspx [28 Oct 2013]

"NRNA says nine maids repatriated from Oman since May," Muscat Daily, 11 Jun 2013, http://www.menafn.com/1093643284/--NRNA-says-nine-maids-repatriated-from-Oman-since-May?src=RSS [13 Jun 2013]

"Number of Nepali workers going to Malaysia sees fall," *Nepal News* [27 Feb 2009]

"On Human Trafficking into Prostitution in India," http://mail.google.com/mail/h/u00yuytmbiwr/?view=att&th=1203e2117eb3be20&atti.... [6 May 2009]

"One Nepali dies in Malaysia," *Nepal News*, 18 Jul 2013, http://www.nepalnews.com/archive/2013/jul/jul18/news18.php [22 July 2013]

"One Nepali killed, two injured in Malaysia quarry blast," *Nepal News*, 21 Jul 2013, http://www.nepalnews.com/archive/2013/jul/jul21/news05.php [22 July 2013]

"Outbound and beleaguered," *Ekantipur*, 8 Jul 2012, http://www.ekantipur.com/2012/07/08/national/outbound-and-beleaguered/356796.html [31 Jul 2012]

"Over 50 Nepali migrant workers deserted in Kuwaiti desert," *Nepal Human Rights News*, 19 Mar 2011, http://nepalhumanrightsnews.com/news.asp?id=1272 [20 Dec 2011]

from Mar 2011
Passage to India, WFP & NDRI, 2008
"Philippine authorities nab Singaporean, Nepalese for smuggling drugs," *Global Times*, http://www.globaltimes.cn/NEWS/tabid/99/ID/722508/Philippine-authorities-nab-Singaporean-Nepalese-for-smuggling-drugs.aspx [30 Jul 2012]
"Preparation to bring back 125 Nepali from Libya," *Ekantipur*, 8 Mar 2011, http://www.ekantipur.com/2011/03/08/national/preparation-to-bring-back-125-nepali-from-libya/330626.html [31 Jul 2012]
"PUTRAJAYA: The Cabinet has agreed to reinstate a 1992 ruling putting the burden of levy on foreign workers instead of their employers," Mar 2013
"Qatar asks Nepal to send skilled workers," *Nepal News*, 4 Jul 2013, http://www.nepalnews.com/archive/2013/jul/jul04/news01.php [5 Jul 2013]
"Qatar court sentences Nepali to 3 years in jail," *Ekantipur*, 11 Jul 2012, http://www.ekantipur.com/2012/07/11/top-story/qatar-court-sentences-nepali-to-3-yrs-in-jail/356915.html [31 Jul 2012]
"Qatar: End corporate exploitation of migrant construction workers," Amnesty International Annual Report, 2013, http://www.amnesty.org/en/news/qatar-end-corporate-exploitation-migrant-construction-workers-2013-11-17 [22 Nov 2013]
"Qatar is top hirer of Nepali migrant workers," *Ekantipur*, 18 Jul 2012, http://www.ekantipur.com/2012/07/18/top-story/qatar-is-top-hirer-of-nepali-migrant-workers/357349.html [31 Jul 2012]
"Qatar releases Nepali teacher held for 'insulting Islam'," *Nepal News*, 12 May 2013, http://www.nepalnews.com/archive/2013/may/may12/news18.php [15 May 2013]
"Ray of Hope – Nepali migrant workers," *Republica*, 25 Jul 2012
"Re HIV/AIDS and substance abuse," INF/Nepal Annual Report, 2012-13
"Record Nepalis migrate for overseas jobs," *The Himalayan Times*, http://www.thehimalayantimes.com/fullNews.php?headline=Record+Nepalis+migrate+for+overseas+jobs+&NewsID=300152 [20 Dec 2011] from Aug 2011
"Recruiting Nepali Manpower," http://www.visitnepal.com/nepal_information/recruiting_nepali_manpower.php [20 Dec 2011]
"Recruitment Agencies seek legal remedy," *The Kathmandu Post*, 5 Dec 2013, http://www.ekantipur.com/the-kathmandu-post/2013/12/05/nation/recruitment-agencies-to-seek-legal-remedy/256586.html [5 Dec 2013]

"Remittance Economy," Dept of Foreign Employment, 2010

"Remittance sustains 30pc families," *The Kathmandu Post,* http://www.kantipuronline.com/capsule.php?&nid=209002 [11 Aug 2009]

"Repeat migrant workers account for half of worker departures," *Ekantipur*, 27 Jan 2012, http://www.ekantipur.com/2012/01/27/business/repeat-migrant-workers-account-for-half-of-worker-departures/347929.html [31 Jul 2012]

"Report sheds light on plight of Nepali women in Qatar, Lebanon," *Nepal News*, 6 Feb 2013, http://www.nepalnews.com/archive/2013/feb/feb06/news17.php [8 Feb 2013]

"Returnee Women," *Ekantipur*, 19 Oct 2012, http://ekantipur.com/2012/10/19/national/returnee-women-want-to-be-their-own-masters/361780 html [21 Nov 2012]

"Sept. 1 Black Day," Sep-13-2010, *Manpower News*, http://www.manpoweragencynepal.com/Manpower-News-67-1.html [9 Jan 2012]

"Seven arrested for gang-rape of Nepali law student in Bangalore," *Nepal News*, 21 Oct 2012, http://www.nepalnews.com/archive/2012/oct/oct21/news04.php [22 Oct 2012]

"South Korea to hire 8,200 Nepalis next year," *Himalayan Times*, 26 Jul 2013, http://www.thehimalayantimes.com/fullNews.php?headline=South+Korea+to+hire+8%E2%80%9A200+Nepalis+next+year+&NewsID=385186 [1 Oct 2013]

"South Korea wants 6,000 Nepalis in EPS roster to re-register," *Nepal News,* 20 Nov 2012, http://www.nepalnews.com/archive/2012/nov/nov20/news15.php [22 Nov 2012]

"Stranded in Madagascar: Missions asked to rescue Nepalis," *Ekantipur*, 20 Jul 2012, http://www.ekantipur.com/2012/07/20/top-story/stranded-in-madagascar-missions-asked-to-rescue-nepalis/357443.html [31 Jul 2012]

"Suicide cases rising among Bhutanese refugees in US: report," *The Kathmandu Post*, http://my.news.yahoo.com/suicide-cases-rising-among-bhutanese-refugees-us-report-045002035.html [21 Apr 2013]

"The attaché case – the government has decided to station labour attachés at last," *The Kathmandu Post,* kantipuronline [26 Aug 2009]

"The Challenge for Nepal's Migrant Workers," *The Diplomat*, 26 Dec 2012, http://thediplomat.com/2012/12/26/the-exploitation-of-nepali-migrant-workers/ [28 Dec 2012]

"The Dark Side of Migration Spotlight on Qatar's Construction Sector Ahead of The World Cup," *Amnesty International*, Index: mDe 22/010/2013, http://www.amnesty.org/en/library/asset/MDE22/010/2013/en/ca150 40d-290e-4292-8616-d7f845beed7e/mde220102013en.pdf [22 Nov 2013]

"The Nepal Project", *Esther Benjamin's Trust, Stop the Traffick*, http:/www.stopthetraffic.org/projects/Nepal.aspx [13/03/2007]

"Three held in Manali gang-rape were Nepalis, say police," *Nepal National*, http://www.nepalnational.com/index.php/sid/215015381/scat/739998 5502eaed63/ht/Three-held-in-Manali-gang-rape-were-Nepalis-say-police [6 Jun 2013]

"Three migrant workers killed in accident," *Ekantipur*, 25 Mar 2012, http://www.ekantipur.com/2012/03/25/business/three-migrant-workers-killed-in-accident/351215.html [31 Jul 2012]

"Three Nepali drivers held for US national's gang-rape," *IANS*, 6 Jun 2013, http://en-maktoob.news.yahoo.com/three-nepali-drivers-held-us-nationals-gang-rape-123417841.html [10 Jun 2013]

"Three Nepalis injured in Malaysia gang attack: MoFA," *Nepal News*, 25 Mar 2013, http://www.nepalnews.com/archive/2013/mar/mar25/news02.php [26 Mar 2013]

"Top Destinations for Nepali Migrant workers," 2009

"Tortured Nepali to expose Japanese justice," *The Standard HK*, http://www.thestandard.com.hk/breaking_news_detail.asp?id=27510 [21 Nov 2012]

"Trafficking racket unearthed in Bihar," *The Times of India*, New Delhi / Chandigarh, 15 Feb 2012, p8

"Two Nepali migrants hurt in clash in Malaysia," *The Himalayan Times*,http://www.thehimalayantimes.com/fullNews.php?headline=Two+Nepali+migrants+hurt+in+clash+in+Malaysia&NewsID=370675 [26 Mar 2013]

"Two-year old Nepali girl 'raped' by relative dies in India," *Nepal News*, 26 Dec 2012, http://www.nepalnews.com/archive/2012/dec/dec26/news07.php [27 Dec 2012]

"UK arrest highlights Nepal's failure to address torture," http://www.amnestyusa.org/news/news-item/uk-arrest-highlights-nepal-s-failure-to-address-torture [9 Jan 2013]

"UK charges Nepalese colonel for 'inflicting torture' during 2005 civil war", *Nepal National*, http://www.nepalnational.com/index.php/sid/211755229/scat/739998 5502eaed63/ht/UK-charges-Nepalese-colonel-for-inflicting-torture-

during-2005-civil-war [9 Jan 2013]
"UK defends decision to prosecute Nepalese colonel accused of torture," *The Guardian*, 6 Jan 2013, http://www.guardian.co.uk/law/2013/jan/06/uk-defends-prosecute-nepalese-colonel [9 Jan 2013]
"UN to question Nepal after peacekeeper Colonel charged with torture," *Global Times*, http://www.globaltimes.cn/content/754068.shtml [9 Jan 2013]
"UNHCR says over 20,000 Bhutanese refugees resettled abroad," *Nepal National*, 8 Sep 2009
"US honours three Nepalis for combating trafficking in Nepal," *Nepal News*, 5 Jun 2008
"Why Britain's arrest of Nepali army colonel should serve as lesson for South Asia," *Nepal National*, http://www.globalpost.com/dispatches/globalpost-blogs/commentary/Nepal-Civil-War-torture-impunity-conflict-zones-political-risk [3 March 2013]
"Women & HIV/AIDS: Experiences & Consequences of Stigma & Discrimination – Nepal," *Family Health International*, nd
"Workers forced to grease TIA officials' palms," *Ekantipur*, 30 Jan 2012, http://www.ekantipur.com/2012/01/30/top-story/workers-forced-to-grease-tia-officials-palms/348092.html [31 Jul 2012]
"Women going to banned Oman from TIA," *Karobar Daily*, 9 Jan 2013, http://www.karobardaily.com/news/2013/01/Women-going-to-banned-Oman-from-TIA [24 Oct 2013]
"You and AIDS", *UNDP*, 31 Aug 2007
"Young pregnant woman burnt alive by family in Nepal," *Nepal National*, http://www.nepalnational.com/index.php/sid/213705468/scat/7399985502eaed63/ht/Young-pregnant-woman-burnt-alive-by-family-in-Nepal [9 Apr 2013]